JEFFREY MASSON

AGAINST THERAPY

With a Foreword by Dorothy Rowe

HarperCollins*Publishers*

HarperCollins*Publishers*
77–85 Fulham Palace Road,
Hammersmith, London W6 8JB

This paperback edition 1997
5 7 9 8 6 4

First published in Great Britain by
Collins 1989

First published in paperback by Fontana 1990
Reprinted six times

ISBN 0 00 637387 9

Set in Meridien

Printed and bound in Great Britain by
Caledonian International Book Manufacturing Ltd, Glasgow

CONTENTS

FOREWORD

Jeffrey Masson is a trouble maker. Every one of his books has been written to create trouble.

Masson was a Sanskrit scholar before becoming a psychoanalyst, and his first book, *The Oceanic Feeling: The Origins of Religious Sentiment in Ancient India*, set out to show that there are no gurus, that is, people so perceptive and wise that they can be trusted totally and implicitly. As Projects Director of the Freud Archives he edited and translated *The Complete Letters of Sigmund Freud to Wilhelm Fliess, 1887–1904* (not actually published until after his next book). The work he did on this correspondence laid the basis for his attack on Freud and the cornerstone of psychoanalytic theory, the Oedipal complex. In his second book, *The Assault on Truth: Freud's Suppression of the Seduction Theory*, he launched this attack, aiming to show that Freud, unable to confront any longer the real and terrible traumas which his clients as children had suffered, came to regard their stories as fantasies motivated by childish sexual desires. Although at the same time as Masson the psychoanalyst Alice Miller was writing about how the real sufferings of children affected them for life, and a host of women were speaking and writing about their experiences of incest, the psychoanalytic community rejected Masson and his work totally. After all, if you pull the cornerstone out, the whole building might come tumbling down.

A traitor to his profession, Masson now became a traitor to his sex. His next book, *A Dark Science: Women, Sexuality and Psychiatry in the Nineteenth Century*, took the side of women against the men who claimed to help them and from whose work came the medical model of mental illness and psychiatry as we know it today. Not content with that, Masson has now moved on to attack the whole philosophy and practice of psychotherapy.

Psychotherapy, like television and credit cards, is big business in the USA. British people who comment scathingly on the way each American is supposed to consult a psychoanalyst daily may not realize that psychotherapy is big business here in the UK. This is not so much in the private sector of health care, though the number of psychotherapists in private practice is burgeoning, but in the National Health Service and amongst voluntary mental health care organizations. Psychiatrists do psychotherapy, so do psychologists, nurses, social workers and occupational therapists. If people feel that 'psychotherapy' is too pretentious a word to apply to what they do, they describe what they do as counselling, and so we have student counsellors, marriage guidance counsellors, Samaritan counsellors, co-counsellors, bereavement counsellors, alcohol counsellors, drug counsellors, tranquillizer counsellors, clergy counsellors, policewomen counsellors, counsellors at day centres and drop-in centres, counsellors on radio and television. More recently, many of these psychotherapists and counsellors have turned into experts. Though sexual abuse of children has only recently come to be seen as a prevalent and serious problem, there are now dozens of counsellors and psychotherapists who are experts on sexual abuse, just as there are counsellors and psychotherapists who are experts on disasters like the sinking of the P & O car ferry off Zeebrugge and the underground fire at King's Cross Station. Indeed, there are so many counsellors and psychotherapists that I sometimes wonder if we are going to run out of people who want to be counselled. That would never do, for I am one of the people in the psychotherapy/counselling business.

There was not always a plethora of psychotherapists. When I first came to England from Australia in 1968 I went to work at a university psychiatric clinic where the professor and the other consultant psychiatrists were devotees of the medical model of mental illness. Freud was discussed only to be dismissed as unscientific and implausible. There the psychologist's role was to administer tests, the psychiatrist's role to diagnose mental illness, prescribe drugs, and to supervise the administration of ECT (electroconvulsive therapy) and the occasional pre-frontal lobotomy (making some incisions in a patient's brain).

All this came as a surprise to me. Back in Sydney, Freud and psychoanalysis occupied a major part of the training of clinical psychologists and of some psychiatrists, particularly child psychiatrists. Amongst my colleagues in Sydney there was general agreement that people found it easiest to talk about themselves in an egalitarian setting, and that traumas and disappointments create fear and despair. It was strange to find myself among men who maintained their prestige in a strict hierarchy in which, on the lowest rung, the patients had no hope of advancement, and who believed that despair and fear are occasioned not by the terrors of this world but by an aberrant metabolism or gene.

However, they were tolerant men. They saw no reason why I should not spend time talking to patients, and they even endured my reports containing all kinds of specious nonsense derived from the Rorschach Test (where patients give their interpretations of a set of inkblots). 'Endured' is the right word, for in the way that Christian missionaries feared the witchdoctor, they feared that through these inkblots I might psychoanalyse them and thus know their innermost secrets. They were relieved when my interest in the Rorschach waned and instead I entered case conferences armed with sheaves of computer paper. I had discovered that if I asked, say, Mrs Smith her opinion of herself and her relatives, her answer would have no value or interest to the people at the case conference, but if I organized my questions and Mrs Smith's answers into numbers (e.g. 'Out of a scale of 7, where 7 is the most and 1 is the least, how much do you get angry with your husband?' '7.'), and got my friend Patrick Slater to put these numbers through his computer, then Mrs Smith's replies, in the form of computer-printed numbers, took on an impressive degree of truth and significance.

Today, in that same psychiatric clinic, repertory grids, as these computer numbers were called, are quite passé. As in all psychiatric hospitals in the UK, the drugs and the ECT still remain, but there is as well a plethora of therapies – individual therapy, group therapy, family therapy, art therapy, and so on. Instead of interviewing the patient from behind an impressive desk, the consultant and patient, at touching distance, relax in comfortable armchairs. Forgotten are the days when a young psychiatric senior registrar and I attempted to introduce discussion groups for patients, something which the nurses and older psychiatrists welcomed as readily as the printers on our national newspapers welcomed computers. However, progress is inevitable. Group therapy is as common now in psychiatric hospitals as computers are at *The Times*. Not that group therapy meant that psychiatrists and nurses lost their jobs, as some printers did. In all psychiatric hospitals the patients can still be seen sitting disconsolately and silently in the day room. Group therapy has not proved as effective as we thought it would be.

Perhaps the reason that group therapy, individual therapy, family therapy, behaviour therapy, and all the other therapies have not been so effective is because, in effect, nothing has changed. In the bad old days patients were ordered to take the drugs their psychiatrist had prescribed, and so patients worked out all kinds of ways of not taking their drugs – dropping them down sinks, behind radiators, trading them for cigarettes from drug addicts, slipping them to someone saving up for a suicide. Now patients are ordered to go to group therapy, so ways have to be found for not going, or, if attending, of saying enough not to be punished for being uncommunicative, but not so much that what you say can be used against you, either in the group or, when reported to the consultant, in the case conference. Patients are still being locked up alone in a cell. It used to be called 'seclusion', and now it is called 'time out', but, whatever it is called, it is unpleasant.

Plus ça change, plus c'est la même chose. Nothing has changed, because the function of psychiatry has remained the same. Psychiatry is not concerned with cure. After all, if mental illness is inherited, no cure is possible. Thus psychiatrists talk not of curing patients, but of 'managing' them. Psychiatry is concerned with power, the power of individual psychiatrists and the power of the State.

When the medical model of mental illness reigned supreme, the aim of psychiatry could be clearly seen and accepted as the maintenance of the status quo. Mad people who threatened the status quo were confined and subdued. People who failed to accept or to fulfil the roles that society decreed for them – a docile wife and mother, a hard-working man, an obedient child – could, by the judicious application of drugs and ECT, be restored to the required role or else locked away from society's sight. When psychotherapy loomed on the horizon of British psychiatry, British psychiatrists felt threatened. Psychotherapy can (but does not always) offer patients a choice.

The harbingers of psychotherapy in Britain in the early seventies were chiefly clinical psychologists. These were a heterogeneous bunch, in the psychiatrists' eyes, undisciplined, unreliable and untidy. The aim of the different kinds of psychotherapy these psychologists practised was to encourage their patients to enjoy life and make their own decisions. It was no wonder that psychiatrists preferred the psychologists who espoused behaviour therapy, a technique well fitted for promoting obedience and conformity.

At first the Royal College of Psychiatrists treated psychotherapists in the same way as they treat all charlatans and parvenus – by scorning and ignoring them. Gradually it dawned on the Royal College that the clinical psychologists in the NHS were gaining power and prestige because they were doing all sorts of putatively curative things which psychiatrists could not do. So, following the old principle of 'If you can't beat 'em, join 'em,' many psychiatrists became psychotherapists.

Of course, many psychiatrists chose to study psychotherapy because they were wise and caring people and because they could see that the unquestioning application of the medical model of mental illness to the multifarious problems of life creates more problems than it solves. However, a medical education trains people to think in a particular way, and so, when psychiatrists turned to psychotherapy, their way of thinking went with them.

A medical education is an education in problem-solving: take an amorphous situation; structure it into a problem; and solve the problem. This is clear, black-and-white thinking, sensible, rational, down to earth, whereas psychotherapy requires a great deal of woolly thinking and the capacity to hold several points of view at one and the same time. Another problem is that psychotherapists write books, on and on, endlessly, and if you want to be a psychotherapist you have to read an awful (and I mean awful) lot of this stuff. If, at university, you have majored in English Literature or History, Psychology or Sociology, you have learned how to read fast and skip the dull bits, but if your subject is medicine you have learned to read as a scientist should, slowly and carefully.

Many psychiatrists who say they do psychotherapy have decided against actually studying psychotherapy and reading all that stuff. Instead, they have noted that psychotherapists talk to patients and that – to these psychiatrists -- is all that psychotherapy is. So they talk to their patients. They ask questions, give advice, tell stories, spend, good heavens, up to ten or twenty minutes with their patients instead of the usual five. Sometimes the patient finds this talk reassuring (if nobody in your life takes any notice of you, ten minutes' conversation can seem wonderful), sometimes the stories are entertaining and the advice helpful, but often such so-called psychotherapy is in the same authoritarian, patient-humiliating mode that has become the tradition in psychiatry. I read Masson's chapter on the pre-history of psychotherapy with horror, not just for what happened then to those women, but for the patients, men and women, I have seen suffer in the same way. What is so appalling about cruelty (and why I write about it so much) is that we find it very hard to see the cruelty which is right before our eyes. Nurses and administrators who would be horrified by a television picture of soldiers beating a defenceless civilian see nothing cruel in a psychiatrist humiliating and punishing a patient, as happens every day in case conferences. Not for nothing did Goffman in his study of asylums call case conferences 'degradation ceremonies'.

By the end of the seventies a number of psychiatrists had realized that not only should they recognize the existence of psychotherapy but that it was imperative they should claim it as their own. Not only did the Royal College recognize that studying psychotherapy was a valid choice of speciality for a psychiatrist (as against specializing in, say, forensic psychiatry or mental handicap), but it created a new consultant post, Consultant Psychotherapist. Thus the psychiatrists crowned themselves Emperors of Psychotherapy. 'Lay' people might call themselves psychotherapists, but only a psychiatrist could be a Consultant Psychotherapist.

A Consultant Psychotherapist is a psychiatrist who, during or following his traditional training first in medicine and then in psychiatry, has undergone some training in one or more of the different kinds of psychotherapy. For some such psychiatrists studying psychotherapy dissolves those habits of mind and behavior which their medical and pyschiatric training had created.

No longer are they special people with authority, knowledge and prestige to command and control. They are now ordinary people, warm, caring, prone to doubt and ignorance, letting others speak before them, treating patients as fellow human beings, eschewing expensive dark suits for something idiosyncratic and comfortable, feeling undemeaned by making coffee, playing with child patients, being indistinguishable from the nurses, social workers and psychologists they work with, inspiring affection and never fear. They are a shame and a disgrace to their profession, and, worse still, this does not worry them.

Fortunately, there are psychiatrists who, in becoming psychotherapists, have not rejected the basic principle of psychiatry: power. They have recognized that psychotherapy can be used most effectively in the pursuit of power.

Just how psychotherapy can be used to manipulate, control and humiliate people is the theme of this book. As Masson notes, out of psychoanalysis came a form of psychotherapy called 'dynamic psychotherapy'. There are strict rules about how dynamic psychotherapy should be done, and those therapists who trained in dynamic psychotherapy and then failed to keep the rules are renegades and unbelievers.

In dynamic psychotherapy there is a hierarchy, just as there is in psychiatry. The psychotherapist is superior, the patient inferior. The psychotherapist, by virtue of his knowledge, training and special insight has access to truths above and beyond the capacity of the patients. The psychotherapist's truths have a higher truth value than the patient's truths. The psychotherapist interprets the patient's truths and tells him what they *really* mean.

The demonstration of the psychotherapist's superiority uses the same techniques employed in religion and royalty. The psychotherapist, like the priest and monarch, can choose to approach the patient, but the patient cannot approach the psychotherapist without being bidden. The psychotherapist, like the priest and monarch, can question the patient on any topic, but the patient cannot question the pyschotherapist. The psychotherapist, like the priest and monarch, has a ritual to mark his separateness from the patient. The psychotherapist, like the priest and the monarch, decides how much time the patient can spend in his presence.

Part of the ritual concerns how the patient enters the presence of the psychotherapist. The psychotherapist approaches the patient, gives a formal greeting, and invites the patient to his office, leading the way *in silence*. Passing the time of day on the journey from the waiting room to the office is considered, in the theory of dynamic psychotherapy, as the psychotherapist trying to gain the patient's affection. Not trying to gain the patient's affection is one way of maintaining distance, and distance is essential for power. Once in the psychotherapist's office the psychotherapist invites the patient to sit and to talk. In the psychoanalytic tradition, the psychotherapist is silent except when interpreting what the patient has said. Everything that the patient says is taken, not as a statement of the patient's truth, but as a projection of the patient's fantasy. Thus, as Masson shows in his chapter on Dora and Freud, did Freud turn aside Dora's observation that he, like Herr K., had deceived her. Though Freud professed an interest in Dora's truth, he was actually concerned with proving his theory. This is how the psychotherapist can refuse to accept responsibility for his own actions and can push responsibility and blame on to the patient. 'You have misperceived reality,' the psychotherapist says to the patient. 'You must try harder. If you don't get better, it is your fault.'

A friend of mine, John, underwent a course of dynamic psychotherapy. His psychotherapist's office was four flights up from the waiting area at the foot of the stairs. He told me, 'She could have just leaned over the banisters and called, "Oi, come on up," but she never did. She always came all the way down and then led me all the way up in total silence.'

Silence was something John found hard to bear. It made him feel frightened and helpless, the very feelings which undermine our self-confidence. All authoritarian systems instil obedience, conformity and acceptance of the authority's version of the truth by undermining the self-confidence of their recruits, novices, pupils, children, patients. The less self-confident the patient is, the more likely he will accept without question what the psychotherapist says.

John felt his self-confidence to be quite thoroughly undermined, and was relieved when his psychotherapist told him that the course of psychotherapy would be coming to an end. But at least he had been selected for psychotherapy. Many people get referred to a Consultant Psychotherapist only to be told that they are 'not suitable for psychotherapy'. The criteria for selection are never explained to the patient, who is then left feeling that the psychotherapist has identified in him some flaw which renders him hopeless and incurable. The cruelty of this act is not even seen, much less condemned, by pyschotherapists.

The reason that psychotherapists divide prospective patients into suitable and unsuitable for psychotherapy is that they wish to avoid those people whose lives have been filled with tragedies beyond repair and recompense and whose education has not fitted them to speak of their experiences in the way typical of the white, middle-class English. Such people render their would-be helpers helpless, and, since the helpers are usually people who pride themselves on their competence in helping, being rendered helpless makes them frightened. Rather than admit their fear, they label such people as 'unsuitable for psychotherapy', or 'from a problem family', or 'chronic depressive', or 'psychopathic', or 'inadequate personality', or 'schizophrenic', and deal with them in rejecting and controlling ways which, not surprisingly, do not help these people and often actually harm them.

Over the years that psychiatrists were turning themselves into psychotherapists, clinical psychologists in the NHS were increasing in number and significance. Back in the early seventies the few psychologists who were interested in psychotherapy would say to one another, 'When there are more of us, all these abuses in the psychiatric system will disappear,' just as we women in pre-Falklands days used to say to one another, 'When there's a woman Prime Minister there will be no more wars.' How wrong we all were!

In the fifties and sixties in psychiatric hospitals a lone psychologist might be found up in the attics or in a far-flung outhouse, marking tests or, if psychotherapeutically inclined, conversing with a patient. Their salaries would have been low and most of their energies expended in resisting the psychiatrists' attempts to order them about. Prestige and good salaries would have resided with the academic psychologists in universities. Then, in the early seventies, the NHS raised the salaries of clinical psychologists, created more jobs, and allowed them to organize themselves into departments. With these changes came prestige and power. Warm and wonderful though all the members of my profession are, there are still many of them who have allowed themselves to be seduced and corrupted by power.

Henceforth, clinical psychologists were no longer just the people who gave IQ tests. They were in the business of making people change. Their methods, and the words they used to describe their methods, changed. Behaviour modification became behaviour therapy and then behavioural psychotherapy. Group leaders created challenging experiences for the participants in the group. (Fritz Perls had put a most delicious form of power into the hands of group leaders.) Individual psychotherapy ceased to be a meandering conversation going on for months or even years. It was marshalled, organized, time-limited and researched. Patients were given contracts and homework, and were reprimanded and rejected when they failed to do as they were told. No longer was psychotherapy seen as it was in my day: the gentle building-up of the patient's self-confidence by creating a trusting relationship between patient and therapist (a model still used by many of those people who call themselves counsellors). Instead, the patients were trapped in paradoxes, advised and confronted. Indeed, confrontation became an important aspect of the kind of therapy espoused by those thrusting and ambitious men who regarded clinical psychology not as a vocation but as a prestigious and competitive profession.

Masson has noted that Sándor Ferenczi was the first analyst to consider that a psychoanalytic interpretation of what the patient says can actually be an act of aggression. Ferenczi thought that such an interpretation was a mistake. Masson commented, 'Years later this mistake was elevated into a principle of therapy, when confrontation therapy became an established form of modern therapy.' Someone who confronts another person is convinced that he is in possession of the truth and that the other person is wrong and must be made to see the error of his ways.

In the final analysis, power is the right to have your definition of reality prevail over all other people's definition of reality. Military forces, police, weapons, prisons, abuse, instructions, laws, rituals and such like are simply the tools by which one definition of reality can be made to prevail over others.

Many people who wish to impose their definition of reality would deny that they are involved in gaining power. They would say that because of their greater knowledge, wisdom, training and experience they know what is best. *The most dangerous people in the world are those who believe that they know what is best for others.*

People who believe that they know what is best for other people are denying other people's truths. Whenever our own truth is denied, ignored or invalidated we experience the greatest fear we can ever know: the threat of the annihilation of our self.

Terrible though death is, we can come to terms with the thought of our death when we feel that our lives have significance and that some important part of ourselves – our soul, or our children, or our work – will continue on after we are dead. But if our self is annihilated, our life has no significance, for we have never existed, and there is nothing left of us to carry on. Facing this threat, we have to protect ourselves.

Freud threatened Dora with the annihilation of her self when, as Masson wrote, Freud had 'trivialized her deepest concern, and had demonstrated a total inability to understand her search for historical truth. It is not that he denied the "seduction" had taken place, but he stripped it of any significance, by giving it a totally different meaning, by "interpreting it". He treated her like a patient, not like a human being. Freud never believed that Dora could be concerned with external truth.' Dora saved her self from annihilation by leaving Freud and never returning. Mark, a seventeen-year-old lad, committed suicide after receiving treatment from a therapist called Albert Honig whose style of therapy in the sixties is described by Masson. Of course, it cannot be shown that Mark's suicide was connected with the treatment he received and it is possible that he might have taken his life irrespective of what therapy he was offered. In such circumstances, the Coroner will absolve doctors for the patient's death, since the doctors have done what they thought was best for the patient. The risk run by every doctor is that, when patients feel their self is threatened and that there is no escape, they will perform the only act of self-determination they feel is left to them. They will kill themselves.

We can feel that we know what is best for others only when we have failed to become aware that, being fallible human beings, we are likely to misinterpret reality and to mistake our motives for doing what we do, being always inclined to impute more noble motives to ourselves than is actually the case. To overcome these errors Freud had insisted that all would-be analysts should first be analysed, and this tradition has persisted in psychiatry and psychology in the USA. It is quite possible to go through a training analysis or years of psychotherapy and emerge with all one's prejudices and blind spots intact, but at least in the USA there is general agreement among psychologists and psychiatrists on the importance of the therapist's self-awareness. No such tradition exists among psychiatrists and psychologists in the UK. A few psychiatrists and psychologists seek personal psychotherapy in their training years, but this has to be done in their own time and at their own expense. Usually a person seeking such psychotherapy needs to keep this secret from his fellow students and teachers, for the 'tough-minded' stance of his colleagues is considered to be the correct one. And, of course, it is, for what is important is not to understand and accept as valid the patient's perception of reality, but to learn just enough of it to label it 'depressive', or 'schizo-phrenic', or 'psychopathic', or 'abnormal', or 'irrational', or 'dysfunctional', then to eradicate it and replace it with the therapist's correct interpretation of reality.

Psychologists and psychiatrists share a number of prejudices, but one which affects their clients greatly is how the religious beliefs that patients hold are, at best, unimportant, and, at worst, evidence of a neurosis or psychosis. Psychiatrists and psychologists are, on the whole, an irreligious lot, and as such are untypical of the general population. Surveys show that between 60 and 90% of the population in the UK and the USA believe in God and in a relationship between God and human goodness and wickedness. Thus, most of the people who come to psychiatrists and psychologists for help are not asking, 'How can I be happy?', but 'How can I be good?' Lacking a belief in God and the life hereafter, psychologists and psychiatrists consider that the only sensible question to ask is, 'How can I make the most of my life (my only life)?' When the therapist and the patient have different and unspoken aims, the course of therapy is doomed to failure. Dora and Freud differed on the aims of their encounter. They were, in Masson's words, 'two strong-willed, forceful and courageous human beings, set on a collision course: one wants to change the other, the other merely wants to be vindicated.'

Another pattern set by Freud and repeated ever since is what I, from years of observing psychiatrists and psychologists, call 'the natural history of a therapist.'

Ferenczi was a close friend of Freud from 1906 to Ferenczi's death in 1933. In 1932 Ferenczi wrote in his diary that Freud

> said that patients are only riffraff. The only thing patients were good for is to help the analyst make a living and provide material for theory. It is clear we cannot help them. This is therapeutic nihilism. Nevertheless, we entice patients by concealing these doubts and by arousing their hopes of being cured. I think that in the beginning Freud really believed in analysis; he followed Breuer enthusiastically, involved himself passionately and selflessly in the therapy of neurotics (lying on the floor for hours if necessary next to a patient in the throes of a hysterical crisis). However, certain experiences must have first alarmed him and then left him disillusioned more or less the way Breuer was when his patient [Anna O.] suffered a relapse and he found himself faced, as before an abyss, with the countertransference. In Freud's case the equivalent was the discovery of the mendacity of hysterical women. Since the time of this discovery, Freud no longer likes sick people. He rediscovered his love for his orderly, cultivated superego. A further proof of this is his dislike and expressions of blame that he uses with respect to psychotics and perverts, in fact, his dislike of everything that he considers "too abnormal", even against Indian mythology. Since he suffered this shock, this disappointment, Freud speaks much less about trauma, and the constitution begins to play the major role. This involves, obviously, a degree of fatalism. After a wave of enthusiasm for the psychological, Freud has returned to biology; he considers the psychological to be nothing more than the superstructure over the biological and for him the latter is far more real. He is still attached to analysis intellectually, but not emotionally. Further, his method of treatment as well as his theories result from an ever greater interest in order, character and the substitution of a better superego for a weaker one. In a word, he is becoming a pedagogue ... He looms like a god above his poor patient who has been degraded to the status of a child.

*

Like Freud, many psychiatrists and psychologists begin their career believing that they are in possession of a special truth, a theory which, once explored and expanded, will restore the insane and the misguided to their rightful roles in life. The theory might concern the function of dopamine in the brain, or genetic engineering, or the discovery of insight through psychotherapy, or the learning of good habits through behaviour modification, or the acquiring of the right attitudes through cognitive therapy. They embark on their mission enthusiastically. For a time all goes well. A satisfactory number of patients behave in the way that the theory predicts. Unaware of how the advent of a bright, enthusiastic, cheerful young man or woman in the life of a sad and lonely person is likely to make that person feel much better, they claim success for their brand of therapy, and look forward to fame, riches, and the Nobel Prize.

As I am often wont to say, 'All therapies work, but no therapy works perfectly.' You can take a ward full of patients of whatever diagnosis, age and sex, and you can give them all a new drug, or a new kind of therapy, or simply a change in their routine, and a third of them will get better, a third will stay the same, and a third will get worse, give or take a few each way. Of course, a few weeks or months later, some of those who got better will get worse, and some of those who got worse will get better. But you cannot be sure that when patients say they are better they really are. Patients, who are always trying to be good, kind people, are likely to tell the therapist what he wants to hear. After all, if this nice young chap has gone to all this trouble, it's a pity to disappoint him.

So, when the psychologists and psychiatrists write their research papers, they find that they cannot announce, as they had hoped, a breakthrough, the dawn of a new era. Instead they have to end their papers with the time-honoured words, 'More research is needed.' They press on, but with diminishing enthusiasm, casting eyes in other directions. They pay more attention to advancing up the career ladder; they look at jobs overseas; they take an active interest in their profession's learned societies; they take training courses in neurology and genetics, or move restlessly from rational emotive therapy to Gestalt to Ericksonian hypnotherapy. As their career advances they change their style. Becoming Consultant Psychiatrists they can indulge their idiosyncrasies, their temper and their wit at the expense of their patients. Becoming Principal

Psychologists they can go into management, and by the time they are in charge of a department of clinical psychology they are so busy 'developing the service' and attending committees that they have no time to spend with patients.

Not that not having anything to do with patients stops these psychologists and psychiatrists from knowing what is best for patients. After all, they know all about patients. They know that patients are incorrigible and have to be managed for their own good.

The natural history of a therapist is a testament to how difficult we all find it to gaze upon life's implacable tragedies with a steady and courageous eye and to tolerate our own helplessness. We do not wish to see how poverty maims and cripples, especially when we benefit from the system which both increases poverty and creates wealth. We do not wish to admit that no degree of goodness, or cleverness, or hard work, no mind-altering drug, no brilliant therapeutic intervention, can save us from loss, disappointment and death, nor recompense us for the humiliations and pain in childhood. Lacking that courage, we blame the victims of life's tragedies for their own misfortunes. If we become victims ourselves, we look for someone to save us. If our parents cannot and God is otherwise engaged, we can put ourselves in the hands of therapists and hope that they will have a magic pill or a magic word which will take our pain and confusion away. Even as we do this, we know that anyone who has, or says he has, the power to save us also has the power to harm us. We must be careful not to do everything that the therapist tells us to do.

David Smail, Professor of Clinical Psychology at Nottingham University, head of Clinical Psychology Services in Nottingham, and once a practising psychotherapist, has proposed an alternative to therapy in his book *Taking Care*. He wrote,

> Psychological distress occurs for reasons which make it incurable by therapy but which are certainly not beyond the powers of human beings to influence. We suffer pain because we do damage to each other, and we shall continue to suffer pain as long as we continue to do the damage. The way to alleviate and mitigate distress is for us *to take care of* the world and the other people in it, not to *treat* them . . . Most of the evils of our society, and certainly by far the greater part of the so-called

"pathological" emotional distress experienced by its members, are more or less directly attributable to the unequal distribution of forms of (usually economic) power which are abused and corrupting . . . Instead of abusing power, we need to use whatever power we have to increase the power of others, to take care rather than treat, to enlighten rather than mystify, to love rather than exploit, and, in general, to think seriously about what are the obligations as opposed to the advantages of power. Ideally, the foremost obligation on power is to "deconstruct" itself . . . Changes of heart would have little impact on the real world unless accompanied by highly organized and concerted action . . . But unless our society *does* mend its ways we may expect no improvement to occur in our private lives, no greater satisfactions in "relationships"; there will be no "breakthroughs" in scientific or psychological understanding to patch up our unhappiness and allow us to carry on as before.

The 'change of heart' of which Smail speaks I would describe as being the rejection of that sense of intrinsic badness and unacceptability which was instilled in us when, as children, we were in the power of our parents and teachers. Losing the sense of intrinsic badness is something we can do without pain, or trauma, or hard work, or even the guidance of some expert therapist. Indeed, the superior–inferior, therapist–patient relationship actually stops us from coming to value and accept our own self. Friends and equals can help us discover the ancient wisdom that we should simply be, and that if we choose to do good things, it is not because we are trying to overcome our sense of badness but because being loving and kind and helpful and all those things that we call good gives us pleasure.

When we accept and value our own self we cease to be afraid of other people. We no longer have superiors and inferiors, but only equals with whom we can co-operate and share while we take responsibility for ourselves. We no longer feel deprived and envious, so we can abandon revenge and greed. We have learnt the wisdom of Lao Tsu: 'He who knows that enough is enough always has enough.' Because we value ourselves, we value others, now and to come, and the planet on which we all live. We reject those who seek to dominate and manipulate us, and who, in elevating greed, revenge and pride to virtues, place our lives and our planet in jeopardy.

Obviously, if we all decided to accept and value ourselves, we would cause those who have power over us a great deal of trouble.

This is just the kind of trouble that Jeffrey Moussaieff Masson wants to make.

DOROTHY ROWE

REFERENCES

Goffman, Erving. *Asylums: Essays on the Social Situation of Mental Patients and Other Inmates*, New York, Doubleday & Co., 1961

Rowe, Dorothy. *Beyond Fear*, London, Fontana, 1987

Rowe, Dorothy. *The Construction of Life and Death*, London, Fontana, 1989

Smail, David. *Taking Care: An Alternative to Therapy*, London, Dent, 1987

PREFACE

This is a book about why I believe psychotherapy, of any kind, is wrong. Although I criticize many individual therapists and therapies, my main objective is to point out that the very *idea* of psychotherapy is wrong. The structure of psychotherapy is such that no matter how kindly a person is, when that person becomes a therapist, he or she is engaged in acts that are bound to diminish the dignity, autonomy, and freedom of the person who comes for help.

I began training to become a psychoanalyst at the Toronto Psychoanalytic Institute in 1970. Eight years later, in 1978, I was admitted to the International Psychoanalytic Association as a psychoanalyst. In the course of my training at a classical, orthodox psychoanalytic institute, much of it in the theory and technique of what is termed 'dynamically oriented psychotherapy,' I was beset with doubts that I assumed were typical: Did any of this make sense? Was I really helping people during therapy? Was I any better off than my so-called patients? As part of my training, I was in analysis five days a week for five years; my 'patients' were also in analysis five days a week for five years. Couldn't we easily have changed places? Did I really understand 'emotional problems of living' any better than anybody else, including people who had absolutely no training or background? Was I learning anything that had any practical application? Were there 'skills' that could be acquired, e.g., learning to listen, learning to be 'empathic' or merely sympathetic, learning to suspend judgment, and so on? If so, was I acquiring them? These doubts were fairly typical of my colleagues at the initial stages of psychoanalytic training. But I still had these doubts after eight years of training.

I saw three possibilities: there was something wrong with me;

there was something wrong with the particular training I was undergoing; or there was something wrong with the theory and the practice. I chose to believe the second, and least threatening, explanation, and decided that once I graduated from Toronto and gained a wider acquaintance with the world of psychoanalysis both in the United States and in Europe, I would be able to resolve my doubts concerning psychotherapy.

I moved to California in order to start a psychoanalytic practice. My doubts persisted; in fact, they increased. I realized that until I felt clearer about these issues, it would be better for me not to practice. I turned my energies to historical research. The issue that most intrigued me was Freud's abandonment of the so-called seduction theory. As a psychoanalytic student I had been taught that Freud initially believed the women who came to him for therapy when they said they had been sexually abused as children, often by members of their own family. Then he made what he thought to be a momentous 'discovery': What he heard from these women were not genuine memories; they were, Freud said, fabricated stories, or madeup fictions. They were fantasies, not memories. Or they were memories of fantasies. They were, Freud believed, important, but they were not real; they referred to internal, not external, events. The implications of this 'discovery' – it never occurred to Freud that it was only a point of view – were enormous. It has affected the course of psychoanalysis and therapy in general from that time on, and has caused incalculable suffering for patients who were in fact sexually abused. Therapists accepted Freud's belief that the best judge of what really happened is not necessarily the person to whom it happened. In therapy, the person's account of a traumatic event is not to be taken literally, as referring to something real that happened in the real world. It may be no more than a symbol, a sign pointing to an obscure internal area of confused desires and fantasies, a nest of unacknowledged needs, impulses, drives, and instincts said to be hidden in the heart of every human being.

To find out what happened, in this view, requires an external, objective source, a person trained in a demasking procedure: the therapist. Freud's views became the testing ground for the training of a later generation of therapists. The therapist thought he knew when patients were confusing internal fantasy with external reality because he had the previously analyzed experiences of the patients of the founder of psychoanalysts to serve as a guidepost. Many people believed that a major breakthrough in the alleviation of human suffering had been achieved: If people could so confuse inner with outer reality that they could mistake an obscure (and never conscious) desire with a frightening and vivid memory of having been sexually assaulted, then how much else might they have distorted in their lives? How could they be trusted to know the real intricate relationship they had with their mothers, their fathers, their siblings, even their spouses? The idea that only the analyst can judge whether something is real or merely a fantasy became standard doctrine, and the very foundation of psycho-analytically oriented psychotherapy. I was taught during my psychotherapeutic training that statements about relationships should always be regarded as no more than an account of wishes, fantasies, desires, and projections. They could not be taken at face value any more than could accounts of sexual assault in childhood. Thus, when I began my investigation of Freud's momentous about face, I was not investigating some obscure corner of psychoanalytic history that held no more than antiquarian interest for a small number of historians. I was examining one of the cornerstones of psychoanalytic therapy.

The results of my investigation were initially received by the psychoanalytic profession with somewhat less than cordial and objective interest. I should not have been surprised that when my book *The Assault on Truth: Freud's Suppression of the Seduction Theory* appeared in early 1984, the attention of reviewers was riveted on the character of the author rather than on an examination of the issues. I had assumed that the implications for psychoanalytic therapy of the new documents I had found – for example, pre-viously unpublished letters by Freud, new material from the Paris morgue about child abuse, unknown pages from Ferenczi's private diary – would be pursued by members of the profession with more clinical experience than I had. I was entirely mistaken. Instead, wherever I lectured, even in France, Italy, Spain, and Holland, the discussions focused on my physical appearance, my clothing, my motivation in researching child abuse, my relationship with my father, my mother, my analyst, Anna Freud, and others. It seemed that neither the findings nor their implications could be regarded with any dispassion. I learned that people who criticize establish-ment dogmas are not accorded a serious hearing. I took some comfort in the recognition that the pain I felt over the personal attacks against me was due to my political naïveté.

But if psychoanalysts, academics, and some members of the public sympathetic to psychoanalysis were not prepared to deal with the issues, another vocal and important part of the public was: the feminists. Many women were interested in the historical material and documentation I had gathered. Feminist writers, including Florence Rush, Judith Herman, Diana Russell, and Louise Armstrong, commented favorably on the research. My book joined a long line of recent works exposing the reality of sexual abuse of girls and women, the most recent of which is the excellent book by Diana Russell, *The Secret Trauma: Incest in the Lives of Girls and Women*.

I received many letters in response to an article on the history of sexual abuse in March 1984 issue of the *Atlantic* and another in *Mother Jones* in December 1984 about my findings. These letters, almost all from women who had been sexually abused in childhood, showed me that many of the facts I uncovered as a result of my archival research were correct and relevant today.

The purely intellectual satisfaction I experienced with the publication, in 1985, of *The Complete Letters of Sigmund Freud to Wilhelm Fliess, 1887–1904* and the largely favorable reviews it received helped restore some of my faith in the value of pure research. But I think this is only because most reviewers did not see the relevance of these letters, which contain the most elaborate exploration we have of Freud's fluctuating views on sexual assault in childhood, to the issues I raised in my earlier book. No review looked at sexual abuse in the light shed by these letters. I believe the letters make it clear that Freud had considerable clinical evidence, material from his own patients, that the abuse he later repudiated as fantasy was, in fact, real.

I had yet to come to terms with one important point: Why would I expect that Freud or Fliess would behave any differently toward their patient Emma Eckstein than they did? Freud had handed her over to Fliess, who "diagnosed" her to be suffering from a 'nasal reflex neurosis' and performed an experimental operation on her nose. She nearly died when she hemorrhaged as a result of surgical gauze Fliess left in the wound he created. Freud later told Fliess that her bleeding was 'hysterical' – psychological, and not the consequence of Fliess's incompetence. This was to be expected, some feminists told me, because the whole legacy of medicine and surgical intervention on women was a violent one. Was this true? Official psychiatric histories presented the nineteenth century as the age when psychotherapy as we know it today was born. Many authors had argued that this official history omitted the violent aspects of nineteenth-century psychiatry. But by and large most confined their research to material available in English. The materials for exploring this in any depth for German and French psychiatry, so influential in England and America, were hard to come by. My knowledge of the primary literature was limited to what I knew from my readings in preparing the Freud/Fliess letters for publication. To place the controversy over sexual abuse in a wider historical context, it was necessary to spend the next few years examining the nineteenth-century psychiatric, pediatric, and gynecological periodical literature in some depth. The result was *A Dark Science: Women, Sexuality and Psychiatry in the Nineteenth Century*, a reader of the horrors inflicted on women in the name of 'mental health.'

Feeling my historical obligations at an end, I have one task remaining to do justice to my many years of psychoanalytic training. Most of that training was not theoretical, but practical – as psychiatrists like to say, clinical. During my training, I was much too close to psychotherapy, either being in it myself or dispensing it, to be able to examine it critically. Now I was unencumbered by any need to protect the profession or my place in it. Perhaps the response of the profession to my findings about child abuse in Freud's time and by implication today was so obtuse, vicious, and self-serving that it would prejudice me against therapists in general. There is some truth in this. Nevertheless, I no longer feel the personal bitterness I once felt. I am left with a strong need to examine what I learned about practicing therapy on 'patients,'[1] and to examine the theoretical assumptions of psychotherapy in general more critically than I feel has yet been done.

This book, then, fulfills my obligation to the reading, the training, and the preoccupations of the last sixteen years of my life. Now

[1] I wish there were another term than 'patients,' which is condescending and has false medical overtones, but there is not. Carl Rogers's term 'clients' lacks the medical implications but perversely seems to underline the condescension. The lack of a term that is not condescending or intimidating is an ironic proof of the reality I argue for in this book.

these years feel like an intellectual detour. I became fascinated with what appeared at the time to be the intellectual beauty of psychoanalytic theory. Perhaps the more profound lesson I learned is that investigation of psychoanalysis was not really a detour at all. Had I studied medicine, or law, or philosophy, the kinds of discoveries I have made would have been duplicated in those fields. I learned something, in the end, about the pretensions to knowledge. I learned something of the frailty of our ability to help another person who is in emotional distress, and especially about the pretensions to this ability. I learned about power, and hierarchies, and dominance, the rationalizations for abuse, and the inability of many people to comprehend the suffering they cause others.

Perhaps it was not a detour after all. When I began my psychoanalytic training, I was a Sanskrit scholar who had become disillusioned with the notion that life could ever provide a guru, a person with unique insights into the internal life of another person. I thought this claim was unique to Indian culture, one that had caused people a great deal of unhappiness, though no doubt many would claim that it had also brought them great happiness, even joy and bliss (just as some people who have had electroshock claim that it did them a great deal of good). I wrote an unpopular book on this theme in 1980, *The Oceanic Feeling: The Origins of Religious Sentiment in Ancient India*. And yet, here I was, eight years later, coming to the same unhappy conclusion about psychotherapy: There are no gurus. Maybe I was touching on one of the characteristics of the human animal, the need to seek somebody apparently stronger, wiser, better, happier, from whom guidance could be sought.

Some who have listened to my ideas have agreed that I may be right, but have then asked a question. Granted that psychotherapy is flawed, what would I put in its place that would be better?

In reply I would note that, as one feminist friend put it, nobody thinks of asking: What would you replace misogyny with? If something is bad, or flawed, or dangerous, it is enough if we expose it for what it is. It is almost as if once it has been determined that something exists, we decide it must be there for a reason (undoubtedly true) and then slide into the false position that it must be there for a *good* reason, which is undoubtedly *not* true. Or it is as if we believed that if we finally rid ourselves of something heinous (like apartheid), then we must replace it with something similar in nature. The truth is we do not know all the wonderful things that could happen once something hateful is abolished. Anyone who has ever oppressed another human being invariably asks what will happen once the oppression is over. What will happen to children once we stop beating them in schools? What will happen to slaves when they are freed from the plantations? What will happen to animals when we stop slaughtering them for food? What will happen to women when we stop subordinating them? What will happen to nonconformists when we do not incarcerate them in psychiatric institutions? What will happen to the wife when her husband no longer beats her? These questions are not real questions at all. What is required is a shift of focus, to the people who *do* these things, the aggressors, not their victims. Why do men hunt? Why do psychiatrists torture people and call it electroshock therapy? Why do men rape? And, perhaps just as important, why does society tend to blame the victim for all these acts of violence? Why do psychologists search for what they think to be the flaw in the victim that caught the attention of the predator?

I have some ideas about how people could live without psychotherapy or psychiatry. I am thinking of self-help groups that are leaderless and avoid authoritarian structures, in which no money is exchanged, that are not grounded on religious principles (a difficulty with Alcoholics Anonymous and similar groups, since not all members share spiritual or religious interests), and in which all participants have experienced the problem they come to discuss. I know that some women who have been sexually abused have been helped by getting together with other sexually abused women to share experiences, survival strategies, political analysis, and just their own outrage. What we need are more kindly friends and fewer professionals.

ACKNOWLEDGMENTS

For the writing of Chapter 1, I am grateful first of all to Wolfgang Binswanger, for allowing me to spend three weeks working in the splendid archives of the Sanitarium Bellevue. I am also indebted to members of the board of directors of the sanitarium for granting me permission to use unpublished material I collected from those archives for this book. I was accompanied to Switzerland by Marianne Loring, who assisted me in every possible way in collecting material for this chapter. I am also grateful to her for going over all the German passages I have translated especially for this book and for making certain that I did not commit errors. As with my previous three books, she was a help in many other ways as well.

For Chapter 3, I am grateful to Dr. Judith Dupont, who holds the Ferenczi copyright, for allowing me access to the original German typescript of Ferenczi's private diary and also for permission to cite from this diary.

For Chapter 5, I am especially grateful to Sally Zinman for providing me with many of the documents necessary to write this chapter. She read it and made a number of important corrections. I am grateful, too, to Virginia Snyder, the private detective who brought charges against John Rosen, for sending me supplementary material and also for reading the chapter.

For Chapter 6, I am especially grateful to Wilma Caffentzis for sending me many of the documents I used in preparing the chapter.

My friend Bob Goldman helped me shorten the Jung chapter, and my friend Catharine MacKinnon helped me in writing the Preface.

I want to thank Sue Doell, who has read every word of this book, and spent many hours making me see the political implications of what I was writing. Her experience with psychiatry and the friendship she has offered to me have been extremely valuable in writing this book. She has improved it beyond measure. Leonard Frank also read the entire book and has made innumerable improvements. His extraordinary library and collection of articles have been of enormous help. I also appreciate the many talks we had on psychiatry, about which he is highly knowledgeable. Other members of what has been called the Psychiatric Inmates' Liberation Movement have been of value to me as friends and teachers. I also want to thank Barbara Quigley and Dee Dee NiHera for many helpful conversations. I am equally grateful to Svea Oster for our discussions of issues associated with psychotherapy abuse. And I wish to thank Drs. Peter Breggin and John Friedberg for their inspiring books.

I have been very privileged to have as my editor Thomas Stewart, president and publisher of Atheneum. He has a very delicate hand and a fine mind, so that his corrections, deletions, and queries always proved helpful and respectful. He made specific comments on the manuscript that seemed so right I have incorporated them into my text. It was a great pleasure to work with him on this.

I wish, too, to thank my agent, Elaine Markson, who has been a true friend to many a writer in need of support.

I know that living with me during the writing of this difficult book has not been easy for Denise, and her lively daughter, Karima. But I am grateful for their humor and their patience.

Finally, my lovely daughter, Simone, has been my true friend for the last thirteen years, and I love her for it. I would like to dedicate this book to Daidie Donnelley, a precious friend who is leading me into new country.

ACKNOWLEDGMENTS · 33

The author is grateful for permission to use excerpts from the following material:

Hermann Hesse's letter, translated by Jeffrey Masson, from *Kindheit und Jugend vor Neunzehnhundert: Briefe und Lebenszeugnisse, 1877–1895*, edited by Ninon Hesse, vol. 1 (Frankfurt am Main: Suhrkamp Verlag, 1972). *Selected Letters by Hermann Hesse* is to be published in 1990 by Farrar, Straus & Giroux, Inc., copyright © 1972 by Suhrkamp Verlag, English translation copyright © 1988 by Farrar, Straus & Giroux, Inc. Reprinted by permission of Farrar, Straus & Giroux, Inc.

The Complete Letters of Sigmund Freud to Wilhelm Fliess, 1887–1904, edited and translated by Jeffrey Moussaieff Masson, and published by Harvard University Press. Reprinted by permission of Harvard University Press.

The diary of Sándor Ferenczi, translated from the German by Jeffrey Moussaieff Masson. Published by permission of Dr. Judith Dupont.

Direct Analysis: Selected Papers by John N. Rosen. Reprinted by permission of the author.

'Responses to Cumulative Trauma and Indoctrination in Chronic Schizophrenia' and *The Awakening Nightmare: A Breakthrough in Treating the Mentally Ill*, by Albert M. Honig, and a brochure on the film *Other Voices* published by the Delaware Valley Mental Health Foundation. Used by permission of Albert M. Honig, D.O., F.A.C.N.

'The Punishment Cure,' which appeared in the March 1979 issue of *Philadelphia Magazine*. Reprinted by permission of the publisher.

A Secret Symmetry: Sabina Spielrein between Jung and Freud by Aldo Carotenuto, translated by Arno Pomerans, John Shepley, and Krishna Wilson. Translation copyright © 1982 by Random House, Inc. Reprinted by permission of Pantheon Books, a division of Random House Inc.

The Freud/Jung Letters: Correspondence between Sigmund Freud and C. G. Jung, edited by William McGuire, translated by Ralph Manheim and R.F.C. Hall, Bollingen Series 94. Copyright © 1974 by Sigmund Freud Archives Ltd. and Erbengemeinschaft Professor Dr. C. G. Jung. Reprinted by permission of Princeton University Press.

Conversations with Milton H. Erickson, M.D. Reprinted by permission of Jay Haley, editor, and Triangle Press.

Jay Haley's conference paper, published in *The Evolution of Psychotherapy*. Reprinted by permission of Jay Haley and Brunner/Mazel Publishers.

A NOTE ON TERMS
AND CONCEPTS

Below I list some of the more common terms that readers will encounter in almost any book about psychotherapy, and which are used throughout my book. The definitions that follow are the commonly accepted ones.

A *psychiatrist* is always a medical doctor who has undergone further training in psychiatry. In private practice most psychiatrists tend to offer psychotherapy as well as prescribe drugs. If that therapy is based on the principles of psychoanalysis, they usually call it *dynamic* psychotherapy. A *psychoanalyst* in the United States is almost always a medical doctor and a psychiatrist who has undergone further training in psychoanalysis. He usually does not dispense drugs. Sometimes a person with a Ph.D. in psychology or a related field is allowed to train as a psychoanalyst. Training to become a psychoanalyst involves a personal analysis (with somebody who is designated a training analyst, i.e., one able to train others to become psychoanalysts), coursework in the basic principles of psychoanalysis, and supervision by a senior analyst of cases handled. Until the work is completed, a person in such training is called a 'candidate.' *Psychoanalysis* generally takes place with the patient lying on a couch and the analyst sitting behind him or her; it is intense and takes place four or five times a week for fifty minutes. A typical analysis will last from two to ten years. *Psychotherapy* is a term that refers to sessions between a patient and a person trained in psychotherapy in which almost everything that happens involves talking. It is currently offered by psychiatrists, psychoanalysts, clinical psychologists (people with a Ph.D. in psychology), psychiatric social workers, and family and marriage counselors (who have taken a two-year postgraduate program). It is less formal than psychoanalysis; typically, it means a once-a-week session, and it lasts from a few months to a year or two.

Among the many terms used by therapists in general, the most common ones are: transference, projection, countertransference, unconscious, repression (defense mechanisms), interpretation, insight, acting out, resistance, empathy, neurosis, psychosis, schizophrenia. *Transference* refers to the feelings that a patient 'transfers' from an earlier important person (primarily in childhood and most commonly a parent) onto the person of the therapist. The behavior of the therapist is considered irrelevant to the origin of these feelings. They belong to the earlier figure and hence are considered to be *projections*. *Countertransference* refers to the equally irrational feelings of the therapist toward the patient, which derive not from any real qualities in the patient, but from the therapists's own past. *Unconscious* refers to something unknown to the person, but whose effects are nonetheless active. *Repression* is the activity that permits something to remain in the unconscious. It is one of the defense mechanisms; others are denial, undoing, reaction formation. It is not a willed activity. *Interpretation* is the activity the therapist engages in when something unconscious is made conscious to the patient or when a truth is declared. *Insight* refers to the intellectual and emotional recognition of the truth of an interpretation, whereby something that has been, until then, repressed is made conscious. Ideally, insight is followed by behavior changes. *Acting out* is the opposite of insight. It refers to acting on impulses whose origin or meaning is not understood, as opposed to remembering and making a conscious connection. If an emotion is unconscious, almost any behavior can be understood as a form of acting out. Generally, however, therapists mean by this term any action taken outside of therapy that is considered detrimental to therapy or a defense against emerging insight, for example, impulsively getting married, or changing jobs, or starting an affair. *Resistance* is the rejection of the therapist's interpretations or any other activity that, in the opinion of the therapist, impedes, delays, or obstructs the psychotherapeutic process, i.e., the gaining of insight. Any disagreement with the therapist can be (and often is) interpreted as resistance. *Empathy* is the quality the therapist is supposed to have that permits sympathetic understanding of the patient's circumstances, mental suffering, and so on. It is a form of identification with the patient's feelings. *Neurosis* refers to the less serious forms of emotional suffering. They are considered ideal reasons for somebody to see a therapist. *Psychosis* is the general term for the more serious forms of emotional suffering, such as manic-depressive illness. *Schizophrenia* is a subcategory of psychosis and is a diagnosis applied quite liberally to people who are judged to have a 'thought disorder.'

I should point out here that I don't think much of any of these terms. All of them have been used to insult, humiliate, and otherwise degrade patients. I am hardly the first to point this out. However, it is important to bear it in mind when reading. None of the terms refer to real, objective entities. They are more like flags waved to indicate the user's intellectual allegiance. When I use them throughout this book, I am always thinking of them in quotation marks. I do not accept any of them at face value.

INTRODUCTION

This is a book about the fundamental presuppositions of psycho-therapy. It is not an attempt to question the effectiveness of psychotherapy – that is, I do not question that some people *believe* they are helped in therapy (though I do question whether they are *in fact* helped by therapy). I am not impressed by the statistics on the failure of therapy. They seem to me beside the point. The value of psychotherapy cannot be decided by statistics. The bias of these studies is all too evident: Organic methods of 'cure' fare better, especially for what are called 'real mental diseases,' such as 'schizo-phrenia' and 'manic-depressive psychosis.' My purpose in ques-tioning psychotherapy is not to replace it with psychiatry, which Hans Eysenck (*Decline and Fall of the Freudian Empire*) called a 'truly scientific psychology,' for psychiatry, in my opinion, has always been intrusive, destructive, and vicious. Generally, what is sub-stituted for psychotherapy (behavior modification, or organic therapies, including medication) by authors, including Eysenck and Garth Wood (*The Myth of Neurosis*), who criticize it is worse.

This book differs from other books that have criticized psychotherapy in a number of important ways. I am skeptical of anybody who profits from another person's suffering. I do not believe that drugs or other forms of psychiatry are preferable to psychotherapy. On the contrary, I think they are less helpful and almost always harmful. I do not subscribe to the position that there are people who are 'mentally ill' and require 'real treatment,' meaning psychiatric drugs (Martin Gross in *The Psychological Society* takes this position) and then there are the rest of us, who merely need to be talked to. I believe, on the contrary, that while there is no such medical entity as mental illness, there are innumerable kinds of suffering and terrible emotional pain that many people, in fact most, undergo at some time or various times in their lives. I am not denying the magnitude of the problem, only the certainty of the solution. I want to make it clear that I am, in this book, not criticizing those who seek out therapy. People go to therapists for good reasons. They are in pain, they are unhappy, they feel some lack in their lives. When people seek out a therapist one of the things they go for is to relieve the burden of their own memories. They may never have talked about these memories in any depth with another person. Tragic things have often happened to them, especially in childhood, which other people deny, especially those who caused them to happen. When we read almost any modern autobiography, we see that what was most painful was living in a reality that others did not see or would not acknowledge or did not care about.

The questions really begin when we think in depth about the ability of any therapist to respond to people's unhappiness. What is needed, I believe, is a sustained examination of the basic underlying assumptions. There are already excellent critiques of the organic therapies. Survivors of electroshock and psychiatric drugging and forced incarceration have done a great deal to alert the public to the destructiveness of these so-called treatments. Thanks to many articles, often in underground or narrowly circulated newsletters and journals, by many former inmates of psychiatric institutions, we know the dangers of modern psychiatric hospitals (which should be called 'institutions,' because that is what they are). There is a heightened awareness of the dangers inherent in labeling somebody with a disease category like schizophrenia, and many people are beginning to realize that there is no such entity. So far, however, there has been no sustained attack on the basic underlying assumptions of psychotherapy, no attempt to clarify just what it is that is problematic about psychotherapy in general, as opposed to any particular therapy. Every criticism of psychotherapy that I have seen either wishes to substitute a different form of psychotherapy for the ones it criticizes, or in some ways seeks to reform or restructure therapy. These analyses do not penetrate to the core of psychotherapy to examine what is wrong with the very idea of engaging in any kind of psychotherapy.

We go to therapists expecting them to possess certain qualities: compassion, understanding, kindness, warmth, a sense of justice, integrity. But why should we believe that anybody possesses these qualities? Are they, after all, something that can be learned? Freud thought they were, and he has been followed by the majority of psychotherapists. But how are these traits acquired? Are they acquired in a classroom, in a 'training program'? Can even the less exalted qualities be objectively taught? Can we acquire the ability to listen, for example? And even if we were to suppose that these qualities could be learned (and who is to judge whether they have been?), how would the prospective client know that the therapist actually possessed them? Are a few sessions enough? Why would they be, when all around us is evidence that it often takes years for anybody to possess an accurate picture of another person's virtues and vices? How can they be when most therapists are taught that they should attempt to reveal little of themselves to their patients? The fact that some psychotherapists are decent, warm, compassionate human beings, who sometimes help the people who come to them, does not shelter the profession itself or the practice of that profession from the criticism I make in this book. It only means that they function in this manner in spite of being psychotherapists, and not because of it.

The virtues and skills listed above are universally acknowledged in any training program for any type of therapy. These are the qualities sought in applicants by every institute that trains psychotherapists. Once in practice, the therapist is encouraged to believe that he or she is in possession of these qualities. The therapist who admitted to not possessing them would probably not feel qualified to treat a patient. Thus a built-in imbalance is inevitably created. Sometimes this is explicitly recognized by therapists, who believe that they serve as 'role models' for their patients. Thus Freud, in 'On the History of the Psycho-Analytic Movement,' wrote that analysis is a 'situation in which there is a superior and a subordinate.' Therapists certainly expect their patients to look up to them. If 'transference' does not take place, therapy is considered, at least by psychoanalytically oriented therapists, to be impossible. In any area of disagreement between the patient and the therapist, it is assumed that the therapist is more likely to be right (more objective, more disinterested, more knowledgeable, more experienced in interpreting human behavior) than is the patient. When a disagreement arises about a course of action, the therapist does not admit to bias, or personal views having nothing to do with the patient.

The therapist claims that she or he is always attempting to determine what will benefit the patient. All behavior on the part of the therapist and all prohibitions with respect to the patient are being done for the patient's 'own good.' Yet this is what everybody says who wants to change another person's behavior. Parents say it, teachers say it, the police say it, and the government says it. How do we know it is actually true? The more sophisticated therapist may well say: 'No, I cannot possibly know what is best for my patient. But I can help her to decide by exploring, with her, all the alternatives and their implications. If she chooses to do something that I think is unwise, still it is her decision to make.' It sounds good, but can we really expect this kind of impartiality and tolerance from a therapist? How many people have any of us met in real life of whom we could say this? Many patients have direct experience of situations that arise in therapy where they fear they cannot count on true tolerance and objectivity.

An example is from a conversation I had recently with a woman who is active in Women Against Pornography. When she told her analyst that she was engaged in political action against *Playboy*, he responded testily by saying that *he liked Playboy*. She was alert and realized that her analysis was doomed. So she left. But suppose the analyst had kept his private opinion to himself? How would she know that she was locked in a struggle that could not possibly benefit her with a person who was in no position to understand her or appreciate the seriousness of her struggle against pornography?

A woman to whom I was very close for many years was in classical psychoanalysis. The woman grew up in the Warsaw ghetto and selected an analyst whose name suggested he was Jewish (in fact, he was German) and would therefore probably know of the problems she had faced as a child in war-torn Poland. Well trained, he never answered her question as to whether he was Jewish or not. She believed he was Jewish, and he did nothing to correct her. Unfortunately, her assumption (he was later to call it a fantasy) had devastating results for her and none for him. He was completely ignorant of the history of the Warsaw ghetto and could make little sense of what she told him, insisting to her that many of her perceptions and observations were distorted by internal aggression. The 'Aryan side,' an expression that came up often in her memories, was for him nothing more than a metaphor for her internal life. The therapist may have benefited from the cloak thrown over the dreadful reality by this metaphor, but she did not. All she gained was the task of freeing herself from yet another tormentor. His insensitivity, historical bewilderment, and general incomprehension were weapons with which he punished this woman for not viewing the universe the way he did: narrowly and benignly. Her 'paranoid' belief that she was pursued came to grief in the breathtaking sweep of his ignorance. A more sophisticated apologist for this man may well claim that he was in no position to alter her past, and the only way he could be of use to her was to focus on her internal life. For the therapist, the terrible realities of the Warsaw ghetto or Auschwitz are, like any other reality, simply the raw clay of our fantasies, of which the master sculptor is the psychotherapist. But it seems that the people who make this claim most vocally are the very people who in their own lives have been furthest removed from traumatic events of this magnitude. It is simply beyond their own experience.

An exception I remember was a Freudian analyst who told me that he found it unbearable to treat concentration-camp survivors, for the simple reason that he had been there, too, and he felt such an urge to reach out to his fellow sufferer. This, in his eyes, disqualified him from helping. He could not be objective. But he remained unaware of the tragedy that would often await the person whom he sent elsewhere: he or she is sent to an analyst with no real understanding and hence no urge to reach out. Non-Jewish German analysts have recently become active in treating Jewish concentration-camp survivors and the International Psycho-Analytic Association sponsors meetings on the topic of holocaust survivors and therapy. This can be a subtle (or not so subtle) form of revictimization.

To attempt to impose one's own views on patients goes against the canons of most forms of therapy. But in reality this is what most therapists do. Freud, at the age of eighty-two, wrote a strong statement against attempts to turn patients into mirror images of their analysts:

> However much the analyst may be tempted to become a teacher, model and ideal for other people and to create men in his own image, he should not forget that this is not his task in the analytic relationship, and indeed that he will be disloyal to

his task if he allows himself to be led on by his inclinations. If he does, he will only be repeating a mistake of the parents who crushed their child's independence by their influence, and he will only be replacing the patient's earlier dependence by a new one.[1]

But two sentences later, Freud ruins these noble sentiments by adding the comment: 'Some neurotics have remained so infantile that in analysis too they can only be treated as children,' thus leaving open the door to any and every form of abuse under the guise of necessary 'educative' efforts.

Most therapists believe that the unhappiness over which patients come to therapy is not socially caused, but is self-created, that the patients are at least partially responsible for the dissatisfaction that is felt. The therapist will often state that he or she is not in a position to alter society, to change a patient's past, or to intervene in the life of the patient. What the therapist claims to offer is understanding. But implicit in this offer is the belief that the understanding is an internal one, an understanding of what the patient has brought to the situation to create unhappiness or at least to intensify it. Here we have a rich soil for creating deep and lasting misunderstandings, and even greater misery. This is one area where psychotherapy ceases to be a harmless pastime and passes over into being oppressive.

To offer but one example, it must not be forgotten that *all* the professions, until very recently, denied the very existence of the sexual abuse of children. Pediatrics, psychoanalysis, psychiatry, psychology, social work, and therapies of all schools were not prepared to acknowledge the reality and extent of the sexual abuse of children until the last few years. To now set themselves up, as many have done, as 'experts' in the cure of a condition they only reluctantly and belatedly recognized does not inspire confidence.

It might be argued that therapists, even if they are not more likely to show a sense of social justice, are not less likely to do so than any other professional. That there are individual therapists who feel outrage over social injustice I am certainly prepared to believe. But has any particular group of psychotherapists ever

[1] 'An Outline of Psycho-Analysis' (1938), in vol. 23 of *The Standard Edition of the Complete Psychological Works of Sigmund Freud*, trans. by James Strachey (London: The Hogarth Press, 1964), 175.

taken a stand against abuse? Did Freud? We know that his insistence (in 1896) that women were telling him the truth about having been sexually abused in early childhood did not last, and that, by 1903, he had retracted this statement. Equally significant, when he published the last of his *New Introductory Lectures on Psycho-Analysis*, in 1933, he was silent about the rise of fascism. Sebastiano Timpanaro, in *The Freudian Slip*, puts it very well:

> Nor is there, in this last lecture, which surveys obscurantist or falsely progressive 'world views,' a single word against the Fascism that held sway in Italy and Hungary, against the clerical Fascism of Seipel and Dollfuss in Austria, or the Nazism which was about to triumph in Germany.

In the ban on electroshock by the voters in Berkeley, California, in 1982, not one group representing any form of psychotherapy took a public stance in favor of the ban, though in private many psychotherapists have told me how appalled they are at the continued use of this largely discredited technique.

Carl Jung, as even some of his staunchest allies have now admitted, was prepared to cooperate with Nazi psychiatry in Germany, making anti-Semitic comments about 'Jewish psychotherapy' in the hope, he unbelievably claimed, of keeping it alive. When the Argentine government began locking up and torturing some politically active psychoanalysts, their local psychoanalytic institute would not defend them. Perhaps this was merely from fear. But then, how does one explain the fact that the parent organization, the International Psycho-Analytic Association, though asked by a small number of politically aware colleagues, would not take a public stance, or write a letter of protest to the Argentine Psychoanalytic Society or to the Argentine government?

The nefarious role of psychiatrists in the euthanasia program in Germany during the Second World War has been investigated in a devastating recent book by Lenny Lapon, a former psychiatric inmate, now a political activist. The message of *Mass Murderers in White Coats: Psychiatric Genocide in Nazi Germany and the United States* was so unpopular that Lapon had to publish the book himself. Susan Brownmiller in her 1975 book *Against Our Will* has shown that psychiatric attitudes about rape created a climate in which it took the rise of the women's movement in the 1970s to convince the larger public that rape was real and endemic to male-dominated societies everywhere. Had not Helene Deutsch, an influential psychiatrist and psychoanalyst, written, in her two-volume *Psychology of Women*, that 'rape fantasies often have such irresistible verisimilitude that even the most experienced judges are misled in trials of innocent men accused of rape by "hysterical women"'?

Are there values inherent to psychotherapy that encourage, albeit silently, passivity in the face of injustice? Are the examples just given (and the ones examined in the chapters to come) fortuitous, chance lapses? I am afraid not. Blaming the victim, the subject of a brilliant social exposé in a book by that name by William Ryan in 1971, is the hallmark of psychotherapy. The values essential to psychotherapy deflect a person from deep reflection on the sources of human misery.

The tools of the profession of psychotherapy are insight and interpretations. But one person's insight is another's nonsense. The term 'insight' was first used in Germany psychiatry, where the expression was *Krankheitseinsicht*, which refers to the patient's recognition of his or her own illness. When a patient said, 'I am sick,' he or she was considered to have improved. In other words, a cure was begun as soon as society's definition of illness was accepted personally. As the reader will see, what the German nineteenth-century physician defined as 'sick' would probably today be called 'independent.' 'Moral insanity' was the term most often applied to a young woman who did not accept her subordinate role in society. The same criteria are at work in today's psychiatric institutions, where a patient cannot be released until willing to admit that the reason for being there is a good one. A few brave souls like Janet Gotkin, in *Too Much Anger, Too Many Tears*, have already recognized the absurdity of this position, and how it turns reality on its head: The truly 'healthy' are those who see through the pretense of psychiatry in the institution. But while some therapists might be sympathetic to this position when the description of the psychiatric institution is put to them, they are less 'insightful' when it comes to their own work. Freudian analysts find it as difficult as anybody else to examine critically their own psychoanalytic prejudices. Yet when somebody who has been stigmatized as 'mentally ill' staunchly maintains his or her own vision in the face of social disapproval, this courage is considered by therapists as further proof of the illness. Psychotherapy is still a living legacy to its forebear: a confining institution.

Psychotherapy is no less immune to political, guild, and ideological pressures than any other profession. The purpose of this examination of the foundations of psychotherapy is to demonstrate that the pretensions of psychotherapy are not accidental. By its very nature, psychotherapy must pretend to supply an objective, kindly, and humane atmosphere to those who wish to express their deepest feelings of pain and sorrow. The tragedy is that this legitimate need is exploited, even if with the best of intentions, by 'experts' who claim to offer what has never been theirs to give.

1

THE PREHISTORY OF PSYCHOTHERAPY:
Hersilie Rouy in the Asylums of France
and the Story of Julie La Roche
on Lake Constance

The medical and psychiatric journals of the late nineteenth and early twentieth centuries reflect a society that was not in any great intellectual turmoil. The serene view of the world of mental illness was particularly comforting to the status quo. This view maintained certain postulates: Heredity is all-important; a vital sexual life is pathogenic; masturbation in particular leads to a dangerous disease; children should be protected from all forms of sexuality, especially their own. When exposed, children should immediately be isolated to prevent their infecting other children. When children have been exposed to any kind of stimulation, they often grow up to be mentally unstable. This instability will manifest itself in certain symptoms, one of the most important of which, for the nineteenth century, was 'moral insanity,' that is, doing things that the rest of society, especially a parent or male psychiatric society, considers wrong. Given this wide application, almost anything a person did, any choice of profession, any choice of partner, could be considered a form of moral insanity, just as today anything a patient in psychotherapy does that conflicts with the values of the therapist is often labeled 'acting out.'

Carl Emminghaus, Professor of Psychiatry and head of the Psychiatric Clinic in Freiburg, wrote a book, often quoted, called *Emotional Disturbances of Childhood* in 1887.[1] In that book he spoke of a child's 'instinctive inclination to the obscene' or, even more generally, 'to the bad in particular.' Yet many of the examples he

---

[1] *Die psychischen Störungen des Kindesalters* (Tübingen: H. Laupp, 1887), 206–13.

provided bring to light instead the terror of a small child caught in a world of brutality and horror from which it has no possibility of escape and which nobody will even acknowledge. Emminghaus told of an eight-year-old girl who often ran away from home, and who showed great anxiety whenever her mother and father attempted to come close to her. Her head would grow hot and red, her face would break out in a profuse sweat, and she would race out of the house screaming: 'My father has murdered a child.' Finally, she attempted to hang herself, explaining, truthfully and sadly: 'I did it so that I could be in peace.' Emminghaus described her as paranoid, and had her removed to an asylum.

An adolescent boy was locked away because he suffered from 'sexual hallucinations.' This was adduced from the fact that he once told the doctor: 'You are a pig and crazy. You are the same person who did those immoral things in my room, and you are doing precisely to me what the people at home did to me too.' Emminghaus and his colleagues considered such a statement to be clinical proof of insanely inappropriate speech and of paranoia. Emminghaus did not ask: Did anything happen to this child at home? And, had he asked the question, there is little doubt that he would have said that nothing had happened to the child, because for Emminghaus such things could not take place. A twelve-year-old boy 'for absolutely no reason,' wrote Emminghaus, was plagued by the 'mad fantasy that his own father wanted to murder him.' As soon as he saw his father, he would become terribly anxious and would try to flee the house. He even jumped out of a window. This was evidence of his mental instability.

For Richard von Krafft-Ebing, the most famous psychiatrist of his day, education must start at a very early age in the case of children who are 'predisposed to mental illness.' Such children should not be permitted to read fairy tales. They should be permitted to read only the blandest of literature. Such children (whom Krafft-Ebing called 'nervous') show an 'abnormal intellectual development,' that is, they often display a desire to learn and to read very early in life. This must be discouraged. They should not be given lessons in language or music. They should be taught, above all, to be obedient and must be 'weaned away from any form of sensitivity.' Such children should be trained to become innkeepers in the country, far away from things that will only excite their emotions and intellects and lead them straight into a mental institution.[2]

Hermann Oppenheim (1858–1919), Professor of Psychiatry in Berlin and director of a private sanatorium, in a popular series of lectures on children's 'mental disturbances' advised that children should not be permitted to read newspapers, or be taken to picture galleries, museums, or theaters; they should not be permitted to demonstrate strong emotions of any kind, whether positive or negative; they must learn, above all, 'renunciation,' 'order,' 'cleanliness,' 'simplicity,' and 'freedom from desire.' The final words of the book are these:

> Although we are not in a position to replace an inherited and inborn neuropathic constitution with another one, nevertheless it is in our power, through the manner of education and the way a child is handled, and especially through keeping at a distance certain harmful things which I have indicated in the above lectures, to see to it that the bud is not allowed to develop luxuriantly, to fully flower, and in that way to prevent the creation of a disease.[3]

Oppenheim's words seem benign enough on their surface: what reasonable person could gainsay the effort of a 'professional' to lead a child away from a life of mental torment? And, given the authoritarian role of parents in the nineteenth century, who would question the right of a parent – or a physician he hired – to prescribe treatment for a 'troubled' child? But more disturbing questions lie beneath the surface of Oppenheim's comments. The entire medical profession encouraged among its patients a belief in specialized knowledge, experience, and a complete trust in authority. If the physician did not advise and warn, he did not know, and if he did not know, he soon lost his authority, and without his authority he could not practice. Psychiatry was the tool of medicine, and medicine was the tool of society.

Society demanded that these very children who showed any

[2] These sentiments are described in Krafft-Ebing's book *Nervosität und Neurasthenische Zustände* (Vienna: Alfred Hölder, 1895). The ideas cited come from the chapter on treatment, 299ff.
[3] *Nervenkrankheit und Lektüre* (Berlin: S. Karger, 1907).

signs of sensitivity should, as adults, and sometimes even as children, be sent to psychiatrists for treatment. In order to understand how psychiatric treatment evolved into psychotherapy, we must know something of the history. I propose to give some of that history in the form of two stories from the nineteenth century, which will illustrate better than any retelling of the history what it meant then to be judged 'insane.'

MEMOIRS OF A MADWOMAN
Hersilie Rouy in the Asylums of France

One of the most extraordinary documents in the history of psychiatry remains almost totally unknown. It is a book published in Paris in 1883. No copy of the book is to be found in any library in the United States, and only with great difficulty was a copy found in France. Yet the book ranks, in my opinion, as the single most important document of the social history of madness in the nineteenth century.

The book was written by Hersilie Rouy, and is entitled *Mémoires d'une aliénée* (Memoirs of a Madwoman).[4] The long book, 540 pages, is the story of Hersilie Rouy's incarceration, when she was forty, in the Salpêtrière (the famed psychiatric hospital where Jean Martin Charcot worked) in Paris and in many other French asylums over a fifteen-year period. The book, written in French, has never been translated into any other language, and has never been referred to in the history of psychiatry.

What happened to Hersilie Rouy was to happen to countless

---

[4] Published by E. le Norman des Varannes (Paris: Paul Ollendorff, 1883). Preface by Jules-Stanislas Doinel. A book has recently come out in France, which I have seen too late to discuss here, that talks about the experiences of · Hersilie Rouy: Yannick Ripa: *La ronde des folles: Femme, folie et enfermement au XIXe siècle* (Paris: Aubier-Montaigne, 1986). In 1882 a novel appeared, written by Le Norman des Varannes, director of the asylum in Orléans (the same man who published her autobiography), under the pseudonym of Edouard Burton: *Mémoire d'une feuille de papier, écrits par elle-même* (Paris: Ollendorf), but I have not been able to find a copy. Perhaps my earlier comment about the uniqueness of Rouy's book should be tempered. Paul Gotkin recently sent me another very unusual book by a nineteenth-century woman author on the same theme as the book by Rouy: *A Secret Institution*, by Clarissa Caldwell Lathrop (New York: Bryant Publishing Co., 1890). She, too, writes well and with great indignation about the indignities inflicted on the 'mentally ill.'

women in France, Germany, England, the United States, and elsewhere, down to the present day. What makes her work almost entirely unique is the clarity of her vision, her ability to understand what the French psychiatrists were doing to her. She was never in any doubt as to her basic sanity, and the reader cannot help but be struck by the power and passion of her writing. The book can serve as a paradigm for all victims of psychiatry, everywhere and always. It deserves to be known.

I could learn nothing about the author beyond what she herself tells us in her book. All information comes from the book. Hersilie Rouy was born in Milan, Italy, in 1814. She was the illegitimate daughter of the astronomer Henri Rouy. She was a moderately successful pianist, and was known to musical society in Paris for her concerts. She lived with her father until his death in 1848, when she was in her thirties. Nothing is known of her mother.

Her troubles began under mysterious circumstances a few years later. Her half-brother apparently was involved. On September 8, 1854, she was, without warning, removed from her Paris apartment, her belongings, including her jewelry, were seized (never to be recovered), and she was taken to an asylum, Charenton. Later she was taken to the Asile de Maréville, and then to the Salpêtrière, where she was told: 'Crazy or not crazy, you will be considered to be crazy. Once you have been incarcerated, everything is against you' (66). She was also told, in so many words, what many 'mental patients' take years to discover. A well-known French psychiatrist by the name of Lasègue saw her. Rouy described what happened:

> He saw me for only a minute or two . . . and he sentences me on the strength of doctor Calmeil, who sentenced me on the strength of a doctor who had never seen me at all, who took me away as a favor to somebody else, on the strength of what they had told him! [92–93]

A problem that was to plague her for the rest of her life began early in this famous asylum: her name. The first person who saw her at the Salpêtrière was named Chevalier. He decided to call her by his name. When she insisted that she was really Rouy, the doctor told her that this was the product of her sick imagination. She had no family, he explained to her, 'except in your sick imagination. You could not know who you are, since nobody knows who you are' (101).

The attempt to deprive her of an identity no doubt began as a prejudice against children born out of wedlock: they had no legitimate, legal name. The issue soon took on far more nefarious overtones. Once she stood up for her right to exist as a separate person, with her own name, she was calling into question values that nobody in this or any other asylum was likely to countenance. The authorities said she was without an identity except the one they chose to give her.

This must have been the fate of many patients. But in Rouy's case something untoward happened. Some workmen came to wash the windows and were evidently impressed by her regal bearing and her elegant speech. They took her for the daughter of the Duke of Bordeaux:

> This became all the more serious because there were current negotiations to merge the two branches of the Bourbons, and it was known that the Salpêtrière was often used as a kind of dungeon to swallow up victims [of intrigue] under the pretext that they were insane]106].

Rumors spread quickly that Rouy might be the illegitimate daughter of King Henry V. Rouy, deprived of her real identity, decided to strike back by using this rumor to the discomfort of her tormentors in the asylum. She had decided by this time that she could expect no help from French psychiatry, the French judicial system, or even the French government, yet she fought on alone in a remarkable battle, pitted against a vast and immovable structure, with only her wit to enable her to survive. Her doctor told her: 'Your delusion is total, and all the more dangerous and incurable in that you speak just like a person who is fully in possession of her reason' (133).

Once her talent as a pianist was discovered, the asylum doctor ordered her to play. She refused. He threatened to punish her. She continued to refuse. The doctor then refined his 'diagnosis' of her illness by telling her: 'You are proud.' She answered: 'Doctor, pride is the wealth of the poor, and a poor person has the right to refuse to act as the toy of the rich' (160). Many of the inmates congregated around her, and she saw that she was more helpful to them than the doctors: 'I brought, from my heart, more hope and consolation to my poor companions than did all the medical specialists together' (173).

Because of the trouble she had been causing in the Salpêtrière, she was sent to another asylum, in the country, at Auxerre. She says that when she arrived it looked, from the outside, so beautiful, so carefully laid out, with gardens and flowers. But the appearance was deceptive. For inside the building were cells 'where one can lock up those who complain in dark cells . . . saying "I curb and I cure"' (202). Dr. Poret promised to release her in three months if she remained silent, but she refused. He told her: 'Crazy or not, as long as you are here you will be considered crazy, and with such a large number of certificates concerning you, one more or less will not make a great difference' (180).

She bitterly conceded the point. Clearly doctors at both the Salpêtrière and Auxerre were puzzled by Rouy, who showed no signs of being what they considered crazy. Yet she was there and must, therefore, be crazy.

She was kept at Auxerre for five years. One day, years after her release, she found the note that had kept her incarcerated for five years on locked wards:

> The woman named Chevalier, age 50, who has been treated in various asylums, arrived in Paris a few days ago . . . with a delusional letter containing threats to the police station of the Seine. She is in a state of reasoned mania. Signed: Lasègue [204].

After the five years, she was returned to the Salpêtrière, on July 3, 1863, and, as she tersely noted, 'the word "relapse" was sufficient to keep me there' (204).

The very attributes that make Rouy such a valuable witness, the clarity of her style, the eloquence of her writing, the sharpness of her intellect, were regarded as 'pathognomonic,' as signs of her illness. Back at the Salpêtrière, she had a fateful, brief conversation with Dr. Payent, which was to have important consequences. He wrote that she had a high opinion of her personal worth and expressed herself with the greatest facility (212). She was suffering from what the French called *folie lucide* and what the English and Germans later called 'moral insanity.' She had, he went on, 'somewhat ridiculous pretensions to have her incarceration recompensed' (212–213). He told her that it was unfortunate that the ordinary world did not recognize her illness. Only the expert could recognize just how sick she was. She acidly rephrased his comment: 'My insanity would not be appreciated in the real world' (213). Payent was disturbed by her rationality, her ability to perceive the doctors' intentions. He arrived at a new 'diagnosis': 'The woman suffers from *orgeuil incurable*,' incurable pride! (212) It was a diagnosis that was to stay with her for the rest of her life.

But while the doctors in the asylum regarded Rouy's ability to write, and her insistence on her right to do so, as symptomatic, she knew it was her only tie to reality: 'If I had not been able to write, I would have died, or become crazy' (214).

The problem centered increasingly on her name. She signed her letters The Antichrist, the Devil, Sylphide, or Polichinelle. She explained that she liked the name Polichinelle (that of a deformed puppet of the French theater) because it was what the patients called her when they were threatened by the staff for criticizing the doctors and sought her help: 'I am accused of insane vanity, of ideas of grandeur. This, name that belongs to a puppet, taught me that I was loved by the poor, by the miserable, the abandoned, not for my name, but for myself' (148).

At one point, her doctor asked her if she still signed her letters in this manner. Her answer was perceptive: 'Of course! There is no law forbidding the use of pseudonyms, especially when one is officially anonymous' (216). When the interview was over, Rouy commented devastatingly on his departure: 'He left, limping on his tiny feet which were ensconced in his faded slippers – his corns hurt him – pulling his big head into his small threadbare frock coat' (217).

While she was being considered for release, a doctor who had not seen her for many years wrote to a member of the family: 'I do not hesitate to state that her release would be a terrible tragedy for her first of all, and for all of your family it would be an endless source of the most plaguing worries' (250). But Rouy had a way of totally deflating these comments:

> This letter shows how a doctor is able to claim that somebody is still insane (and thereby have her continue to be held against her will in an asylum) even when he has not seen her for ten

years and who might, therefore, have been cured in the meantime, if, in fact she were ever crazy to begin with [251].

Finally, Rouy met the Inspector General of Asylums, who reviewed her history, and the many asylums she had been put in:

> *Inspector:* You don't seem to be happy anywhere.
> *Rouy:* Would you be happy if you were in my place? [He stopped laughing when I asked this question.]
> *Inspector:* No, of course not! He offered me his hand [254].

On Christmas Day 1865, in Orléans, two high functionaries came to see her:

> They came to test my thinking, my beliefs, to see if there were grounds for keeping me in perpetuity. Was I, then, in front of the grand inquisitors? . . . How can you destroy the future of a woman and allow her liberty to be assaulted simply because she carries her head high and has the audacity to want to live from her own talent and her own writing? I have been buried alive [257].

Meanwhile, her half-brother had become the director of the newspaper *La presse* in Paris. He did not wish to see her released. He had informed her relatives that she had died. She knew that nobody would be able to sympathize with her because 'one has to have gone through this pain to understand fully the bitterness' (264). The doctors considered her paranoid, she wrote, because of her complaints that the inadequate lighting in her cell prevented her from writing. And what, they asked, did she have to write about in the first place? Rouy was in despair. She wrote:

> For fourteen years I have lived under an incarceration that cut me off from the real world, took away my civil rights, deprived me of my name, took away everything I owned, destroyed my entire existence without even being able to say why [275].

In spite of this she was able to say: 'You can kill me, but you cannot dominate me and you cannot silence me' (290).

Soon after writing this, fourteen years after her incarceration began, her fortunes began to change. Her papers arrived from Milan, her birthplace, and the authorities were able to see that she was, in fact, the person she claimed to be. A cousin was discovered: he was Laurence Rouy, Commander of a Division of the Haras, cavalry of the household of the Emperor, Napoleon III. And astonishing things began to happen because of her highly placed Rouy cousin:

> From the day that Dr. Payent learned that I was the cousin of a Commander of a Division of the Haras, he decided I was already much better. I improved even more after the visit of the Chief of Police. The doctor decided I was completely cured the day the administrator decided to refer the case to the courts [304].

She was granted another audience with the Inspector General of Asylums, whom she had seen earlier. After listening to her story, he advised her:

> *Inspector:* Believe me, you would do better to keep silent.
> *Rouy:* Thank you for your advice, sir, but I cannot continually be sacrificed for the reputation and peace of mind of those who ought to protect me and show me justice [318].

The authorities were alarmed. They could look very bad. Rouy asked them to take responsibility for what had happened to her:

> *Rouy:* You could simply say that you made a mistake.
> *Inspector:* That is impossible. We put you away because you were crazy. We set you free because you are cured.
> *Rouy:* Of what have I been cured?
> *Inspector:* That is for the doctors to say [320].

Rouy's many letters and many complaints to government officials were beginning to have an effect. The authorities had now to explain how Rouy, not crazy, was incarcerated in an asylum. Among the first of the doctors who had been her was a certain Pelletan. The authorities now believed that he wanted to get rid of her for reasons of his own, and so had her committed. But there were problems with this theory, as became evident during her cross-examination by the Ministry of Health:

> *Ministry:* You will perhaps deny that he was your lover?
> *Rouy:* Certainly I will, for I never saw him before the day he took me away [324].

A letter from Rouy to one of her psychiatrists was published in *La France médicale* (vol. 16, August 12, 1871). It reads:

> You have, you say, fifteen years of experience as a doctor in mental asylums. I have had fourteen years as a patient in these same asylums. You deny that my correspondence was intercepted and that my windows were sealed because you cannot believe that such acts are probable, or even possible. Permit me to say, Doctor, that you are like every other psychiatrist. The minute something strikes you as out of the ordinary you cry: 'Insanity!' and certify the patient without any further examination. The science of psychiatry must be clairvoyant if its practitioners are able to do this without any examination [372].

The authorities wanted to know exactly who she was and what her family background was. Rouy was not as interested as they were: 'For me it was not a question of knowing whether I was legitimate, the product of adultery or a bastard, but rather why was I locked up as crazy without being crazy and under a name that was not mine' (403). She knew that the embarrassment she had created went beyond her own case and clearly indicted the entire profession: 'In everything, everywhere, always, the ministry, the prefectures and the police had no other concern than to exonerate themselves and each other and did not look in any way for the truth' (411).

The Attorney General made an inquiry for the Ministry of Justice. He wrote to the Keeper of the Seal, on October 18, 1868:

> Miss Chevalier [*sic*] talks and writes a great deal. I have read with great care several of her letters. . . . This correspondence seemed to me to indicate in truth that the author was suffering from mental problems [418].

As proof he noted that she wrote, on July 16, 1867, to the Administrator:

> I think it is my duty to repeat that today there are two Hersilies. The proof of this is that for the last fifteen years I speak, and I write, and I repeat that the other Hersilie disappeared during a single afternoon and no trace has been found of her [419].

Here Rouy was making fun of the psychiatrists for insisting that she was not who she said she was. They used her ironic humor as evidence that her thinking was disordered. She answered then:

> A foreign woman played music under the name of Hersilie Rouy . . . as soon as I was locked away, the rumor of the death of Hersilie Rouy was spread. But which one died? Her death was announced to my relatives, friends and acquaintances [421].

Rouy appealed to the Ministry of Justice again. The Ministry's position was revealing:

> This does not concern us at all. All we have done is harbor an *unknown* person whose identity is a doubtful as her name. But our doctor who knows more about it than we do has the conviction that she is mad and we bow before his infallible science [421].

Rouy was not fooled by this response. She was beginning to recognize how difficult her position was, for 'in exonerating Dr. Pelletan, it was necessary to exonerate as well all those who later kept me incarcerated' (421). Once the mistake (if that is what it was) was made, it would be necessary to cover the trail of everybody who had ever participated, and of course the solidarity of the medical profession, of the court system, of the Ministry of Justice would prevail over the truth and the need of one woman to discover that truth.

Soon, however, thanks to the tireless efforts of Rouy, the Minister of the Interior became involved as well, and he demanded an inquiry. Dr. Calmeil, at Charenton, the first asylum to which

Rouy was committed, wrote to the Minister of the Interior defending his actions on the grounds that when he saw her she may well have *appeared* sane, but only because she was in an *état latent d'aliénation* (i.e. remission). On May 22, 1869, at the Minister's request, he explained the source of her insanity: 'She tired her nervous system by an excess of late nights and by her diligence in study and in her devotion to music . . . her life was filled with emotions' (428). However, he went on, one must exercise caution, since 'she has preserved her ability to reason in a logical fashion and even in a specious manner . . . The day after she arrived she was overexcited and talking volubly' (428).

Rouy defended herself: 'Psychiatrists are wonderful! I would very much like to know if *they* would be joyous and satisfied if they were to suddenly find themselves locked up in an insane aslyum . . .' (431).

Calmeil continued: 'In the end, we avoided the inconvenience of letting the public know about the tragedy that had happened to her' (432). But Rouy did not let him off the hook, and rightly asked who would have been inconvenienced:

> The psychiatrists were well able to avoid this inconvenience by causing me to vanish from my house as easily as a conjurer's pea. They changed my name so that nobody would know where I was. They said I was dead so that nobody would try to find out what had become of me [432].

On June 29, 1865, Payent, the doctor at Orléans, defended himself in a letter to the Administrator:

> When I look at her file, I see that all the doctors, Trélat, Métivier, Falret, Lasègue, Calmeil, Husson, considered her crazy; that the directors and the doctors of the asylums at Fains, Maréville, Auxerre, Doctors Auzouy, Teilleux, Foville, etc., etc., etc., all had the same opinion. . . . She encourages insubordination wherever she goes. Diagnosis: Pride, vanity, envy. . . . We consider, along with all our colleagues, that she is suffering from a kind of incurable insanity of pride [*folie d'orgueil incurable*]. She must, therefore, be kept in an insane asylum [443].

When the Ministry indicated that Rouy was demanding an outside hearing, the psychiatrist, because she was now quieter and more restrained, wrote:

> Would it not compromise this result to expose her to the emotions of the personal hearing she seeks? After all, we are not dealing here with a person who is guilty and who could be usefully listened to in her own defense, but rather to a person who has been sick for a long time . . . who needs not justification, but protection and help [446].

How clear is the voice of the nineteenth-century psychiatrist! But Rouy refused to be quiet:

> Do the people in the ministry by any chance believe that the insane have no emotions? . . . Had I been seen, and questioned in a serious and honest fashion, this laboriously constructed 'insanity' would no longer have been credible, and it is this result that was so strenuously avoided under the guise of commiserating with my situation [446].

The Inspector General wrote to the Minister of the Interior, d'Aboville. He conceded that one doctor might have made the initial mistake of admitting her. But

> I cannot grant that ten, fifteen people with official titles, esteemed, honored, of whom several are justly cited in the scholarly world as being masters, could have each of them become complicit in a bad action, in a crime . . . and please note that you are accusing not only these men, but also all the functionaries, judges, and others who had, during the long seclusion of your protégée, been forced to hear, listen to and judge her numerous and incessant protests [457].

She knew, and had been told by the authorities, that 'we cannot condemn ourselves by admitting an error.' But she was not to be put off:

> I am as sane today as I was twenty years ago. I will persist until I am vindicated. I do not wish to disappear again under a

> fictitious name by means of a certificate prepared in advance by order of the police under the pretext that my style, my ideas, make it necessary to lock me away and take away my civil liberties [460].

She was implacable:

> I have no intention of either hiding what I have suffered, which was such a valuable lesson, nor excusing those who first threw me in that hell and did not recoil from any slander in order to keep me there and once I got out to see to it that I would vanish [466].

In 1878 the Ministry of Justice offered Hersilie Rouy the sum of twelve thousand French francs as compensation and an annual pension of three thousand six hundred francs (467).

She died of pulmonary congestion in Orléans, on September 27, 1881.

Hersilie Rouy's book is a remarkable document in its own right, and also for what it can say to readers today. We have almost no reports by patients from the nineteenth century of what it was like to be in an institution. What we have, instead, are the reports by doctors. Comparing Rouy's account with almost any 'case history' by a nineteenth-century psychiatrist shows it to be not only fuller, more detailed and elaborated, but also clearly more authentic. She wrote from her direct experience, not from any theoretical point of view. Another reason her account is important is that increasing attention is being paid today to the fact that women in particular are often victimized by being labeled or given a specific psychiatric diagnosis. Rouy's book, which is unknown to people who are writing about this issue, provides perhaps the first account of such victimization. Many feminists, and some women psychiatrists who identify themselves as feminists, are critically examining the *Diagnostic and Statistical Manual* (the *DSM* III), the official manual of the American Psychiatric Association for classifying the 'mentally ill.'[5] Rouy's account is an invaluable example of the wrongs

---

[5] See, in particular, Patricia Perri Rieker and Elaine (Hilberman) Carmen, *The Gender Gap in Psychotherapy: Social Realities and Psychological Processes* (New York: Plenum Publishing Co., 1984).

associated with diagnosis. Finally, an influential article by David Rosenhan, 'On Being Sane in Insane Places,' showed experimentally how easy it is for a perfectly normal person to be committed to a psychiatric institution, and how difficult it is to be released, even when the experiment is described to the psychiatrist.[6] Rouy's is the very first account demonstrating the truth behind Rosenhan's experiment.

Nothing that happened to Hersilie Rouy would be described today as 'therapy.' But let us remember that the psychiatrists who saw Rouy were convinced that they were incarcerating her for her own good. Rouy's psychiatrists described what they were doing as 'therapy' even though that therapy consisted of nothing more than an attempt to break her will. The practice of psychotherapy has changed enormously in these one hundred years, but the questions I raise in this book are disturbing: Is it possible that there was nothing unusual or unique about Hersilie Rouy's experience, then or now? Is it possible that what happened in the middle of the nineteenth century to Hersilie Rouy, the attempt to break her will, to label her as 'sick' and in need of treatment, represents the very heart of psychotherapy, its basic underpinning? Whether we put people in psychiatric institutions or simply interpret their dreams, once we allow any group of people in our society to define what is sane and insane, we have begun to set up the structure upon which psychotherapy as we know it today is built. Hersilie Rouy is one of the first people ever to question that structure, and she deserves to be remembered for that.

But even while these things were happening to Hersilie Rouy, and countless other people in psychiatric institutions throughout Europe, a new approach was beginning to manifest itself in Switzerland, one that was to have fateful consequences for the development of psychotherapy.

[6] *Science* 179 (1973): 250–58. This article caused an enormous controversy, especially in psychiatric circles. Robert L. Spitzer, the main author of the *DSM* III, responded in 'On Pseudoscience in Science, Logic in Remission, and Psychiatric Diagnosis: A Critique of Rosenhan's "On Being Sane in Insane Places,"' which was published with other criticisms and Rosenhan's response in the *Journal of Abnormal Psychology* 84, no. 5 (1975): 433–74.

MORAL INSANITY
The Story of Julie La Roche
on the Lac de Constance

The term 'moral insanity' was coined by the British psychiatrist James Cowles Prichard, in his *Treatise on Insanity*.[7] Here is what Richard Hunter and Ida Macalpine have to say about moral insanity in their *Three Hundred Years of Psychiatry, 1535–1860: A History Presented in Selected English Texts:*

> At his time it was a considerable advance, almost revolutionary, to equate with insanity proper cases without those twin features delusion and hallucination which had long been and indeed still are considered the hallmark of the mad.[8]

This definition is interesting because it clearly shows that diagnosing people as suffering from moral insanity was a necessary precursor to offering them psychotherapy, since the term, in effect, means that they do not live the way you would wish them to live. It is really impossible to offer them psychotherapy until you have made the judgment (which they are somehow coerced into accepting) that they are not living well, or as well as other people, and are therefore in need of 'help.' We often claim that the people seeking psychotherapy make this moral judgment on their own, but this is almost never true. The tyranny of judging another person's life to be inadequate was and is the very wellspring of psychotherapy.

A few years ago I visited the Sanitarium Bellevue in Kreuzlingen, Switzerland, on Lake Constance.[9] I was looking for new material on Ida Bauer (Sigmund Freud's Dora), and I believed I might find it there. We know that Anna O. had been a patient in

---

[7] London: Sherwood, Gilbert & Piper, 1835.

[8] London: Oxford University Press, 1963, 838.

[9] The sanitarium (also known as the Binswanger Clinic Bellevue) is renowned for many reasons. Ludwig Binswanger, the founder of 'existential psychiatry,' was a student of Carl Jung, and went with Jung, in 1907, on Jung's first visit to Freud in Vienna. Freud visited Binswanger at Bellevue in 1912. Anna O. (Bertha Pappenheim), the famous patient of Josef Breuer, about whom he wrote in *Studies on Hysteria* in 1895, was there, as was the great Russian dancer Nijinsky in later years. Edmund Husserl, Martin Buber, Karl Jaspers, Martin Heidegger, and many other well-known figures of European intellectual life visited there.

Bellevue, and we also know that Freud sent other patients there during the 1890s.

I can remember my first visit to Bellevue and the strange feelings that came over me as I went through the iron gate into the enormous, quiet, parklike garden in which the buildings of Bellevue were set. Bellevue had recently been closed (after more than one hundred fifty years) and was empty of people. It was autumn, everything was quiet, and, as I walked on the leaves and looked up at the giant trees, I could not help imagining the feelings of patients one hundred years ago, when Bellevue was at the height of its fame, as they first arrived to take up their strange new life.

How many women, filled with inexpressible sadness and fear, had taken this same path before me? I remembered the opening of Thomas Mann's novel *The Magic Mountain*, in which Hans Castorp paid his first visit to the Swiss tuberculosis sanatorium Schatzalp (the fictional counterpart of the mountain town Davos), intending to spend three weeks but remaining seven years. And I remembered Thomas Mann's lecture at Princeton in which he described the making of *The Magic Mountain* and how, in 1912, he went to visit his wife in Davos for three weeks, and the physician in charge of the sanatorium examined him, found a wet spot on his lung, and suggested he stay for six months. Mann knew that if he did, he might, like the fictional Hans Castorp, enter a magic time zone, when seven years of his life would be taken from him.

A stranger, with 'expert knowledge,' tells you that you are ill and require specialized care. How much more powerful was the compulsion to believe this if you were a young woman and your father brought you, for a consultation, here to the most advanced, the most elegant, the most prestigious clinic in all of Europe.

Wolfgang Binswanger, the son of Ludwig and the last medical director of the clinic, took me into one of the houses and led me to a room that contained thousands of files; they were the case histories of every patient who had been in Bellevue from 1875 to its closing in 1975. Looking through them, I found that they contained not just the case histories written by the doctors, but also letters from the patients to family members, letters from the senior Binswanger to other doctors, letters from people connected with patients, photographs, and more. I spent two weeks reading all the cases of women who were in Kreuzlingen between 1880 and 1900. It was like a *Magic Mountain* with original documents. But unlike

Mann's characters, these women were real; they were not mouth-pieces for one persons' views (however interesting) of the world of prewar Europe.

So many lives, so much suffering, and so little remained! It made me sad but also resolved to attempt to understand something of what happened to these women. Their true stories, their real lives, not fiction, would help me understand the buried history of psychotherapy.

A common scenario, as revealed by the case histories, was the following.[10] A young woman is told by her father (from whom she is somewhat distanced) that he is taking her to visit family members in Switzerland. On the way, the train stops at the rather desolate railway station of Kreuzlingen. It is a quiet winter day. The woman looks out of the window, notices the bleak trees, the stillness of this little place, the streets bare of people, the silent buildings. She sees the dark lake and the mist, and remembers that people call it romantic. Nothing could happen here. (Is it any wonder that one patient wrote, 'Nothing exists here,' and another, 'I was hoping it was a bad dream – that it would go away, that I would wake up'?) She shudders, glad that she comes from Berlin, or Munich, or Vienna. Her father calls her out of the train and introduces her to a man she has never seen: 'Herr Doktor Binswanger.' The father looks embarrassed, shuffles his feet, then abruptly turns away and boards the train, saying, as he leaves: 'Go with him.' This is no vacation; this is her destination. She has been brought, by trickery, to a clinic for hysterical women, a sanitarium for *Nervenkranke*, those ill in their nerves. Binswanger knows little about her. But solely by virtue of her having been brought to him, he 'knows' she is sick, suffering, hysterical. The look she gives her father in parting makes the diagnosis easy: This young woman is suffering from moral insanity. That is, in the opinion of her family

[10] Here, abridged, is a letter to Dr. Binswanger, dated Meran, March 9, 1894: 'Dear Doctor: On the morning of the 11th I shall come to Constanz directly from Innsbruck. I would appreciate it if you could send somebody to meet us since I do not know my way around. My daughter and I are in mourning. She is a tall, slender girl, somewhat taller than I am, very pretty, with black eyes. I will be wearing a hat and shall carry an umbrella with a golden handle in my right hand so that you will be able to recognize me. My daughter does not know that I intend to leave her there. I will tell her that she and I are going to stay in a Pension so that we can rest. Everything will then fall into place. Sincerely yours.'

and her doctors, there is nothing wrong with her intellect, or her senses, yet she cannot live like other women. She wants too much, she has too many ideas, she is too independent. She does not know what is best for her. She does not know what correct behavior is. She is morally insane.

Binswanger was much taken with the term invented by the English doctor. It fit his patients well. What was wrong with them was that they were morally insane. There were so many of them, and there seemed to be more all the time. He could barely cope. He had to hire assistants, distinguished doctors like himself: Dr. Hermann Smidt from Bremen and Dr. Otto von Holst from Livonia. Somewhat to Binswanger's credit, he did not wish to use any kind of physical or chemical restraint, and was rather interested in what he called *traitement moral* or what we would to-day call 'psychotherapy.' A moral treatment for a moral disease seemed to make sense. Some of the wealthier patients, from the upper classes, 'could be offered an entire villa, so that they could be looked after by their own servants as well.'[11] But the genteel picture of quiet rural care for slightly eccentric European nobility does not really correspond to the reality. Access to the archives of the sanitarium permitted me a more realistic evaluation of what actually went on there. Following are some of the case histories, beginning with that of Julie La Roche.[12]

On February 25, 1896, a certain Herr La Roche (also spelled

---

[11] See Ludwig Binswanger, *Zur Geschichte der Heilanstalt Bellevue in Kreuzlingen, 1857–1932,* a privately printed history of Bellevue. More information on the clinic is found in the Zurich weekly *Tagesanzeiger Magazin* (no. 14, April 5, 1980), in an article by Jör Aeschbacher, which contains some fine photographs (pp. 16–23). The last prospectus describes Bellevue as follows: 'Bellevue Sanitarium is a private hospital devoted to the cure and treatment of all forms of neuroses, mild and severe psychoses and chronic addictions. Education facilities are available for young psychopaths undergoing treatment here. The institution is also particularly well adapted to the needs of those requiring physical and nervous rehabilitation.'

[12] The information for the first case history comes from the files of Julie La Roche contained in the archives of Bellevue. With the assistance of Marianne Loring, my research associate, I was also able to find the original newspaper articles and some of the important court documents relating to the case in Canton Thurgau in Switzerland. Much of the information has been reprinted in a small, rare booklet: *Irrenanstalt und Millionenerbe: Streiflichter aus einer Basler Millionärsfamilie und einer thurgauischen Irrenanstalt,* a reprint from the *Schweiz. Wochen-Zeitung* (Zurich: J. Enderli, 1897).

Laroche) wrote a brief letter in German from Basel to Dr. Robert Binswanger, which reads as follows:

Dear Sir:

May I be permitted to inquire whether you would be willing to admit for observation a young lady aged nineteen who has been diagnosed by her doctors as 'psychically perverse.'

The lady is presently not here, however I could send you a telegram advising you of her arrival in Kreuzlingen so that she might reach your institution, properly accompanied, without a stop in Basel, in order to be placed there, in the event you are willing to accept the patient. Please let me know if you are willing to admit the patient.

The lady must be placed under strict surveillance so that any attempt at escape can be prevented.

Looking forward to your reply, I am, sincerely yours,

LA ROCHE-RINGWALD.[13]

On February 28, 1896, R. Massini, a gynecologist who was the family doctor, wrote a letter, at Mr. La Roche's request, to Binswanger. The letter reveals a great deal about the attitude of physicians in the nineteenth century toward women like Julie La Roche. It is worth quoting in full:

Dear Dr. Binswanger:

At the request of Mr. L. La Roche-Ringwald, I am quickly sending you a brief report on his daughter Julie. Miss Julie La Roche is 19 years old. Six years ago her mother died of diabetes; her father's age is 52. After his wife's death, he led what must be described as less than a model life; he has a mistress who as recently as two years ago frequently accompanied him and his children on walks. The fact that the woman's husband joined them on these walks, and tolerated the relationship because of the financial support he received from Mr. La Roche, did not make matters any better.

[13] All the translations that follow in this chapter were done by the author and Marianne Loring, from original German and French texts. All this material has recently been transferred to the university archives at Tübingen.

Mr. La Roche, himself in poor health, often in a bad mood and given to violent temper outbursts, hardly offered his children a loving home. Miss La Roche went through her adolescence in this environment, watched over by maids and a somewhat stupid governess. About two years ago she met a girlfriend with whom she probably had a lesbian relationship. At the same time she manifested a steadily increasing tendency to lie. On the one hand this tendency made the unpleasant conditions in the home appear to be worse than they really were, and on the other hand it created a veritable romance based on pure fantasy. Her relations with her family as well as her experiences were woven into a fabric of untruth. Until last year Miss La Roche was kept in a pension in Lausanne. She returned home suffering from metritis [an inflammation of the uterus] and after a probably somewhat violent altercation with her father she ran off to Berlin with her friend Miss Schmitter. Thereupon a life of adventure began. At New Year's she is said to have bled from the stomach; from Wiesbaden she made a sudden trip to Berlin and entered the sanatorium of Dr. Aronsohn and was treated by Professor Dr. Ewald. In mid-January she ran off from there, supposedly with her brother, but in fact with the adventurer von Smirnoff, and suddenly appeared in Basel, presenting him as her fiancé. Here of course the relationship was not approved, and after a few days the daughter disappeared, leaving behind a letter to the effect that she would either marry von Smirnoff or kill herself. Since that time all efforts of the police to trace her have been unsuccessful. The flight from Basel can only have been realized with the help of employees who were bribed. It appears that even in Berlin Miss La Roche employed detectives.

Von Smirnoff lives with his mother, who is separated from her husband, in Berlin, probably on borrowed assets. It is clear that he exploits Miss La Roche, who likes to exaggerate her financial assets. All of this leads me to conclude that Miss La Roche, who is otherwise a thoroughly lovable girl, is heading toward 'moral insanity,' which makes medical supervision advisable. Dr. Aronsohn also found his patient to be emotionally ill. It is unlikely that Miss La Roche will submit freely to stay in Bellevue. She will surely attempt to escape, perhaps at the least pretend to commit suicide. It will therefore be necessary to put her in the charge of incorruptible guards who will watch over her very closely. Of course in view of the above circumstances a pregnancy is not impossible. A cousin of the patient got herself pregnant by an ugly coachman a few years ago; a cousin and brother-in-law of her father (he married Mr. La Roche's sister, his cousin Germaine) was mentally ill but is back home now. I do not believe that Mr. La Roche ever mistreated his daughter, though he may well have reprimanded her harshly. As you can see it is not a pleasant picture I unfold before you. Also I am at a loss to know what should be done with the unfortunate, corrupted girl. Unfortunately, I cannot influence her in any way because she considers me her father's ally. I feel sorry for her father in spite of his faults for which he must now pay heavily.

It goes without saying you will observe the patient, and in case no sufficient grounds are found to diagnose a psychosis (mental illness), will discharge her.

However, I still hope that the discipline inherent in institutional life and appropriate treatment will bring the poor patient to the point where she can be returned to society.

Please exuse my long letter, but I could hardly express myself more briefly since it is very important to me that I give you as clear a picture as possible.

Respectfully yours,
DR. R. MASSINI
Basel, Feb. 28, 1896

Julie La Roche entered the Binswanger clinic on April 12, 1896. There are enough case histories in the archives of Bellevue to let us know what could well have happened to her. There are cases where a young woman was admitted in the full bloom of youth, only to stay there for forty years and then be discharged to an old persons' home. Such did not happen to this spunky, independent, and resourceful woman. Less than a week later, she was out. And not only was she gone, but she took what was, for the time, the brave step of writing her own story, and publishing it in a respected German-language Alsatian newspaper, the *Strassburger Bürgerzeitung*, on July 24, 1896. In many ways it is a unique document:

I, Julie von Smirnoff, born La Roche, daughter of Louis La Roche and Louise La Roche, born Ringwald, from Basel, find myself forced to offer to the public my life history, or at least a part of it, in as few words as possible, in order to seek public support. I was born on the 8th of March, 1877, in Basel, Switzerland, the eldest child of my parents. Until 1887 my childhood could be called a completely happy one, since I was constantly watched over by a loving mother. But in 1887 my mother died, and from then on my life became a painful struggle. My father, who had always disliked me, now gave evidence of this in every possible way. He treated me with exquisite cruelty and even managed to turn my younger brother, whom I loved very much, against me so that our sibling relationship suffered. In 1893, at my urgent insistence, I was put in a pension in Lausanne, since I could no longer bear living at home. My father abused me in a terrible manner, and his drunkenness as well as his immoral life, which reached into our very home, made my existence in Basel unbearable. In 1895 I returned from Lausanne to Basel. Once I fell down the steps and unfortunately spilled some ink on the stairs, which sent my father into a terrible rage and as a result of this accident I had to put up with the most terrible scene for hours. At the beginning of March in that year, I saw myself obliged to say something to my father about his immoral life, which was taking place more and more often in our house. At 10 o'clock at night he showed me the door, after he had thrown a sharp object at my head with such force that my face was covered with blood, to which a deep wound testified. There are witnesses to all these events. I went to Berlin, where I had friends, and wrote my father from there. In Berlin I became very ill. When I was better, I went to Wiesbaden, where I was taken into a pension for women. In December, 1895, I was forced to leave Wiesbaden to go to Berlin and have a consultation there with a famous professor (on the advice of a doctor in Wiesbaden) since I had a stomach ailment. I notified my father. In Berlin I met a young Russian nobleman, Edgar von Smirnoff; his sister had been a friend of mine. We fell in love, and when my condition permitted it, I traveled with his next of kin to Basel, so that I could inform my father. I had barely begun to tell him about my love for this Russian nobleman, when he fell into a terrible rage, and abused me in the most awful manner with his cane, threw dishes at me, and kicked me. The next day, Edgar von Smirnoff came to the house to ask my father for my hand. The only answer he received was rude insults. From then on, my father locked me in the house and garden. I was subjected to the most terrible abuses and diabolical harassments with reference to Edgar von Smirnoff and my dead mother. On February 3, 1896, I escaped. The abuses, the drunkenness and the immoral life of my father, as well as the love I felt for Edgar von Smirnoff, encouraged me to take this step. I went to France, while Edgar von Smirnoff stayed in Berlin. A friend of Edgar von Smirnoff, Dr. Taunay in Saarburg, allowed us to use his house. From there we traveled in the middle of February, to England, to be married. I was sick, and the bad pains and bleeding in my lungs resulting from the terrible beatings with a cane inflicted by my father while I was in Basel made everything worse. It was only the great care, concern and selfless sacrifice on the part of my husband that had so far prevented my condition from becoming dangerous. One day in Saarburg, where we returned after our marriage, and where I had to remain in bed, we were surprised by the police and then by my father. My father pretended to be a broken man, which is something he often did in front of other people. My husband and Dr. Taunay were taken into custody. I was not even allowed to touch my husband. Though sick, I was dragged off through storm and rain by Mr. La Roche. My marriage certificate, everything, was in vain. With court transportation, I was taken to Kreuzlingen, which is a private insane asylum (as can be ascertained by looking it up in any directory). There, on the first day, I was diagnosed as melancholic and insane. My father made the most dire threats against me, but when anybody was present, he behaved in a most charming manner. I was put to bed and I was guarded day and night by two women nurses. The mocking response to my persistent request to be permitted to see a clergyman was: 'What for, we are all descended from the apes.' The last words my father addressed to me were: 'Here you can remain for a long time.' [The word used, *sitzen*, is applied to a prisoner in jail.] My sole nourishment was coffee and dry bread in the morning, watery soup at noon and again coffee and a piece of bread at night. During the six days I was forced to lie in bed, my bed was never made up. Upon questioning by the doctor and Mr. La Roche, I said that I had been pregnant for a month. Every day, while at Kreuzlingen, upon strict orders from Dr. Binswanger, I was given medication seven times a day. This caused me extreme pain, which still persists. The night from Saturday to Sunday was to see my release. I had already planned to flee the previous night, but did not succeed. All the doors were locked and my guardian woke up. But God helped me the following night. I managed to pack up a few things without waking the guardian, and creep out of the room. The door to my room, which normally was locked day and night, was open. The door to the house responded to the pressure of my hand and when I reached the great iron gate in the garden I found it open, and could take flight. What a miracle, for normally this gate, which I could see from my window, was heavily bolted. One can imagine my feeling of bliss when the walls of the private insane asylum of Dr. Binswanger in Kreuzlingen were behind me. Two able physicians, one of them a 'Kreisphysicus' who had treated me for a long time, testified in writing that my mental state was completely normal, that I am not even nervous. They are willing to testify any time in court. It is evident from this inhuman act of incarcerating one's own child, who is mentally completely normal, in an insane asylum, that matters of inheritance could be at the bottom of this action. According to the law of Basel, upon reaching the age of twenty, or earlier if I marry, I inherit my mother's fortune, which amounts to several million Swiss francs. I am absolutely certain, had I remained for several weeks longer in that insane asylum, treated as I was, malnourished, given drugs which caused the most awful abdominal pains, surrounded by guards who tried to convince me that I was insane, worried about my husband, from whom I had been so brutally separated, and of whom I knew nothing and whom I was not permitted to write, surely Mr. La Roche-Ringwald and Dr. Binswanger (who must have been in communication with my father for some time, since he knew of my coming, as I found out), as well as Dr. von Holst and Dr. Smidt, would have reached their goal. Is it conceivable that a doctor can declare a patient insane after two hours without having spoken to her? I would like to address myself to public opinion, to inquire whether there is any defence against such acts.

A Swiss newspaper, the *Thurgauer Tagblatt*, gave a one-page summary of this remarkable autobiographical account on August 9, 1896. Dr. Robert Binswanger sued the newspaper for slander. The court appointed a psychiatrist from Göttingen, Dr. D. Kolb, to investigate the charges. He fulfilled his duties by visiting Dr. Binswanger and his clinic. He did not meet Julie La Roche. His report, which we were able to find in the court records of the city of Thurgau, is another remarkable example of the thinking of the time and an indication of the extraordinary bravery of Julie von Smirnoff. Dr. Kolb wrote:

> The care and treatment of the patient was appropriate to her condition at the time according to the depositions of all persons and as can be expected *a priori*, with all certainty, in the case of an institution with the renown of Dr. Binswanger's. The demeanor of the patient during her stay, her repeatedly expressed satisfaction, are in noticeable crass contrast to her publication. She behaved graciously, obediently, was content, communicative and cheerful. The article published in the *Strassburger Zeitung* written by the patient reveals a mendacity and shamelessness which in the case of a young lady of standing and supposedly good upbringing can only be the result of intellectual and moral defects. My observations are weighty points in support of Dr. Massini's judgment of the patient. Certainly we have before us in the person of Frau Smirnoff someone who since her childhood has shown exceptionally bad habits, has a tendency toward perversions, toward reckless spending, gets into debt, runs about seeking adventure, lies and is sexually aberrant. However, her upbringing was made difficult on the one hand because of unfortunate family circumstances, but also because of her personal constitution. She suffers from weakness of character, as demonstrated in particular through lying and shamelessness. These are the main characteristics of a mental illness which, for simplicity's sake, we call 'moral insanity,' a state of moral and intellectual weakness. This view is shared by Drs. Binswanger and Smidt, even though they did not go so far as to give an

expert opinion as requested by Mr. Laroche. They did not do so out of caution and because the short time did not permit them to make an accurate observation upon which they could base such an expert opinion. Such patients are able to hide their defects or keep them a secret depending on the time, circumstances and their surroundings. Therefore there is nothing remarkable when these patients are judged to be mentally normal by laymen, nor in the fact that the press can publish medical testimony to the effect that they are healthy. Therefore it is my conclusion, based on my subjective opinion, that all accusations made against the private insane asylum of Dr. Binswanger in regard to the sick Frau von Smirnoff Laroche in the article are pure inventions without any foundation in fact.

DR. D. KOLB, Göttingen
September 7, 1896

The paper was fined, and on February 11, 1897, published a retraction which contained the following comment:

It appears that Julie Laroche has been eccentric from the time of her childhood on, and as she grew up she developed a distinct inclination to mendacity, to keeping bad company, to wasting money, to perversions, in short, she carried all the signs of the disease known today as 'moral insanity.'

So much is transparent in these texts. We have here a paradigm for what was to become psychotherapy in the years to come. Julie La Roche (perhaps we should now call her by her married name, Julie von Smirnoff) was a woman of substantial character. At a very early age she had developed what the doctors came to see as her first symptom, ideas of independence. At the age of ten she realized, when her mother died, that her father did not love her, a remarkably courageous perception in a child. She knew, too, that her father wanted the several million Swiss francs she was to inherit from her mother when she turned twenty or married. The only way for her father to gain control over her inheritance was to have her declared insane and become her legal guardian. Once she actually married (in England, because she could not marry at nineteen in Switzerland without parental consent) it would be necessary for him to have her declared incompetent, in order to nullify the marriage. Clearly Dr. Massini, the family physician, wrote the letter to Binswanger, declaring her to be 'morally insane,' with at least some reluctance. He provided enough information in the letter to show the reader that the father was, even in the view of this man who was in his pay, not entirely a paragon of virtue. But he alerted Dr. Binswanger to the fact that what they were hoping for was a verdict of at least one type of insanity, the most benign – moral insanity. That would permit Binswanger to treat her with his *traitement moral*, that is, psychotherapy, which in this case would mean to convince her that she should not marry, should not seek to be independent of her father, and, above all, should not seek to manage her large inheritance on her own. The hint that something should be done about her pregnancy seems to have been taken seriously, for at the clinic she received a drug that she felt was in order to cause her to abort.

Julie von Smirnoff was at no time under any illusions about what to expect from her father, or the medical doctors in his employ. She must have known that these men shared her father's views, which were the prevailing views of the time. She courageously escaped from the asylum. Even more remarkable was her moral outrage (were there such a thing as moral insanity, then surely those suffering from it were the father and his henchmen-psychiatrists, not Julie von Smirnoff), which led her to submit to a daily newspaper an account of her life that bears all the authenticity of directly lived experience. She is speaking with her own voice, about her own life, and there can be no mistaking the truth of what she is telling. The very fact that Binswanger agreed to receive her (after the father's peculiar and empty letter) suggests that he was, at least in principle, in agreement with the father's aim. It seems very likely, as well, that Julie's belief that he attempted to abort her with medication is correct. Naturally, when the account appeared in a Swiss newspaper, Binswanger's reputation was bound to suffer. He did not attempt to dispute the truth of her account. Instead he appealed to the state to appoint a psychiatrist. This was a shrewd move, since the psychiatrist was bound to believe that anybody who did the things Julie von Smirnoff did was suffering from moral insanity. Moreover, he was a psychiatrist from Göttingen, no doubt well acquainted with Binswanger himself and his illustrious brother, Otto Binswanger, Professor of

Psychiatry at the University of Jena. Dr. Kolb never saw Julie von Smirnoff, but nevertheless was willing to diagnose her, no doubt on the basis of the letter by the father's physician and the account by Binswanger. He provided, of course, no medical evidence, only moral judgment disguised as an admittedly 'subjective' medical diagnosis. He concluded that she was suffering from moral insanity. The Swiss newspaper was quick to recognize its error, and also joined the male chorus: Yes, she was sick, morally insane, and sexually perverse to boot.

To his credit, Robert Binswanger did not believe in an unchangeable *abnorme Keimanlage*, an abnormal constitution, but what he wished to substitute for it was an uncritical reflection of the pedagogical principles of his own society and class. This is an essential ingredient of psychotherapy, seen here as an early attempt to browbeat the patient into conforming to what society expected of her. What Binswanger felt his patients lacked, primarily, was 'discipline,' and it was the basic duty of the physician to provide the patient with education, or, rather, what he called a *Wiedererziehung*, a re-education. Binswanger wished to reach the point where

> the doctor, through detailed examination of the experience of the patient, through the study of the peculiarities, and through empathy and encouraging words, wins his trust so that the patient allows himself to be led by the doctor . . . into being punctual and to obeying the medical procedures recommended by the doctor.[14]

There were many cases like that of Julie von Smirnoff. It is clear from my reading of the archival records of the patients in Bellevue that many of the women were branded as morally insane merely because they did not conform to what their parents or society or medicine expected of them. There is the case of the Countess Ilona E., who was in Bellevue from 1893 to 1899. Her mother explained to the doctors that she 'read novels by Zola, had a love affair with her tutor, and wishes to earn her living as a piano teacher.' A report from a certain Dr. Svetlin, from another asylum in which the woman had been confined, stated:

[14] Ludwig Binswanger, *Zur Geschichte der Heilanstalt Bellevue in Kreuzlingen, 1857–1932,* 25.

Patient protests against being labeled ill, saying 'one could not help but become neurotic in my family.' Her most pronounced ethical defect is the total lack of any love for her mother. A further indication of her moral pathology is her complete irreligiosity and the lack of any faith in authority. . . . It is clear from these reflections, which are the result of a five-month observation of the Countess, that she suffers from a light case of 'moral insanity.' It is definitely inadvisable to allow her to be independent.

Not unlike Julie von Smirnoff's, the Countess's father wished to enlist Binswanger's aid in depriving his daughter of any possible inheritance. In a letter dated July 7, 1894, he wrote:

In the course of this year I have to petition the court to be made Ilona's legal guardian before she turns 24. She tends to fall into a 'moral marasmus.' May I ask you, then, to testify in writing that Ilona is not able to conduct her own affairs, nor, as a result of her illness, is she able to make appropriate plans in the various circumstances of life or take care of herself. I need this in case she has any plans once she is of age.

In another case from the Bellevue archives, the famous Viennese psychiatrist Julius Wagner-Jauregg, who later received a Nobel Prize, wrote to Binswanger about a certain Baroness M.:

Dear Director:
Baroness M., about 19 years old, is hereditarily heavily tainted; she has good intellectual gifts and even attempted to write, though the achievement was dubious. She has always been moody, bizarre, and difficult to guide. In the last few years she has presented an ever-growing picture of 'moral insanity.' She is boastful and a spendthrift, a liar and malicious. The emergence of a lack of self-restraint in the sexual sphere, manifested in cynical conversations, entering into nonsensical, compromising love affairs, scandalous public accusations against her own mother and other very respectable persons — all this necessitates placing her in an asylum. The only real sexual excesses that seem to have arisen are in the form of masturbation. She should be kept in the locked ward, [even

though] I believe she will prove very docile in the asylum, at least in the beginning in particular, because she lives in holy terror of being truly locked away, for example, in an insane asylum. Therefore the knowledge that the possibility of such an internment hangs over her will have an excellent disciplinary effect on her.

The mother wrote Binswanger a letter confirming everything Wagner-Jauregg had written, adding: 'Even when she was only seventeen my daughter had the insane desire to be free and independent.'

Was it only women who suffered from the diagnosis of moral insanity? No, but the majority of cases were women. Where the label was attached to men, they were apt to be young, talented, and rebellious. A tragic example, which was only revealed in 1966, concerns the well-known writer Hermann Hesse.[15] In June 1892, his father was convinced that Hermann had a secret life, filled with 'unnatural and unhealthy thoughts and feelings and excited fantasies.' The father decided to commit his fifteen-year-old son to the Stetten Asylum for Epileptics and the Feeble-Minded. When the son realized where he was being taken, he became terrified. The head of the asylum, Inspector Pfarrer Schall, noted that the way Hermann knitted his brows was a sign of moral insanity, and, moreover, that he had been reading the Russian writer Turgenev, an evil influence. From the asylum, the boy wrote one of the great letters of the nineteenth century. On September 11, 1892, he wrote to his father:

And now I ask you, purely as a human being (for I permit myself, in spite of your desire and my 15 years, to have an opinion): Is it right to send a young person, who, apart from a minor weakness in his nerves, is pretty much completely normal and healthy, to an *Insane Asylum for Epileptics and the Feeble Minded*, and thereby to rob him, violently, of his belief in love and justice and hence in God? ... Now, when I am

---

[15] The material that follows comes from Hermann Hesse, *Kindheit und Jugend vor Neunzehnhundert: Briefe und Lebenszeugnisse, 1877–1895*, ed. by his wife, Ninon Hesse, vol. 1 (Frankfurt am Main: Suhrkamp, 1972). The translations are my own.

apparently cured, I am inwardly sicker than ever. Would it not be better to throw me, with a millstone tied to my neck, into the deepest part of the ocean so that I could sink to the bottom? . . . It is indeed strange, very very strange in fact, that for a young man of 15, nervous, true, but otherwise completely healthy . . . there is not a single spot on this whole wide globe of ours but Stetten im Remstal, the Castle, Number 29. . . . You are proper, real Pietists. You are Christians. I am only a human being. . . . If you could look inside me, you would see a black hole, the only light a hellish gleam and burning – you would wish me to die, you would allow me to die. . . . I would like to run away, but where? It is cold outside. It is autumn and I have no money, no place to go, simply into the gray world out-side. . . . Please don't write me any more about Christ. . . . Everywhere here is written Christ and Love, but all is filled with hatred and enmity. . . . I am a human being, as good as Jesus. . . . Write to me, but please, no hollow phrases . . . [262].

And yet, Paul Flechsig, Professor of Psychiatry at the University of Dresden, delivered a celebrated address before King Albert of Sachsen, on April 23, 1896, 'Die Grenzen geistiger Gesundheit und Krankheit' (The Borderline between Health and Sickness), in which he said: 'In reality, in Germany to this day, there has never been even a single solitary case of a person who was not mentally ill who has been declared to be mentally ill.'[16]

Most historians would agree that psychotherapy began with Freud. Anna O., whom many consider to be the first psycho-analytic patient (in actuality, Breuer's patient) and who appeared

---

[16] Published in Leipzig: Veit Verlag, 1896, 7. Leonard Frank has drawn my attention to the fact that a similar statement was made to the United States Senate in 1961. 'It is well known that there are legal safeguards against what is commonly called railroading of people into mental hospitals, and we contend that people are very well protected in all of the States. I have never in 30 years of constant living with this problem seen anyone whom I thought was being railroaded,' said Dr. Francis J. Braceland, former President of the American Psychiatric Association. From *Constitutional Rights of the Mentally Ill*, Hearings before the Subcommittee on Constitutional Rights of the Committee on the Judiciary, United States Senate, 87th Congress, First Session, March 28, 29 and 30, 1961, Part I: Civil Aspects (Washington, D.C.: U.S. Government Printing Office, 1961), 65. See, for similar statements, 37, 146, 155, 177.

in the *Studies on Hysteria*, was, as mentioned earlier, sent to Bellevue. Early in his career as a psychotherapist, Freud sent some of his patients to Bellevue.[17] The psychiatrist and sexologist Richard von Krafft-Ebing received a letter from a nineteen-year-old woman, Nina R., who told him that she had sexual dreams. Krafft-Ebing wrote to Freud that this patient was suffering from 'psychic masturbation.'[18] In 1891 Freud wrote a case history in which he stated:

> Nina R. has always been overexcited, full of romantic ideas, thinks her parents did not like her. Has the occasional fantasy that her father does not love her. The patient does nothing but read and write. Life appears to her to be transitory and everything seems unreal.

Two years later, Freud wrote out this woman's case history for Dr. Binswanger:

> The inborn crookedness of her character manifested itself in her forgetting her immediate duties, her adjustment to her milieu, while she strove to gain interests on a more idealistic level and absorb more exalted intellectual stimuli.[19]

Here, clearly, was a woman up in arms about the life that awaited her, attempting to find a way out. This, in the eyes of the world

[17] See Albrecht Hirschmüller, 'Eine bisher unbekannte Krankengeschichte Sigmund Freuds und Josef Breuers aus der Entstehungszeit der "Studien über Hysterie,"' *Jahrbuch der Psychoanalyse* 10 (1978): 136–68.

[18] In 1888, in an article entitled 'Über pollutionsartige Vorgänge beim Weibe' (*Wiener medizinische Presse* 29: 466–69), Krafft-Ebing describes a particular patient as a model of the person afflicted with psychic onanism: 'Her main complaint is an almost continuous restlessness and excitation in her genitals. It behaves like a stomach when it is hungry. She feels, in her genitals (objective examination negative), a painful burning, a heat, a pulsating, a restlessness, as if the internal mechanism of a clock had gone crazy inside her.'

[19] *Jahrbuch der Psychoanalyse* 10, 159. *Die angeborene Schiefheit ihres Wesens offenbarte sich darin, dass sie an die Erfüllung ihrer nächsten Pflichten, an ihre Ausgleichung mit ihrem Milieu vergass, während sie sich bemühte idealere Interessen zu gewinnen und höhere geistige Anregung auf sich wirken zu lassen.* Freud was writing a private letter to a colleague, not meant for publication. Hence the clumsiness of some of the wording. The German is not easy to translate. This is why I have given the original.

around her, constituted her illness. Breuer, Freud, and Krafft-Ebing all agreed, as would the entire medical world of the time, that she was sick, and needed 'treatment.'

During the next ten years, Freud developed a special kind of treatment for such 'sick' people that came to be the model for today's psychotherapy. Freud, no doubt, transformed the prevailing methods of psychotherapy. In a few short years, the procedures used by men like Binswanger and Krafft-Ebing would no longer be recognized as psychotherapy. Nevertheless, Freud shared with these men, and others like them, most of the underlying moral judgments about the lives of his patients. Freud's great case histories are replete with presuppositions about the correct way to live. He was treating people who, for one reason or another, did not fit into the standard mold. Very often he shared the views of the parents and other guardians of his patients that their misery was caused by their own refusal to conform to what society demanded. Freud found it difficult to side with the patients, and yet the technique he developed was, in theory, uniquely suited to uncovering precisely the kinds of hypocrisies in society that made the patients so unhappy in the first place. Unexpectedly, Freud found himself learning about things he was not equipped to evaluate, but which, as a therapist, he felt he must evaluate. The tragedies that ensued can be clearly seen in many of his case histories. The Dora case is one of the most poignant of these tragedies. Freud, as therapist, was confronted with the dilemma that what society called 'moral insanity' in Dora (and for which her parents demanded a cure by psychotherapy) Dora knew to be 'moral vision.' The direction of psychotherapy was decided in this one historic case.

2

DORA AND FREUD

Asked to pinpoint the beginning of what we know as modern psychotherapy, many people would cite Freud's treatment of the patient he called Dora (Ida Bauer).[1] Many, in fact most, of the issues that are current today concerning treatment, its drawbacks and its strengths, were first raised by Freud in the paper he wrote on the Dora case. It contains the first discussion ever of the effects of 'negative transference,' that is, what happens when a patient thwarts the efforts of the therapist, does not wish to get well, does not wish to see him, does not wish to accept his interpretations or play the game by his rules. It also contains many explicit statements as well as underlying assumptions about what is normal and healthy for a sixteen-year-old girl that have had a great influence on what we label 'pathological' today. What Freud did *not* do looms almost as large as what he did do, and we are able to deduce a great deal about what is considered the proper sphere of psychotherapy. Although no Freudian therapist would accept without question all of the assumptions of this important paper, none would claim it is basically outdated or unsound. It is still a living force, an influence of some magnitude in psychotherapy. Freud was at the height of his powers when he wrote the paper,

[1] Sigmund Freud, 'Fragment of an Analysis of a Case of Hysteria,' trans. by James Strachey, *Standard Edition* (*S.E.*), vol. 7 (London: The Hogarth Press, 1953), 3–122. All page numbers refer to this edition. All translations from the case are by Strachey unless I indicate in the footnote where I differ from the *S.E.* The German is 'Bruchstück einer Hysterie-Analyse' and was first published in 1905 in the *Monatsschrift für Psychiatrie und Neurologie* 18: 285–310, 408–67. For the German text I have used the one published in the *Gesammelte Werke* (*G.W.*), ed. by Anna Freud, E. Bibring, W. Hoffer, E. Kris, and O. Isakower, vol. 5 (London: Imago Publishing Co., 1942), 163–286. Reprinted by Fischer Verlag in 1972.

and it contains the essential ingredients of what is today called 'dynamically oriented psychotherapy.' It is Freud's first and longest psychoanalytic case history and the one most often cited on the origins of hysteria in women.

When one has read, as I have done, hundreds of nineteenth-century case histories, to come upon Freud's Dora case is like coming upon an oasis in the desert. It is beautifully written, cogently argued, elaborately developed. One is quickly drawn into Freud's world, and the writing has an immediacy that most case histories written since simply lack. It is elegant and eloquent, possibly the single greatest case history in the literature of psychiatry.

On October 14, 1900, Freud wrote to Wilhelm Fliess that 'it has been a lively time and has brought a new patient, an eighteen-year-old girl, a case that has smoothly opened to the existing collection of picklocks' (427).[2] On January 25 he wrote to Fliess:

> I finished 'Dreams and Hysteria' [the Dora case] yesterday, and today I already miss a narcotic. It is a fragment of an analysis of a case of hysteria in which the explanations are grouped around two dreams; so it is really a continuation of the dream book. In addition, it contains resolutions of hysterical symptoms and glimpses of the sexual organic foundation of the whole. It is the subtlest thing I have written so far and will put people off even more than usual. Still, one does one's duty and does not write for the day alone. The essay has already been accepted by Ziehen, who does not realize that I shall soon inflict the 'Psychopathology of Everyday Life' on him as well. How long Wernicke will put up with these cuckoo's eggs is his business [433].

Later that month, January 30, Freud wrote, almost apologetically, to Fliess to say about the case:

> The main thing in it is again psychology, the utilization of dreams, and a few peculiarities of unconscious thought

---

[2] All quotes from the Fliess letters are from *The Complete Letters of Sigmund Freud to Wilhelm Fliess, 1887–1904*, ed. and trans. by Jeffrey Moussaieff Masson (Cambridge, MA: Harvard University Press, 1985).

processes. There are only glimpses of the organic [elements], that is, the erotogenic zones and bisexuality. But bisexuality is mentioned and specifically recognized once and for all, and the ground is prepared for detailed treatment of it on another occasion. It is a hysteria with tussis nervosa and aphonia, which can be traced back to the character of the child's sucking, and the principal issue in the conflicting thought processes is the contrast between an inclination toward men and an inclination toward women [434].

Freud first met Dora in October 1900, and wrote his case history in January 1901. But he did not publish it until 1905, nearly five years later. Why? The publication of the full letters from Freud to Fliess suggests an explanation. In a letter omitted from the earlier edition of the letters, Freud wrote to Fliess on March 3, 1901:

> At his request I let Oscar [Rie, a close family friend] read 'Dreams and Hysteria,' but he derived little joy from it. I shall make no further attempt to break through my isolation. Otherwise these are very bleak times, outstandingly bleak! [438]

Freud did not expect his colleagues to find any pleasure in the Dora case. Two years later, when it became apparent to him that Fliess, like so many of his medical peers, had rejected his ideas and his friendship, Freud wrote him, on March 11, 1902, to say, 'I withdrew my last work from publication because just a little earlier I had lost my last audience in you' (456). With the loss of Fliess's friendship and interest in his work, Freud felt that there was no one who would care about what he was writing. He sensed, no doubt, that the Dora case was superior to anything similar that had been published in the psychiatric literature, and it must have been a deep disappointment to him to see how little understanding his closest friends had of his achievement.

Dora (Ida Bauer, 1882–1945) was brought to Freud by her father, Philip Bauer, a wealthy industrialist. Freud tells us that when he accepted Dora for treatment she was 'in the first bloom of youth – a girl of intelligent and engaging looks.' Presumably Freud was struck that 'the child had developed into a mature young woman of very independent judgment' (*S.E.*, 7:22). Her main 'symptoms' (presumably according to the father) were depression (*Verstimmung*; Strachey's 'low spirits' is too mild) and a change in her character. By this the father meant that she was no longer on good terms with him or with her mother. And, even more important in his eyes, she was on particularly bad terms with close friends of the Bauers, Herr K. and his wife. Once, during an argument with her father, she lost consciousness, and Freud believed her fainting was accompanied by convulsions and delirious states, though the subsequent amnesia never yielded to analysis. She also wrote a suicidal farewell letter, though her family felt it was not serious. In addition, Freud said she suffered from a feeling of *taedium vitae*, and, at least earlier, a nervous cough, hoarseness, and loss of voice. Dora made it clear that she did not wish to be analyzed, but 'it was determined, in spite of her reluctance, that she should come to me for treatment' (*S.E.*, 7:23).

Before beginning his account of the analysis, Freud tells the reader that in his *Studies on Hysteria* he postulated an original psychic trauma, a conflict of emotions, and 'an additional factor which I brought forward in later publications – a disturbance in the sphere of sexuality.' The reference here (as Freud makes clear in a footnote on page 27 of his case) is to his controversial paper, published in 1896, 'The Aetiology of Hysteria,' in which he had stated that hysteria originated in a sexual seduction at an early (prepubescent) age. There can be no doubt that Freud intended the present case to be read in the light of this paper, one that his colleagues furiously rejected and that has, even now, ninety years after it was written, recently provoked heated and acrimonious debate.[3]

The rest of the case history is Freud's attempt to reveal and analyze what he called 'the sphere of sexuality' in Dora's external and internal life. Dora's father had told Freud what he thought was the root of her problems. He explained that he had formed an intimate friendship with the K. family, that Frau K. had nursed him during a long illness, that Herr K. was always most kind to Dora, that Dora was very fond of Frau K. and of their two children.

[3] I consider that essay to be the greatest that Freud ever wrote. I have included it in Appendix B to my *Assault on Truth*, along with some corrections of Strachey's translation.

But when she was sixteen, Dora and her father visited the K.'s at a summer resort on an Alpine lake. Dora suddenly told her father that she would not remain there after all. A few weeks later she told her mother, who told the father, that Kerr K. had made sexual advances to her on a walk after a trip on the lake. Herr K. vehemently denied Dora's accusation, saying that he knew from his wife that Dora read books about sexuality, in particular Paolo Mantegazza's *Physiology of Love*, and that she had merely 'imagined' the whole scene she described. The father told Freud:

> I have no doubt that this incident is responsible for Dora's depression and irritability and suicidal ideas. She keeps pressing me to break off relations with Herr K. and more particularly with Frau K., whom she used positively to worship formerly. But that I cannot do. For, to begin with, I myself believe that Dora's tale of the man's immoral suggestions is a fantasy that has forced its way into her mind; and besides, I am bound to Frau K. by ties of honourable friendship. . . . But Dora, who inherits my obstinacy, cannot be moved from her hatred of the K.'s. She had her last attack after a conversation in which she had again pressed me to break with them. Please try and bring her to reason [*S.E.*, 7:26].

This was in fact the second 'trauma.' The first sexual incident, which Freud regarded as a psychic trauma, took place when Dora was fourteen. Herr K. contrived to be alone with her in his office, and 'suddenly clasped the girl to him and pressed a kiss upon her lips.' Dora had a 'violent feeling of disgust, tore herself from the man,' and left, but never brought up the incident to anyone until she told Freud about it during her analysis (*S.E.* 7:28). For some time afterward she avoided being alone with Herr K. and was in fact very agitated whenever he appeared in her presence unaccompanied.

While Freud did not see his task in the same light as the father (he agreed with Dora that these scenes were real, not imagined), he did agree with the father that Dora was ill and in need of treatment. Freud soon learned that Dora believed that her father was having an affair with Frau K. – and that she was correct. She also felt that her father's denial and hypocrisy about it revealed strains in his character that she found unattractive. She told Freud that her father was deceitful (*unaufrichtig*) and dishonest (*falsch*). Freud remarks:

> I could not in general dispute Dora's characterization of her father; and there was one particular respect in which it was easy to see that her reproaches were justified. When she was feeling embittered she used to be overcome by the idea that she had been handed over to Herr K. as the price of his tolerating the relations between her father and his wife; and her rage at her father's making such a use of her was visible behind her affection for him.[4]

But to Dora there was something even more upsetting, something that seemed to corrode the very basis of her sense of what was real:

> None of her father's actions seemed to have embittered her so much as his readiness to consider the scene by the lake as a product of her imagination. She was almost beside herself at the idea of its being supposed that she had merely fancied [*eingebildet*, imagined] something on that occasion [*S.E.*, 7:46].

Freud was clearly taken, at least initially, with the intelligent, lively, and independent-minded young woman in his office. He was determined to find out what she really felt, at a level outside her awareness. He thought that making these discoveries (interpretations) would permit Dora to achieve insight and thereby to

[4] *S.E.*, 7:34. It is peculiar that Freud cannot allow his recognition of Dora's correct perception to stand without challenge. And so he feels obliged to add: 'At other times she was quite well aware that she had been guilty of exaggeration in talking like this. The two men had of course never made a formal agreement in which she was treated as an object for barter; her father in particular would have been horrified at any such suggestion.' But what Dora said was no exaggeration of the reality at all; on the contrary, she was merely highlighting for Freud the deeper emotional reality of her father's behavior. She was being 'insightful' and 'analytic,' whereas Freud was insisting on being 'literal.' Dora, clearly, did not believe that there was a written agreement between her father and Herr K., but this hardly diminished the impact of the emotional trauma on her of being selfishly and callously used by her father, and Freud knew that she was perfectly correct.

carry on her life with some degree of emotional freedom. That it did not turn out the way Freud wished it to turn out tells us a great deal about the underlying assumptions of psychotherapy.

It is a genuine paradigm: two strong-willed, forceful, and courageous human beings, set on a collision course; one wants to change the other, she merely wants to be vindicated. They began, then, with completely different goals. Dora did not come on her own seeking insight; she was forced into treatment by her father. The fact that Freud, unlike everybody else in her environment, however, did not dispute her vision of reality (at least at first) must have convinced her that there was something unusual about this man that made speaking to him worthwhile. It is unlikely that Freud told Dora what he tells his readers at the end of the paper on the case:

> It must be confessed that Dora's father was never entirely straightforward. He had given his support to the treatment so long as he could hope that I should 'talk' Dora out of her belief that there was something more than a friendship between him and Frau K. His interest faded when he observed that it was not my intention to bring about that result [S.E., 7:109].

This is an impressive recognition of Dora's reality, and one that she would no doubt have appreciated.

This was not the only problem faced from the beginning of the analysis. Of even greater significance were the prejudices (I do not know what else to call them) that Freud brought to the analysis. One of these prejudices, in particular, has not previously been commented upon. At the beginning of his presentation, in the 'Clinical Picture,' Freud, in describing Dora, says of her:

> She tried to avoid social intercourse, and employed herself — so far as she was allowed to by the fatigue and lack of concentration of which she complained — with attending lectures for women and with carrying on more serious studies [S.E., 7:23].

It is true that we cannot know, from the text, what Freud means by 'lectures for women' (*Vorträge für Damen*); most likely, he meant lectures on female emancipation.[5] But it is clear from the passage that he disapproved of these lectures, since he speaks of 'more serious studies.'[6] He therefore makes it plain from the outset that he did not approve of Dora's educational interests, and hence her intellectual ambitions.

But perhaps even more important for the outcome of the case were the views that Freud brought with him concerning female sexuality, since Freud himself said that the case and its resolution centred on the sexual sphere. These views are explicitly stated in the text. Freud refers first to the scene of the kiss and states that

[5] Freud's views on feminism were not positive. This is clear from a letter to his fiancée, Martha Bernays, written on November 15, 1883, in which he tells her that he has been translating John Stuart Mill: 'He lacked the sense of the absurd, on several points, for instance in the emancipation of women and the question of women altogether. I remember a main argument in the pamphlet I translated was that the married woman can earn as much as the husband. I dare say we agree that housekeeping and the care and education of children claim the whole person and practically rule out any profession . . . It seems a completely unrealistic notion to send women into the struggle for existence in the same way as men. Am I to think of my delicate sweet girl as a competitor? . . . I believe that all reforming activity, legislation and education, will founder on the fact that long before the age at which a profession can be established in our society, Nature will have appointed woman by her beauty, charm and goodness, to do something else.' *Letters of Sigmund Freud, 1873–1939*, by Ernst L. Freud, trans. by Tania and James Stern (London: The Hogarth Press, 1961), 90.

[6] Perhaps the reason this prejudice has not been previously commented upon in this context is because James Strachey, the translator of the case into English in the *Standard Edition*, misunderstood a critical sentence in the German text and mistranslated it. The German text reads: *beschäftigte sie sich mit dem Anhören von Vorträgen für Damen und trieb ernstere Studien* (G.W., 5:181). Strachey translates it as 'with attending lectures for women and with carrying on more or less serious studies.' *Ernstere* is simply a comparative, and Freud is not saying 'more or less,' but simply 'more.' In other words, 'lectures for women' were not serious. The translation into French was done by Freud's close friend and pupil Marie Bonaparte, who had no doubt discussed the Dora case with Freud personally. It is interesting, therefore, to see that the French translation is even faultier than Strachey's. Bonaparte translates it: *elle s'occupait, autant que le lui permettait l'état de fatigue et de manque de concentration dont elle souffrait, à suivre des conférences mondaines et faisait des études sérieuses*. In other words, 'women's lectures' is transformed into *conférences mondaines* (worldly lectures) and 'more serious studies' is obliterated in favor of 'serious studies.' There is thus absolutely no way of knowing from the French that Freud disapproved or that Dora's ambitions had anything to do with women's studies. Was this translation a result of Bonaparte's talks with Freud? The French text was published as *Cinq psychanalyses*, traduit par Marie Bonaparte et Rudolph M. Loewenstein (Paris: Presses Universitaires de France, 1954).

'this was surely just the situation to call up a distinct feeling of sexual excitement in a girl of fourteen who had never before been approached' (*S.E.*, 7:28). The reader is no doubt taken aback by this statement, wondering how Freud (or anyone else) could know this. Freud makes his views even more explicit in the next paragraph:

> In this scene . . . the behaviour of this child of fourteen was already entirely and completely hysterical. I should without question consider a person hysterical in whom an occasion for sexual excitement elicited feelings that were preponderantly or exclusively unpleasurable [*S.E.*, 7:28].

This is, needless to say, a highly mechanistic view of the human person, for it implies that such things as context and relationships play no role in one's reactions, which must be purely physical. Dora, only fourteen years old, is sexually approached (deviously, at that) by a man old enough to be her father (and with two children of his own), married to a woman who is having an affair with her father, and she is expected by Freud immediately to yield, ecstatically and without hesitation, to his sudden, unwanted sexual advance. Dora's behavior, then, is for Freud *proof* that she is suffering from hysteria, that she is denying (or repressing) feelings she should have had.

By the time of the second scene, the sexual request at the lake, Dora's refusal is symptomatic, for Freud, of a more serious psychopathology. But now it is no longer a question of Freud's preconceived views, but of what he claims to have uncovered during the course of Dora's analysis.

Dora told Freud that she had been quite close to her governess, 'an unmarried woman, no longer young, who was well-read and of advanced views' (*S.E.*, 7:36). Freud clearly disapproves of her. (See his footnote: 'This governess used to read every sort of book on sexual life and similar subjects, and talked to the girl about them.') What Dora found out was that the woman was in love with her father and that 'she herself was a subject of complete indifference to the governess, whose pretended affection for her was really meant for her father.' Freud, instead of feeling some sympathy for the disturbing recognition that Dora was being callously exploited, used the story as a means of 'throwing a most unwel-

come light on a part of Dora's own behaviour.' Freud concludes
that Dora's great affection for the K.'s children must be feigned,
and only a means to her goal: 'all these years she had been in love
with Herr K.' Dora does not agree with Freud. Nowhere in the text
does she state any physical attraction to Herr K. But Freud does. At
one point he says that Herr K., whom he had met, was 'still young
and of prepossessing appearance [*einnehmendem Äusseren*]' (*S.E.*,
7:29). Freud then asks the following important question:

> If Dora loved Herr K., what was the reason for her refusing him
> in the scene by the lake? Or at any rate, why did her refusal
> take such a brutal form, as though she were embittered against
> him. And how could a girl who was in love feel insulted by a
> proposal which was made in a manner neither tactless nor
> offensive, as we shall hear later? [*S.E.*, 7:38].[7]

His explanation is this:

> Her having felt so injured by Herr K.'s proposal seemed to me
> in general to need explanation, especially as I was beginning to
> realize that Herr K., too,[8] did not regard his proposal to Dora a
> mere frivolous attempt at seduction. I looked upon her having
> told her parents of the episode as an action which she had
> taken when she was already under the influence of a morbid
> craving for revenge. A normal girl, I am inclined to think, will
> deal with a situation of this kind by herself [*S.E.*, 7:95].

The revenge that Freud refers to is clarified later, after he repeats
Dora's account of a young governess in the K. household:

> She then told me that Herr K. had made advances to her at
> a time when his wife was away for several weeks; he
> approached and ardently courted her and implored her to

---

[7] Strachey's translation accidentally omitted the last five words, which are,
in German, *wie wir später hören werden.*

[8] Again Strachey has mistranslated: 'I was beginning to realize that Herr K.
himself . . .' But the German text (*G.W.*, 5:257) reads: *dass die Werbung um Dora
auch für Herrn K.*, 'for Herr K. as well.' In other words, Freud is saying that both
Dora and Herr K. took the proposal seriously.

yield to his entreaties, saying that he got nothing from his wife, and so on [S.E., 7:105–6].[9]

Freud noticed that these words were the same ones with which Herr K. had asked Dora, in the scene by the lake, to accept him as her lover. (Also, by the way, they were the same words that Dora's father had used about his wife when explaining to Freud his relationship with Frau K.) Freud could then triumphantly say to Dora:

> Now I know your motive for the slap in the face with which you answered Herr K.'s proposal. It was not that you were offended at his suggestions; you were actuated by jealousy and revenge. . . . 'Does he dare,' you said to yourself, 'to treat me like a governess, like a servant?' Wounded pride added to jealousy . . . [S.E., 7:106].

This is a rather simple-minded explanation. Surely Dora had every right to be insulted, whether she was interested in Herr K. or not, merely given the fact that he had, as Dora told Freud, just seduced the governess of the house, and after that conquest treated the governess with contempt. And then he made the exact same proposal to Dora, and, to top injury with insult, used the same clichéd formula. It was, to Dora's sharp ears, a rehearsed speech. There was nothing spontaneous and genuine about it, and, especially, there was nothing personal in it, nothing directed to *her* as a separate person. So yet again Dora was being treated as a cipher, an object of Herr K.'s lust, not of his genuine affection, let alone love. She was not, then, activated by jealousy or wounded pride or a desire for revenge. She was simply disgusted, as well she might have been.

Why could Freud not see this? Because in fact Freud had decided that a good outcome for all concerned would have been for Herr K. to divorce his wife and marry the sixteen-year-old Dora! First he told Dora that, in his opinion, Herr K. had perfectly honorable intentions, and then he went on to tell her explicitly that

---

[9] Strachey translates: 'he made violent love to her and had implored her . . .' But the German (G.W., 5:268) reads: *genähert, sie sehr umworben*, which clearly means that he approached her and courted her ardently.

the scheme would by no means have been so impracticable. Your father's relations with Frau K. – and it was probably only for this reason that you lent them your support for so long – made it certain that her consent to a divorce could be obtained; and you can get anything you like out of your father. Indeed, if your temptation at L— had had a different upshot, this would have been the only possible solution for all the parties concerned [*S.E.*, 7:108].

Could Freud really have believed that this nest of deceit and deception could so easily and so happily be cleared up? It was a very sunny view of sexual love. But Freud had not entirely finished with his interpretation. He still needed to explain, to his satisfaction, precisely why Dora was so angry at having her memory of the scene by the lake treated as a fantasy. He told her:

You will agree that nothing makes you so angry as having it thought that you merely fancied the scene by the lake. I know now – and this is what you do not want to be reminded of – that you *did* fancy that Herr K.'s proposals were serious, and that he would not leave off until you had married him.[10]

These were Freud's last words to Dora. 'Dora had listened to me without any of her usual contradictions. She seemed to be moved; she said good-bye to me very warmly, with the heartiest wishes for the New Year, and – came no more' (*S.E.*, 7:108–109).

It is not surprising that she came no more, because it makes far more sense to believe that Dora was not moved, but appalled. Freud had just trivialized her deepest concern, and had demonstrated a total inability to understand her search for historical

[10] The German text reads: *Ich weiss nun, woran Sie nicht erinnert werden wollen, dass Sie sich eingebildet, die Werbung sei ernsthaft und Herr K. werde nicht ablassen, bis Sie ihn geheiratet* (*G.W.*, 5:272). Strachey did not notice that Freud deliberately used the word *einbilden* in two different senses here, the first time to refer to Dora's 'imagining' the scene by the lake, and the second time (*sich einbilden*) to refer to her pride that he would ask her to marry him. By means of this pun, Freud entirely took away from Dora the full meaning of her concern with a validation of her perceptions. Freud in effect told Dora that she merely imagined the whole scene, not in the real sense of the word 'imagine,' but in what he regarded as the deeper sense, namely, that she had the proud notion that she would be married to Herr K. Freud substituted for Dora's legitimate concern with the truth his own limited views of what women really want.

truth. It is not that he denied that the 'seduction' took place, but he stripped it of any significance, by giving it a totally different meaning, by 'interpreting' it. He treated her like a patient, not like a human being. Freud had never believed that Dora could be concerned with external truth. When he said, early in the case, that 'she was almost beside herself at the idea of its being supposed that she had merely fancied something on that occasion,' he went on to say: 'For a long time I was in perplexity as to what the self-reproach could be which lay behind her passionate repudiation of this explanation of the episode' (S.E., 7:46). In other words, Freud did not believe that Dora had a legitimate concern with historical truth; it must be neurotic, serving a defensive function. In this case Freud believed she was merely deluded; it was an internal pretense. Now we know that even torture victims often find the fact of not being believed as painful as the torture itself.

Freud's interpretations of Dora's behavior (most of them made, let us remember, directly to her) were in the service of disavowing the apparent reality in favor of his deeper reality. Not only did this come to take on an automatic quality (the fate it was invariably to suffer at the hands of lesser intellects), but it was also patently false in many instances. Thus, for example, Freud explained Dora's 'pretence at suicide' (S.E., 7:23) as the expression of a longing for sexual love at the hands of Herr K. (S.E., 7:33, n. 1) because she had seen her father pretend to attempt suicide in order to account for a secret rendezvous with Frau K. This 'explanation' ignored the simpler and, in this case, more profound significance: Dora was deeply unhappy. Dora's own perceptions and her own instinctive, uninstructed response to her environment were often strikingly more perceptive than Freud's interpretations. Thus Freud said that Dora felt that her thoughts about her father 'required to be judged in a special way' (S.E., 7:54). Freud said she was right, but only because he went on to discuss his theory of what he called 'supervalent thought,' that is, thoughts that occupy the mind to the exclusion of other thoughts. For Freud, the only possible explanation was that these thoughts were charged with energy from other, deeply repressed and unconscious, trains of thought. Freud then used this theory to explain Dora's preoccupation with her father and the affair he denied having with Frau K. Freud insisted that Dora was, in an unconscious fantasy, identifying both with her mother and with Frau K. because she was in love with her father. But Dora was obviously right to claim that her thoughts about her father, like any daughter's thoughts about any father, 'required to be judged in a special way'; the father-daughter relationship is a special one. What else should a child think about when she is the object of deception, deceit, and indifference on the part of the person who has been closest to her in her life? Surely the suffering this produces in the daughter is of a magnitude that justifies the absorbed thinking. Is a wish for paternal protection pathological? What made this wish so tragic for Dora was the fact that her father's protection was unavailable. In Freud's analysis of Dora's first dream, he said that in the dream

> the child decided to fly *with* her father; in reality she fled *to* her father; she summoned up an infantile affection for her father so that it might protect her against her present affection for a stranger. Her father was himself partly responsible for her present danger, for he handed her over to this strange man in the interests of his own love-affair. And how much better it had been when that same father of hers had loved no one more than her, and had exerted all his strength to save her from the dangers that had then threatened her! The infantile, and now unconscious, wish to put her father in the strange man's place had the potency necessary for the formation of a dream [*S.E.*, 7:86].

But there was nothing 'unconscious' about this wish; Dora knew, or could have known very easily, that she wanted protection and love from her father, as everybody wants from a father. That Dora's father, like so many others, not only was incapable of providing this protection, but was also directly responsible for the danger itself, was Dora's tragedy, the very tragedy that Freud simply could not face, in spite of the fact that he could openly admit that Dora's father was the very person responsible for her danger. Dora wanted protection, not because she did not acknowledge that she loved Herr K., but because she needed protection from him. Naturally she turned to her father. How could she know that he had no interest in her interests, in protecting her from danger, but was interested only in himself?

By now we can see that the relationship between Dora and Freud was doomed from the very beginning. Each wanted something entirely different from the other person. Or, rather, each needed something entirely different from the other person, since Dora presumably did not want anything from Freud. They met with different expectations, and different views of the world, and when the work of analysis was finished, they parted with these views simply strengthened. I do not know if it is true, as has been suggested a number of times, that Freud did not like Dora.[11] But it is certainly true that he did not learn anything from her about the real world, only about the world of psychoanalysis. And she did not learn anything from Freud about the real world, only about the world of psychoanalysis. At the end of the analysis, Freud felt he knew what was wrong with Dora. It is important to see precisely what he claimed.

Freud asked himself, many times, why Dora fell ill. His answer is that she was in love with too many people, and loved them too much. First, she was in love with her father: 'I told Dora that I could not avoid supposing that her affection for her father must at a very early moment have amounted to her being completely in love with him' (S.E., 7:57). Then she was in love with Herr K. 'So you see that your love for Herr K. did not come to an end with the scene, but that (as I maintained) it has persisted down to the present day – though it is true that you are unconscious of it' (S.E., 7:104). Note that Freud never believed Dora's conscious 'no' but also believed that 'there is no such thing at all as an unconscious "no"' (S.E., 7:57). So there was no logical way that Dora could contradict him.

Freud also claimed that 'Dora had a deep-rooted homosexual love for Frau K.' (S.E., 7:105). In fact Freud believed that this was the most deeply buried of her unconscious feelings (S.E., 7:110). Freud felt he failed Dora by not telling her about this love: 'I failed to discover in time and to inform the patient that her homosexual (gynaecophilic) love for Frau K. was the strongest unconscious current in her mental life' (S.E., 7:120 n.). Proof of this buried homosexual love was the fact that Dora did not seem to hold it

[11] At one point Freud says impatiently that Dora 'kept on repeating her complaints against her father with a wearisome monotony' (S.E., 7:46). One cannot help wondering if Dora's complaints might not have ceased had Freud acknowledged their truth.

against Frau K. that she was the one who betrayed her by revealing to her husband, whom she despised, the fact that she and Dora read sexual manuals together. Freud could not believe she did this out of any kind of generosity or loyalty; it must be homosexual love (cf. *S.E.*, 7:120 n.). But she was also, paradoxically, in love with a young German engineer, though the only evidence Freud seemed to have of this was his own wish that this should be so. (Cf. *S.E.*, 7:96, 100, and the curiously optimistic statement on the last page of the case that 'unless all the signs mislead me – she has married the young man' [122]. But all the signs did mislead Freud, as he admitted in a footnote to some, but not all, of the later editions of the Dora case, and she did not marry this engineer.)

Freud was still left with the question of why Dora loved so much. Here he entirely abandoned his new psychology and fell back on standard nineteenth-century ideas about heredity, since he said, for example, that Oedipal love for a father 'must be assumed to be more intense from the very first in the case of those children whose constitution marks them down for a neurosis, who develop prematurely and have a craving for love [*nach Liebe hungrigen Kindern*]' (*S.E.*, 7:56). Of course Freud believed that men fell neurotically ill as well as women. But I cannot think of a case in any of the twenty-four volumes of the *Standard Edition* in which Freud talks of a man falling ill for these reasons. Are Freud's views about the genesis of neurosis in women different from those he holds about men? After all, is there any evidence whatever that Dora was different from any other young person who wished to love and be loved for her own sake? What child, after all, does not 'hunger for love'?

Are there other features peculiar to women that mark them down for a neurosis? Yes.

The pride taken by women in the condition[12] of their genitals is quite a special feature of their vanity; and disorders of the genitals which they think calculated to inspire feelings of repugnance or even disgust have an incredible power of

[12] Strachey speaks of 'the pride taken by women in the appearance of their genitals' but the German word is *Gestaltung*, which refers not to the appearance, but to the condition, i.e., the health or otherwise, of the genitals, which is a perfectly normal concern.

humiliating them, of lowering their self-esteem, and of making them irritable, sensitive, and mistrustful. An abnormal secretion of the mucous membrane of the vagina is looked upon as a source of disgust [S.E., 7:84].

Is this really surprising, and is it really a feature of vanity? What is Freud's source here? I do not believe that women were telling him about their concern for their genitals unless they were legitimately concerned with their physical condition. The concern with the appearance of female genitals is a male concern, and primarily a concern of pornography. Moreover, any fears Dora had were entirely legitimate. But when Dora gave as one of her motives for being angry at her father that he had contracted syphilis (no doubt a source of Dora's mother's dislike of her husband, since he passed it on to her, a fact that Dora knew) and she was afraid she herself might have been contaminated, Freud used this concern as further evidence of her neurosis: 'I was careful not to tell her that . . . I too was of the opinion that the offspring of syphilitics were very specially predisposed to severe neuropsychoses' (S.E., 7:75).

Freud thought of the Dora essay as an appendix to *The Interpretation of Dreams* (hence the original title of the paper, 'Dreams and Hysteria'). One of the central concerns of that book is the existence and effects of emotions that operate outside the sphere of awareness. In Dora's case, her dreams revealed a host of feelings of which she was consciously unaware: love, hatred, jealousy, disgust. But Freud's brilliant discovery that there exist emotions outside our knowledge did not address the question of the *source* of those emotions. Dora may well have had fantasies of revenge that were unknown to her and that dictated her behavior, but her unconscious feelings were anchored in reality. If her dreams revealed that she was disappointed, she had every right to be disappointed. When Freud interpreted Dora's dream about her father's protecting her from a fire, Freud made a sexual interpretation to the effect that the fire symbolized the desire to sleep with Herr K. (S.E., 7:89–90). The father in the dream, according to Freud, was there to protect Dora from her own 'temptation.' But Freud also noted that 'in actual fact, it was he [the father] who had brought the girl into danger' in the first place. A more straightforward explanation of the dream, then, is simply that Dora wished her father would protect her not from a temptation but from a danger to which he had exposed her. That is a perfectly legitimate desire on the part of a young girl, yet it is a possibility that Freud, ever eager to trap Dora, could not see. He took every opportunity to use Dora's dreams against her, and to interpret them in directions he wished, rather than she wished. This is no doubt why, after two hours of dream interpretation, Freud told Dora he was satisfied with the result, only to have her say 'in a depreciatory tone: "Why, has anything so very remarkable come out?"' A good question, which was to remain unanswered.

What Dora thought was wrong with her was entirely different. Freud did not, of course, tell us, but we can see, from her concerns, that she was preoccupied with matters of truth and honesty. She felt conspired against. She was conspired against. She felt lied to. She was lied to. She felt used. She was used. She was beginning to lose her faith in justice, in integrity – in short, in the world. She was right. And it was as if she were giving Freud one last chance to demonstrate to her that he, at least, was not going to use her the way others did, that he was interested in her for her own sake, or, at least, that he could be objective and recognize and acknowledge the truth when he saw it. She knew her father, the person who should have stood by her, had failed her, and she was right. So, Freud wrote, 'she was constantly comparing me with him consciously, and kept anxiously trying to make sure whether I was being quite straightforward with her, for her father "always preferred secrecy and roundabout ways"' (*S.E.*, 7:118). It is not, really, that Freud disagreed with Dora. He simply ignored her needs in the service of his own, which was to find more evidence for the correctness of his psychological theories. His task, he felt, was not to corroborate her vision of the world (even when he shared it), but to probe beneath and behind it, in short, to interpret: 'He that has eyes to see and ears to hear may convince himself that no mortal can keep a secret. If his lips are silent, he chatters with his finger-tips; betrayal oozes out of him at every pore' (*S.E.*, 7:78).

There is almost a certain cynicism in the way Freud plodded along with his agenda. No doubt he would have agreed that the world, certainly Dora's world, was precisely the way she saw it. But that kind of vision did not interest him very much. And so he simply ignored one kind of reality in his search for another, for one that *he* regarded as deeper. He may even have been right. (Clearly, though, I think he was wrong). But whether he was right or wrong, he was no help to Dora. In the end he even withdrew his sympathy from her and, like the others, pushed her to accept the solution that society wanted for her: to close her eyes to what was happening around her. Freud had presented Dora with an interpretation that could only have been welcome to the very people who had accused her of mendacity, when in fact she was the only one in her environment who was willing to face the truth. But what could she, at eighteen, do against a powerful industrialist backed by the whole of Viennese society? If Freud could not take up the struggle on her behalf (and on behalf of his other women patients similarly abused), he could at least have walked away from their tormentors in disgust and washed his hands of the emotional and intellectual corruption that surrounded him.

But Freud did not defend Dora. Instead he turned his attention to one of his great discoveries, 'transference.' The Dora case contains Freud's first extended discussion of transference and its effects on treatment. But Freud's explanation of transference in this case is self-serving. Dora was not 'transferring' to Freud; she was simply 'comparing' Freud with other significant people in her life. She compared her analyst with her father, and found them both wanting. This may well have been unconscious to Dora. But of far greater significance is the fact that it was also unconscious to Freud. With all his psychological sophistication, this eighteen-year-old was wiser than he was about psychological realities. Freud *was* like her father. He cared about his own interests far more than he cared about hers.

Freud's technique, his method, was to discount Dora's perception of reality and substitute a psychological task for it. If Dora complained about anybody, Freud turned it back against her: 'A string of reproaches against other people leads one to suspect the existence of a string of self-reproaches with the same content. All that need be done is to turn back each particular reproach on to the speaker himself' (*S.E.*, 7:35).[13] And to the extent that Freud

[13] Dora, as we know, was most upset at not being believed. Freud remarks: 'For a long time I was in perplexity as to what the self-reproach could be which lay behind her passionate repudiation of this explanation of the episode' (namely, that it was a product of her imagination) (*S.E.*, 7:46). But why would there need to be anything more? Given the enormous consequences for Dora's life of everybody believing that she had merely invented this episode, it is no wonder that she was 'almost beside herself' at the thought that nobody

would admit that Dora was correct in her perception of the world, he would nonetheless tell her to adjust to that world whether it was right or wrong. Dora looked at the world around her and was horrified at the hypocrisy and dishonesty. Freud told her, in effect, yes, you may be right, but it is the only world you have, and you had better make your peace with it. Actually, he did not tell her that. Maybe if he had, the outcome would have been better.

Freud was to claim that Dora had a hidden agenda. He stated that she wished to take vengeance on men and, more generally, on the hypocrisy of adults, that her dreams showed that she felt that 'men are all so detestable that I would rather not marry. This is my revenge' (S.E., 7:120). Dora had good reason. Every single person in her environment had used her to achieve his or her sexual end: her governess, who wished to sleep with her father, pretended to be her intimate friend; the impoverished Frau K., who also wished to sleep with Dora's wealthy father, pretended to be her close friend, handed over the care of her children to her (when Dora herself was still a child), and read books on sexuality with her, but she used this feigned friendship with Dora as a means to her own ends and also betrayed her when Dora told the truth (which she knew as well) about her husband; her father claimed to love her but was willing to offer her to Herr K. as the price for continuing his affair with Herr K.'s wife; Herr K. was prepared to accept the father's offer and permit the affair with his wife to continue, but not out of genuine feelings for Dora (he was, at the same time, having an affair with the governess of his children).

In the case history Freud mentions a patient who thought she had dreamed of swimming in a blue tropical ocean, but realized she had in fact dreamed that she was 'swimming in a frozen sea and was surrounded by icebergs' (S.E., 7:93). This is an accurate pictorial representation of the coldness and lack of feeling on the part of people who surrounded Dora. Like the dreamer, Dora too wanted to believe that she was in the midst of warmth and sunshine. Who would not fall ill in such an environment? Freud did not manage to extricate himself from this web of deceit woven around Dora. He was yet another man in authority who knew best what was best for Dora.

believed her. We should also remember that she knew perfectly well that *everybody* at some level knew she was telling the truth. If such a situation is not ideally suited to drive a person insane, I don't know what is.

Dora's solution was one that did not appeal to Freud, and it has not appealed to other men, especially analysts in the years that followed. Freud described it as taking her revenge on the K.'s:

> To the wife she said: 'I know you have an affair with my father'; and the other did not deny it. From the husband she drew an admission of the scene by the lake which he had disputed, and brought the news of her vindication home to her father. Since then she had not resumed her relations with the family [*S.E.*, 7:121].

In other words, she confronted them with the reality of what they had done to her, and they could no longer deny it. Once they had admitted the truth, she was finished with them. It was a brave and remarkable act. But in 1961 Erik Erikson, in an influential talk delivered before the plenary session of the American Psychoanalytic Association in New York, asked: 'Why did Dora confront Freud with the fact that she had confronted her parents with the historical truth? This act may impress some of us even today as "acting out."'[14] But is this 'acting out' or simply acting bravely? Dora's hidden agenda turned out to have been far more straightforward than Freud or Erikson would be prepared to admit. She merely wanted the truth established.

Moreover, though Freud did not admit it, he actually did have a hidden agenda. Freud's views on the importance of real external events in the life history of his 'hysteric' patients – in short, his seduction theory – had set him at odds with his medical colleagues. The 1896 paper that Freud referred to at the beginning of the Dora case, in which he had put forth those views, had received, as Freud told Fliess, 'an icy reception.' 'The word,' Freud said, 'has been given out to abandon me and I am isolated.'

The Dora case was Freud's first published case since this debacle, what everybody regarded as his public disgrace (his 'error' concerning the seduction theory). What is most conspicuous is that Freud was no longer, in this case, looking for a real trauma. The Dora case stands at the threshold of Freud's change of theories (the

---

[14] 'Reality and Actuality,' *Journal of the American Psychoanalytic Association* 10 (1962): 451–74. Many of the essays I quote from have been reprinted in a useful collection, *In Dora's Case: Freud-Hysteria-Feminism*, ed. by Charles Bernheimer and Claire Kahane (New York: Columbia University Press, 1985).

abandonment of the seduction hypothesis). It is his declaration to his colleagues, as if he were telling them: 'Look, Dora was suffering from internal fantasies, not external injuries. The source of her illness was internal, not external; fantasy, not reality; libido, not rape.'

On a personal level, it is also an appeal to Fliess not to abandon him, not to abandon their friendship, which meant so much more to Freud than to Fliess. In writing about a case he treated in 1897, Fliess said:

> Among the pains which derive from masturbation, I would like to emphasize one in particular, because of its importance: neuralgic stomach pain. One sees it very early on in the case of women who masturbate, and it is to be found among 'young ladies' as frequently as masturbation itself.

In Freud's private copy of Fliess's book, he had marked this passage for special attention.[15] It is not surprising, then, that Freud refers to Fliess and to this view (possibly this very passage) when he seeks what he considers the ultimate origin of Dora's illness, the true source of her hysteria, namely, that Dora masturbated as a child:

> The circumstantial evidence for her having masturbated in childhood seems to be complete and without a flaw. In the present case I had begun to suspect the masturbation when she had told me of her cousin's gastric pains, and had then identified herself with her by complaining for days together of similar painful sensations. *It is well-known that gastric pains occur especially often in those who masturbate.* [Italics added.] According to a personal communication made to me by Wilhelm Fliess, it is precisely gastralgias of this character which can be interrupted by an application of cocaine to the 'gastric spot' discovered by him in the nose, and which can be cured by the cauterization of the same spot [S.E., 7:78].

[15] Wilhelm Fliess, *Ueber den ursächlichen Zusammenhang von Nase und Geschlechtsorgan* (Halle an der Saale: Carl Marhold, 1902), 7. Freud's copy carries the dedication 'To my dear Sigmund.' The book was published in 1902, but represents Fliess's views from 1893 on. A similar passage is found in Fliess's major work, *Die Beziehungen zwischen Nase und weiblichen Geschlechtsorganen* (Leipzig and Vienna: Franz Deuticke, 1897), 108, where he discusses 'stomach-ache spots.'

Moreover, at the very end of the case, Freud wrote a sentence that reads like a personal appeal to his erstwhile friend: 'It is the therapeutic technique alone that is purely psychological; the theory does not by any means fail to point out that neuroses have an organic basis' (S.E., 7:113).

While all of Freud's colleagues found his theory of the external genesis of neurosis, via seduction, to be incredible, the majority of them were comfortable with finding that same genesis in masturbation. Here is something that could be blamed on the patient. Masturbation, especially in women, was something that was frequently written about in medical literature in Freud's time.[16]

We know that when Freud handed over an earlier patient, Emma Eckstein, to Fliess for nasal surgery because of masturbation, she nearly died from the bungled operation.[17] Freud eventually exculpated Fliess from any blame, and achieved the 'insight' that the patient had nearly bled to death because she was a hysterical bleeder. The operation, he decided, played no part. This was in 1897. Three years later Freud was once again prepared to sacrifice a patient to Fliess's inane theories. Dora did not know how lucky she was to have left Freud before he could achieve his final cure.

The topic of seduction per se occurs only once in the Dora case, in a footnote on page 57, where Freud writes: 'The decisive factor in this connection is no doubt the early appearance of true genital sensations, either spontaneously or as a result of seduction or

---

[16] An influential and popular book by Dr. Thésée Pouillet was De l'Onanisme chez la femme (Masturbation in Women), 7th ed. (Paris: Vigot Frères, 1897), which recommended for a cure 'the moderate cauterization of the entire surface of the vulva, without forgetting the clitoral gland, nor the two sides of the hood of this organ. The initial pain of the burn, which lasts about two hours, is followed, for six to eight days or more, by a morbid sensitivity, which is bearable only as long as one does not touch the mucous membrane of the vulva, but which becomes a very sharp pain at the first contact with any object whatsoever, and even more so should the fingers rub the genitals.' (My translation from the French on page 205.) Should this fail, Dr. Pouillet does not hesitate to perform an excision of the clitoris, and gives several examples (200–205) of the results he has had after surgical removal of the clitoris. A vast literature from the nineteenth century exists on this topic, and I cite from it in my Dark Science: Women, Sexuality and Psychiatry in the Nineteenth Century (New York: Farrar, Straus & Giroux, 1986).

[17] I discuss Emma Eckstein in my book The Assault on Truth: Freud's Suppression of the Seduction Theory (New York: Farrar, Straus & Giroux, 1984: paperback, with New Preface and Postface, New York: Penguin Books, 1985).

masturbation.'[18] What Freud is discussing is when a libidinal tie becomes truly precocious, or fixated. Of course, without saying so, he has touched here on the very heart of the Dora case, even in his own terms. For according to his own formula Dora is sick because she cannot acknowledge her love for Herr K. She cannot do this because she cannot acknowledge her love for her father. She cannot acknowledge her love for her father because she has never freed herself from it in the normal course of development. Now comes the question why this has happened, why Dora did not pass through what Freud would regard as the normal developmental stage of a slow disillusion with the father, or, more kindly put, a slow detachment from exclusive sexual love for him. (I think it is only fair to acknowledge that Freud may well be right in thinking that all children go through such a stage, though here I would defer to the actual experience of women on this point.) The question is clearly critical to Freud's theories and in particular to Dora's case. His answer is that either she was seduced or she masturbated, and this produced a premature libidinal fixation.[19] Now if we think back to the 1896 paper on hysteria, we know that at that point Freud said the answer had to be seduction, and by seduction he meant something very serious, what we today call 'sexual assault.' It corresponded pretty much to incest. He did not consider masturbation (which he had already written about at some length) a sufficient traumatic moment. Most of those who have written about Dora have recognized the centrality of this question of seduction (which ultimately includes the notion of fantasy versus reality). Thus Steven Marcus, when he compared Freud and Coleridge (using the comment from *Lyrical Ballads* about the willing suspension of disbelief), said:

> We know very well that Freud had a more than ordinary capacity in this direction and that one of the most dramatic moments in the prehistory of psychoanalysis had to do

[18] The words 'in this connection' are not in the German text, but have been added by Strachey.

[19] Later Freud said that 'if Dora felt unable to yield to her love for the man, if in the end she repressed that love instead of surrendering to it, there was no factor upon which her decision depended more directly than upon her premature sexual enjoyment' (*S.E.*, 7:87). But here he is referring to her bed-wetting!

precisely with his taking on faith facts that turned out to be fantasies.[20]

Jane Gallop, too, in her piece 'Keys to Dora,' wrote:

> It has become a commonplace of the history of psychoanalysis to mark as a turning point the moment in the 1890s when Freud stopped believing in a 'real' seduction at the origin of hysteria and realized that the source of neurosis is the child's fantasies. This is the monumental break with theories of traumatic etiology and the discovery of infantile sexuality.[21]

The discovery of a seduction, of an external trauma of this kind, is a part of the truth. But as Philip Rieff, in his introduction to the Collier edition of the Dora case, shrewdly noted, 'Freud is not interested in all truths, and certainly not in Dora's, except in so far as they block the operation of his own. Because Dora's insights are part of her illness, Freud had to hammer away at them as functions of her resistance to his insight.'[22] Marcus, too, in discussing the Dora case ended up believing that 'reality turns out to be something that for all practical purposes is indistinguishable from a systematic fictional creation' (81).

Clearly the Dora case marks Freud's first muted message to his small but ever-growing audience that he has shifted his allegiances, that from now on he will seek for the cause of mental suffering in the person, not in the external world.

Later analysts were to speak of Dora with contempt. Ernest Jones, Freud's biographer, for example, said of her many years later: 'Dora was a disagreeable creature who consistently put revenge before love; it was the same motive that led her to break off the treatment prematurely, and to retain various hysterical symptoms, both bodily and mental.'[23] Jones, of course, never met Dora. He is speaking of his impressions derived from Freud's case history or from things Freud told him later.

---

[20] 'Freud and Dora: Story, History, Case History,' from *In Dora's Case*, 75.

[21] 'Keys to Dora,' from *In Dora's Case*, 213–14.

[22] Sigmund Freud, *Dora: An Analysis of a Case of Hysteria*, ed. by Philip Rieff (New York: Collier Books, 1963), 11.

[23] *Sigmund Freud: Life and Work*. Vol. 2, *Years of Maturity, 1901–1919* (London: The Hogarth Press, 1958), 287.

And Felix Deutsch, who had been Freud's personal physician and later a prominent analyst, writing in 1957, said about Dora:

> The inability to 'clean out her bowels,' her constipation, remained a problem to the end of her life. Being accustomed to this trouble with her bowels, she apparently treated it as a familiar symptom. Her death from a cancer of the colon, which was diagnosed too late for successful operation, seemed a blessing to those who were close to her. She had been, as my information phrased it, 'one of the most repulsive hysterics' he had ever met.[24]

This 'information' came not from Deutsch himself, but from an unnamed informant! A single anonymous opinion, however, when it is repeated by a psychoanalyst, and when it corresponds to the unstated message from Freud himself, is powerful and impervious to contradiction. Deutsch's informant's opinion was to become widely cited, not as malicious opinion, but as fact. For example, Marcus, in his much-cited article 'Freud and Dora,' wrote that 'Dora refused to be a character in the story that Freud was composing for her, and wanted to finish it herself. As we now know, the ending she wrote was a very bad one indeed.'[25] This is a reference to Deutsch's account. Note the certainty. Even a feminist account of Dora, by Toril Moi, for example, said:

> It may be gratifying to see the young, proud Dora as a radiant example of feminist revolt (as does Cixous); but we should not forget the image of the old, nagging, whining, and complaining Dora she later becomes, achieving nothing.

From what does Moi derive this certainty? How does she know that Dora became this person? How does she know that she

---

[24] "A Footnote to Freud's "Fragment of an Analysis of a Case of Hysteria,"' *Psychoanalytic Quarterly* 26 (1957): 159–67. Deutsch met Dora in the late fall of 1922, and she told him of her deep disappointment with men, and how her husband had been unfaithful to her. Deutsch took this as a sign of her paranoia. He states, 'At the time of her analytic treatment she had stated unequivocally: "men are all so detestable that I would rather not marry." Thus her marriage had served only to cover up her distaste of men.' But Deutsch has made an error. What he quotes are not Dora's words, but Freud's interpretation of one of Dora's dreams! Hardly unequivocal.

[25] 'Freud and Dora: Story, History, Case History,' from *In Dora's Case*, 88.

achieved nothing? Only because Deutsch said that somebody told him so. No other information is available.'[26]

Jones wrote:

> This first case history of Freud's for years served as a model for students of psycho-analysis. . . . It was the first of Freud's postneurological writings I had come across, at the time of its publication, and I well remember the deep impression the intuition and the close attention to detail displayed in it made upon me. . . . At the present day it is hard to convey what an amazing event it was for anyone to take the data of psychology so seriously. Yet that it should less than half a century after seem a commonplace is a measure of the revolution affected by one man [288–89].

This strikes me as a fair estimate, and I believe it accounts for the extraordinary vitality of the work. If I am right in believing that Freud completely misunderstood Dora, and did her no service with his interpretations, what do I find to like about this case history? Part of the answer is supplied in a fine passage by Marcus:

> Freud's creative honesty was such that it compelled him to write the case of Dora as he did and that his writing has allowed us to make out in this remarkable fragment a still fuller picture. As I have said before, this fragment of Freud's is more complete and coherent than the fullest case studies of anyone else. Freud's case histories are a new form of literature; they are creative narratives that include their own analysis and interpretation. Nevertheless, like the living works of literature they are, the material they contain is always richer than the original analysis and interpretation that accompany it, and this means that future generations will recur to these works and will find in them a language they are seeking and a story they need to be told [90].

There is a further reason the Dora case is so interesting to read. It

[26]'Representation of Patriarchy: Sexuality and Epistemology in Freud's Dora,' *Feminist Review* 9 (1981): 60–73. I am quoting Moi from the book edited by Charles Bernheimer and Claire Kahane, *In Dora's Case*, 192.

is because it allows us a glimpse into the depths that Freud did *not* plumb. Everything I have said about Dora, which runs so counter to Freud's interpretations, is based on the information that Freud provided. Unlike Marcus, however, I do not believe the reason was that Freud was writing literature. I think, quite the contrary, that it was because Freud was writing, some of the time, and to some extent, about the real world. What distinguished Freud from *all* his colleagues was that he was willing to concede the complexities in *all* the cases he saw. He did not cover them up to the extent that his colleagues did, by simply passing over them in silence. Here, for contrast, is a typical case history from Krafft-Ebing's classic *Psychopathia Sexualis:*

Mr. Z., aged twenty-two, single, was brought to me by his father for medical advice, because he was very nervous and plainly sexually abnormal. Mother and maternal grandmother were insane. His father begat him at a time when he was suffering from nervousness. Patient was said to have been a very lively and talented child. At the age of seven he was noticed practicing masturbation. After his ninth year he became unattentive, forgetful, and did not progress in his studies, constantly requiring help and protection. With difficulty he got through the Gymnasium, and during his free time had attracted attention by his indolence, absentmindedness and various foolish acts. Consultation was occasioned by an occurrence in the street, in which Z. had forced himself on a young girl in a very impetuous manner, and in great excitement had tried to have a conversation with her. The patient gave as a reason that by conversing with a respectable girl he wished to excite himself so that he could be potent in coitus with a prostitute! His father characterized him as a man of perfectly good disposition, moral but lazy, dissatisfied with himself, often in despair about his want of success in life, indolent, and interested in nothing but music, for which he possessed great talent. The patient's exterior – his plagiocephalic head, his large prominent ears, the deficient innervation of the right facial muscles about the mouth, the neuropathic expression of the eyes – indicated a degenerate neuropathic individual. Z. was tall, of powerful frame and in all respects of masculine appearance. Pelvis masculine, testicles well developed, penis remarkably large, mons Veneris with abundant hair. The right testicle much lower than the left. . . . patient asked to have his will strengthened. His awkward, embarrassed manner, timid glances and drooping posture pointed to masturbation. The patient confessed that from his seventh year until a year and a half ago he practiced it, years at a time . . . he had constantly grown more bashful and indolent, less energetic, and more cowardly and apprehensive.[27]

When we read this, we realize just how extraordinary Freud's account is, in spite of its many weaknesses. No doubt it marked a turning point in the history of Western man, but although we may admire it for many reasons, we can nevertheless decide that the influence it was to have, down to the present day, on psychotherapy was not a good one. Whereas reading the Krafft-Ebing may make us laugh at it (even if our laughter is mixed with horror) and recognize how absurd it is, reading Freud produces a response that is not the same at all. In fact, while many feminist historians would agree that Freud and Dora had a tragic encounter, they are not at all certain that the fault lay with Freud.

This is especially true of French feminists, who have been deeply impressed with psychoanalysis,[28] and particularly with Jacques Lacan, and the sympathetic reading he gave to the Dora case in one of his most celebrated lectures on transference. The lecture was first given in 1952, and may have been the first to recognize what many have called the 'misalliance' between Freud and Dora, that is, Freud's prejudices in terms of what he deemed a healthy solution for Dora. On the other hand, Lacan merely substituted prejudices of his own for those of Freud:

As is true for all women, and for reasons that are at the very basis of the most elementary forms of social exchange (the very reasons that Dora gives as the ground for her revolt), the

---

[27] My translation from the German, *Psychopathia Sexualis: Eine medizinisch gerichtliche Studie für Aerzte und Juristen*, 15th ed., ed. by Alfred Fuchs (Stuttgart: Ferdinand Enke, 1918), 120, case 67. The first edition appeared in 1887.

[28] See in particular Hélène Cixous and Catherine Clément's book *La jeune née* (Paris: 10/18, 1975).

problem of her condition is fundamentally that of accepting herself as an object of desire for the man.[29]

Suzanne Gearhart, commenting on the importance of Lacan's early essay, wrote:

> The 'return to Freud' inaugurated by Jacques Lacan has served to underscore the fundamental importance of Freud's remarks to Fliess. This is especially clear in Lacan's interpretation of the Dora case in 'Intervention sur le transfert,' for the psychoanalytic procedure of treating even coherent, logical accusation on the patient's part as screens or symptoms was first set down there.[30]

Lacan's final word on transference was a celebrated phrase which describes the movement of analysis as that of a search for truth, but this truth is *le vérité du désir du patient*, the truth of the desire of the patient.[31]

By all accounts, one of Freud's goals was to get Dora to see her own complicity in the tragic situation she was in. The feeling generally held by psychotherapists about this case is that only by accepting her own responsibility would Dora have been able to free herself from what all agree was a terrible situation. Freud acknowledged that he failed in his goal. He attributed his failure, in the famous Postscript (the date of which cannot be determined, but was some point between April 1902, when Dora visited Freud for the last time, and October 1905, when the case was published in the *Monatsschrift*), to his failure to recognize the negative transference, that is, the fact that Dora ascribed to Freud qualities that really belonged to Herr K., and was therefore bound to treat Freud as she wished to treat Herr K.: vengefully. Freud wrote that he ought to have said to Dora:

---

[29] Lacan's essay was first published in the *Revue française de psychanalyse* in 1952, and was reprinted in *Ecrits* (Paris: Editions Seuil, 1966), 215–26. I have used the translation by Jacqueline Rose that appeared in *In Dora's Case*, 99.

[30] 'The Scene of Psychoanalysis: The Unanswered Questions of Dora.' From *In Dora's Case*, 107.

[31] I have taken this from Anika Lemaire's book *Jacques Lacan* (Brussels: Pierre Mardaga, 1977), 329.

Have you noticed anything that leads you to suspect me of evil intentions similar (whether openly or in some sublimated form) to Herr K.'s? . . . Her attention would then have been turned to some detail in our relations, or in my person or circumstances, behind which there lay concealed something analogous but immeasurably more important concerning Herr K. And when this transference had been cleared up, the analysis would have obtained access to new memories, dealing, probably, with actual events [S.E., 7:118].

Freud felt that Dora *acted out* these memories, rather than talk about them, by deserting Freud, 'as she believed herself to have been deceived and deserted by him.'

It is a nice piece of analysis, but is it true? Freud assumes that *any* negative qualities Dora could find in him that were reminiscent of Herr K. would be due exclusively to the transference; that is, they would be fantasies. But the evidence seems to suggest that Dora did, in fact, perceive similarities between Herr K. and Freud that were *not* the product of her imagination. They were real. Freud was not interested in Dora's truth any more than Herr K. was. This is the hidden quality that they had in common. Herr K. did deceive Dora. So did Freud, for he led her to believe that his only concern was for the truth. There was nothing neurotic in Dora's decision to 'desert' Freud. She left merely out of disappointment. She did not even seem to be angry at Freud. No doubt she had come to realize that no more could be expected of men in general. Her greatest anger, appropriately, was reserved for the man who had done her the greatest harm, Herr K. (Freud may have disappointed her, but Dora no doubt felt that he had not actively harmed her.) And she found, quite on her own, without any help whatever from Freud, the courage to confront him with the truth and force a confession. This is not 'neurotic acting out.' This is a political statement of remarkable maturity.

3

FERENCZI'S SECRET DIARY
AND THE EXPERIMENT IN
MUTUAL ANALYSIS

Sándor Ferenczi, Freud's most beloved disciple, profoundly affected the growth of psychoanalysis in Europe and in the United States, though sometimes his predominance has not been acknowledged or even recognized. In the United States his ideas have significantly influenced Clara Thompson, Karen Horney, Harry Stack Sullivan, Erich Fromm, Frieda Fromm-Reichmann, Sandor Lorand, Sandor Rado, Harold Searles, and Gregory Bateson (the 'double-bind'). In England he played a leading role in the formation of many analysts, including Michael Balint, Donald Winnicott, and Masud Khan.

In my book *The Assault on Truth*, I drew on unpublished letters to trace the complex dispute that arose between Freud and Ferenczi over the reality of sexual abuse in childhood. This dispute had even wider implications for the entire process of psychotherapy. Freud acknowledged that Ferenczi was a remarkably gifted healer. Of all the analysts working during Freud's time, he had the greatest reputation for being what was called a 'natural therapist,' or a superb clinician.[1] But Ferenczi began to develop doubts about the very notion of performing therapy, doubts he did not confide to Freud, only to a private diary, written toward the end of his life.

Sándor (Alexander) Ferenczi, born in Hungary in 1873, a medical doctor with interests in spiritualism and psychology, met Freud in Vienna in 1908, and that same year spent his vacation

[1] I should make it clear that, although I regard Ferenczi's ideas as a move in the right direction, I still feel that he remained a 'therapist,' somebody who wished to impose his own views of the world on somebody else. Throughout this chapter it is necessary to keep in mind that Ferenczi was writing in 1932. Nobody else, at that time, was writing the way Ferenczi was, and he should be given credit. But that does not mean that I endorse what he says as true today.

with him in Berchtesgaden. The next year, Ferenczi, Jung, and Freud visited the United States together. From that time on, Ferenczi became Freud's closest analytic friend, and later was considered the person who, after Freud, had the greatest impact on psychoanalytic psychotherapy. Until about a year before his death, on May 22, 1933, Ferenczi and Freud were in agreement on the fundamental questions in psychoanalysis; in fact Freud often deferred to what he considered to be Ferenczi's greater talent for therapy. Freud believed that Ferenczi had more compassion for his patients than he did. But Ferenczi began to undergo a change in his attitudes. This change, revealed to some degree in his publications, and hence to his colleagues, was never really known in any detail. The details Ferenczi put into a private diary. The first entry was made on January 7, 1932, and the last on October 2 of the same year. The diary, which was written in German, was not published for fifty-three years. When it appeared for the first time in 1985, it was in a French translation, and has still to appear in German and in English.[2]

There are two major themes in the diary: sexual traumas and mutual analysis.[3] In mutual analysis, the patient and the analyst trade places on the couch, and the analyst is analyzed by his patient. It would seem that Ferenczi came to the idea of mutual

[2] Sándor Ferenczi, *Journal clinique* (January–October 1932), translated from the German by Le Groupe de Traduction du Coq-Héron: Suzanne Achache-Wiznitzer, Judith Dupont, Susanne Hommel, Georges Kassai, Françoise Samson, Pierre Sabourin, Bernard This (Paris: Payot, 1985). The work contains a posthumous introduction by Michael Balint, Ferenczi's pupil, and a much more useful preface by Judith Dupont. The translation is a very faithful rendition of the German original. Dr. Dupont, a Hungarian analyst living in Paris, owns the Ferenczi copyright. An English translation is scheduled to appear soon from Harvard University Press.

[3] Of course I have selected only those passages from the diary that I found most interesting. They tend to be those in which Ferenczi questions the underlying assumptions of therapy. It is only fair to the reader to state that many of the other passages take the usefulness of therapy for granted (a position I obviously do not share) and are fairly standard psychanalytic fare. No doubt these are the very passages that permitted the diary finally to be published. What kept it from being published for so many years are the other passages, the ones I comment on here. Some account of the suppression of the diary is to be found in my book *The Assault on Truth*, in the chapter on Ferenczi. My translations are from the original German text, which I have in transcript form, rather than from the published French text. But wherever my translation differs from the French version, I will signal it in the notes. (All page numbers are from the French translation.)

analysis because of his own growing doubts about the nature of psychotherapy, the very profession for which he was most praised and for which he seemed most suited. He began to wonder about the covert sadism involved in psychotherapy. In a startling confession on July 27, he wrote:

> We greet the patient in a friendly manner, make sure the transference will take, and while the patient lies there in misery, we sit comfortably in our armchair, quietly smoking a cigar. We make conventional and formulaic interpretations in a bored tone and occasionally we fall asleep. In the best of cases the analyst makes a colossal effort to overcome his yawning boredom and behave in a friendly and compassionate manner. Were we to encourage our patients to real freedom [of expression], and to overcome their anxiety and embarrassment toward us, we would soon learn that patients at some level are actually acutely aware of all our real feelings and thoughts [246].

This is an altogether new voice. One could search the entire analytic literature to date in vain to find such a personal, deeply honest account of what goes on in the analyst. And this is by no inexperienced beginner in psychotherapy; this is written by a man who, by all accounts, was one of the great clinicians of his day.

Ferenczi became more and more aware of his own faults (and by implication those of the profession of therapist). Thus, on August 17, he gave an example of how insensitive he had been with a patient. This patient told Ferenczi that when she was about nine years old her mother left and she was alone with her father. Ferenczi, instead of allowing the woman her own thoughts, made a sarcastic (and psychoanalytic) comment which hid an interpretation. He said: 'It was really a happy marriage between you and your father.' The woman had told Ferenczi that her father, upon the loss of her mother, had turned to her with increasing demands for her affection. (One cannot help wondering if she was trying to tell Ferenczi about sexual demands.) In adolescence she formed friendships with boys her own age, something that her father resented. Ferenczi says that he wanted her to gain some insight into her own incestuous fantasies. Hence his interpretation. But it did not work. As Ferenczi wrote:

The next day I learned that the patient had spent the entire day in a deep depression, having given up on me. She said: 'If I get so little understanding from *him*, what can I expect from others? He too calls it "a happy marriage," as if it were something I actually desired, instead of seeing that perhaps as a child I had desired something similar in fantasy, but nothing was further from my mind than to have this wish realized in actuality. This actuality was forced on me and thus the path to normal development was blocked. Instead of loving and hating, all I could do was identify. . . .' I admitted that I had been enslaved by my theoretical expectations and this led me to superimpose in a superficial and thoughtless manner the feelings belonging to a sexually mature person in a case where probably only infantile, unreal erotic fantasies were present . . . [276].

This may be the first occasion when an analyst recognized (or at least acknowledged) that an interpretation can be an act of aggression. Ferenczi had intruded, in an invasive manner, on the thought process of another person. And he knew it. Years later this mistake was elevated into a principle of therapy, when confrontation therapy became an established form of modern therapy. In a sense, every interpretation is an invasion, an intrusion, and a confrontation.

The meaning of Ferenczi's comment was apparently clear to the woman. He was telling her that she must have harbored the fantasy that her mother would disappear, leaving her alone with her father, to be the sole object of his attention. This is what she desired; now it had come to pass, and she had replaced her mother, to become her father's wife. Ferenczi was telling the woman that she did not realize that she had desired this all along. How did Ferenczi know this was true? He didn't, of course. And this is what he admitted to the woman when he said that he reached this conclusion only because of theoretical prejudices.

Psychoanalytic theory demanded and even Ferenczi himself postulated that all girls desire to be left in sole possession of their fathers, and Ferenczi accepted this as true just as blindly as did everybody else. Ferenczi did not in fact know that the woman wanted this. He assumed that she did. That was what made the comment, for Ferenczi, a confrontation (needless to say, a confrontation is a genuine confrontation only if the truth of what is asserted is taken for granted). Ferenczi believed that he was 'confronting' her with knowledge she did not possess. The goal? The 'aha' of insight. But, as it must in many cases, the confront-ation backfired. Instead of behaving like a well-trained analytic patient, this woman reacted in a more directly human manner: she became sad, or, as she explained it, she despaired of being understood, or, even more fundamentally, of being believed.

Ferenczi was unable, at that point, to imagine a real-life situa-tion completely different from the Freudian paradigm of a girl desiring her father exclusively for herself. Even in his imagination, he could not accommodate the thought that the girl hated being alone with her father, for fear of what he might do to her. Alternatively, he could not imagine that the girl mourned her mother's departure, her feelings uncomplicated by a lust (repressed or otherwise) for her father. Or she may have felt something entirely different. The point is that Ferenczi did not know. And the only possibility his thinking permitted was the one that psychoanalytic theory had taught him.

At this point a modern Freudian therapist might object by maintaining that there is nothing in psychoanalytic theory that makes such an interpretation mandatory. Ferenczi was being overzealous. Or the modern therapist, not necessarily a Freudian, may claim that Ferenczi made a technical error, that an interpret-ation need not be a confrontation or an intrusion or an invasion, that the analyst's interpretations can be tactful and tentative, and he must be ready to withdraw them at the first sign that they are off the mark or are experienced by the patient as intrusive.

But the Freudian therapist then must overlook the fact that Ferenczi was talking of something he actually *did*. Can Ferenczi really be accused of being ignorant of Freud's intentions when he had the benefit of constant and continual contact with Freud himself, as well as all the other 'great clinicians' (of which he was a prime example) of his time? If making the error happened to Ferenczi, we can be fairly certain that it happened to others as well; indeed, the very reason that Ferenczi gave this example was that he knew how typical it was. The claim that only Ferenczi and a few other analysts were guilty of such technical errors is hardly convincing.

To the modern eclectic therapist we can point out that there would be no point in making an interpretation at all if one did not have a theoretical framework in which to make it. If the therapist is going to do anything more than listen, then she or he must have some foundation for comments of an interpretive kind.

It is greatly to Ferenczi's credit that the woman's despair at being misunderstood struck a responsive chord in him. He did not merely dismiss it as resistance (to the truth of his remarks) or seek to interpret her 'no.' Freud, we saw, did this with Dora, arguing, tendentiously, that the unconscious knows no 'no.' Ferenczi, on the other hand, took her 'no' seriously, and reflected, for a change, not on her, but on himself. And since he knew very well (he had by then supervised hundreds of budding analysts, and so knew their work at first hand) that what he was doing was not unique to him, but was an integral part of psychotherapy, he began to reflect on that as well. He continued the anecdote by saying:

> We analysts have projected God knows how much of our sexual theories onto children and certainly no less onto our patients when we discuss transference. We simply cannot accept the fact that our patients, although adults, have really remained small children and only wish to play ... they pretend they are in love with us to satisfy our own expectations. ... We behave like the father who, overwhelmed by the sexual play of the daughter, rapes her. It is this forced adult sexuality that then causes the arrested developments of the child in this early stage. The Oedipal fantasies turn into reality through the father's demeaning scoldings and beatings. Even worse is the fixation that occurs when the father takes these fantasies as real, acts upon them, and then as a result of his bad conscience withdraws from the child emotionally and punishes her (in order to cause the child to forget and to soothe his own conscience) [277].

In this unusual passage, Ferenczi made some statements about what happens in psychotherapy that have not, as far as I know, been stated anywhere else in print, at least by a therapist.[4] For here

[4] When a friend of mine, a woman who is involved in the Psychiatric Inmates' Liberation Movement, and is herself a survivor of incest, read this passage (and my explanation), she told me she was offended. Once again, she said, men were telling women what really happened, what they really did,

Ferenczi completely reversed the usual understanding, certainly in 1932, about what happens in adult/child sexuality. Freud had told Ferenczi, and the rest of the world, that when women reported such abuse in childhood, they were merely imagining the events. They were, said Freud, the product of childhood fantasies. But Ferenczi gave back to fantasy its innocent meaning. What the child has, according to Ferenczi, is a fantasy of being loved in the nonsexual sense of the term. The father, however, responds by raping the daughter. And as if this weren't bad enough, he then denies the event, and devises methods whereby the girl is made to believe it never took place ('you are crazy'; 'you dreamed it'; 'you cannot distinguish between a thought and an action'). He also can no longer provide the daughter with affection of any kind, and withdraws from her emotionally, thereby abandoning her and refusing her the help she originally came to the father for. Not only does this appear to be an accurate rendition of what sometimes happens in incest (as we now know from the many recent books on the topic, for example, Diana Russell's *The Secret Trauma: Incest in the Lives of Girls and Women*), but Ferenczi drew a parallel with the analytic situation that had never been made previously, nor since, as far as I know. He likened the transference, the feelings that the patient supposedly develops for the analyst on the basis of other feelings in the past, to the original play/affection/needs of the child. And just as the father took advantage of these needs, either misunderstanding them or ignoring their import, so the analyst takes advantage of the transference. Therapy is, Ferenczi said, like a rape. This is a powerful analogy and an equally powerful indictment. What exactly did Ferenczi mean? How does the analyst take advantage of the transference? Ferenczi gave many examples in the diary, all of them unsettling. On August 13, he wrote:

> *Index of the Sins of Psychoanalysis* (Reproaches made by a woman patient): Psychoanalysis entices patients into 'transference.'

what they really wanted. You have, she said honestly, no possible way of knowing any of this. I have to admit that she is completely right. I see, from this experience, how hard it is to overcome one's usual habits of thought. Much as I wish to escape thinking like a therapist, I sometimes fall into old and bad habits. I am glad that I know such women, who try to keep me honest.

Naturally the patient interprets the [imagined] deep understanding of the analyst, his great interest in the fine details of the story of her life and her emotions, as a sign of deep personal interest, even tenderness. Since most patients have been emotionally shipwrecked, and will cling to any straw, they become blind and deaf to signs that could show them how little *personal* interest analysts have in their patients. Meanwhile the unconscious of the patient perceives all of the analyst's negative feelings (boredom, irritation, and hate when the patient says anything unpleasant or provokes the analyst's complexes) [232].

In other words, just as the father ignores the separate autonomy and dignity of the child, and responds to her affection with brutality, so the analyst ignores the request for understanding (that is, validation) on the part of the patient and, instead, responds with needs of his own (for example, validation of psychoanalytic theory about transference or the Oedipus complex). Ferenczi continued in a darker vein:

Analysis is an easy opportunity to carry out unconscious, purely selfish, unscrupulous, immoral, even criminal acts and a chance to act out such behavior guiltlessly (without feeling guilt), for example, a feeling of power over the numbers of helplessly worshipful patients, who admire the analyst unreservedly; a feeling of sadistic pleasure in their suffering and their helplessness; no concern for how long the analysis lasts, in fact the tendency to prolong it for purely financial reasons; in this way, if the analyst wishes, the patient is made into a lifelong taxpayer. As a result of infantile experiences similar to this it becomes impossible for patients to detach themselves from the analysis even after long and unsuccessful work . . . just as it is impossible for a child to run away from home, because, left on its own, it would feel helpless [232].

Ferenczi said that the analyst infantilizes patients. Far from helping them to overcome infantile problems, the analyst resubmerges them in an infantile relationship in which it is the analyst who emerges as all-powerful.

What conclusions did Ferenczi draw from these profound observations on the nature of the therapeutic relationship? We have to remember that Ferenczi, for his entire adult life, regarded himself as a medical 'healer.' It would be expecting a great deal for him simply to turn his back on therapy. Instead, he sought to reform it. While many analysts before Ferenczi sought to reform psychoanalysis (Adler, Stekel, Jung, Rank, among others), Ferenczi's reform was different in quality and kind. His insights into the problems of analysis were far more fundamental than any before. Ferenczi's questions went to the very heart of psychotherapy, not just to one or another aspect of psychoanalysis. Owing to this, Ferenczi was, in my opinion, far more honest than Jung or others who rebelled against Freud. And he was, above all, far less self-concerned. Jung, as we will see, sought to restore to analysis the preoccupations of his own youth, religious crises, for example. He never called into question the practice of psychoanalysis or psychotherapy, only Freud's version. His solution was to substitute his own views for those of Freud. Ferenczi's vision was far more inclusive: *all* therapists were doing something wrong, and it seemed to lie in the very nature of therapy that they did, he appeared to be saying. It was not just this or that theory, but the very nature of therapy, that Ferenczi brought into question.

But if Ferenczi did not go so far as to ask for the total abolition of psychotherapy, he did something that was nevertheless extremely radical. As we saw, Ferenczi felt that something of the hypocritical, harmful atmosphere of analysis was caused by a wrong theoretical expectation, namely, that patients could not distinguish between what really happened to them and what they imagined happened to them. This, in Ferenczi's opinion, was Freud's great initial error, which had started psychoanalysis in a wrong direction, and from which it had never really recovered. If this is so, then he is left with an even greater problem: Were this theoretical mistake corrected, could the practice of psychoanalysis remain intact? What would happen to the daily practice of the psychoanalyst? Would a change in theory automatically solve the problems he saw? Casting about then for a solution that would leave the underlying structure of psychotherapy intact, Ferenczi came up with one that was as radical as one might expect for the time: He attempted to democratize it.

Ferenczi reasoned that underlying the abuse of children was

an imbalance of power. This same power structure, and the same imbalance, existed in the analytic situation. How could it be done away with? Ferenczi thought that if the patient were given the opportunity to analyze the analyst, it would benefit both. Needless to say, this was a novel idea, but one that was also dangerous to the very existence of analysis and therapy. Ferenczi never wrote about his ideas concerning mutual analysis in any publication. The first notice of it is to be found in the diary entry for January 17. There he spoke of a patient, to whom he gave the initials R. N., who felt that Ferenczi might wish to torture patients, and that the only protection she could envisage would be for her to analyze Ferenczi in order to rid him of this tendency and thereby protect herself. The exact passage reads:

> R. N. demands an analysis methodically carried out, as the only possible protective measure against the tendency perceived in me of killing or torturing patients. At first I was strongly opposed: the patient could abuse the situation . . . and analyze me instead of herself. Surprisingly, things turned out differently [54].

It was certainly a novel proposition. Ferenczi accepted it. We have only the vaguest hints as to how it was carried out, for how long, and what, precisely was said. Ferenczi gave some more details of this patient, R. N., on May 5: He explained that he had seen her for a number of years, and had already 'experimented' to the extent that he saw her for double sessions, on Sundays, and even at her own house, rather than his office. For over a year she had insisted that Ferenczi had hidden feelings of hatred for her and that her own analysis could not progress until she was able to analyze these in him. Ferenczi gave in and allowed her to analyze him. He wrote that 'it was my confession of personal and physical dislike [of the patient] that made the greatest impression on her, as well as my confession that the friendliness shown earlier was exaggerated.' This is, indeed, strong stuff (though not as strong as the passage on February 16, in which Ferenczi envisaged saying to a patient: 'Actually, I find you very disgusting, I can't stand the way you smell, your face and your manners are equally ugly') and undoubtedly convinced R. N. that her perceptions of Ferenczi's sadism were not ill-founded (83–84). Here is one of the dilemmas of analysis: undoubtedly Ferenczi did find her unlikable. This happens all the time. When a therapist finds a patient unlikable, can therapy proceed? The theory of analysis claims, of course, that it can. It would be economic disaster to admit otherwise. But Ferenczi, by agreeing to mutual analysis, tacitly admitted that such feelings will interfere with the therapy. He seemed to believe, along with R. N., that these feelings can be 'analyzed away.' But can they? Is there any reason to believe that an initial dislike will change, with time, into affection? It may do so, but there is no guarantee; and what if it does not? Ferenczi, in this same passage, said that many patients told him that they felt that love coming from the therapist could cure them, that if Ferenczi could simply be there, more or less silent, without any attempt to interpret, this would help them. Ferenczi found this was true, and wondered if this love acted as a salve for the wounds left by early traumas. But he also recognized that the feeling the patient had of being helped did not always last beyond the end of the session. He asked whether this is not because 'our imagination endows us with more love than we in fact possess.' After all, he pointed out, when the analytic hour is over, the therapist simply sends the patient away and ushers in the next.

In this context I remember some remarks that Anna Freud made to me when we were talking about her father's attitudes toward Ferenczi. She and Ferenczi once discussed this very topic, and Ferenczi said to her that the one hour of treatment was a very artificial time barrier, and that he preferred to give his patients however much time they wanted. Anna Freud said she raised the obvious objections: What if the patient wanted all afternoon; what did one say to other patients who were waiting? Ferenczi thought for a while and then said to her: 'Maybe one should have only one patient.' Anna Freud told me she was very impressed by this remark. But surely part of the implication that follows is that therapy per se is not possible. Having one patient is not an artificial situation; it is more like ordinary situations, such as living with somebody, having children, having friends. Indeed, Ferenczi, in the entry for the next day, pointed out that he was in need of the soothing effects of love as much as his patients were; he, too, needed to be somebody's 'only patient.'

Ferenczi was now lost in the dilemmas he had perceived. For he pointed out, on January 31, that it is not a play that the patient is engaged in when reliving a traumatic incident. The therapist cannot be an indifferent spectator to the suffering. If one is to take it completely seriously, then one must really enter the past with the patient, that is, really believe in the reality of the event. 'Freud would not permit me to do this,' Ferenczi complained. He wrote that to remain on an intellectual plane, without allowing one's feelings to enter, is subtly to encourage the patient to feel that the event could not have taken place. The child who has been abused often attempts to protect herself against the full realization of what was done by saying, according to Ferenczi, 'It cannot be true, that all of this happened to me; for surely if it had, somebody would have come to my assistance.' It is preferable for the child (and, later, the patient and the analyst) to doubt the veracity of memory than to become aware of the world's coldness and badness. How do children survive knowing that fathers can be so cruel, and that they can expect nothing but disbelief, derision, or indifference from the rest of the world when they attempt to talk about it? A similar dilemma takes place, according to Ferenczi, immediately after the trauma:

> In most cases of infantile traumas, the parents have no interest in engraving the incidents in the memory of the child, and, quite the contrary, almost always employ a kind of repression-therapy: 'It is nothing.' 'Nothing happened.' 'Don't think about it any more' . . . the events are silenced to death, the hesitant hints given by the child are not taken in, or are rejected as impossible, and this is done so systematically and is in such conformity to what everybody else believes that the child's own judgment cedes [72].

Analysis, Ferenczi maintained, simply continues this denial. One way it does so is by the refusal to take the emotional content seriously. The sharp eyes of the patient perceive that the analyst is not really interested. It would be better, and more honest, wrote Ferenczi, to say to the patient: 'I have so many personal difficulties of my own that it is only with great difficulty that I can hear about yours.' Often, said Ferenczi, when the analyst smiles in a friendly and encouraging manner, he is really thinking: To hell with you, I wish I could throw you out of my office. Ferenczi then confessed: 'I have yet to see a single case of a training analysis, my own included, that was so complete that such corrections, both in life and in analysis, would be unnecessary' (73).

A few days later, on February 2, he began a mutual analysis with a patient who, after a few days, decided to break off the analysis: she wanted to travel to the hometown of an affectionate relative, because that person could give her the love and tenderness she felt Ferenczi could not give her. Ferenczi was very sympathetic, and noted that when a child has been the victim of trauma, she or he needs an enormous amount of genuine love:

> otherwise, the child remains in mute and proud suffering, and if there is not at least one human being to whom it can open up, the child is suspended in majestic solitude above the events, whereas in the symptoms, such as nightmares, etc., and in trance states, the suffering is carried out without leaving any trace of conviction [as to the reality of what happened] [75].

On February 20, Ferenczi made a bold experiment. He decided to be entirely honest with a patient (probably R. N.) who had had an early traumatic experience involving a murder – Ferenczi did not give the details – a story that nobody was willing to believe. At the beginning of the session he told her (cruelly, to my mind): 'I have something to tell you that is extremely embarrassing, something that one ordinarily does not say to a patient.' He went on: 'I have promised you a successful analysis. But in reality I often fear that the whole thing will be a failure and that you will end up insane or will commit suicide.' Unexpectedly, the patient responded positively:

> 'Had I, early on, been able to bring my father to make such a confession about the truth, and to recognize the danger I was in, it would have saved my mental health. For this confession would have shown me that I was right when I spoke about things that seemed to be impossible . . .' [86].

And then Ferenczi was able to wonder whether 'the whole plan of "mutuality" was not . . . an unconsciously sought antidote against the hypnotic lies of childhood.'[5] On the very same day, another patient was more skeptical, and wondered whether Ferenczi could possibly understand what she had gone through. Ferenczi admitted that her skepticism was justified.

Ferenczi's comments about mutual analysis on March 13 carry us to the very heart of his ideas:

> Certain phases of mutual analysis represent the total giving up of all force and all authority, on both sides. They give the impression of two children of the same age, who had been terrified, and who tell each other about their experiences. Because they have the same fate, they understand each other completely, and instinctively seek to comfort one another. The knowledge that each has experienced a similar fate permits the partner to appear totally harmless, a person to whom one can safely entrust oneself [106–7].

With characteristic directness, Ferenczi bypassed the less interesting issues of mutual analysis (such as who would pay) and focused on what he considered to be the heart of what psychotherapy should be. To give up authority was something that Freud had never even considered. It was an idea totally absent from medicine in Europe in Ferenczi's lifetime and was in fact antithetical to medical practice. Ferenczi envisaged a therapy based on mutual traumas. But he meant this quite literally, and not in the metaphorical sense that analysis has always taken it. After all, one formal requirement of analytic training – that the candidate must be analyzed – has for its justification the fact that everybody has been to some extent 'traumatized.' Interestingly enough, this requirement is one that Ferenczi himself suggested to Freud. But Ferenczi here clearly had something quite different in mind. He was referring to two survivors comforting one another. That is not

[5] 'Hypnotic lies' refers to a theory held by Ferenczi that an abusing parent often puts the child into a kind of hypnotic trance, giving the child the post-hypnotic suggestion that it will remember nothing of what happened. Sometimes, Ferenczi suggested, children will put themselves into such an altered state during the abuse, as a way of blotting it out. Michelle Morris, in her extraordinary contemporary novel about incest, *If I Should Die Before I Wake* (Los Angeles: J. P. Tarcher, 1982), confirms this. Robert Fliess has also written about this trancelike state, in his *Symbol, Dream and Psychosis* (New York: International Universities Press, 1973).

analysis. Analysis has never had anything comforting about it. In analysis, there is no sense of solidarity, of two people who have come through some tragedy still alive but wounded in similar ways. This comes closer to what we find today in groups of women survivors of sexual abuse, or self-help groups such as Alcoholics Anonymous and Al-Anon.

Ferenczi seems greatly concerned with safety. At one point (March 13), he says that 'to undo infantile amnesia, one must enjoy total freedom from fear of the analyst.' The original trauma was one that was pervaded by fear, the original fear of being killed or badly hurt, and the later fear of not being believed, of being thought 'crazy.' Why should one assume that the analyst will behave differently? Indeed, it was Ferenczi's experience that *the* analyst, the very first analyst, did *not* behave differently, and this was what sensitized Ferenczi to the harm that could be done. He had experienced this very harm at the hands of Freud. He felt that Freud had treated him as he had treated all his patients, with a certain callous indifference to their *real suffering*. This is the significance of what is certainly the single most remarkable passage in the diary (May 1, 1932), in which Ferenczi tells, for the first and only time, what he thought had happened with Freud on the question of the believability of his women patients:

> Why should the patient place himself blindly in the hands of the doctor? Isn't it possible, indeed probable, that a doctor who has not been well analyzed (after all, who is well analyzed?) will not cure the patient but rather will use her or him to play out his own neurotic or psychotic needs? As proof and justification of this suspicion, I remember certain statements Freud made to me. Obviously he was relying on my discretion. He said that patients are only riffraff.[6] The only thing patients were good for is to help the analyst make a living and to provide material for theory. It is clear we cannot help them. This is therapeutic nihilism. Nevertheless, we entice patients by concealing these doubts and by arousing their hopes of being cured. I think that in the beginning Freud really believed in analysis; he followed Breuer enthusiastically, involved himself passionately and selflessly in the therapy of neurotics

---

[6] *Die Patienten sind ein Gesindel.*

(lying on the floor for hours, if necessary, next to a patient in the throes of a hysterical crisis). However, certain experiences must have first alarmed him and then left him disillusioned more or less the way Breuer was when his patient [Anna O.] suffered a relapse and he found himself faced, as before an abyss, with the countertransference. In Freud's case, the equivalent was the discovery of the mendacity of hysterical women. Since the time of this discovery, Freud no longer likes sick people. He rediscovered his love for his orderly, cultivated superego. A further proof of this is his dislike and expressions of blame that he uses with respect to psychotics and perverts, in fact, his dislike of everything that he considers 'too abnormal,' even against Indian mythology. Since he suffered this shock, this disappointment, Freud speaks much less about traumas, and the constitution begins to play the major role. This involves, obviously, a degree of fatalism. After a wave of enthusiasm for the psychological, Freud has returned to biology; he considers the pyschological to be nothing more than the superstructure over the biological and for him the latter is far more real. He is still attached to analysis intellectually, but not emotionally. Further, his method of treatment as well as his theories result from an ever greater interest in order, character and the substitution of a better superego for a weaker one. In a word, he is becoming a pedagogue. . . . He looms like a god above his poor patient, who has been degraded to the status of a child. We claim that the transference comes from the patient, unaware of the fact that the greater part of what one calls the transference is artificially provoked by this very behavior [148–49].

What Ferenczi has offered here is a unique explanation of the direction that therapy took after Freud's abandonment of the seduction theory. Ferenczi explains that once Freud no longer believed in the reality of these early, terrifying traumas, he posited an explanation for their having been fantasized that is strictly biological. They are, Freud argued, universal fantasies. They cannot, therefore, evoke in the therapist any degree of real compassion for real human suffering. The therapist's only task is that of the educator, to explain to his patient that these apparent memories are nothing but biologically determined fantasies; they are mistakes in perception. Therapy, Freud maintained, does not require any deep emotional commitment, but merely a certain intellectual grasp of theory. In effect, said Ferenczi, Freud's heart was no longer in therapy, because he could no longer believe in the uniqueness and the reality of each separate human being's experience of suffering. He had universalized suffering, thereby robbing it of its power to move us individually. Just as the educator believes that the young student who must be educated is hopelessly inferior when in fact the child is merely younger, so also the analyst believes the patient has simply misunderstood the world around him, as an adult often believes a child does. Ferenczi knew that Freud had lost something uniquely valuable; the greater tragedy is that, with its loss to Freud, it seems to have been lost to therapy in general. And the greatest tragedy is the suffering this has caused so many people since.

On May 18, 1932, Ferenczi acknowledged that too many analysts feel superior to their patients, wanting to instruct them in how to live. He maintained:

> No analysis can succeed in which we do not succeed in really loving the patient. Every patient has the right to be regarded, and treated, as an abused and unhappy child. It demonstrates, therefore, a weakness in the psychic organization of the analyst if he treats more kindly a patient he finds sympathetic than one he does not [190].

But of course analysts do not want to admit to such a weakness, and so they simply claim (who, after all, could ever verify it?) that they treat all their patients with the same sympathy. If we follow Ferenczi's reasoning and agree that every patient has the right to be considered an abused and unhappy child, we nevertheless must ask: How did such persons come to analysis? Because they believe, mistakenly, that the analyst will treat them differently than they have been treated until then. After all, if they are seeking treatment, they have failed to get the kind of understanding they seek in their everyday life. But what Ferenczi failed to see was that if Freud gave up on these patients (as Ferenczi maintained) because he could not tolerate the suffering they went through as children and denied its reality, and if Ferenczi himself could spend twenty-seven years analyzing patients with the same attitudes that Freud and other analysts had, how could he expect things really to change? Clearly there were strong forces at work in society that made recognizing what happened to all these patients something that would not be rewarded. Ferenczi himself saw what happened when he attempted to convince Freud that what his patients had been telling him was true all along. He was dropped, quickly, by Freud and every other analyst at the time.[7] Since he knew perfectly well that until that point he had been universally admired, even loved, he must have known that the real reason for his disgrace had to do with the nature of the subject he was bringing up. It made everyone uncomfortable. The very denial that Ferenczi recognized to have played a major role in the lives of these patients was now to become his lot as well, as analysts rushed to deny the truth of what he was telling them. Ferenczi had become, at last, and like his patients, somebody whose knowledge made him unwanted. He fared no better than they did. Did this deeper truth still elude him, or did it kill him?

Ferenczi died on May 22, 1933, at the age of fifty-nine, soon after struggling with what all his colleagues considered his heretical views, and before he could write about them in any detail. The world had to wait until 1985 before gaining access to the diary to which he consigned these thoughts. Will they make a difference to therapy now? There are many therapists in the United States who

[7] I have told the full story, based on previously unpublished letters between Freud and Ferenczi, in a chapter called 'The Strange Case of Ferenczi's Last Paper' in my *Assault on Truth* (145–87). In brief, what happened was that Ferenczi came to believe, toward the end of his life, that women who told him they had been sexually assaulted as children were telling the truth. He wrote a paper about this, 'Confusion of Tongues between Adults and the Child,' which he wished to give at the Wiesbaden Congress of psychoanalysts in 1932. Freud and all the other analysts at the time urged Ferenczi not to give the paper, saying that it would damage his reputation. Ferenczi insisted on meeting Freud and discussing it with him face to face. It was the last meeting the two close friends were to have. Freud was adamant and insisted that he had been right to give up the seduction theory. He told Ferenczi that he was being deceived by his patients, that what they reported to him were fantasies, not memories. Ferenczi was deeply disappointed, and he died soon after the meeting. Jones started a rumor that Ferenczi was mentally ill (for believing the women) and, since he disagreed with Freud, that he had homicidal tendencies. (To disagree with Freud was tantamount, in Jones's psychology, to killing him.) Ferenczi's paper, which he insisted on giving and publishing, was not published in English (in the *International Journal of Psycho-Analysis*) for sixteen years. Today, many would consider it Ferenczi's most beautiful essay.

proudly trace their lineage back to Sándor Ferenczi. Will they take seriously these, his most profound reflections on the nature of therapy? Will any therapist have the courage to take Ferenczi's thoughts to their logical conclusion? Ferenczi may have wished merely to stop the abuses of therapy, to improve it and reform it. Is it possible that Ferenczi was about to take the further step of acknowledging that there is something in the very nature of engaging in therapy that leads to abuse; that it is not this or that therapist, but therapy itself, which has to be questioned?

4

JUNG AMONG THE NAZIS

Ferenczi, as we saw in the last chapter, wanted to think of therapy as harmless, as a comforting activity engaged in by survivors of trauma. But he became deeply concerned that therapy was anything but harmless. Carl Jung seems like the incarnation of Ferenczi's fear. While many people have acknowledged Jung's sympathetic actions toward German Nazis in the early 1930s, nobody has attempted to link this sympathy with elements of Jungian psychotherapy. Jung's interest in the real world was limited to his own preoccupations. I believe that Jung's remarkable degree of self-absorption allowed him to shut out the real traumas that fill people's lives, and to ignore political tragedies as well as personal ones.

· Carl Gustav Jung (1875–1961) was a Swiss psychiatrist who trained in the Burghölzli Clinic in Zurich under Eugen Bleuler, and for some years (1907 to 1912) was closely associated with Sigmund Freud. To the general public his name is second only to Freud's, and his fame has spread perhaps even more widely around the world than has Freud's. His first book was published in 1902 and his last book was published posthumously. His collected works have been published in twenty volumes. After breaking with Freud, he went his own way, founding a school called 'analytic psychology,' which is still active today. It has had a greater impact on the general educated public than it has had on psychiatry proper. Nevertheless, most eclectic psychotherapists have incorporated some ideas that originated with Jung.

[1] As we shall see, Göring never hesitated to cite Hitler in this journal, as Jung well knew. The Nazi party daily, the *Völkischer Beobachter*, in 1938, reported a speech by Göring in which he mentioned an exchange of telegrams with

JUNG AND THE NAZIS

Many people have accused Jung of having collaborated with Nazi psychiatrists in Germany during the Second World War. Jung and his followers claimed that, by accepting the presidency of the International Medical Society for Psychotherapy (until then a uniquely German society), Jung was only attempting to protect his Jewish colleagues, since they could not become members of the German branch, but could become members of the International Society. Here are the facts.

In 1930 the German psychiatrist Ernst Kretschmer became President of the Allgemeine Ärztliche Gesellschaft für Psychotherapie (the General Medical Society for Psychotherapy), which had been founded two years earlier. Jung was Vice-President.

In 1933, when a general ruling was proclaimed in Germany that all societies (artistic, scientific, and so on) had to conform to Nazi ideology (*Gleichschaltung*), Kretschmer, who was not a Nazi and who also wished to keep psychotherapy under the control of psychiatry, resigned his position. Jung then became the President of the International Medical Society for Psychotherapy, and Matthias Heinrich Göring (1879–1945), a cousin of Hermann Göring (the Prussian Prime Minister), became President of the German branch of the society. The main function of the society, apart from meetings, was the publication of a German-language journal, published in Leipzig, entitled *Zentralblatt für Psychotherapie und ihre Grenzgebiete* (Journal for Psychotherapy and Related Disciplines), of which Jung became the editor in chief. In the issue in which this announcement was made, December 1933, Vol. 6, page 1, two things were published that captured the world's attention, and they have continued to be written about over the years. The first was a momentous statement by Göring:

> It is expected of all members of the Society who write articles that they will have read through with great scientific care the path-breaking book by Adolf Hitler, *Mein Kampf*, and will recognize it as essential [to their work].[1]

Hitler, quoted approvingly from *Mein Kampf*, praised hereditary biology, and decried the former influence of Jews in the field of depth psychology. This is cited in Geoffrey Cocks, *Psychotherapy in the Third Reich: The Göring Institute* (New York: Oxford University Press, 1985), 115.

Equally important was an editorial that Jung wrote. It is less than one page long. He explained that he had taken over the presidency of the society and the editorship of the *Zentralblatt*. He spoke of the prevailing confusion in psychotherapy, 'not unlike the previous state of affairs in politics,' a pointed reference to Hitler and a subtle commendation of the 'accommodation process,' since he was hinting that the confusion had now ended. Then Jung made the statement for which he has been so bitterly condemned over the years:

> The differences which actually do exist between Germanic and Jewish psychology and which have long been known to every intelligent[2] person are no longer to be glossed over, and this can only be beneficial to science [*C. W.*, 10:533].

The storm broke a few months later, when a Swiss psychiatrist and psychoanalyst, Gustav Bally, published an article in the *Neue Zürcher Zeitung* on February 27, 1934, in which he quoted Göring's words, pointed out that the journal had been *gleichgeschaltet* (conformed to Nazi ideology), and that a Swiss national, Jung, had become the editor. Jung responded at length on March 13, 14, and 15. Among other things, he wrote:

> Should I, as a prudent neutral, withdraw into security this side of the frontier and wash my hands in innocence, or should I — as I was well aware — risk my skin and expose myself to the inevitable misunderstandings which no one escapes who, from higher necessity, has to make a pact with existing political powers in Germany? [*C. W.*, 10:535–36].

[2] Actually the German word is *einsichtig*, which means reasonable, sensible, discerning. Since the word comes from *Einsicht*, literally, 'insight,' it also connotes psychiatric wisdom. Thus, Jung is making a psychiatric statement here. The quotations come from *Collected Works of C. G. Jung:* Vol. 10, *Civilization in Transition*, 2d ed., ed. by Gerhard Adler, Michael Fordham, Sir Herbert Read, exec. ed. William McGuire; trans. by R. F. C. Hull, Bollingen Series XX (Princeton: Princeton University Press, 1970; first published 1964. Referred to here as *C.W.*) Most of the material related to these issues is contained in the Appendix. For comparison with the German text, I have used *Gesammelte Werke*, Vol. 10, *Zivilisation im Uebergang*, ed. by Lilly Jung-Merker and Elisabeth Rüf (Olten: Walter-Verlag, 1974).

The 'higher necessity' that forced Jung to 'make a pact with the existing political powers in Germany' apparently was the fear that psychotherapy was in danger of disappearing in Nazi Germany:

> As conditions then were, a single stroke of the pen in high places would have sufficed to sweep all psychotherapy under the table. That had to be prevented at all costs for the sake of suffering humanity, doctors, and – last but not least – science and civilization [C.W., 10:536].

Jung then explained that he had been told that the statement by Göring would appear in a special German issue, and would not be included in the international issue with his name on the cover: 'In this way my name unexpectedly appeared over a National Socialist manifesto, which to me personally was anything but agreeable. And yet after all – what is help or friendship that costs nothing?' (C.W., 10:538). Jung went on to say:

> Medicine has nothing to do with politics . . . and therefore it can and should be practiced for the good of suffering humanity under all governments. . . . The doctor who, in wartime, gives his help to the wounded of the other side will surely not be held a traitor to his country [C.W., 10:538 – 39].

Jung was no doubt aware of the real charge, namely, that the 'other side' to which Jung had given his help was not the victim, the Jew, but the oppressor, the Nazi:

> Admittedly I was incautious, so incautious as to do the very thing most open to misunderstanding at the present moment: I have tabled the Jewish question. This I did deliberately. . . . The Jewish problem is a regular complex, a festering wound, and no responsible doctor could bring himself to apply methods of medical hush-hush in this matter [C.W., 10:539].

But if we go back to the words that Jung actually wrote in the journal in 1933, we find that he did not raise the 'question' (a few lines later to become the 'problem') of the Jews in order to help them, or to convince the Germans that their attitude was a pernicious one. For whom was the 'Jewish problem' a problem, a 'festering wound'? The very terms, even here, in his so-called explanation (it is certainly not intended as an apology), were cast in the language of the aggressor. Jung then said that 'my public will object, why raise the Jewish problem today of all days and in Germany of all places?' (*C.W.*, 10:543). Jung justified himself by pointing out that he had made similar statements in his career: 'If I am to be exploited for political ends, there's nothing I can do to stop it' (*C.W.*, 10:543). But he could easily have stopped it by not having made the statements in the first place, or he could have stopped it by taking an explicit position against the persecution of the Jews, something he did not do. Yet Jung wrote (in the same article), 'I must confess my total inability to understand why it should be a crime to speak of "Jewish" psychology' (*C.W.*, 10:541). This lack of awareness does not absolve Jung; it simply adds ignorance (which is another form of oppression) to opportunism.

Had Jung really been outraged, as he claimed, he could have immediately announced his resignation. In fact he remained editor until 1939. In a letter to the head of the society's Danish branch, Dr. Oluf Brüell, dated March 2, 1934, Jung wrote of the Göring manifesto as if it were only 'a tactical blunder' and stated that he would 'try everything possible in the future to eliminate political influences from the *Zentralblatt*.' His own statements about 'Jewish' and 'Aryan' psychology he did not consider political.[3]

On the same day, March 2, Jung also wrote to Walter Cimbal, a German psychiatrist who was Secretary of the German General Medical Society for Psychotherapy from 1933 to 1935. Jung certainly did not complain vociferously of the 'blunder' in including Göring's manifesto, but only asked for some influence on the make-up of the journal, and promised that he would not 'under any circumstances use this influence for the publication of anything that is politically inadmissible,' a promise he was to keep (*Letters*, 145–46).

It is useful to keep in mind the person Jung was addressing. Walter Cimbal joined the Nazi party in 1933. An article he wrote for the *Deutsche Seelenheilkunde* (cited in Cocks, 83) concludes with a warm recommendation of *Mein Kampf*. Freudian psychoanalysis

---

[3] *C. G. Jung Letters*, ed. by Gerhard Adler and Aniela Jaffé, trans. by R. F. C. Hull, vol. 2, *1906–1950* (Princeton: Princeton University Press, 1973), 144–45.

was under vicious attack, most notably by Julius Streicher, the Nazi editor of *Der Stürmer*. Jung must have been aware of this. He must also have known that these attacks were often led by the very men who were responsible for the *Zentralblatt* that he edited, since these men were appointed by Göring. To his European colleagues, Jung attempted to minimize the significance of these affiliations. Thus he reassured the Dutch psychiatrist J. H. van der Hoop by writing, in a letter dated March 12, 1934, that 'you can be assured that the Nazi outpourings of the German members are due to political necessity rather than to the religious convictions of the gentlemen in question' (*Letters*, 146–47). Jung wanted very much to convince others, and perhaps himself, that what was happening in Germany was unrelated to real persecution. In a letter dated May 26, he attempted to defend himself to James Kirsch, one of his Jewish students, who was then living in Palestine: 'Neither have I addressed Hitler over the radio or in any other manner, nor have I made any political statements.' Jung evidently did not consider his earlier comments to be political. In the same letter his anger showed when he wrote, 'As you know, Freud previously accused me of anti-Semitism because I could not abide his soulless material- ism. The Jew directly solicits anti-Semitism with his readiness to scent out anti-Semitism everywhere' (*Letters*, 160–63).[4]

After the war, of course, Jung claimed that he often spoke up for Jewish doctors in Germany and elsewhere. But I have not been able to find contemporary evidence supporting this claim. In fact, it appears, from a letter Jung wrote to Eric Benjamin Strauss, a British psychiatrist who was a member of the organizing commit- tee for the Tenth International Medical Congress for Psychother- apy held in Oxford in 1938, that there was some objection on the part of the German members to Jews being permitted to speak at the congress. Jung wrote: 'I cannot and shall not exclude non- Aryan speakers' (*Letters*, 242). However, he went on to state: 'The only condition on which I insist is that everybody, Aryan or non-Aryan, refrain from airing remarks apt to arouse the political psychosis of our days.' In other words, Jung was taking what he

---

[4]The reference to Freud is no doubt to 'On the History of the Psycho- Analytic Movement,' which was published in 1914, in which Freud wrote: '[Jung] seemed ready to enter into a friendly relationship with me and for my sake to give up certain racial prejudices which he had previously permitted himself' (*S.E.*, 14:43).

claimed to be a strictly neutral position in public. By not speaking out, he was eloquently silent *for* the Nazis. Moreover, he was closely associated with men who were, in his own society, demanding that Jews not be heard. *All* of the Germans with whom Jung worked in the society were Nazis or Nazi collaborators.[5] Thus the German psychiatrist Gustav Richard Heyer was a staunch supporter of the regime from the beginning, becoming a party member in 1937. His colleagues recall him as an enthusiastic Nazi (Cocks, 61). He was also a student of Jung (see Jung's letter to him dated April 20, 1934). Hans von Hattingberg, another member of the inner circle connected with Jung's journal, 'responded enthusiastically to the events of 1933; if he had reservations then, or regrets later, we do not know about them' (Cocks, 70).

In 1934, in the *Zentralblatt* again, Jung returned to the 'Jewish problem,' so important to his German colleagues, in an article entitled 'The State of Psychotherapy Today' (*C.W.*, 10:157–73): 'The Jews have this peculiarity in common with women; being physically weaker, they have to aim at the chinks in the armor of their adversary.' Jung's next passage ranks as one of the most disturbing things he ever wrote:

> The Jewish race as a whole – at least this is my experience – possesses an unconscious which can be compared with the 'Aryan' only with reserve.[6] Creative individuals apart, the average Jew is far too conscious and differentiated to go about pregnant with the tensions of unborn futures. The 'Aryan' unconscious has a higher potential than the Jewish; that is

[5] The members of the managing committee were: Walter Cimbal, Carl Haeberlin, Hans von Hattingberg, Gustav Richard Heyer, Fritz Künkel, I. H. Schultz, Harald Schultz-Hencke, Leonhard Seif, and Viktor von Weizsäcker. For information on the Nazi activities of these men, see Cocks's *Psychotherapy in the Third Reich*, and the 1983 issue of the German journal *Psyche* (vol. 37). One eyewitness account of a meeting in 1936 or 1937 at which Jung was present tells of a German psychiatrist who 'went up to the speaker's place in an SS uniform. He stretched out his hand and started out with "Heil Hitler."' See the outstanding book *Mass Murderers in White Coats: Psychiatric Genocide in Nazi Germany and the United States*, by Lenny Lapon (Psychiatric Genocide Research Institute, P. O. Box 80071, Springfield, MA 01138–0071), 147.

[6] The quotation marks are due only to the squeamishness of the translator, as if to indicate that Jung was using the word in a special sense. But he was not. The German text (*G.W.*, 10:190) (*das sich mit dem arischen nur bedingt vergleichen lässt . . .*) makes it clear that Jung used the word without quotation marks. It is not capitalized in German only because it is an adjective.

both the advantage and the disadvantage of a youthfulness not yet fully weaned from barbarism. In my opinion it has been a grave error in medical psychology up till now to apply Jewish categories – which are not even binding on all Jews – indiscriminately to Germanic and Slavic Christendom. Because of this the most precious secret of the Germanic peoples – their creative and intuitive depth of soul – has been explained as a morass of banal infantilism, while my own warning voice has for decades been suspected of anti-Semitism. This suspicion emanated from Freud. He did not understand the Germanic psyche any more than did his Germanic followers.[7] Has the formidable phenomenon of National Socialism, on which the whole world gazes with astonished eyes, taught them better? Where was that unparalleled tension and energy while as yet no National Socialism existed? Deep in the Germanic psyche, in a pit that is anything but a garbage-bin of unrealizable infantile wishes and unresolved family resentments. A movement that grips a whole nation must have matured in every individual as well. That is why I say that the Germanic unconscious contains tensions and potentialities which medical psychology must consider in its evaluation of the unconscious. Its business is not with neuroses but with human beings – that, in fact, is the grand privilege of medical psychology: to treat the whole man and not an artificially segregated function.[8] And that is why its scope must be widened to reveal to the physician's gaze not just the pathological aberrations of a disturbed psychic development, but the creative powers of the psyche laboring at the future; not just a dreary fragment but the meaningful whole.

Lest it be lost on his audience that he is agreeing with the common Nazi criticism of Freudian (i.e., Jewish) psychoanalysis, Jung, on the next page, is more explicit:

---

[7] The German text (*G. W.*, 10:191) is stronger: *Nachbeter* is pejorative, not just a follower, but a parrot, somebody who uncritically or thoughtlessly repeats.

[8] The German reads *nicht nur behandeln darf, sondern auch soll*, which is omitted from the English. This means that medical psychology 'not only *can* but *should* treat' the whole person.

The poison of the 'low-down'[9] interpretation has bitten so deeply into the marrow of these people's bones that they can no longer think at all except in the infantile-perverse jargon of certain neurotics who display all the peculiarities of a Freudian psychology.

Jung writes that Jews are overintellectual compared to the 'decent' German:

And if he [the Freudian] degrades everything to the level of a 'dirty joke' psychology,[10] then we must not be surprised if the patient become spiritually blighted and compensates for this blight by incurable intellectualism. . . . To treat such people reductively, to impute ulterior motives to them, and to suspect their natural wholesomeness of unnatural obscenities is not only sinfully stupid but positively criminal.

Jung's claim that he was duped into accepting Göring's praise for Hitler becomes highly suspect when we examine the actual issues of the *Zentralblatt* published under Jung's name from 1933 to 1939. In reading through the issues, the first thing that struck me was that the infamous comment by Göring that psychotherapists must from now on take as their scientific model Hitler's *Mein Kampf* was actually made in the section titled 'News' (*Aktuelles*) on the very first page of the issue of January 1933 (the year in which a party-directed boycott against Jewish businesses, doctors, and lawyers took place for four days in April) and right after Jung's short announcement that he is taking over both the presidency of the society and the editorship of the journal, and his *cri de guerre* that Jewish and Aryan differences will no longer be dissimulated. The volume begins with Göring's statement that the new society was founded on September 15, 1933, under the guiding principles of National Socialism (Nazism), continues with the comment about Hitler's book, and goes on to name the new members of the committee. Since the remark about Hitler's book is embedded in a

[9] *Entwertende Deutung*, that is, a 'devaluating' interpretation, one· that debases the individual.

[10] The translator has omitted a phrase here. Jung (*G.W.*, 10:192) actually writes: . . . *alles und jedes in den infantil-perversen Sumpf einer obszönen Witzpsychologie*, i.e., the analyst drags 'everything into the swamp of the infantile and perverse morass of an obscene-joke psychology.'

commentary providing news to the membership of the society, it would seem that, contrary to Jung's claim, this message was never intended to be published in a separate issue, but was obviously meant for this place, right after Jung's remarks. If this is true, it would mean that Jung was *not* deceived by Göring, or any other member of the committe, into believing that this statement would not be published in 'his' journal.

The evidence for Jung's collaboration continues to mount. The subsequent volumes display the influence of Hitler and the racism that Jung explicitly claimed, after the war, could not have been tolerated in a journal of which he was editor in chief. Volume 7 of the *Zentralblatt*, 1934, was the first with Jung's name on the cover. It contains an account of the first congress, which was held in Bad Nauheim from May 10 to 13, 1934. On Friday, May 11, the congress was opened by three speeches. One was by Dr. R. Sommer on the history of psychotherapy, one by Jung, and one by M. H. Göring in which he speaks of the 'impregnation of German psychotherapy through the ideas of the Führer' (*Befruchtung der deutschen Psychotherapie durch die Ideen des Führers*) (130). In this same issue is an article by K. Gauger entitled 'Psychotherapy and a Political World View,' which contains these words:

> Since Adolf Hitler, the words *Volk*, and country, discipline, fidelity and honor have regained their biological importance in Germany. . . . All in all, medicine in the new Germany has taken on a political significance that no one would have dared to imagine previously. I have only to point to the grand political designs in regard to population, which are medically oriented, on the part of the Führer, his extraordinarily significant measures in regard to racial hygiene, and other matters [168].

This is clearly a reference to the plans, which Hitler carried out with the help of German psychiatrists, to murder mental patients.[11]

---

[11] The subject of the mass killing of mental patients (estimates are 350,000 killed) has been dealt with by Alexander Mitscherlich and Fred Mielke, *The Death Doctors* (London: Elek Books, 1949). Mitscherlich, a German psychoanalyst, was shunned by his colleagues after writing this book, as he explains in the preface. Fredric Wertham has a chapter on it in his book *A Sign for Cain:*

A Danish Nazi sympathizer, the psychiatrist Oluf Brüell, published an article in the same issue with the title 'Psychotherapy in the North.' It is the account of a young blond northerner who is 'traumatized' by seeing a film about the Hunchback of Notre-Dame. The author ends by saying:

> As we saw, the case presented is concerned with a person of northern Germanic extraction of exceptional racial purity, who in her tender childhood was exposed to an artificial-psychic traumatization in which the ugliness of life [i.e., the existence of dark, deformed human beings] swept over her budding idealism. In contrast many individuals who are not as high-bred could have weathered similar experiences with ease [277–86].

[11] *Cont.* An Exploration of Human Violence (New York: Paperback Library, 1969). Robert Jay Lifton, in *The Nazi Doctors: Medical Killing and the Psychology of Genocide* (New York: Basic Books, 1986), has also written on the subject. But the best book I have seen in English is Lenny Lapon's *Mass Murderers in White Coats: Psychiatric Genocide in Nazi Germany and the United States,* which he had to publish himself. Wertham notes that one young psychiatrist, Dr. Theo Lang, 'made a serious attempt to stem the whole program. He was at that time in Germany and later became chief physician of the institution Herisau in Switzerland. On January 20, 1941, he obtained an interview with Dr. M. H. Göring at the German Institute for Psychological Research and Psychotherapy. His plan was to get Dr. Göring to sign a declaration against the extermination of mental patients. When he tried to tell Dr. Göring the whole story of the program, which at that time had been going on for more than a year, he found that Dr. Göring knew all about it and confirmed its truth. However, he refused to sign the declaration' (174). Whether Jung knew about the killings has never been addressed. In the last few years a large number of outstanding books have been published in Germany on this topic. I have received some twenty-five volumes that explore this theme. I will mention here only the excellent book by Benno Müller-Hill: *Tödliche Wissenschaft: Die Aussonderung von Juden, Zigeunern und Geisteskranken 1933–45* (Reinbek: Rowohlt, 1984), which is scheduled to appear in English translation this year from Oxford University Press in England. See, too, Ernst Klee: *'Euthanasie' in NS-Staat: Die 'Vernichtung lebensunwerten Lebens'* (Frankfurt am M.: Fischer, 1986) and, by the same author, *Was sie taten – Was sie wurden: Aerzte, Juristen und andere Beteiligte am Kranken- oder Judenmord* (Frankfurt am M.: Fischer, 1987). An excellent article by a German pediatrician was published in *The Lancet* (August 2, 1986, 271–73): 'From Nazi Holocaust to Nuclear Holocaust: A Lesson to Learn,' by Hartmut M. Hanauske-Abel. The article became a *cause célèbre* in Germany when the head of the German medical association attacked Dr. Hanauske-Abel publicly. (See *Die Zeit,* No. 46, 6 November 1987, 45 ff., and the article in *Der Spiegel,* No. 3, vol. 42, 18 January 1988, 76–80, under the title: *Aerzte unter Hitler: 'Mission verraten.'*)

So here, in a journal of which Jung was editor in chief, and at the very congress where he was to become the President, racist comments were made, Hitler was praised, and northern, as opposed to Jewish, psychology was recognized. Could Jung claim that he had no idea this was going to happen, or that he could not prevent the publication of these articles in his journal?

In volume 9, 1936 (a year after the enactment of the Nuremberg Laws, which defined Jews as a separate race whose marriage or sexual contact with 'Aryans' was forbidden, and in which illegal sexual relations were called *Rassenschande*, race defilement),[12] with Jung's name again on the cover, Göring had an article, 'Worldview and Psychotherapy,' in which he quoted extensively from Hitler. He wrote:

> Whoever lives in the national-socialist state and supports it must recognize racial contrasts and act accordingly. It certainly is understandable that the Party looked with great suspicion on everything connected with psychotherapy because the idea of a racial worldview is totally alien to psychotherapy.

Jung must have been aware of the deep anti-Semitism of the organization of which he had now become president. His claim, after the war, that he was only trying to help Jews rings deeply hollow and false to whoever takes the trouble to go back and examine what was actually printed.

It is clear to me that Jung's views, at the time, were often in sympathy with those of the Nazis.[13] Thus he gave an interview on

[12] See Sarah Gordon, *Hitler, Germans and the 'Jewish Question'* (Princeton: Princeton University Press, 1984), 121.

[13] A Canadian psychiatrist, George Maclean, in an article, 'Jung the "Protector,"' published in *Midstream* (April 1987, 39–41) notes the parallels between the comments by Jung cited previously, and very similar quotations from Hitler's *Mein Kampf*. He quotes Hitler: 'Of two forms the strongest is the Aryan . . . the Jew was never in the position of a culture of his own . . . for his spiritual activity has always been furnished by others at all times. His intellect has developed through the culture that surrounds him. Never did the reverse process occur.' Jung, in 'The State of Psychotherapy Today,' which was published in the German *Zentralblatt* in 1934 (*C.W.*, 10:165), says something very similar: 'The Aryan unconscious, on the other hand, contains explosive forces and seeds of a future yet to be born, and these may not be devalued as nursery romanticism without psychic danger. The still youthful Germanic peoples are fully capable of creating new cultural forms that still lie dormant in

Radio Berlin on June 21, 1933, to his student Adolf Weizsäcker, a German neurologist and psychiatrist.[14] The interviewer introduced Jung by stressing his Protestant background, in contrast to the Jewish background of Freud and Alfred Adler. He then said that the Germans were surrounded by misunderstanding on the part of the other European nations. Jung was sympathethic and explained that the German people's 'enthusiasm for the reconstruction of the German community remains incomprehensible to Western Europeans.' Then he quoted Hitler, and I believe it is the only time he ever did:

> Only the self-development of the individual, which I consider to be the supreme goal of all psychological endeavour, can produce consciously responsible spokesmen and leaders of the collective movement. As Hitler said recently, the leader must be able to be alone and must have the courage to go his own way.

In 1938 Jung was interviewed by the American foreign correspondent H. R. Knickerbocker. The interview was published in *Hearst's International-Cosmopolitan* for January 1939, and it brought Jung's name to the attention of many people in the United States.[15] What is so extraordinary about this interview is Jung's clear admiration for Mussolini and his decidedly positive words about Hitler. About Mussolini he said that he was a man of style and good taste who was 'warm' and 'human'; 'I couldn't help liking Mussolini.' His comments about Hitler are no less disturbing:

---

[13] *Cont.* the darkness of the unconscious of every individual – seeds bursting with energy and capable of mighty expansion. The Jew, who is something of a nomad, has never yet created a cultural form of his own and as far as we can see never will, since all his instincts and talents require a more or less civilized nation to act as host for their development.' It seems hard to avoid the conclusion that Jung, aware of Hitler's remarks, was echoing them deliberately in a publication that would certainly catch the eyes (in 1934) of the Nazi authorities.

[14] *C. G. Jung Speaking: Interviews and Encounters*, ed. by William McGuire and R. F. C. Hull (Princeton: Princeton University Press, 1977), 59–66.

[15] Jung's remarks have been published in *C. G. Jung Speaking*, under the title 'Diagnosing the Dictators,' 115–35.

> There is no question but that Hitler belongs in the category of the truly mystic medicine man. As somebody commented about him at the last Nürnberg party congress, since the time of Mohammed nothing like it has been seen in this world. This markedly mystic characteristic of Hitler's is what makes him do things which seem to *us* illogical, inexplicable, curious and unreasonable. . . . So you see, Hitler is a medicine man, a form of a spiritual vessel, a demi-deity or, even better, a myth. . . .

Jung reduced an entire political ideology and a murderous political reality to a psychological interpretation: 'You could say that he has a tremendous mother complex, which means that he will be under the domination either of a woman or of an idea. Idea is always female.' Does this mean that Hitler's 'idea' of killing the Jews, mental patients, homosexuals, Gypsies, and Slavs is 'feminine'?[16] In these passages, Jung did not distance himself in any way from the men he was discussing. Later, as we shall see, he stated that his intention was to warn people of the dangers he saw. Jung claimed, for example, that he warned the world about the German's identification with Wotan early on. Here is a passage from this 1938 interview:

> Again, you take the widespread revival in the Third Reich of the cult of Wotan. Who was Wotan? God of wind. Take the name *'Sturmabteilung'* – Storm Troops. Storm, you see – the wind . . . And all these symbols together of a Third Reich led by its prophet under the banners of wind and storm and whirling vortices point to a mass movement which is to sweep the German people in a hurricane of unreasoning emotion on and on to a destiny which perhaps none but the seer, the prophet, the Führer himself can foretell – and, perhaps, not even he [118].

After the war Jung's tone changed entirely. His most famous piece is entitled 'After the Catastrophe.' It was published in Zurich

---

[16] Later, in 1945, Jung said about Hitler: 'It is also difficult to understand how his ranting speeches, delivered in shrill, grating, womanish tones, could have made such an impression' (*C.W.*, 10:204).

in the *Neue Schweizer Rundschau* in 1945 (*C.W.*, 10:194–217).[17] Because of the controversy that had raged over Jung's earlier statements, there can be little doubt that he wrote this piece as a response. Indeed, in his Preface he more or less explicitly acknowledged this: 'My statements have evidently led to all manner of misunderstandings . . .' (*C.W.*, 10:177). Although Jung did not have to wait until the end of the war to explain his position (he could easily have done so, from neutral Switzerland, before or during the war), he was surprised that people took his silence badly: '. . . it certainly never occurred to me that a time would come when I should be reproached for having said absolutely nothing about these things before 1945' (Epilogue, *C.W.*, 10:236).

'After the Catastrophe' had a peculiarly impersonal quality to it. Jung is writing from a certain distance, as if it had nothing to do with his personal conduct during the war. And clearly, to judge from the two passages quoted above, he knew that his response would be judged to be an explanation for his personal behavior. But Jung sought to avoid this aspect of the essay when he explained his reasons for writing: 'Questions are being asked on all sides about the meaning of the whole tragedy. People have even turned to me for an explanation, and I have had to answer them there and then to the best of my ability' (*C.W.*, 10:194).

Now Jung heaped contempt on Hitler and the Germans. He called what had happened 'the most monstrous crime of all ages.' He mentioned, several times, the concentration camps. He called Hitler a 'megalomaniac psychopath' (201); 'a psychic scarecrow . . . rather than a human being' (204); 'he was an utterly incapable, unadapted, irresponsible, psychopathic personality, full of empty, infantile fantasies, but cursed with the keen intuition of a rat or a guttersnipe' (223, 'The Fight with the Shadow').

Then Jung launched a sudden, unexpected diatribe against modern painting, atonal music, and James Joyce, exclaiming that 'here we already have the germ of what was to become a political reality in Germany.' But far from explaining Nazism, this is remarkably similar to Nazi writing during the war about the

---

[17] Jung collected three of his essays written between 1936 and 1945, including this one, and published them together in 1946. These were brought out in England as *Essays on Contemporary Events*, trans. by Elizabeth Welsh, Barbara Hannah, and Mary Briner (London: Kegan Paul, 1947). Preface and Epilogue by Jung.

corrupting effect of modern art. Jung also complained bitterly (201) that his warnings were not recognized and said that he felt like the lonley prophet, though the passages we have seen earlier could hardly be considered to contain a prophetic warning. The following lines may offer some clue as to what Jung was evading:

If only people could realize what an enrichment it is to find one's own guilt, what a sense of honor and spiritual dignity! But nowhere does there seem to be a glimmering of this insight. Instead, we hear only of attempts to shift the blame on to others – 'no one will admit to having been a Nazi' [202].

Who is the very best example of this complete lack of insight if not Jung himself? For nowhere in the essay did he apologize for anything he ever did or failed to do. No matter what his explanation was, surely Jung must have realized that many of his remarks before and during the war *could* be used against the Jews. As we will see below, Jung's words were actually quoted by Nazi authors and thus added to the general climate in which it was considered permissible first to denounce Jewish values and eventually to destroy the Jews themselves. The main point of Jung's essay was that 'the history of the last twelve years is the case-chart of an hysterical patient' (209), but this psychiatrization only served to screen Jung all the more from any direct involvement.[18] Surely 'hysteria,' with its overtones of 'unconscious' lying and so on, is irrelevant when one considers what Jung did, in fact, quite consciously say.

Jung's student and secretary, Aniela Jaffé, wrote an article, 'C. G. Jung and National Socialism,' in which she attempted to defend Jung.[19] Her claim, unsupported by any evidence, is that Jung acted correctly, since 'there was no other conceivable way in which his German-Jewish colleagues might have been helped.' But she did have the honesty to say that what Jung did was a 'grave human error' (85).

Jaffé states that Jung 'was pitiless in his public criticism,' but she

---

[18] 'When I say that the Germans are psychically ill it is surely kinder than saying that they are criminals' (209). Fortunately the world chose, in the Nuremberg trials, to avoid psychology and apply the law.

[19] In Jaffé's *From the Life and Work of C. G. Jung*, trans. by R. F. C. Hull (New York: Harper & Row, 1971), 81. First published in German in 1968.

admits that this became clear from his writings only 'after the gruesome drama was over' (91). Clearly Jaffé, herself Jewish, did not feel good about what Jung did, or even about his later pronouncements. However, she has a remarkable explanation:

> Three decades have passed since the Hitler terror. Jung died in 1961, and in retrospect even his mistakes at that period fall into place in his life and work without diminishing the stature of his personality. To adopt the language of analytical psychology, one could speak of a manifestation of his shadow which, as an archetype, clings to every man and is often all the blacker the brighter the light his personality sheds. Jung gave mankind too much for his shadow ever to dim his spiritual significance and his greatness as a man [95].

What Jung did was wrong. To call this wrongdoing 'a manifestation of his shadow' is merely to play with words. My own view is that Jung's anti-Semitism and, more important, his sympathy for fascism ran deep.

Many of Jung's later students took it upon themselves to clear Jung of these charges. Laurens van der Post, for example, in his book Jung and the Story of Our Time, wrote:

> . . . not only were his remarks misunderstood and taken out of context to be used by the Germans as additional justification for stepping up their inhuman campaign against German and Austrian Jews but they also gave grave offence to the Jews and opponents of Hitler everywhere in Europe.[20]

Van der Post admitted to the poor timing, but explained that this failed to take into account the fact that Jung 'was engaged in a totally different dimension of reality' and hence could not be expected to be aware of the exact time. I cannot imagine that Jung did not know what he was saying, and when. He certainly knew where: in a German publication sponsored by a Nazi group.

A number of rumors, including one about Jung being placed on a Nazi death list, seem to have been started by E. A. Bennet, in his book of conversations recorded from 1946 to 1961, Meetings with Jung.[21] The first entry in his diary, on March 29, 1946, reads:

[20] New York: Random House, 1975, 195.
[21] Zurich: Daimon, 1985, 14.

He said that until 1935 it had seemed possible, in Germany and Italy, that some good had come from Nazism. Germany was transformed; instead of roads crowded with people without work, all was changed and peaceful. Then he saw other things and knew it was evil. He began to speak against – as at the Oxford Congress for instance – and did so increasingly. He showed me an American article which had been falsely translated, misquoting him on the subject: his phrase 'looking with amazed eyes' (at the trend of events in Europe) had been transcribed as 'looking with admiring eyes.' He became so outspoken in his criticism of Germany that Mrs. Jung was afraid he would get into trouble, with so much German influence in Zurich. Referring to the rumors of his so-called Nazi sympathies, C. G. told me that his name was on the black list in Germany because of his views, and that he would certainly have been shot at once had he fallen in Nazi hands.

If we look at Jung's address to the Oxford congress, we do not find any criticism of Nazism, indeed, any mention of Germany at all (C. W., 10: 564–67). Nobody has ever confirmed that Jung's name was on a blacklist, and in fact we know, from his own account, that he met Goebbels in Berlin, that he had been invited by Hitler's doctors to examine him, and finally that 'a student of Jung's, Wolfgang Kranefeldt, recalled that when he went to Berlin in 1935 to give a series of lectures on archetypes, he was received with great joy and admiration, especially by Heinrich Göring, specifically because of his affiliation with Jung.'[22]

Most of those who knew Jung do not want to deal with the matter of his association with the Nazis in any way. Thus Barbara Hannah, in her book *Jung: His Life and Work*, wrote:

> To anyone, who, like myself, was with Jung in Berlin in July, 1933, and who saw and heard him frequently during the next twenty-eight years, the libel that Jung was a Nazi is so absurd and so entirely without foundation that it goes against the grain to take it seriously enough to contradict it.[23]

[22] Cocks, *Psychotherapy in the Third Reich*, 12.
[23] New York: G. P. Putnam's Sons, 1976, 213.

The fact is that Jung made statements and took actions that harmed Jews and others, and whether he joined the Nazi party or not is irrelevant. Jung's words speak loud and clear, and the message they give is one of collaboration. The reason it is so important to recognize this fact is that Jung's psychotherapy contains attitudes that are compatible with his collaboration. With its coercion and disdain for the real traumas that people experience, there is a deep strain of fascism running through Jung's psychotherapy.

Surely what Jung did, at that critical moment in history, was central to who Jung was. Jung did not take a principled stance against fascism, ever. He did not speak out on the suffering of the Jews or any other group persecuted by the Nazis.[24] I get the impression from reading what he wrote that his actions haunted him for the rest of his life. Never again, after 1945, did Jung write about the Second World War, or Hitler, in any sustained fashion, in all the many years of writing that lay ahead of him until his death in 1961.

I know that Jung had many Jewish pupils, both before and after the war. I know, too, that Harvard in 1936 gave him an honorary doctorate, as did Oxford in 1938, and that in 1937 he was invited to give the Terry Lectures at Yale University. I know that Jung's life was filled with honors too many to mention. But I also know that he never fully faced what he had done, and this, almost as much as the actions themselves, is inexcusable.[25]

---

[24] Lenny Lapon, in *Mass Murderers in White Coats*, drew attention to the Nazi killings of mental patients in the 1930s. I cannot believe that Jung knew nothing about it, given his close association with doctors high in the psychiatric hierarchy of Germany. Needless to say, he never mentioned it, and we will probably never know whether this is because he knew nothing about it or chose not to reveal what he knew.

[25] Some other accounts of this episode in Jung's life can be found in Edward Glover's excellent *Freud or Jung?* (New York: Meridian Books, 1956); Vincent Brome, *Jung* (New York: Atheneum, 1978); Paul J. Stern, *C. G. Jung: The Haunted Prophet* (New York: George Braziller, 1976), who gives a fair, balanced account. Henri Ellenberger has a long chapter with much documentation, 'Carl Gustav Jung and Analytical Psychology,' in his *Discovery of the Unconscious* (New York: Basic Books, 1970), 657–748. A defense of Jung is to be found in E. A. Bennet's *C. G. Jung* (London: Barrie & Rockliff, 1961), 56–62. Gerhard Wehr's *Carl Gustav Jung: Leben, Werk, Wirkung* (Munich: Kösel Verlag, 1985) is the latest complete biography. As far as I know, Freud never made any public statement about Jung's actions. However, his student Franz Alexander

JUNG'S PSYCHOTHERAPY

A psychotherapist with a neurosis is a contradiction in terms.

CARL JUNG

In 1937 Jung addressed the annual meeting of the Bund der Köngener, on the subject of psychotherapy. He said:

> I am Mr. Jung and that is all I am, and there is Miss So and So. It would not be at all nice were I to refuse to treat sick people like her. Moreover I enjoy the work. I like to be busy. I have a pioneer mentality. When a crazy chicken like this one comes through my door, it awakens my joy in discovery, my curiosity, my spirit of adventure, my sympathy. It touches my heart, which is much too soft, and people of my stature generally have such a heart. They try to hide it, but, stupidly, they don't succeed. I enjoy seeing what I can do with such a nut. It has become a game for me to cure the most difficult cases. This is merely a form of curiosity and spirit of adventure.[26]

This little-known quotation from Jung reveals a side of the man that is not generally written about. However, I do not believe that the flippant and callous attitudes he gives expression to here are so different from the ones for which he is generally known. When a therapist writes as much as Jung did, one is bound to learn his attitudes toward many contemporary issues that are less openly addressed in general by psychotherapists. (A Freudian analyst, by contrast, often gives no clues to what he or she feels about many urgent issues of the day.)

Jung certainly did not believe that the therapist must remain

---

apparently spoke to Freud about them, for he wrote, in *The History of Psychiatry* (New York: Harper & Row, 1966), 409: 'What moved Jung to play a prominent role in a newly racially oriented psychological movement? Since it was obviously neither racial prejudice nor Nazi conviction, what was it then? It is difficult to evade the answer that it was sheer *opportunism*. Freud's suspicion was that Jung, to achieve acclaim, was not immune to allowing his views to be influenced by public opinion. This is strongly supported by Jung's activities and writings during the Hitler era.'

[26] My translation from the German text in Wehr, 294.

anonymous, or that the therapist's ethical stance is irrelevant. In 1933, in *Modern Man in Search of a Soul*, Jung wrote that 'the latest advance of analytical psychology [the name Jung gave to his own system of psychology] makes an unavoidable problem of the doctor's ethical attitude.'[27] In 'Principles of Practical Psychotherapy,' written in 1935, Jung wrote that 'the doctor must emerge from his anonymity and give an account of himself, just as he expects his patient to do.' In 'Psychotherapy and a Philosophy of Life,' published in 1942, he wrote:

> The art of psychotherapy requires that the therapist be in possession of avowable, credible, and defensible convictions which have proved their viability, either by having resolved any neurotic dissociations of his own or by preventing them from arising. *A therapist with a neurosis is a contradiction in terms.* [Italics added.][28]

In other words, Jung firmly believed that the therapist is, by definition, a healthy person. That is why he is able to help others. In his autobiographical work, *Memories, Dreams, Reflections*, Jung wrote that 'in any thoroughgoing analysis the whole personality of both patient and doctor is called into play . . . the doctor's whole being is challenged.'[29]

It is clear, from these statements, that Jung, as a psychotherapist, wished to be judged as a human being. He acknowledged the importance of ethics. Questions about his own ethics are therefore in keeping with his own teachings. Jung's prejudices about Jews would have to interfere were he to see a Jew in therapy. Even if his own prejudices somehow did not interfere, he would have to recognize that for the Jewish patient, the stance Jung took during the war would make therapy impossible. Moreover, as Jung's comments about modern art, modern literature, and modern music demonstrate, there were other areas in which he had strong

---

[27] Trans. by W. S. Dell and Cary F. Baynes (New York: Harcourt, Brace & World, 1955), 53.

[28] The last two quotations come from C. G. Jung, *Collected Works*, vol. 16, *The Practice of Psychotherapy: Essays on the Psychology of the Transference and Other Subjects* (Princeton: Princeton University Press, 1966), 18, 78.

[29] Recorded and edited by Aniela Jaffé, trans. by Richard and Clara Winston (New York: Pantheon Books, 1973; first published in 1965), 132–33.

biases. How could he see people who worked in these areas and expect to help them? But these are not the only ideas about which Jung had strongly held prejudices. His views on women, even as late as 1955, were hardly enlightened:

A man's foremost interest should be his work. But a woman *is* her work and her business. Yes, I know it sounds like a convenient philosophy of the selfish male when I say that. But marriage means a home. And home is like a nest – not enough room for both birds at once. One sits inside, the other perches on the edge and looks about and attends to all outside business.[30]

When Jung recorded his autobiography, toward the end of his life, he spoke about his travels to Africa:

I asked myself whether the growing masculinization of the white woman is not connected with the loss of her naturalness . . . whether it is not a compensation for her impoverishment; and whether the feminizing of the white man is not a further consequence [263].

Since, at the same time, Jung wrote, 'I have had mainly women patients' (145), one cannot help wondering how he dealt with those who did not, like him, feel that they should 'stay in the nest.' Perhaps they could overcome Jung's prejudices in this regard, but why should they have to try? And what if they were timid and dared not confront him? What if they were afraid to speak about their desire to 'flee the nest'? Would not Jung automatically interpret this as an 'impoverishment'? How could he help women to feel good about themselves when he did not feel good about women?

Jung's appalling attitude toward blacks and his sympathy for colonialism is clear from various sources. He wrote:

In South Africa the Dutch, who were at the time of their colonizing a developed and civilized people, dropped to a much lower level because of their contact with the savage

---

[30] From 'Men, Women, and God,' in *C. G. Jung Speaking*, 244.

races. The savage inhabitants of a country have to be mastered. In the attempt to master, brutality rises in the master. He must be ruthless. He must sacrifice everything soft and fine for the sake of mastering savages. Their influence is very great; the more surely they are dominated, the more savage the master must become. The slave has the greatest influence of all, because he is kept close to the one who rules him.[31]

Jung, in a paper read at a congress in Freud's presence, said:

The causes for the [sexual] repression can be found in the specific American Complex, namely in the living together with lower races, especially with Negroes. Living together with barbaric races exerts a suggestive effect on the laboriously tamed instinct of the white race and tends to pull it down.[32]

In an oft-quoted passage from 1933, Jung claimed that all of his patients over thirty-five were struggling with religious problems:

I should like to call attention to the following facts. During the past thirty years, people from all the civilized countries of the earth have consulted me. I have treated many hundreds of patients, the larger number being Protestants, a smaller number Jews, and not more than five or six believing Catholics. Among all my patients in the second half of life – that is to say, over thirty-five – there has not been one whose problem in the last resort was not that of finding a religious outlook on life. It is safe to say that every one of them fell ill because he had lost that which the living religions of every age have given their followers, and none of them has been really healed who did not regain his religious outlook.[33]

This is a most extraordinary statement. What Jung wrote are not 'facts,' of course, but only his opinions. The inference is clear,

[31] From a 1912 interview in the *New York Times* reprinted in *C. G. Jung Speaking*, 12. One might argue that many people held such views in 1912. But what was to prevent Jung from adding a footnote in later editions saying that he no longer accepted such a position?
[32] Quoted by Fredric Wertham in *A Sign for Cain*, 91.
[33] *Modern Man in Search of a Soul*, 299.

however: anybody who went to Jung as an atheist or an agnostic, or somebody indifferent to religious problems, would be subtly or not so subtly coerced into dealing with something the person did not wish to deal with. Because, for Jung, they would be avoiding a religious problem, and his system demanded that they deal with this problem before he could call them 'cured.' So, by his own standards, he would be remiss in his medical duties if he ignored religious questions, no matter how much his patients protested to him that they were not concerned with such questions. Jung interpreted 'unhappiness' to mean 'not having found religion.' Thus he said, in the same 1933 essay:

> About a third of my cases are suffering from no clinically definable neurosis, but from the senselessness and emptiness of their lives. It seems to me, however, that this can well be described as the general neurosis of our time. Fully two-thirds of my patients have passed middle age [61].

In other words, if any patient came to Jung complaining of the 'senselessness' and 'emptiness' of his or her life, Jung would immediately interpret this to mean a religious crisis, and would also envisage a religious solution. 'However far-fetched it may sound, experience shows that many neuroses are caused by the fact that people blind themselves to their own religious promptings because of a childish passion for rational enlightenment' (67).

There were, no doubt, areas that interested Jung that did not interest other psychotherapists. These included alchemy, para-psychology, Teutonic mythology, the *I Ching*, the occult, Yoga, UFOs, symbols, and so on. Jung was convinced that his own interests corresponded to the reality of the world: 'For the present, at any rate, only two groups of facts have been established with any certainty: firstly the congruence of individual symbols and mythologems; and secondly, the phenomenon of extra-sensory perception' (*C.W.*, 16:125). Perhaps if Jung had confined himself to patients with these very interests, he could have been helpful. But it seems highly unlikely that all his patients shared his pre-occupations. It would appear from accounts by ex-patients, that when they did not, he imposed his own interests very quickly. Thus one of his pupils, Aniela Jaffé, wrote:

Personalia never played a prominent part in Jung's life; the real and important thing was the impersonal. Once when in a consultation I wanted to tell him about my relation to my parents — the *pièce de résistance* of a classic analysis — he wouldn't let me get a word out. 'Don't waste your time! Anyway I know a person's relation to his parents at first glance.'[34]

This is nonsense, but obviously impressive nonsense, and many of his patients must have believed him and refrained from speaking about matters that clearly did not interest him. It is obvious from reading Jung's published case histories in which early relationships were ignored that Jung was serious in his lack of interest. He decided *in advance* that the patients who came to see him did not have the problems they thought they had.

It is not entirely clear what Jung actually did with his patients. It seems, from his published accounts, that he played the wise old sage from the town of Küssnacht. He seems to have imposed his views about mythology and spiritual redemption and the wisdom of the collective unconscious and archetypal memories on his patients. His personal preoccupations became the subject matter of therapy. We see an example of this in the story of one of his patients recounted in 'The Realities of Practical Psychotherapy,' which he wrote in 1937 (*C.W.*, 16:327). The patient was a twenty-five-year-old woman who, he said, 'suffered from a high degree of emotivity, exaggerated sensitiveness,' and 'compulsive argumentativeness' (i.e., she tended to disagree with Jung). He interpreted one of the woman's dreams to mean she wished to marry:

> She produced the most violent resistances against any such possibility. Behind these resistances, it then turned out, there was hidden a most singular fantasy of a quite unimaginable

[34] In *From the Life and Work of C. G. Jung*, 116. Perhaps as a carry-over from his days with Freud, Jung had a particular distaste for examining the past: 'There is the danger of perpetually brooding on the past, of looking back wistfully to things that cannot be remedied now: the morbid tendency, very common among neurotics, always to seek the cause of their inferiority in the dim bygone, in their upbringing, the character of their parents, and so forth' (*C.W.*, 16:135).

erotic adventure that surpassed anything I had ever come across in my experience. I felt my head reeling, I thought of nymphomaniac possession, of weird perversions, of completely depraved erotic fantasies [C.W., 16:331–32].

Jung then provided some background and explanation:

The patient was a full-blooded European, but had been born in Java. As a child she spoke Malay and had an *ayah*, a native nurse. When she was of school age, she went to Europe and never returned to the Indies. Her childhood world was irretrievably sunk in oblivion [C.W., 16:334].

As chance would have it, at the same time that he was treating this patient, he happened to come upon a book by Sir John Woodroffe (alias Arthur Avalon), *The Serpent Power*, about the symbolism of Tantric Yoga, in particular, the *kundalini*, a serpent supposedly coiled at the base of the spine that rises under special mystical conditions to produce blissful feelings.[35] Jung was then able to 'interpret' all her symptoms in terms of Tantric symbols and 'this little bit of Tantric philosophy helped the patient to make an ordinary human life for herself, as a wife and mother, out of the local demonology she had sucked in with her *ayah*'s milk' (C.W., 16:337). But there is absolutely no indication that the woman ever heard anything at all about Tantrism from her nursemaid in Java, or at least, if there is, Jung never provided it. I fail to see the connection between Indian Tantric texts and this woman's strange dreams and fantasies, which Jung acknowledged he could not understand. (He understood her dreams as little as he understood the Tantric texts.) This is an example of Jung imposing his own limited concerns and interests on a patient. It is, of course, inevitable that *all* therapists do this. But it is rare that it is so transparent as in the case of Jung. Most therapists attempt, with varying

[35] Jung clearly believed that the study of these ancient texts on Tantrism was dangerous. Thus in a 1958 paper on 'Schizophrenia' (C.W., 3:259), he told of a patient who attended his lectures on a Tantric text and then began to have dreams of earthquakes, collapsing houses, and floods. Jung forbade her to attend his lectures, and insisted instead that she read Schopenhauer's *The World as Will and Idea*, because Schopenhauer, too, had been influenced by Buddhism.

degrees of success, to keep their preoccupations from surfacing as readily as Jung's did. Yet what Jung did is typical of the function of therapy. To argue that Jung made mistakes other Jungians would not make is absurd; surely one cannot argue that Jung was atypical of Jungian analysis, or that Freud was a poor representative of Freudian analysis.

Interpreting another person's dream is at best a subjective and hazardous undertaking. (Listening to another person's dream and talking about it with him or her is a different matter — it is not therapy.) Any therapist's claim to 'understand' another person's dream is foolhardy. To provide somebody with a coherent, complete account of a dream is itself a difficult, often impossible, undertaking. But beyond these ordinary difficulties, Jung added another dimension of difficulty. For he had a special way of using dreams, a method he called the 'anagogic' or spiritual interpretation of dreams. (This corresponded to what he called the 'progressive' method of interpretation in general, 'synthesis' as opposed to 'analysis.') This device allowed Jung to claim that dreams were often clairvoyant, especially certain of his own dreams that he felt clearly foretold important world events. Thus in a 1952 interview with the historian of religions Mircea Eliade, Jung spoke of a dream he claimed to have had in 1913 that he felt predicted the First World War:

> I found myself on the Southern seas near Sumatra, in summer, accompanied by a friend. But we learned from the newspapers that a terrible cold-wave had swept over Europe, such as had never been known to occur before. I decided to go to Batavia and board a ship to return to Europe. My friend told me he would take a sailing ship from Sumatra to Hadramaut and from there continue on his way through Arabia and Turkey. I arrived in Switzerland. All around me I saw nothing but snow. Somewhere an enormous vine was growing; it had many bunches of grapes. I approached and began to pick the grapes and distributed them among a throng of people who surrounded me but whom I could not see.[36]

Jung claimed to have had this dream three times. There are many elements of this dream that sound improbable as a dream (as

[36] *C. G. Jung Speaking*, 233.

opposed to narrative fiction), but that is not what concerns me at the moment. Jung said that he was to give a talk on schizophrenia in Aberdeen: 'The congress was to take place in July 1914 – exactly the period when I saw myself in my three dreams voyaging on the Southern seas.' Jung claimed that in the dream he had a sense of the exact time it was taking place, July 1914, and that this date in the future (along with all the particulars of the dream) was repeated on three separate occasions! The First World War broke out in Europe on July 31. So Jung claimed to know that the dream did not, as he feared, foretell his own schizophrenia ('as a psychiatrist I became worried, wondering if I was not on the way to "doing a schizophrenia" as we said in the language of those days'), but, rather, that his dream was prophetic of the greater 'madness,' as he called it, that was to overtake all of Europe, except for Switzerland. Jung was certain that he had advance knowledge of the war, and that he was destined to play some healing role in the war (a prophecy that was not realized). I must confess to a certain skepticism. Not only do I believe that the dream had nothing to do with the First World War, but I believe also that Jung did not dream this dream as he related it, and, finally, I believe that Jung did not dream it when he said he did. After recounting the dream, the editors of the collection in which it appeared, William McGuire and R. F. C. Hull, add the following comment:

Jung was glad to receive a second explanation of this dream shortly afterwards. The newspapers were not long in telling of a German naval captain by the name of von Mücke who in a sailboat had crossed the Southern seas from Sumatra to Hadramaut, taken refuge in Arabia, and proceeded from there to Turkey.[37]

They add in a footnote:

Notice of Lieut.-Cdr. Helmuth von Mücke's voyage appeared in the *Neue Zürcher Zeitung*, August 4, 1915, and the route corresponds to that given here. Later that year, von Mücke published an account of his adventures in a book entitled *Ayesha* ([the] name of his schooner).

[37] *C. G. Jung Speaking*, 234.

But this is hardly impressive corroboration of Jung's dream, *unless* Jung had published an account of his dream before the account of the trip appeared in the Swiss newspaper. In fact, Jung told somebody about this dream only in 1952. What proof is there, then, that Jung did not have the dream *after* reading the account, a far more likely event? I realize that this would make Jung dishonest, but this seems to me far more probable than the extraordinary account Jung provides of the dream and its circumstances. Thirty-seven years after the event Jung might have been confused, but what an egotistical confusion! Jungian analysis is best known for dream analysis. But we can see that at the hands of the master, a great deal is missing.

In a similar vein, Jung not only subjected his patients' dreams to the anagogic method, but also used his own dreams to help interpret a patient's reality. Thus in *Memories, Dreams, Reflections*, he told of a dream he had about an unknown patient who came to him, told him about herself, and, still in the dream, he felt he did not understand her until it suddenly occurred to him that 'she must have an unusual father complex.' The next day 'a young woman appeared. She was Jewish, daughter of a wealthy banker, pretty, chic, and highly intelligent . . . She was a well-adapted, Westernized Jewess, enlightened down to her bones.' The next night Jung had another dream, in which he went down on his knees and handed her an umbrella 'as if she were a goddess.' He told the woman his dreams, 'and in a week the neurosis had vanished.' Here is Jung's explanation:

> The dream had showed me that she was not just a superficial little girl, but that beneath the surface were the makings of a saint. She had no mythological ideas, and therefore the most essential feature of her nature could find no way to express itself. All her conscious activity was directed toward flirtation, clothes, and sex, because she knew of nothing else. She knew only the intellect and lived a meaningless life. In reality she was a child of God whose destiny was to fulfill His secret will. I had to awaken mythological and religious ideas in her, for she belonged to that class of human beings of whom spiritual activity is demanded. Thus her life took on a meaning, and no trace of the neurosis was left [138–40].

Jung's dream that preceded the arrival of the woman could not possibly have had anything to do with her. Nevertheless, he claimed that the woman's life was meaningless, and that only a religious conversion to orthodox Judaism could possibly free her from her neurosis. This is sheer psychological tyranny. It is preposterous and self-exalting for Jung to claim that 'she was a child of God whose destiny was to fulfill His secret will.' Even if one were to accept Jung's presuppositions about God, how would Jung know what God's secret will was if it was secret? Perhaps, in recounting the dream, Jung is simply proclaiming his direct communication with God (138–40).

It is not surprising that Jung could easily reverse this apparently saintly activity on behalf of his patients and use dreams to make equally implausible, but horrifying, predictions. Thus in his account of his psychiatric activities, Jung told of meeting a seemingly normal man who wished to become a psychoanalyst. Jung accepted him for analysis, but found he was getting nowhere, until, after the second week, the man produced a dream in which 'an idiot child of about two years old was sitting on a chamber pot and had smeared itself with feces.' Jung was alarmed: 'I knew all I needed to know – here was a latent psychosis! I must say I sweated as I tried to lead him out of that dream. I had to represent it to him as something quite innocuous, and gloss over all the perilous details' (135).

Jung commented that 'even for doctors it is difficult to recognize and treat a latent schizophrenia.' No doubt many patients over the years have been diagnosed as schizophrenic and sent away to psychiatric institutions on no greater evidence than a fragment from a dream. What is apparent, from reading his articles on schizophrenia over the years, is that Jung's attitudes had not changed since he learned them in 1900 from Eugen Bleuler, the Professor of Psychiatry and head of the Burghölzli Clinic in Zurich. I do not mean to imply that modern attitudes are any better than the early attitudes, but Jung claimed to have gone beyond psychiatry. In fact, he had not, and remained a psychiatrist, through and through, all his life. He retained much of the psychiatric arrogance that allowed him to say, for example, that 'it is pointless to subject a simple soul who lacks nothing but a dose of common sense to a complicated analysis of his impulses, much less expose him to the bewildering subtleties of psychological dialectic'

(*C.W.*, 16:9) or 'the simplest cases are those who just want sound common sense and good advice. With luck they can be disposed of in a single consultation' (*C.W.*, 16:19). Of course it is better to give somebody good advice rather than incarcerate him or her in a psychiatric institution, but Jung's assumed fund of 'sound common sense' and his ability to give this good advice is sadly lacking in his own life.

What I find totally absent in Jung's accounts is any sense of all the tragedies that go on in people's lives. The real world is simply absent from his books. I cannot believe that Jung's patients never spoke about the real world. I find it far more likely that these concerns did not correspond to Jung's interests and preoccupations with spiritual matters. His accounts are only as varied as his interests. What is missing from his accounts of his patients' lives are traumas, sexual assault, child abuse, rape, battering, torture, verbal abuse, concentration camps, and many other acts of violence, which happen far more frequently than psychiatry has ever admitted. Are we to suppose that they simply did not happen to Jung's patients, or that if they did the patients never mentioned them? It strains credulity and flies in the face of all logic. It makes more sense to acknowledge that Jung simply did not interest himself in the tragedies that happen to all of us.

I have called this chapter 'Jung among the Nazis.' What is the connection between Jung's links to National Socialism and his psychotherapy? As I see it, the essence of the defect of Jungian psychotherapy is the attempt to avoid touching on those issues that are most concrete, most real, most related to the body and to a specific moment in history. Hence Jung's notorious lack of interest in his patients' sexual histories and their family histories. But it seems to me that this is not accidental. Jung could not afford to urge his patients to examine their pasts, for he needed to avoid thinking about his own past, tainted as it was by collaboration with the Nazis. What better way than to erect a powerful theoretical model of psychotherapy in which the past played only a minor role? Jung's psychotherapy was a screen behind which he could hide his own unpalatable past.

5

JOHN ROSEN AND
DIRECT PSYCHOANALYSIS

A prominent psychiatrist, and Professor of Psychiatry, John Rosen, who had been much praised by his fellow psychiatrists for his 'discovery' of a new method of treatment, 'direct psychoanalysis,' surrendered his medical license in Harrisburg, Pennsylvania, on March 29, 1983.[1] He did this to avoid being tried by the State Board of Medical Education and Licensure of the Department of State of Pennsylvania, which stood ready to accuse him of sixty-seven violations of the Pennsylvania Medical Practices Act and thirty-five violations of the rules and regulations of the Medical Board.[2]

---

[1] 'Direct psychoanalysis is a method of psychotherapy based upon the discoveries of Freud.' 'Direct Psychoanalysis: A Summary Statement,' in *Current Psychiatric Therapies*, vol. 4, ed. by Jules H. Masserman (New York: Grune & Stratton, 1964), 101–7. The second volume of Rosen's collected papers, *Selected Papers on Direct Psychoanalysis* (New York: Grune & Stratton, 1968), includes a bibliography of one hundred twenty-eight items devoted to his work. Included are reviews and commentary, almost all positive, from some of the major figures in psychotherapy, including Donald Winnicott, Margarete Séchehaye, Carl Rogers, Harold Searles, Milton Wexler, Frieda Fromm-Reichmann, Don Jackson, Samuel Lipton, Lawrence Kubie, Fritz Redlich, Theodore Lidz, Michael Balint, Georges Devereux, Ronald Fairbairn, Kurt Eissler, and many others. Clearly at the time Rosen was not a peripheral figure in modern psychiatry. Rosen believed, and many distinguished psychiatrists accepted his assessment, that he had discovered a new method of psychotherapy that could, and should, be widely taught: 'What I envision is a psychiatric "peace corps." It will consists of many young assistant psychotherapists trained for the kind of work that needs to be done at state hospitals and at "community mental health centers"' (ibid., vii). A brave new world, then, which was to remain undisturbed until very recently.

[2] This was not the first time that Dr. Rosen fell afoul of the law. In 1960 he lost a celebrated case known as *Hammer* v. *Rosen* (7 N.Y. 2d 376; 165 N.E. 2d 756; 198 N.Y.S. 2d 65) in New York, where he was accused of beating a patient. Rosen argued 'that the treatment was knowingly and freely consented to by reason of the fact that the patient's mother testified that if beating was a

The investigation itself came into being because a number of Rosen's patients had had enough abuse, and determined to come forward and seek justice. They were reluctantly followed by the Medical Board. The events that took place tell us a great deal about psychotherapy in the United States. To learn about what John Rosen did to his patients may make the reader feel that Rosen belongs to a nightmare world of cruelty and gross excesses. I do not believe this is true. John Rosen is one of many, many therapists who harm their patients under the guise of their greater wisdom. He merely had the misfortune of being caught. There is nothing unusual about what he did to his patients. In many other disguises, this kind of treatment goes undetected in thousands of psychiatric institutions throughout the United States. Indeed, far worse things happen on a daily basis. John Rosen is really only the tip of the iceberg. But he is symbolic because he was so praised by his colleagues when his star was ascending, and, perhaps even more telling for our purposes, once his crimes were exposed for the world to see, those same colleagues became strangely reluctant to speak about them. I am aware of only a handful of psychiatrists who are willing to publicly denounce what John Rosen stands for, though privately, of course, most psychiatrists fulminate as loudly as anyone about these abuses. This solidarity tells us even more about psychotherapy than does the exposure of a single case of abuse. That abuse is worth reporting in some detail because it is indicative of some deeper malaise in the profession.

John Nathaniel Rosen was born in Brooklyn in 1902. He got his medical and psychiatric training in New York. In 1959 he was made Associate Professor of Psychiatry at Temple University Medical School in Philadelphia and Chairman of the Philadelphia Mental Health and Mental Retardation Foundation. In 1953 Grune & Stratton, a New York medical publishing house, brought

[2]Cont. means of cure, she was agreeable to the treatment.' Rosen defended himself by saying that 'beating' constituted a recognized form of treatment. He did not, however, produce expert witnesses to testify on his behalf. 'Mrs. Hammer testified that after treatments she observed her daughter was "beaten up" and had "blue eyes"; that her daughter returned from treatments "black and blue."' The case has been commented on in 'From contract to status via psychiatry' by George J. Alexander and Thomas S. Szasz (Santa Clara Lawyer 13 [1973]: 537–59). See, too, Ronald Jay Cohen, Malpractice: A Guide for Mental Health Professionals (New York: The Free Press, 1979).

out his book *Direct Analysis: Selected Papers*. In a survey of psychiatrists and psychoanalysts published in 1970, John Rosen was rated the second (of fourteen) most controversial living psychiatrist in the United States.[3] In 1971 he won the Man of the Year award of the American Academy of Psychotherapy.

His most influential paper was published in the prestigious *Psychiatric Quarterly* in 1947. It was entitled 'The Treatment of Schizophrenic Psychosis by Direct Analytic Therapy' and was considered so important that it was prefaced by praise from the editors as well as by a published discussion by six prominent psychiatrists (five of whom were psychoanalysts). Rosen claimed to offer a new treatment for schizophrenia, one that he called 'direct analysis,' which consisted of spending long hours with patients and entering into their 'delusional system,' confronting them with its irrationality, and forcing them to face reality. Many psychiatrists felt – wrongly, as we can see from the chapter on Ferenczi – that it was based on Ferenczi's techniques. Possibly this error was due to the fact that Rosen claimed, astonishingly, that he spent up to ten hours a day with a single patient:

> The patient, a married woman in her late twenties, spoke at last. The physician tended her, fed her, treated her like a baby for nine months. For two of them, he had been with her for 10 hours a day, for the next seven, for four [45].[4]

Is this likely or even possible? How many patients could a psychiatrist have if he treated each one for ten hours a day? Rosen is obviously claiming something that cannot be true. Another puzzle is that the psychoanalysts who heard the paper knew that Rosen had never been trained as a psychoanalyst, though he did apparently undergo a personal analysis. For him to call himself a psychoanalyst on the basis of having been analyzed would be like somebody claiming to be a surgeon because of having once undergone surgery. Yet throughout this paper Rosen speaks of his 'ordinary analytic procedures' as if he were practicing

---

[3] Arnold A. Rogow, *The Psychiatrists* (New York: G. P. Putnam's Sons, 1970), 111. Among the others named were Thomas S. Szasz, Rollo May, and Melanie Klein.

[4] Unless otherwise noted, all page references are to *Direct Analysis: Selected Papers* by John N. Rosen (New York: Grune & Stratton, 1953).

psychoanalysis. (For example: 'Some patients have been discharged as "recovered," and others are still in analysis,' page 46.) The point of the paper is to claim remarkable results: Rosen claims to have treated, with his new method, thirty-seven cases (the youngest patient was fifteen, the oldest fifty-two) of 'deteriorated schizophrenia,' and 'in 36 of these cases, the psychosis was resolved.' There is a startlingly uncritical footnote to this astonishing claim, written by the editor:

> The editor of *The Psychiatric Quarterly* and three other members of the editorial board saw and interviewed this patient both formally and through ordinary friendly conversation. The editor agrees, and his three associates concur, that Dr. Rosen's descriptions and evaluation of his results represent what actually occurs [46].

Rosen claims that all his patients were made ill by not having been loved in childhood. He says:

> In the case of direct psychoanalysis the counter-transference [feelings the therapist has for the patient] must be of the nature of the feelings a good parent would have for a highly disturbed child. The therapist, like the good parent, must identify with the unhappy child and be so disturbed by the unhappiness of the child that he himself cannot rest until the child is again at peace [72].

What enabled Rosen, in his own view, to 'cure' these 'incurable schizophrenics'? He tells us on page 73:

> In order to treat the schizophrenic, the physician must have such a degree of inner security that he is able to function independently, whether he is loved by the patient or not. Or perhaps it would be better to state that the physician must be able to manage with the least possible amount of love from the patient. He must make up for the tremendous deficit of love experienced in the patient's life. Some people have this capacity for loving as a divine gift. But it is possible to acquire this the hard way – by psychoanalysis. It is the *sine qua non* for the application of this method in the treatment of schizophrenia.

As an example of this love, Rosen writes: 'My problem was to convince the patient that he was a man, that is, that he had a penis. I tackled it directly at the very next visit. When the patient stood up, I told him to put his hand on his penis *and assisted him in this maneuver*' (74). (Italics added.) Throughout his book Rosen is particularly concerned with homosexual men. None of them, he maintains, was really homosexual, and it was Rosen's task to demonstrate this for them.

Listening to this paper should make anybody suspicious of a man who claims so much for himself. Nevertheless, the analysts in Rosen's audience, or those, like Paul Federn (a distinguished internist, and friend of Freud's, who became a much-sought-after analyst in New York after the Second World War), who read the paper and commented on it for the *Quarterly*, were completely convinced. Thus Federn wrote: 'To a great extent, Rosen is giving belated, but most necessary, sex-education and sex-information to his patients, who are still living in an invisible mental nursery' (78). Of course Federn had an ulterior motive, which he commented on quite openly:

> It is clear to me that this technique and its good results can be used by psychiatrists who are as fully convinced of Freud's interpretation of the unconscious as Rosen is. Rosen's findings are also another proof of the truth of Freud's tenets. . . . I pay my tribute to Dr. Rosen that, as psychiatrist, he has incorporated Freud's work into his own mind, with great clarity combined with pioneer enthusiasm [79].

The only word of caution that Federn uttered was when he said, 'I suggest that for the present it might be well to confine experimentation with this therapy to trained psychiatrists who are also fully qualified psychoanalysts.' This is a peculiar comment. Rosen was not, in fact, a fully qualified psychoanalyst, as Federn knew perfectly well. Would it not be a rather strange undertaking to confine a therapy invented by a nonpsychoanalyst to psychoanalysts? It would be like suggesting that Freud's methods could be used only by nonanalytic psychiatrists. Dr. Jules Eisenbud wrote:

> There's one thing, however, which has impressed me about the work of Dr. Rosen during the time that I have been

privileged to observe it, and that is the fact that, so far as I can observe, Dr. Rosen has absolutely no hostility toward the patient, toward the psychotic patient.

He expanded on this:

I have observed Dr. Rosen with several of his patients, and at first I was astounded to notice the casual way in which he just threw overboard the exquisite instruction of Frieda Fromm-Reichmann. I watched, and I watched, and I said to myself, that *I* could never treat a patient with such a casual attitude. But I noticed one thing, that as far as I could observe, Rosen is not afraid to do this because he has no hostility toward the patient whatsoever [85].[5]

Dr. Hyman Spotnitz ended by saying: 'I want to compliment Dr. Rosen on his courage and on his deep insight into this field. I feel it requires a great deal of courage, devotion, and sincerity to do this type of work' (91).

Rosen's peers, then, felt no hesitation in claiming that he had made a major contribution to psychotherapy.[6] But throughout his

---

[5] Eisenbud was the author of a series of articles arguing in favor of ESP. Was it this that allowed him to divine the internal state of Dr. Rosen?

[6] The distinguished psychoanalyst Leon Stone reviewed Rosen's *Direct Analysis* in a special book section of the *Journal of the American Psychoanalytic Association* 3 (1955): 126–48. There he wrote that 'as time went on Rosen gained the opportunity to demonstrate and explain his work directly before learned societies and remote hospital staffs; his work has been seriously appraised by many, followed as a method by some. Certainly it is known to all.' In the review, Stone spoke of Rosen's 'moving' case histories, of his efforts to cure as nothing less than 'heroic.' He spoke of his 'courage,' 'passionate dedication,' and 'intuitive resourcefulness.' Stone automatically assumed that Rosen's patients were 'desperately ill.' This is so often used (to excuse what would otherwise be considered barbarous practices) that one wonders how the person could possibly know. Clearly Rosen's word is believed, just as it is believed when he insists, over and over, on his love for his patients. Once this is believed, then any evidence from the published writings that suggests something is wrong is explained away in a benign fashion. So much of what Rosen writes simply makes no sense. Stone explained that the wild interpretations he makes 'may mean more to the embattled psychotic patient than accuracy of interpretations, or – in some instances – than the question of whether the interpretations are really relevant to his basic conflict or not.' And

articles (collected in *Direct Analysis*), Rosen provides examples that should have alarmed anybody, even a psychiatrist. The fact that they did not is clear evidence that there was nothing unique about John Rosen in the field of psychiatry.

His basic thesis is that the patient has fled into a psychosis to avoid the pain of being unloved, and that the therapist must use 'cunning, guile, shrewdness, and seductiveness' that are locked away in his own unconscious to hunt out the secrets of the patient. In other words, the therapist gives himself or herself over to unconscious, primitive instincts, the better to stalk the patient. It requires no great leap of the imagination to see how such a view could be used to rationalize any kind of behavior on the part of the therapist. No matter how ugly or violent an action might seem to an onlooker, the therapist could claim it was only a strategy. And, since Rosen postulates that the therapist is by definition, 'loving and protective' (19), it follows logically that all of these actions are done only for the good of the patient. In the chapter on Ferenczi we saw how concerned Ferenczi was with the tendency in therapy to entice, seduce, and infantilize the patient, because it can lead to abuse and even torture. It was almost as if he had John Rosen in mind.

Not only is the therapist all good and loving, but so is everybody who works with him. Thus:

> A patient believed her father was condemned to death in the state capital. I had the family foregather and produced a spurious reprieve from the governor. A celebration befitting such an occasion followed. The patient was dazed and participated in the celebration stiffly. Following this, she began to manifest anxiety relating to food and now she refused to eat for a period of time sufficiently prolonged to result in the loss

this dangerous posture is acceptable because, argued Stone, Rosen has 'a rare capacity for wholehearted empathy with the psychotic patient, for feeling his point of view against his environment while fighting his "crazy" imagination (with no holds barred). Further than this there is an unreserved, uninhibited involvement with the patient, fearless, exuberant, loving, authoritarian, at times combative and punitive, but always strong and affirmative.' But this implies that nobody could spontaneously hate Rosen, or, even worse, that Rosen could not spontaneously hate a patient. It is as if such feelings simply do not exist in the realm of psychotherapy. And Stone made his reputation by exposing the dangers of misusing the transference!

of 40 pounds of weight. It can be surmised that the presence of Father again admitted the possibility of incest which might anger and alienate Mother. Mother would punish her with poison milk [22].

Everything about this scenario is shocking: the clear belief of Rosen that he is omnipotent and can do as he likes; the idiotic interpretations; the danger in which the patient is placed simply to permit Rosen to put his odd beliefs into practice.

Rosen is even more explicit when he comes to the topic of violence. He says that when he perceives a tendency to violence in patients, he tells them: 'If you ever again lay a hand on your mother, father, husband, wife, child, sibling I will give you worse by far than you ever thought of doing to them' (26). He is as good as his word. In a paper on treatment techniques, he writes:

Another way of confronting the patient with reality is to call his bluff dramatically in regard to some delusion and then point out the absurdity of his behavior. I did this with the patient . . . who whined endlessly that he was going to be cut up into little pieces and fed to the tigers. When I could stand no more of this, I walked into his room with a big knife, saying, *'All right, if you're so anxious to be cut up, I'll cut you up'* [149].

A few pages later, he is even more explicit: 'Sometimes, when I have the patient pinned to the floor, I say, "*I can castrate you. I can kill you. I can eat you. I can do whatever I want to you, but I am not going to do it*"' (151).

Equally emotionally violent are the dialogues that Rosen prints (we can assume that these are the dialogues he is proud of; we can only imagine those that did not pass muster). His principle is one of confrontation via insult. Here is an example from an extended dialogue he printed in a paper on the prognostic outlook of schizophrenia:

Patient: I was born a Jew.
Rosen: Who cares?
Patient: So you're probably the crazy one.
Rosen: No, you're the crazy one.
Patient: I know. How do you go about curing it?

Rosen: Well, I'm a psychiatrist and I know how to cure.

Patient: How do you do it?

Rosen: By talking.

Patient: Go ahead and talk.

Rosen: I'm trying to find out what made you crazy. I think your mother did it.

Patient: I was nervous all the time.

Rosen: I know. I don't think your mother cared for you.

Patient: How do you know?

Rosen: I know your mother. . . . Why are you here?

Patient: To get better.

Rosen: What's the matter with you?

Patient: Nothing. I don't know. I was just sick.

Rosen: What is the sickness? Don't hesitate to tell me.

Patient: I don't know.

Rosen: What is your sickness?

Patient: I was nervous. I was upset. I don't know.

Rosen: I don't like a liar.

Patient: No, I don't lie. Why should I lie to you?

Rosen: Because you want to hide the fact that you were crazy [132].

But Rosen does not confine himself to this emotional assault through words. He resorts, as he himself readily and proudly admits, to trickery and deceit. Thus he writes:

On November 6, as I continued my pressure toward reality, I called Mary's attention to the fact that in the three weeks that she was in the hospital her mother had not come to see her once. The patient fainted dead away. I should say, in all fairness, that the mother had been acting on my orders. Perhaps a harsh procedure but not as harsh as schizophrenia. My purpose was to focus the patient's attention on the pathogenic lack of love rather than to allow her to be confused by the mother's loving attitudes [134].

In this extraordinary statement Rosen declares that he knew that although the mother may have *thought* she loved her daughter, in fact she did not, and only Rosen had access to her unconscious and knew this. It would only prove confusing to the woman to have her mother appear and thus demonstrate love that in fact Rosen knew to be absent, and so Rosen arranged for the mother not to visit the daughter, then told the daughter that the fact that her mother did not come was proof of Rosen's assertion that she did not love her. This is not an isolated incident. It is typical of Rosen's published cases. Here is, another example, from an article entitled 'The Survival Function of Schizophrenia,' published in the *Bulletin of the Menninger Clinic 14* (1950): 81–91.

> On the fifth day of therapy, I insisted for the first time that Joan stay in the treatment room with me. She stayed in the room, but when I asked her to lie down on the couch, she gave no indication that she had heard me. She wandered about the room gaily examining my books and furniture. Then, spying a cigarette on the table, she picked it up. When I said, 'Drop the cigarette,' very firmly, she dropped it on the floor and made a dash for the door. I grabbed her, pulled her back in again and forced her down on the couch. While I held her wrists, Joan squirmed, kicked and wrestled violently. She kept up a continuous stream of productions which indicated she was fantasying enormous sexual experiences. The struggle lasted about half an hour and I made no intepretations until she had quieted down from sheer exhaustion.

Rosen then tells her: 'Come on. No more fucking.' Rosen explains: 'I added, "No more fucking," which is an interpretation on the genital level, rather than, "no more rocking," in the hope of forcefully arousing the patient to more mature considerations" (86). He then tells the patient that she can suck his thumb:

> *Rosen:* You can keep it there as long as you want. It's all right. It's all right. Do you get pleasure from it?
> *Patient:* Yes.
> *Rosen:* Is it very exciting?
> *Patient:* Yes. Yes. Hard. Hard. Hard. Hard . . .
> *Rosen:* I am your mother now and I will permit you to do whatever you want.

Finally Rosen tells her, after a series of wild interpretations, that 'you can be certain that between you and me, you will not win. I will win . . . I dominate you to protect you from harm because I love you.'

The nightmare world that Rosen subjected his patients to was one in which he was in total control. One gets the feeling of a dangerous and violent guru who has lost control of himself but not of his peers.

Rosen's published works also reveal a great deal about his attitudes toward women, and even though they were written in the fifties they demonstrate a pronounced bias even for that time:

> Our own psychoanalytic approach, based on clinical material from psychotic and neurotic patients, helps us to understand why women wear men's clothes, try for commanding positions in business, and prefer not to care for their own children but hire nurses to play the role of make-shift mother [101].

The sense of horror I had when reading Rosen's published works was evidently not shared by leading figures in psychiatry. O. Spurgeon English,[7] who for many years was Chairman of the Department of Psychiatry at Temple University School of Medicine, in *Introduction to Psychiatry*, a widely used textbook, praises Rosen and his innovative methods of treatment.[8]

Some psychiatrists were skeptical, not of what Rosen actually did, but of his improvement rate. A number of articles tested his results and found them to be a great deal less positive than Rosen

[7] In an article entitled 'Clinical observations on direct analysis,' in *Comprehensive Psychiatry* 1 (1960): 156–63, English wrote: 'In June 1956 the Institute for Direct Analysis was formed within the Department of Psychiatry at Temple University Medical Center. The original project was sponsored and financed by the Rockefeller Brothers Fund for a period of three years. Cases for treatment were chosen by a committee of three, two psychiatrists and a psychologist.' The psychiatrists were Kenneth Appel, Professor and Chairman of the Department of Psychiatry, University of Pennsylvania School of Medicine, and Robert Bookhammer, Executive Director of the Philadelphia Psychoanalytic Institute. The psychologist was Irving Lorge, Professor of Education, Columbia University. Three years later Temple put Rosen on the staff of the medical school. In other words, John Rosen was backed by powerful members of the psychiatric, academic, and financial community; he was by no means an outsider shunned by his more conservative colleagues.

[8] New York: W. W. Norton & Co., 1954.

had claimed.[9] But none of the authors ever actually criticized what Rosen wrote, or claimed that there was anything peculiar (not to say unethical) in his treatment. In fact, Rosen's reputation as an innovative healer continued to grow. He treated a member of the Rockefeller family, and this fact, which he clearly did not hide, brought many other referrals from prominent and wealthy families. This reputation only increased with the publication in 1968 of a popular novel, *Savage Sleep*, by Millen Brand[10] that is explicitly based on the work of John Rosen and praises his methods in an extravagant and disciplelike manner. (Brand was an ex-aide. He had written the screenplay for *The Snake Pit* some twenty years earlier.)

The fact that Rosen insisted that he loved his patients is obviously not proof that he did. Nor, of course, is it evidence that he did not. But the behavior that he himself chose to reveal in print indicates that we should at least approach his statements with some caution. What is required is observation, rather than interpretation, which seems to be a great deal more than any of his colleagues were publicly willing to do, for they were not willing to reveal the excesses they must have observed. But this is a good deal less than what his actual patients did. And one of them in particular, Sally Zinman, went a great deal further.

Sally Zinman was born in Philadelphia in 1937, the daughter of a prominent local banker. She attended Sarah Lawrence College and received a master's degree from the University of Pennsylvania. In 1964 she was an adjunct instructor of English at

[9]In 1958 a paper entitled 'A Study of Cases of Schizophrenia Treated by "Direct Analysis",' by William A. Horwitz and three other psychiatrists, was published in the *American Journal of Psychiatry* 114 (1958): 780–83. It concludes: 'The findings in our 10-year follow-up of the course of the 19 patients fail to sustain the originally reported statement of therapeutic effectiveness of direct analytic therapy in schizophrenia. Many of the patients who at the time of the original report were improved, subsequently relapsed and required other treatments. Whatever the merits of direct analytic therapy for schizophrenia, the claim that it results in a high degree of recovery remains unproven.' Similarly, four other psychiatrists later published 'A Five-Year Clinical Follow-Up Study of Schizophrenics Treated by Rosen's "Direct Analysis" Compared with Controls' (Robert S. Bookhammer *et al.*, *American Journal of Psychiatry* 123 [1966]: 602–4), which concludes: 'This evaluative study indicates that a group of patients treated by the method of "direct analysis" did not show significantly better results than a random control group or a designated control group.'

[10]New York: Crown Publishers, 1968.

Queens College, in New York. When she was thirty-three years old, in October 1970, she woke one day and felt completely dissociated from her past. She remembered it, but did not believe it was *hers*. A friend of her father, a psychiatrist by the name of Dr. Harvey Corman, went to her apartment and was introduced to her as a business associate of her father who had come for a social chat, but evidently he was really there to evaluate her 'mental status.' He stayed for five minutes. In January 1971, her father showed up with two large aides of Dr. Rosen and several family members, and said, 'We're going.' He chartered a plane, had her flown to Boca Raton, in Florida, and put her in the care of Dr. John Rosen. Rosen was known to Philip Zinman because they belonged to the same country club. The therapy that awaited Sally Zinman was hardly what one would expect from Rosen's articles. (The reality is invariably worse than the theory.)

No doubt sensing something strange, Sally Zinman was frightened from the moment she saw Rosen. Nevertheless, things did not seem, at first, too ominous. She lived in a house (rented and paid for by her father) with two 'therapists'[11] and spent her time walking, swimming, and in general regaining her physical health. Nobody talked to her about her real problems. Instead, Rosen made a few fatuous interpretations to her about her mother's milk having been sour, about having incestuous fantasies about her father, and so forth. Nobody had asked her what was wrong, how it started, what she felt, just the simple facts. During the times she and Rosen saw each other there was no rapport between them. Her mother was living in Boca Raton, and she often took excursions with her daughter. It was a pleasant, but a rather expensive, life: Philip Zinman was paying Rosen five thousand dollars a month for the treatment.

At the end of a month, Sally Zinman felt there was no point in remaining, and she asked Rosen if she could move into her parents' apartment with them and see Rosen daily. He said she could. She packed and was waiting for Rosen to arrive at 5:00 P.M. before leaving. But when Rosen arrived, something totally unexpected happened: Without a word of explanation, he and his main

[11] Rosen conferred this term on any of the people who helped him with patients. As far as I could tell, not one of the many aides, or therapists, who worked for Rosen ever held any kind of license. Rosen himself was not licensed to practice medicine, psychiatry, or psychotherapy in Florida.

aide, an ex-Marine, tore off all her clothes except her underpants and began beating her on the face and breasts (the aide held her down while Rosen beat her). She was then tied to her bed, still with no clothes on, and kept that way for twenty-four hours, under close guard. A week later, she was able to escape, ran to Key West, and called her parents and told them about Rosen, the beating, and the imprisonment. They promised her she would never have to see Rosen again. They met her, and her father accompanied her on a flight to Philadelphia.

At the airport they were met by a chauffeur-driven car, and Sally Zinman was taken, screaming and resisting, to Rosen's Twin Silos Farm in Gardenville, Pennsylvania. She was put into a 'security room' in the basement of Rosen's house for two nights and remained in the house for one week. She ran away but was caught and returned with the help of the police, even though there was no legal document ordering her return. When she got back, Rosen threw her across the room. She stayed for two months, watched constantly by two people, even while she was in the shower or on the toilet. Rosen continued his vacation in Florida. Eventually Rosen returned, and 'treatment' began. Rosen's treatment consisted of telling her that he would not let her out until she said her name was Sally Zinman. Finally, to secure her release, she conceded. She was then free to go.

Sally Zinman now explains her original doubts about who she was in a nonpsychological and very convincing manner. She recently told a San Francisco reporter:

> I hated myself in those days. I was a vain, materialistic person living in a fancy apartment with expensive furniture. I didn't like what I stood for. But I couldn't rebel as other people did, and I couldn't fit in. What happened to me was my way of growing up. It was a break*out*, not a break*down*. I consider that day the beginning of my life.[12]

Over the next two years, Zinman remained an 'outpatient' of Rosen and saw him for very brief (and expensive) sessions. When she expressed the desire to leave and was, with Rosen's permission, actually on the verge of doing so, he told her parents that

[12] 'Liberating Madness,' *Image Magazine, San Francisco Chronicle*, June 29, 1986, 20–25, 36.

she would not be alive in a year unless she was signed over to his custody. He further scared them by telling them that she had gonorrhea and was going to give all her money to black people. These were lies, but they played on her parents' worst fears. The 'therapy' consisted of his suggesting various 'delusions' to her and fondling her breasts when they were alone (often the sessions were groups), and once even her vagina. In explaining why she continued to see Rosen, she explained: 'I was so terrorized, then brainwashed, that I felt there was no place to go for help. All places and persons led back to Rosen, where the punishment would be worse than the first time.' In 1973 she saw him for the last time.

That year she bought a farm in Florida, and for the next several years grew organic vegetables. Gradually, as she began to think about her 'therapy' with Rosen, she became more and more convinced that it was necessary to act. It took that long for her to feel safe enough from Rosen to approach the authorities. Finally, in 1977, she went to see a private investigator in Delray Beach, Virginia Snyder.

Virginia Snyder (who had been an award-winning investigative reporter) is one of America's few female private detectives, and she has, since opening her own office in 1976, at the age of fifty-five, built a reputation for integrity, investigative brilliance, and success. Her reputation is such that those on death row who feel they are innocent often call on her. Of the seventy-seven murder cases she has handled, fifteen of the felons were on death row. Money is not her object; finding the truth is, and these inmates knew that. She has also been the champion of a number of underdogs and people who have been hurt by the system, especially the mental-health system. Sally Zinman could not have gone to a better person. And Rosen could not have been more unlucky. Snyder was somebody who really believed in justice, and believed that injustice should be exposed. She listened to Zinman, believed her, and took action. It was the beginning of the end for John Rosen.

Snyder soon learned that Sally Zinman's was not a unique case. In the very same room where she had been held, another patient, an elderly man, died on June 13, 1977. Rosen signed the death certificate. One of the employees at the time of the man's death later gave an affidavit to the Pennsylvania Department of Public Welfare to the effect that the staff had been told that the patient had gone home, but they later learned that he had died in the security room. Zinman and Snyder compiled documented information, which was sent to all the regulatory, monitoring, and policing agencies in Florida and Pennsylvania. They personally took the report to the Palm Beach County State Attorney, who did nothing.

On Sunday, September 18, 1977, the *Miami Herald*, Palm Beach Edition, ran a major story, 'Dr. Rosen: Praise and Fear in Boca Raton,' by Tim Pallesen, a staff writer. In this article Pallesen wrote that 'five former aides – including one who says she witnessed the former patient [Sally Zinman] being stripped and punched – have told the *Herald* similar stories, although they say such incidents are isolated.' The article tells the story of Sally Zinman. The reporter spoke to the former aide, Jane Purtzer, who was responsible for Zinman, and she confirmed that 'Rosen stripped Zinman to her underpants and then beat with his fists on both her face and breasts.' The article tells also of other patients, including Julia Blythe, forty-four, who was under Rosen's 'care' for sixteen years and who had written a letter in 1975 to the Boca Raton police saying that Rosen had kidnapped her. 'Two former aides and a former patient say Rosen slapped her for talking to imaginary voices.' (Note that this would be entirely consistent with Rosen's stated beliefs, as we saw above.) Later that year, on December 6, parts of this article were confirmed by the *Philadelphia Inquirer*, which quoted from the affidavit filed the day before with the welfare department by Merry Humose, who said:

> While she was employed in Rosen's farm as an assistant therapist, she saw him strike patients on two occasions. She said that Rosen had told his staff 'that the best way to get results is to make patients fear you.' Miss Humose, according to welfare department sources, has told investigators that she approached Rosen for treatment but could not afford the fees, so he offered to employ her as an assistant therapist. She left his employ after about four months because, 'among other reasons, I was concerned about the circumstances of Ted's death.' Ted, she said, was a patient who had been kept locked in a basement security room, which lacked a toilet, in one of the houses on Twin Silos Farm. Rosen, she said, told staff members that Ted had gone home but they later learned that he had died in the security room.

Rosen responded to these allegations by filing a libel suit against the *Herald*, the reporter, Tim Pallesen, who wrote the stories, and the *Philadelphia Inquirer*. The resulting depositions, now part of the public record, are invaluable as a source of information about Rosen, since he was giving, under oath, his own account of matters.[13] Rosen explained that he often charged as little as a dollar an hour, but 'also with X and Y I charged $10,000 a month. And Mr. John D. Rockefeller, III, who was our trustee, Mrs. X's trustee, when I sent him the bill for the year of $120,000, he said if I added a zero, he would have no objection' (162).

Here is Rosen on the death of one of his patients:

Q Did you have a patient by the name of Ted Schwartz?
A Yes, I had a patient by the name of Ted Schwartz.
Q For how long a period of time was Mr. Schwartz a patient?
A Quite a few years.
Q Did Mr. Schwartz eventually die?
A He died . . .
Q Did you ever strike Mr. Schwartz?
A When he wouldn't eat. I didn't strike him. I threatened to strike him and I said, 'You must eat,' because he was losing weight. And he did, too. And I told him he should eat, he was naughty, and he was a bad boy, and I would spank him if he didn't eat. He would eat or try to eat [121].

An example of Rosen's depth of understanding of (not to mention sympathy for) his patient Sally Zinman is revealed on page 98 of the deposition, when he gives his explanation of the cause of her 'psychosis':

From early on, her mother rejected her as the bad child, the ugly duckling, and she had a great deal of trouble in school because her sister, who her mother called beautiful, and she was beautiful, Sally is very ugly, I don't know if you ever saw her, and she never could get – I mean it would be a miracle if she found anyone who would marry her because she is so ugly.

[13] The deposition (No. 78-3053, in the United States District Court for the Eastern District of Pennsylvania) was taken on March 2, 1981. The copy was made available to me through the kindness of Ms. Snyder.

This preposterous statement, this wild and hurtful comment, simply defies characterization. On the next page, Rosen explains, in line with Freudian doctrine, that Sally Zinman had 'incestuous fantasies' about her father. Sally Zinman told me that Rosen was simply lying, just as he had when he claimed that she believed she had had sexual relations with her father. It was simply not true. Rosen said:

> So that her devotion to her father and the need for her father to be the loving one, because the mother wasn't, I felt — was responsible for her incestuous fantasy about her father.
>
> And I asked Phil once, did you ever allow her to come into your bedroom or do anything with Sally. Absolutely not.
>
> But she believed that she had had sexual relations with her father.

The behavior that Rosen found so objectionable in Sally Zinman is described on page 85 of the deposition, when he explained that she had hitchhiked in Italy:

> Q On the basis of this hitchhiking, you felt she needed custodial care? [One can hear the justified outrage in the question.]
> A Yes. And especially she wanted to pick up rides with blacks, and she made up her mind she should have a black baby, which she has, as you know. If you don't know, I am telling you. And I consider this abnormal behavior. A Jewish girl doesn't go out looking for a black to be her date, ordinarily; ordinarily.

In fact, Sally Zinman adopted, as a single parent, a black child. Rosen sets himself up as the standard of behavior, and whatever deviates from what Rosen believes is normal becomes 'pathological.' Sally Zinman was once raped, and it goes without saying that this is not how John Rosen saw the matter:

> She was very much in love with blacks. As a matter of fact, she seduced a black who she claimed raped her. And he broke her arm and beat her unmercifully. And when that happened, she called me and my wife to please come to the house that she

rented for herself. And I took her to Bethesda Hospital with a detective, and she was examined by a doctor and found, as a matter of fact, she had had intercourse. Whether she was raped or not, I don't know. And the upshot of all of that is a complete denial, because when it came out, she thought, when she began to talk more rationally, that she had had intercourse with her own father. And that, I think, was behind the denial, he is my father, because of the horror of incest and why she adopted a black baby [67].

As for her consenting to treatment, Rosen said this:

Q Did you believe you had Sally Zinman's consent to treat her?

A She didn't know anything about treatment. I was some kind of a villain, as we all were. And she was being — she was kidnapped, held prisoner, something like that. [Sally Zinman told me that she never made such a statement.] And she did not know that she was mentally sick.

Did Rosen believe in having sexual relations with patients? He claimed, in the deposition, that he did not. However, he explained that his patients often desired to have sexual relations with him, and then he discussed it as follows: 'I might say something like, if you are cured and when you are cured, if you still wish to have sexual relations with me, we will talk about it then' (64). This is an extraordinarily self-serving comment.

Based on Zinman's complaints and the investigation undertaken by the private investigator, Virginia Snyder, the State Board of Medical Education and Licensure in 1977 began investigating the charges made against Rosen. Nothing happened, however, for two years. Then something dramatic took place.

Claudia Ehrman, thirty-one, an artist from New York City, was one of Rosen's patients. He assigned to her two therapists, Karmen 'Jay' Patete, also thirty-one, and Robin Samuels, twenty-two. Ehrman refused ever to speak to them. On December 26, 1979, she was found dead in her room at a facility run by John Rosen. The report of the investigation by the Medical Examiner (Office of the District Medical Examiner, Broward County, Florida), in the final summary, states that the 'autopsy revealed several bruises (fresh and recent) on the chest and abdomen, extremities and head. Internally the liver was extensively lacerated and there was massive hemoperitoneum with retroperitoneal hematoma.' The 'Narrative Summary of Circumstances Surrounding Death' in the official autopsy report states that two witnesses, both patients, Julia Kester Blythe and Diane Lamberger, 'stated the decedent was held down (usual practice when they are being punished for something) earlier in the day by the three in charge. Then later in the day the decedent was thrown in the pool in her dress . . . and last time she got out, she was having trouble breathing.' Dr. Shashi Gore, the Medical Examiner who signed the autopsy, stated that she died from lacerations of the liver 'caused by blunt force injuries to the abdomen.' Investigators said that Samuels held Ehrman's feet while Patete either punched or kneed Ehrman in the upper abdomen and lower chest. The 'therapy' was an attempt to force her to speak to them. The autopsy also revealed that in the ten hours before her death she was struck in the head several times and in the lower chest and abdomen about ten times.

Robin Samuels pleaded no contest to a reduced charge of battery and was placed on probation for one year. She testified in a hearing before Broward Circuit Court Judge Mel Grossman what she saw happen:

> I saw Claudia on the floor, and I saw Jay [Patete] holding her wrists down . . . trying to awaken her from her insanity. His right knee was on her stomach. He said he was kneeling on her diaphragm and therefore not hurting her. I can't specifically say how she responded, but she was just lying there.

Patete pleaded guilty to manslaughter, and was given eight years' probation. Ehrman's parents sued John Rosen in civil court. It was settled (according to the *Miami Herald*, September 3, 1981) out of court; Rosen's insurance company paid $100,000 in settlement. Rosen commented: 'It's not costing me a thing.'

The police intended to remove the other two patients in the house at Lighthouse Point where Ehrman was murdered, but when the families were contacted, they said they had full confidence in John Rosen and wished their children to remain with him!

And then on July 24, 1981, Janet Katkow sued John Rosen in

the Court of Common Pleas in Bucks County, Pennsylvania. Katkow had been in Rosen's 'care' from 1970, when she was twenty-four, until 1979. The complaint, which is in the public domain, makes for chilling reading; indeed, some people I showed it to found it almost unbearable to read. I believe it must be read, because it is by no means an isolated or unique case. I hesitate to call it typical, but it is certainly not unusual.

Janet Katkow was taken to Rosen by her parents. In front of them, during the very first interview, he asked her if she had enjoyed her first sexual experience. She did not answer. When she said she wished to return to her home in the mountains of Colorado, Rosen made an immediate and 'deep interpretation' to the effect that she liked those 'snow-capped peaks' because they were the next best thing to 'a breast filled with mother's milk.' 'Defendant then told Plaintiff's mother that he had something better for Plaintiff to suck on and he simultaneously patted his groin with one hand.'

She was left in Rosen's care. Over the next few days he explained to her that her mother had had a breast like a rock, with no milk to give her, and consequently she had never 'negotiated her oral phase' of development, and had never properly satisfied her instinct for sucking. 'He then proceeded to lie down and take off his pants and boxer shorts down over his penis and he commanded the Plaintiff to suck on his penis . . . and continued to philosophize: "This is what it is all about, this is when a baby is at peace, when it is sucking."' For the next seven years, she had literally hundreds of such 'therapy' sessions, which were invariably followed by vomiting. He explained this as her vomiting up her mother's bad milk.

Eventually the therapy proceeded to other stages, for example, the anal. 'Defendant told Plaintiff that in order for her cure to come about she must lick his anus and orally take in as much of his faeces as she could, which she did.' He later told her she would have to become involved in three-way sex or 'he would knock her teeth out.' He forced her to engage in cunnilingus with another woman, stating that if she didn't, he would 'beat the shit out of her.'

A federal judge became involved.

On or about June, 1973, Defendant introduced Plaintiff to a federal judge who was also Defendant's patient. Defendant told Plaintiff that the judge was suffering from sexual

impotency and Defendant told Plaintiff that he had a therapeutic plan in which Plaintiff must cooperate as she could
help the judge to solve his problem.

At Rosen's insistence, and under threat of physical violence, she
had intercourse several times with the judge.

In 1974 she escaped to Colorado and tried to kill herself with an
overdose of barbiturates. She was transferred to Colorado
Psychiatric Hospital, where she told the doctors about her experience with Rosen and how frightened she was of being sent back.
On June 14, 1974, she was returned, against her will, to the
custody of Rosen (neither she nor any of Rosen's patients had ever
been legally committed). 'Upon her return, Defendant told Plaintiff she was the most hideous and ungrateful person he had ever
known. Defendant also stated "your insides are rotted," that she
was "hopeless," and told her that she should kill herself.'

At last, after five years of investigation, the State Board of
Medical Education and Licensure of the Department of State of
Pennsylvania (the Commissioner of Professional and Occupational Affairs) was ready to accuse John Rosen of sixty-seven
violations of the Pennsylvania Medical Practices Act, and thirty-
five violations of rules and regulations of the Medical Board.[14] The
citation begins with Sally Zinman's case, goes on to Janet Katkow,
and then cites others, for example (counts 13–20), the case of Julia
Blythe, who was a patient of Rosen from 1963 to 1979. She was,
she claimed, kept prisoner by Rosen and his staff ('she was never
adjudicated incompetent, and was never committed to Respondent's care by virtue of any legal proceeding'), was physically
abused, and 'during the course of said psychiatric treatment,
Respondent did subject Julia Blythe to sexual abuse, in that he did
force and/or induce Julia Blythe to engage in frequent and numerous sexual relations with Respondent and with other parties,
which relations were of both heterosexual and homosexual
natures' (3). Three other women patients made similar accusations. One accusation (35–42) concerned a fourteen-year-old boy:

---

[14] I quote from the Amended Citation, dated October 19, 1982, which is
thirty-seven pages long (File Nos. 77-ME-1221 and 81-ME-889) and in the
public record. A copy was made available to me through the kindness of Ms.
Snyder.

During the course of above-mentioned doctor-patient relationship, Respondent, in the course of a treatment session, forced X's head onto Respondent's lap and did request and/or order X to perform fellatio on Respondent. 41. During the course of the above-mentioned doctor-patient relationship, Respondent unjustifiably accused X of being a homosexual and did thereafter force X to admit same to his mother. 42. During the course of the above-mentioned doctor-patient relationship, Respondent ordered X to solicit homosexual relations with a ten (10) year old male patient.

Several patients complained that they had been kept in the same 'security room' where Sally Zinman was confined, and described conditions in there exactly as Zinman had. The death of Claudia Ehrman was also cited. Rosen was accused, by the board, of 'the commission of acts involving moral turpitude, dishonesty, or corruption as well as misconduct in the practice of medicine, practicing medicine fraudulently, beyond its authorized scope, with incompetence, or with negligence' (13). The document concludes by stating:

> That the course of conduct set forth in Paraphrase I through 180 above, which are incoporated herein by reference as if fully set forth, is evidence that Respondent is unable to practice medicine with skill and safety to patients by reason of illness, drunkenness, excessive use of drugs, narcotics, chemicals or any other type of material, or as a result of any mental or physical condition, the same of which constitutes a violation of the Medical Practice Act of July 20, 1974. Now therefore, this 19th day of October, 1982, you are hereby ordered to answer the foregoing Citation as directed below, and to appear before Hearing Examiner Gene D. Cohen at a time and place to be directed by him, to show cause why your license to practice medicine and surgery in the Commonwealth of Pennsylvania should not be suspended or revoked [37].

Rosen was told he could confront witnesses and cross-examine them or have subpoenas issued. It was signed by Richard C. Lyons, M.D., Chairman of the State Board of Medical Education and Licensure. The Prosecuting Attorney was Walter H. Killian.

The *Palm Beach Post* of March 30, 1983, reported that on the preceding day, John Rosen surrendered his medical license in Harrisburg, Pennsylvania, rather than face trial. He pleaded guilty to three courts: of abandoning Claudia Ehrman into the care of his employees, who beat her to death; of failing to provide proper supervision or regular treatment for Michael Hallinan, who was kept bound and shackled in the security room; and of 'being unable to practice medicine with skill and safety for his patients.' The reporter, Steve Rothman, quoted the Prosecuting Attorney: 'We could have proved all of the complaints filed against Rosen. From our point of view, Rosen's pleading guilty and surrendering his license saved the state a great deal of expense.' The *Bucks County Courier Times*, in an article on the same day, by Don Wolf, quoted a member of the Medical Board, Herbert C. Goldstein, who questioned why the consent agreement was 'sanitized' to exclude any reference to sexual and physical abuse of patients. Killian explained that this was the best the board could get without going through a costly hearing. The board has no power to fine or imprison, only to remove a medical license. And this is what they got.[15]

I am sure that some psychiatrists, reading this account of Rosen, will be indignant and appalled by Rosen's actions. They will angrily reject the possibility that Rosen's antics represent the norm in psychotherapy. The argument would run that Rosen is an exceptionally bad psychotherapist. True, he fooled a number of prominent families, and a number of prominent psychiatrists, and a number of prominent medical schools, granting bodies, licensing agents, and law-enforcement agencies. Yes, they might even argue, we should have known sooner. We should have read his work more carefully, shown ourselves more skeptical. Yes, it is

[15]The Stipulation and Consent Agreement between the State Board of Medical Education and Licensure and John Rosen was actually signed on April 8, 1983. Rosen, in that document, admitted to 'not making provision for the continuing psychiatric medical treatment of Gay Claudia Ehrman'; to 'failing to adequately supervise assistant therapists, whose actions resulted in Michael Hallinan not receiving regular and/or substantive psychiatric therapy'; and, finally, 'Respondent is unable to practice medicine with reasonable skill and safety to patients by reason of illness.' His license was revoked, and 'the Commonwealth hereby dismisses with prejudice all other charges made against Respondent in the Citation and Amended Citation.'

too bad that it took a former patient to expose him for what he really was. Still, Rosen does not represent psychiatry. Rosen is an exception.

The point of this book is to raise precisely this question: Is Rosen an exception, or is there something about psychotherapy, something in the very nature of psychotherapy, that tends toward such abuses? Are these abuses or simply the use that is made of psychotherapy? A prison warden, a slaveholder, and a psychotherapist have in common the desire to control another person. (The analogy may appear inexact, for the person in therapy, many believe, is free to leave or quit. I don't believe this is true, though it would require a discussion of the concept of 'informed consent.' Nevertheless, the parallels are striking. We know for a fact that many slaveholders thought of themselves as kindly and argued that slaves were lucky to have them as masters, for others would be worse. Medical doctors at Auschwitz argued that if they didn't do what they did, others would do it more brutally. People who participate in causing suffering to others often employ this argument.)

I called Dr. Morris W. Brody, a prominent psychoanalyst in Philadelphia who had been in the Department of Psychiatry at Temple University Medical School at the same time as John Rosen. We had an interesting conversation. He is well read and well informed. I explained to him what I was writing. After some initial hesitation, he admitted that he had been suspicious of Rosen from the beginning. It did not take much intelligence, he agreed, to be able to read his writings and see through the man. Clearly something was dreadfully wrong. Nevertheless, Dr. Brody told me that he had witnessed an exchange with a patient who insisted that she heard voices coming from another room, upstairs, talking about her. Rosen told her, as was his wont, that this was crazy. He insisted that she stop making the claim. She persisted. Rosen threatened to hit her if she continued. She continued. Rosen hit her. Then came the amazing part of this conversation. The analyst told me that he was there, and could see that when Rosen hit her he was not being sadistic.

This is, after all, only an interpretation, even if, unlike most interpretations, it is meant to be benign rather than hurtful. For how on earth could Dr. Brody, or anybody else, for that matter, observing Rosen, assert with any degree of probability that Rosen was not being sadistic when he hit the woman? He went on to tell me how this same interpretation was made to a young boy whom Rosen abused, and whose response to this abuse was so positive that he immediately recovered. The boy explained, later, that the abuse Rosen had showered on him (it was, apparently, physical abuse) reminded him of the way in which his football coach treated the players, and how effective this had proven to be.

However, Dr. Brody maintained that, although he and other colleagues eventually grew disillusioned and suspicious of Rosen, they had never imagined that he could be guilty of the kinds of gross misconduct that were eventually established against him by the Pennsylvania Board of Medical Quality Assurance. How, he argued, could they possibly have known that? (True, it took people with a great sense of justice to do this.) But even should we agree that they did not know it at the time, now they did know it. Now they knew that it was true. I said (being tactful and hiding my outrage at Rosen) that what amazed and intrigued me was the fact that this information finally had to come, not from Rosen's peers and colleagues, but from an ex-patient working with a private investigator. That did raise certain important questions about the ethics of psychotherapy, did it not? We had reached a sensitive point in our discussion. Suddenly Dr. Brody shifted ground entirely. He said it was like selling the Brooklyn Bridge. He was intrigued not by the psychology of the seller, but by the psychology of the buyer. Why would somebody be so stupid as to buy the bridge? Similarly, he was interested not in John Rosen or in his psychology (or even what this says about the profession of psychotherapy), but in his patients. Why did they go to him?

Here was yet a new twist to blaming the victim. The introspective analyst was telling me that patients should have been able to see through Rosen immediately. But he did acknowledge that the Department of Psychiatry did not achieve this vision until after many years of contact with the man. Was he saying that patients should have read his articles and reached the same conclusions he did? But those conclusions were hardly shared unanimously by his colleagues. Indeed, had not the Chairman of the Department of Psychiatry, O. Spurgeon English, a distinguished psychiatrist and psychoanalyst, given him an appointment as clinical professor of psychiatry based on those very writings?[16] Should an unhappy patient have been able to see what the Chairman of the Department of Psychiatry could not? Dr. Brody said he could not see why I or anybody else would be interested in John Rosen. The only interesting question, he felt, was how these wealthy patients could allow themselves to be so fooled. But I believe that Dr. Brody has failed to ask himself how it is that members of his profession (he is also a psychiatrist) could remain ignorant of the damage being done by a colleague's treatment until the law acted. And even when they become aware of it, to claim it is but an uninteresting aberration with no implications for the profession is to avoid an unpleasant truth.

Dr. Brody suggested I call Dr. O. Spurgeon English, and on November 1, 1986, I had a phone conversation with him. He told me that he had indeed invited John Rosen to come to the Department of Psychiatry in 1959, and that he stayed on there, as Associate Professor of Psychiatry, until 1964, which is also the year that Dr. English retired. He invited Rosen specifically so that his new methods of therapy for schizophrenic patients could be investigated by members of the department. Two buildings were made available to Rosen, and a special institute was created: the Institute for the Study of Psychotherapy. There were about twenty-five psychiatrists in the department. Many of them were involved in studying Rosen's methods. Rosen demonstrated his work on a daily basis. There were, said Dr. English, many valuable aspects to it. It was, he said, a very interesting period. Many of the psychiatrists who watched Rosen were influenced by his methods, and some of them went on to use them in their own practice, including Dr. English himself. There were, at the time, no objections from the staff, although a few were uninterested. The

---

[16] In an article entitled 'How I Found My Way to Psychiatry,' published in *Twelve Therapists*, by Arthur Burton and Associates (San Francisco: Jossey-Bass, 1972), 78–102, O. Spurgeon English wrote: 'The second colleague with whom I found it interesting to exchange ideas and to work was Dr. John N. Rosen, who joined me at Temple University Medical School in the Department of Psychiatry. We worked actively together over a ten-year period – from 1955 until 1965, when I resigned as department head. John's concepts of the meaning of psychotic thought and behavior were uncannily perceptive . . . It used to be said by many in our field in the thirties and forties that psychotic people were sensitive and easily traumatized and should be treated with great deference and consideration. *But work with them shows precisely the opposite.*' [Italics added.]

analytic community was less interested than the psychiatric community, but there was no criticism. Dr. English had asked the advice of many influential psychiatrists around the country at the time, and all approved his hiring of Rosen, including the Menninger brothers. He said that Rosen's influence had been considerable, that he had tried to apply Rosen's methods, and that he felt they were successful in sixty-six percent of the cases.

There was a pause in our conversation. I asked Dr. English if he was aware that Dr. Rosen had lost his licence because of a charge of abuse by the Medical Board. Dr. English replied that he was. I then asked how his ideas about Rosen and the value of his teachings had been affected by this recent development. Dr. English replied that these charges had no relevance for the effectiveness of Rosen's methods; that his ideas were not necessarily the best in the world, but he had many good ideas. Dr. English no longer saw psychotic patients, so he didn't use Rosen's methods, but if he did, he would continue to use them.

Here, then, is the perfect answer to the psychoanalyst who wondered why I would be interested in Dr. John Rosen. Here is an influential psychiatrist, the author of one of the standard textbooks used in psychiatry, whose positive opinion of John Rosen has not been affected in the least by all the information that has become available. I expected Dr. English to tell me that he did not suspect any of these things about Rosen when he was working in his department (he did tell me this), but that now that he knew them, it would, of course, alter his view. Not at all. He stuck by what he knew of Rosen in the past. Perhaps he was making the point that the man may be faulty, but his views about therapy could still be valid. But his views about therapy, as we have seen, are intimately tied in with the behavior of the man. Or maybe they are not. Maybe many therapists, by the very nature of therapy, engage in activities that are not wholly unlike those of Dr. John Rosen. Maybe it is in the very nature of therapy to encourage abuse. Maybe therapy is the very opposite of what it appears to be. I found the conversation with Dr. English instructive. It took place in 1986 and showed me that Rosen had indeed touched upon some of the very foundation stones of psychotherapy. I am convinced that Rosen was no exception, no aberration. This is therapy.

On November 11, 1986, I received a letter from Dr. Morris W. Brody, the psychiatrist and psychoanalyst who knew Rosen at

Temple University Medical School. He wrote: 'As far as I am concerned, John Rosen is a thing of the past and should stay that way.' No doubt many psychiatrists would share this point of view. But I don't believe that the whole matter can be dismissed so easily or so lightly. For many of his patients, John Rosen is hardly 'a thing of the past.' Dr. Brody is clearly annoyed that I have chosen to write about what he regards as a distasteful subject. But we are not concerned here with aesthetic sensitivities. We are concerned with the truth about psychotherapy. I cannot stress strongly enough that this truth was uncovered not by any psychiatrist (indeed, not by me either), but by Sally Zinman and Janet Katkow and the many other former patients who came forward to testify and speak out, often at great risk. This took courage, and this took the kind of moral sensitivity that therapists claim as their special possession, the quality that permits them the illusion that they need to instill vision in their morally weaker patients.

When Dr. Brody suggests that the Rosen episode be forgotten, he clearly indicates that for him it is an aberration, something that belongs to the dark ages of psychiatry. But is this true? In the next chapter we will see that the influence of John Rosen lives on, and that one of his disciples leads a psychiatric institution in which all the practices of John Rosen continue to be used on patients.[17]

---

[17]Morris W. Brody is also the author of the book *Observations on Direct Analysis: The Therapeutic Technique of Dr. John N. Rosen*, forewords by John N. Rosen and O. Spurgeon English (New York: Vantage Press, 1959). The book is an apologia for Dr. Rosen. The description he gives of his 'technique' is quite terrifying. Brody points out that Rosen does not hesitate to strike a patient, to kick or drag a patient up or down the stairs (71). He gives an example in which a 'paranoid' patient insisted there was a man upstairs and Rosen told her he would go upstairs with her to see if it was so, but that if there was no man there he would 'throw her down all the stairs head first' (73). The group sat transfixed, afraid that Rosen, who 'does not like to back down from a threat,' would harm the woman, but they were unable to take any action. Rosen, according to Brody, would recurrently use the phrase, 'If you continue to act crazy I will crack your skull open' (79). But Brody is convinced Rosen is a kindly man: 'By watching Dr. Rosen a little more closely one becomes convinced that his intentions are in no way meant to be cruel' (79). Rosen has, according to Brody, only a single thought in mind: how to rescue the patient from the throes of a psychosis. On pages 62 through 69, Brody reproduces verbatim dialogue between Rosen and a young woman, and intersperses his own commentary. This dialogue is the most shocking example I have seen of Rosen's abuse. He begins by telling the woman that he disapproves of her being a 'tomboy' and warns her that if she continues he will mutilate her. He

[17] *Cont.* also tells her that 'I can't fuck you if you are a boy, so why do you want to be a boy?' He then asks her to have intercourse with him (with the observers present) and when she hesitates he tells her, 'I will knock you through that wall in a minute. (Patient recoils.) You are ready to have intercourse now' (63). A few statements later he tells her that he will stop loving her if she does not have intercourse with him. At the end of the dialogue she complains of pains in her stomach (68). Rosen tells her it is from intercourse. She objects and says it is from exercise. Rosen's final words to her are: 'The only muscle you should exercise is your vagina. Well, maybe we will have intercourse.' When an unusually large number of observers were present during a meeting of the Eastern Psychological Association of April 11, 1958, Rosen 'demonstrated' this patient to a large audience. In front of the group he told her: 'You're an evil person, Bea. It's no wonder everybody dislikes you. Maybe that's why your poor father went to find other people – tried to get away from you and your family. . . . You have plenty to be ashamed of. You're very low-class' (93). He also told her that she was unbearably stupid and came from the low part of Philadelphia. Brody takes this all in his stride and insists that Rosen is a benign, unusually gifted psychotherapist. In this book we have three respected members of the psychiatric community endorsing what any person can readily see is nothing but abuse. In his Foreword, Rosen boasts: 'Under the terms of a grant from the Rockefeller Brothers' Fund, which established the Institute for Direct Analysis at Temple University Medical Center, we have developed a research program which has among its other goals the definition of direct analysis.' We could have saved the Rockefeller Brothers' Fund a lot of money and told them in two words the definition: naked brutality. The real research would be into why this appealed to so many professionals for so long.

6

SEX AND BATTERING IN
PSYCHOTHERAPY

A number of psychotherapists I spoke to about John Rosen were willing to concede that he was, indeed, a very bad person, and, a greater concession, even a very bad psychotherapist. But surely, they argued, this did not reflect on the entire profession. Even granting me that his fame and influence live on and that many prominent psychiatrists simply will not admit that he is terrible, nevertheless, they point to the fact that he did, a few years ago, lose his medical license. It may have been overdue, but at least such a man is no longer practicing psychotherapy. This is true, but it is more than his influence that lives on. There are many disciples of John Rosen who continue to use the methods he taught them.[1]

One of these disciples is Albert Honig (not a psychiatrist, but a doctor of osteopathy), Medical Director of the Delaware Valley Mental Health Foundation, 'a unique therapeutic community' (to quote from its brochure), in Doylestown, Pennsylvania, a 'non-profit, non-sectarian institution dedicated to the treatment of severe emotional illness, research and training.' The description is idyllic, emphasizing community, the warmth of a familylike, gentle environment in which patients live in little cottages nestled among thirteen acres of rolling hills in Bucks County. It sounds like

[1] In 1981, two years before John Rosen surrendered his license, John Wiley & Sons, in their Wiley-Interscience series, published a massive book, edited by Raymond J. Corsini, entitled *Handbook of Innovative Psychotherapies*, which contains 'authoritative' information on most of the new therapies. Included is 'Direct Psychoanalysis,' written by John Rosen. Departing from his usual procedure, the editor has added a short foreword, in which he writes about how happy he is to be able to include this section: 'Rosen was always spoken of in wonder by those who saw what he accomplished . . . the reader is now in for a thrilling experience – what follows is a chapter that should be read carefully by all those who wish to understand psychotherapy in its fullest.'

what many families are looking for. Indeed, in its April 5, 1966, issue, *Look* magazine featured a major article entitled 'Breakthrough in Psychiatry: Revolutionary Treatment of the Mentally Ill' ('produced' by Chandler Brossard and photographed by Matt Herron) about the Foundation and Dr. Honig, who was described as the 'dedicated and brilliant young director.' The article explained that Honig's method was patterned on 'direct psychoanalysis.' The pictures showed Honig 'interacting' with patients. There is one of an angry Honig with his hand over a patient's mouth. The caption read: 'Following his direct-therapy method, Dr. Honig furiously puts his hand over patient's mouth to stop him from lying.' Most of the article consisted of dialogue between Honig and his patients. Here is a typical comment from Dr. Honig: 'Your obsession is warding off the anxiety which is related to that which is the mother's breast. Our battle is with your compulsion.' But incomprehensible gibberish is one thing, terrifying a patient is quite another; clearly Honig was an expert at both. He asked a young patient, 'Do you know what autistic means?' and then gave him his inarticulate and threatening answer: 'Autistic is somebody that stays by themself and eats candy and lives in a dream world, and doesn't want to have anything to do with anybody else.'

> *Patient:* I know what that means. Maybe there's something that could be . . .
> *Honig:* Let's get him some candy. And I want it right in his room.
> *Patient:* Try to be helped.
> *Honig:* You want chocolate?
> *Patient:* Yes. That's right.
> *Honig:* All right. We're going to put ten pieces right in your room, and you'd better not touch one.
> *Patient:* I understand that. I will not.
> *Honig:* They're going right on your dresser. If one of those is gone . . . Ho! Ho! Just don't show up the next morning.
> *Patient:* That's right . . . the opportunity to make myself sick.
> *Honig:* You'd better not touch one of those.
> *Patient:* Right. I will not touch it. I will not.
> *Honig:* Because you might not be alive.
> *Patient:* I will not touch them. I will not. I'll be careful.

Honig went on to tell this terrified patient to 'stop stuttering so much. Every time you get nervous, you start stuttering.' He then told him that the candies came from his mother, and she put 'some of her own brand of stuff in there,' namely, poison, and so, Honig said, 'We'll have to bury you.'

It is hard to believe that such emotional assaults disguised as therapy could be singled out by *Look* for praise. But there can be no doubt that these things did take place, and continue to take place. At my request, in February 1987, the Foundation sent me a film that was made of Dr. Honig's methods, entitled *Other Voices*. It was nominated for an Academy Award, and, according to the Foundation's brochure, Dr. Erich Fromm said of it, 'I highly recommend this picture to anyone who is interested in man.'[2] I wonder if Dr. Fromm meant 'man's inhumanity to man.' There is a terrifying scene with a seventeen-year-old boy (very fond of dogs – a point that is ridiculed by Dr. Honig) who is physically very slight. Dr. Honig, a large man, well over six feet tall and probably over two hundred pounds, sits on the boy while the boy curses and implores him to get off. In the film brochure, the dialogue is reproduced:

[2]This film may remind readers of a similar film, *Warrendale* (produced in 1966), which was called by *Newsweek* (September 2, 1967) 'a very nearly perfect documentary by Allan King, made at a Canadian treatment center for emotionally disturbed children where the principal therapy is brute love.' *Saturday Review* (September 28, 1969) called it 'one of the most telling, even shattering, documentary films ever made.' It won several festival prizes in the sixties. *Time* (September 29, 1967) said it was the 'most remarkable documentary in the showing – and perhaps the most unusual film in the entire festival.' The reporter spoke about how 'with monumental patience, the young Warrendale staff tries to disarm the children, holding them during their emotional storms, constantly preventing their retreat into themselves with physical force as well as emotional empathy.' Stanley Kauffman, reviewing it in the *New Republic* (September 2, 1967), spoke of it with near awe and explained that 'the basic Warrendale technique is 'holding': when a child has an emotional seizure, an outsize tantrum, one of the attendants – sometimes two or three – pins his arms and legs and lets him rip. Complete freedom of feeling is the essence, with restraint to keep the child from hurting himself and to provide a sense of physical contact, the *caring* for somebody else.' Needless to say, the same kind of arrogant control of another person's emotional life is evinced in the Foundation's film, under the exact same disguise of love and care. What is extraordinary is how much praise these exercises in brutality garner from the critics. Clearly the men who do this kind of thing are not engaging in some aberrant exercise of emotional violence personal to themselves; they are acting in complete conformity to the rest of society.

Mark and Dr. Honig are fighting furiously on a couch. Although the doctor is much larger, Mark's rage makes him very powerful. The following dialogue takes place throughout the violent wrestling match.

Dr. Honig: You'd better sit on this couch or I'm going to sit on you.

Mark: Oh, you, why don't you drop dead, for Christ's sake? Don't give me, 'Well, I love you' – fucking doctor, you bastard you. I'm not taking any more bullcrap from you now, I don't care how much stronger you are than me.

Dr. Honig: Now you'd better sit over here . . .

Mark: (yells) No, I won't!

Dr Honig: Get over here, RIGHT HERE, right here . . . and we'll talk like one human to another.

Mark kicks and hits. He is hysterical with rage.

Dr. Honig: Are you going to sit here and talk like a gentleman?

Mark: (gasping) No. I won't.

Dr. Honig: How were you brought up – like an animal?

Mark: Yeah – you were brought up like a fucking bitch . . . Oh-h-h (roars)

Doctor Honig has a scissor hold on him.

Dr. Honig: Who did I come over to see first this morning?

Mark: You came over to see me first so you could antagonize me – because you know I sleep late!

Dr. Honig: You what?

Mark: You know I sleep late. You know I sleep till 10:30. You came over here so you could wake me up early, huh? So I had to get up early, 7:30 . . .

Dr. Honig: That's part of your mental condition.

Mark: I'm warning you – don't get me mad!

Dr. Honig: Don't get mad? What do you call this? I've never seen so much anger in a guy in all my life – look at this! No wonder you hang around with dogs all the time! Can't even control your own anger! Now you gonna be able to sit up here? . . .

Mark: Leave me alone.

Mark, with a burst of energy, tries again to break the doctor's grip. From a close-up of his face, contorted with rage, we cut to: Doctor Honig, sweat pouring down his face, sitting quietly on the couch. Next to him Mark, equally exhausted, stares into the camera with sullen anger. The two of them sit there for a long time in silence.

It is hard to watch this film without feeling rage at what this man is doing to the boy. Dr. Honig explains: 'I tackled him because I was trying to get him to experience his anger. I wanted him to feel himself, his own body. He was enraged at being roused from the protective lethargy and withdrawal which had shielded his true feelings . . .' I have no idea why Honig did what he did to Mark, but I know that it was cruel. Honig says:

> During the course of the film, Mark went through a greater transformation than any of the other patients. When he first arrived at the clinic he was fat, sluggish, feeling very little except groggy depression. Eventually, he lost fifty pounds and that drugged quality disappeared; he became lean, intense, and angry. He came to feel things he'd never felt before. In Mark's case his growing good feelings were too much for him and made him too uncomfortable and frightened.

This is leading up to Honig's admission that Mark committed suicide while under Honig's care. Honig has this to say about it:

> We were incredibly shocked by his suicide. The changes in him had been so dramatic, we were sure that the healthy forces were going to win the struggle. But, sadly, treatment will sometimes fail at the most critical point – the birth of the person's own real identity. All we can do when this happens is to go on.

It is not only the *Look* article and the nomination for an Academy Award that indicate the favor Honig was held in. An article by Ann Loring, published in *New York* in 1977 (October 31, pages 39–43), entitled 'Emerging from Schizophrenia: A Case History' offers a glowing account of Honig and his therapy. But the account, which is meant to be positive and to show Honig in his best light, chilled me to the bone. It is yet another instance of somebody who is bullying and humiliating a patient and calling it therapy. Confrontation, as Honig calls it, is what is known in everyday life as insult. An example is when he demands to know of a patient called

Benjamin whether he told the writer about his belief that he was searching for the answer to life's problems. I quote from the article; the comments are Ann Loring's.

> *Dr. Honig:* He 'thinks' so he can 'hear' the answer to life's problems. Did you tell your cousin that, Benjamin?
>
> There was a mounting tension.
>
> 'Why do you . . .' Benjamin began, then caught himself mid-sentence. 'No,' he paused. 'I . . . I never talked about it.'
>
> 'Why not? That's what you believe.'
>
> 'It was . . . private.'
>
> 'Private . . . ? Come on, Benjamin.'
>
> Dr. Honig, in his quiet calm voice, was driving a little harder now.
>
> 'Why not? Were you ashamed of it? Like you know it's nuts. Crazy. A nice middle-class American guy like you, trying to act out something you're not. Standing around immobile. And those eating habits of yours. They're crazy too . . .'
>
> By turns gentle, harsh, brutally honest, incisive, humorous, caring, Dr. Honig was attempting to pierce through Benjamin's wall of 'craziness.'[3]

In other words, no matter how brutal the treatment, if the person says he is doing it for the other person's good, it is acceptable.

A book by Dr. Honig, *The Awakening Nightmare: A Breakthrough in Treating the Mentally Ill,*[4] provides proof, in his own words, that this article was no exaggeration. It was Rosen's dialogue, all right,

[3] A woman who actually witnessed the treatment of this man wrote me the following (she has asked that her name not be used): 'This example doesn't convey any of the brutality of Benjamin's treatment. In fact Benjamin, who was himself a Ph.D. psychologist, was one of the most viciously abused patients. I wonder how [the writer] would have responded to seeing Benjamin dragged off, placed in a strait jacket, ankle restraints and blindfold. Then his pants would be pulled down – in a room full of people – a group session – then he would be shocked repeatedly with a cattle prod as he screamed in protest. This happened *often*, almost daily, during months of his "treatment." This is how Honig brought about his great improvement, by forcing him, under penalty of torture, to relate to people in a "normal" way. In this case he did have the resources to do what Honig asked of him. Many other patients, unfortunately, did not. For those who had never been "normal," those too young, or too seriously disturbed for all their lives, this torturous treatment just led to further degeneration.'

[4] New York: Dell Publishing Co., 1972.

in many instances identical, certainly in tone. One patient, frightened of perhaps harboring homosexual tendencies, is told by Honig: 'I think that every moment that you're alive you have thoughts of sucking my dick' (181). Astonishingly, Honig admits that 'soon after, the patient became more withdrawn; it was impossible to get him to come to the office except by force. He was then hospitalized *against his will*.' (Italics added.)

At my request, Dr. Honig sent me a paper, 'Responses to Cumulative Trauma and Indoctrination in Chronic Schizophrenia,' which will be published shortly in the *Bulletin of the Menninger Clinic*, about the experience of concentration camp survivors and schizophrenia. In that article he admits to shaving the heads of some of his patients. (Is he aware that this was done in concentration camps too?) He says that with one 'catatonic' patient 'I sat on his pelvic frame, pried open his catatonic jaws and dripped saliva from my mouth to his.' For one 'paranoid' patient, he reports:

> Since his belief system was that electricity was the method used for his persecution, electricity would also be his cure. He was given his 'last meal,' anything he wanted to eat. He chose steak, potatoes, ice cream and apple pie. Next morning his head was shaved, and he was led by the staff blindfolded to a large chair in an adjoining living room. A pulsating muscle stimulator (a machine used to treat muscle injuries by rehabilitation specialists) with wetted pads was attached to his calves of both legs and to his forearms . . . the staff subdued him and placed him in a strait jacket. . . . He took a nurturing bottle of warm milk and a sign was placed on his chest saying, 'I am hungry for love – please love me.'

What is one to make of this kind of thing? It appears to contain all the basic postulates of psychotherapy carried to absurd extremes. But it made me think that if this is what Honig publishes and advertises himself as doing in the clinic, then the reality must be much, much worse. I was not wrong.

In 1969 Wilma Caffentzis, who had a Ph.D. from Yeshiva University, in New York, took up her duties as Program Director and Staff Psychologist (though only in the outpatient department, never in the inpatient department, which is why she was not a witness to the incidents that went on in that department and found out about them only later) at the Delaware Valley Mental Health Foundation, a position she was to hold for nine years. Before that, she had been Assistant Professor of Psychology at the City College of the City University of New York. In October 1978 she and another therapist, Diane Mann, formed an ad hoc committee to end patient abuse and startled the local District Attorney's Office with charges of serious abuse at the Foundation, accompanied by affidavits, case records, witnesses, and so on. It took remarkable courage to prepare these documents and to bring them to the attention of the authorities.

It is not surprising that we find in them many of the same elements of abuse that we saw in the preceding chapter, about John Rosen. The patients were humiliated, degraded, and abused in very similar ways. The committee's statement[5] described therapists, as part of the sexual humiliation, doing the following:

> using a stick to show the genitals of a female patient to a male patient in an 'anatomy' lesson given by one of the treating doctors; coercing an unwilling male and female patient to share the same bed for sleeping over a prolonged period in an effort to induce them to be sexually active; revealing the genitals of a female patient while cutting off her dirty underclothes and displaying them to a predominantly male group of staff by a treating psychologist; inducing a fifteen year old male patient to masturbate into a condom and displaying it at a group session.

Many other abuses were reported. A remarkable letter written by a woman who was both a patient and later a therapist at the Foundation, but who does not want her name to be used, gives us some flavour of what happened there:

> It is precisely the idea that the clinic is the best place in existence that seems to lead to its worst atrocities towards its patients. I believe that Dr. Honig and most of his staff are firmly convinced that they are saving lives, healing souls, curing those previously thought hopeless – and therefore if they hit and beat these patients, zap them with cattle prods, hook them

[5] This was kindly supplied to me by Wilma Caffentzis.

up to 'relaxicisors' which shock them, and scream at them and constantly demean them in the name of 'confronting their craziness,' that this is all right, that it is different from the brutality of other unenlightened doctors. *I assure you that from a patient's perspective it really does not matter that the authority figure who is shocking you with a cattle prod thinks he is saving your life.* It is still experienced as torture. . . . The incident which ended my illusions about the clinic once and for all occurred in February of this year. But it is really just one incident in a long, long line of incidents. In mid-February, Dr. Sandy Mintz [a psychologist working as a psychotherapist at the clinic] forced N. G. to eat the contents of several ashtrays. When she vomited, he then forced her to eat her own vomit. He did this supposedly to teach her to say 'no' to him — but she did say 'no' strongly enough. Numerous staff members watched this without protest (as is usually the case. Doctors are not questioned at the clinic). Paula Matter came rushing next door where I was to tell me, saying we must get the Patients' Rights Committee together and stop him. From long experience, I was sure the Patients' Rights Committee would have no power to stop Dr. Mintz and I told Paula to get Dr. Strochek, the executive director, which she did. *The result of this was a lot of talk and Dr. Mintz being suspended (whatever that is) for one day!* I was sure that when Dr. Honig returned from vacation he would take some action, but, on the contrary, he felt compelled to defend Dr. Mintz and went around saying that the people who objected to what Mintz did had problems with their aggression! . . . It is difficult to give a sense of what life is like for a patient at DVMHF to someone who has not experienced it. Very few of the staff have any idea what a constant sense of terror, degradation, and diminished sense of self are caused by their tactics. The basic therapeutic technique, demonstrated by the medical director and copied by the uneducated staff, is confrontation. What confrontation means in the patient's daily life is that anything from how long he stays in the bathroom, to how much she eats, to how he's dressed, to her 'attitude' is subject to the possibility of angry, derisive verbal attacks by staff members. What bothers one staff member may not bother another, so the patient's 'craziness' is subject to inconsistent, changing definition. This whole mocking, hostile style of interacting with patients is so habitual that I recently observed an ex-family therapist who has been away from the clinic for five years fall unknowingly into this derision when talking to a current patient. This form of verbal abuse, which is an easy outlet for therapists' aggressions, is called therapy. For the patient being constantly subjected to these scornful, angry outbursts lead to a pervading sense of terror and powerlessness. Any aspect of the patient's behavior can be 'confronted.' As an example, in my case, *Dr. Honig decided that my 50% hearing loss was possibly psychological and he forbid me to wear my hearing aids which he said were a crutch*. Then, whenever I was unable to hear someone, they would get angry with me, accusing me of not wanting to hear them, etc. I found these attacks for something I had no idea how to change to be thoroughly dehumanizing and anxiety provoking. [Italics added.]

On December 29, 1978, the Bucks County District Attorney's Office in Doylestown, Pennsylvania, issued a ten-page report. They found that 'within the past two years cattle prods, relaxicisors, paddles and physical restraints were used by primary therapists (i.e., treating psychologists) on patients at the Delaware Valley Mental Health Foundation . . .' However, the DA's Office also found:

The devices were used in good faith by the therapists and in the sincere belief that they would aid the treatment process. The devices were employed at times as 'punishment' but only as that term is understood within behavior modification theories. The treatment methodology of aversion therapy and behavior modification [though Honig never said he practiced behavior modification; he called it analysis] practiced at the DVMHF falls within the recognized and legitimate treatment techniques for the mentally ill.

In other words, as Thomas Szasz has so often and cogently argued, once somebody is declared 'mentally ill,' you can do anything you want to them, including torture, as long as you claim that you are doing it for their own good.

The report also took note of the ashtray incident:

> After careful investigation, we find the 'ashtray incident' to represent an inappropriate treatment judgment *made in good faith by the therapist.* The Foundation immediately condemned the incident and took steps to internally deal with the lack of judgment it represented. We find the incident to have been an almost unique aberration in treatment at the Foundation. [Italics added.]

The report went on to say: 'Delaware Valley Mental Health Foundation treats as inpatients those persons with severe psychosis, some of whom have homicidal and suicidal tendencies. The Foundation often represents the last chance for patients with extensive previous institutionalization.' This is, of course, the same rationale used by the Foundation (and every other center using methods not generally sanctioned by society). How could the DA's Office possibly know this? How could the Foundation possibly know it? Indeed, how could *anybody* possibly know it? The DA's Office even brought up the same defense that Honig (and Rosen) used, namely, that things are often worse elsewhere:

> Although some inpatient treatment methods used at the Foundation may appear shocking, this facility represents to most of its patients the last in a long line of mental hospitals, many of which practice treatment techniques such as drug therapy, electroshock and even lobotomies. The Foundation does not rely on any of these treatment modalities.

But the fact that other places are even *more* cruel surely does not justify cruelty, brutality, and torture. No doubt the Argentine prison wardens could say that the situation in Turkey was even worse than it was in their country. The way to break this cycle is simply to step out of it, and instead of saying, 'If they were not here, they would be in a mental hospital, where they would receive electroshock or lobotomy,' to say, 'They will not go to any institution at all.' The DA's Office then went on to criticize the ad hoc committee: 'Many allegations in the original affidavits contained out-of-context distortions.' No examples are given. And then, in a piece of ugly bullying and threat, it said: 'Several of the

Ad Hoc Committee probably committed crimes in the process of compiling their allegations. Within the overall context of this report, we find it would serve no useful purpose to prosecute them.' Probably? Again, no examples are given. It is a strange thing to find in an official report. The conclusion (signed by the District Attorney, Kenneth G. Biehn, the Deputy District Attorney, Dana C. Jones, and the Assistant District Attorney, Joanne D. Sommer) stated:

> It is our firm conviction that the work of this facility and its staff has been unfairly characterized. We have studied the basic treatment philosophy and have investigated the various allegations. We believe that at all times treatment was given in an attempt to help the patient overcome his or her psychosis. We have concluded that there was no intent to harm any patient and that treatment was administered in the good faith belief that the patient would benefit. We have documented the success of the treatment program. [No examples were given.] In view of the above and after diligent and thoughtful considerations, we have terminated our investigation of the Delaware Valley Mental Health Foundation and will file no criminal charges.

How could the signers of the report possibly know that there was 'no intent to harm'? Why did they suppose that many patients complained and many therapists (at least fifteen) had been willing to risk public exposure and other forms of possible harm to come forth and denounce what they knew *from direct experience* really to be happening at the Foundation? What benefit could there be in it for them? This reminds me of people who accuse children of making false allegations of sexual abuse. What possible benefit could there be to the children? Is not the opposite, the desire to cover up, a much greater likelihood? It simply makes no sense to believe that a large number of patients and staff would come forth with accusations of serious misdeeds in a private mental facility for no reason at all.

In March 1979, Loretta Schwartz wrote an article for *Philadelphia Magazine* entitled 'The Punishment Cure,' (38–43) in which she told of her conversation with Dr. Honig after the report by the District Attorney's Office. He said that it represented 'a clear mandate to continue our pioneering work with the most hopeless of the mentally ill.' He also explained some of his hiring policies for therapists:

> 'Each living unit is run by a couple. We have married couples working here who are former patients or who have been through drugs. Some have been in jail. These are the kinds of people who we want to have work here. One guy who tried to kill his father is a counselor here now . . . we shave people's heads. We put dunce caps on them. The dunce cap says *you're stupid, you're an idiot*. Why do we shave their heads? Maybe to let out the evil spirits. Evil needs to be exorcised; purging them is part of the cure. I've been doing this for 20 years. I know how to reach them . . . sometimes I'm a mother, sometimes I'm a father and sometimes I'm God. It's a commune and I'm the moral leader . . . the primitive god, the person who is more powerful than the illness. My patients will go to the ends of the earth for me.'

Schwartz quoted Paula Matter, a former patient and then a staff member:

> 'We're dealing with the hopeless throwaway cases, people who may as well be dead. Words will not reach them. If you want to make a break in the case you must *do* something. You must force your way into their system. Often their system is all they have going for them and they don't want anybody messing with it. This is where the arrogance and defiance comes in.'

Here is an example from a patient:

> 'I lost my capacity to open my eyes and to walk as well as to talk. I was told by Honig that he hated my eyes and could not stand to look at them. He made me close them and keep them closed during one entire session . . . after my eyes were closed and I had lost my ability to speak, I was told during another session to get on the floor face down, which I did. However, when Dr. Honig told me to get up, and I did not, he said, "Look at that defiance." At that point he yanked me up solely by my

hair, which was braided in a single braid in the back. I was so frightened by being picked up by my hair alone that I wet my pants. He then, still holding me by my hair, flopped me on the couch. He asked the male staff to hold my arms above my head and others to hold my legs, while he sat on my stomach. Honig then put his hands around my neck and started squeezing, saying, "Open your eyes; I want you to look at me; open your eyes! You know I could kill you." The staff confronted me and threatened that if I did not open my eyes they were going to arrange to have them extracted and donated to an eye bank . . . Then I was taken into the therapist's back room accompanied by Adam Houtz and a young doctor. The doctor told Adam to hook up my legs and Adam did so. The doctor asked me to open up my eyes, but in my catatonic state, I was unable to do so. The doctor then had Adam turn on The Machine. Higher and higher went the voltage in a constant flow. My legs felt like they were actually being torn from my body. Through this, the doctor kept yelling, "Open your eyes! Open your eyes!" I finally turned to him, and although I could not open my eyes, I still could move my body. I turned to him with outstretched arms raised toward him, and beseeched him with the totality of my being, as I could not speak, to turn off The Machine. The pain was so intense that I thought it was about to kill me.'

Another patient, in this revealing article, told the reporter that Dr. Honig offered to kill her father for her (no doubt a 'staged drama' to 'help her get well').

He paused for a moment and then said, 'Do you want to go to bed with your father?'

'No,' she answered. 'Do you want to go to bed with your daughters?'

'I did entertain the thought. Yes, I've thought of it,' Honig said.

'That's sick,' she said, 'that's really sick. What kind of doctor are you talking to me about sex with your daughters and telling me you're willing to kill my father?'

Just then another female patient entered the room. Honig put his arm around her and pulled her down on his lap. He held her hand and rested his head against her hair. 'Do you object to me sleeping with Carol?' he asked.

'I think your behavior is out of line,' Jennie said. 'I think this is a psychiatric farce. I think that any sane person listening to this conversation would say this is not right. I'm being held here against my will and I think *you're* insane.'

'It's you who've been diagnosed a hebephrenic schizophrenic,' Honig replied. 'Is there anything more I can help you with today?'

Several staff members wrote letters in support of the ad hoc committee. For example, in a letter written October 5, 1978, one confessed with admirable honesty:

> This level of vilification and denial of human dignity puts the lie to the insistent claims made by Dr. Honig and others that the assaults made on patients are made with 'love.' And my own inaction during this brutality, rationalized as 'they know what they're doing,' fueled by a high degree of moral confusion and paralysis, and overlain with fear, describes, I am sorry to say, the response of many well-meaning people when confronted by experiences like this at the foundation.

Another staff member, in a letter of October 12 wrote, courageously:

> I blame the whole Foundation for tolerating, even rewarding, this over and over again. In many ways I am as much to blame as the others because I didn't take outside action sooner than I have. I now know better. I just hope it is not too late.

Other letters described further abuses. For example:

> The clinic confused humiliating with the idea of regression. D. shackled by the ankles to a bench was shaved by Buck Strauch, a family therapist, Michael Stone, a live-in ancillary therapist, and Dr. Mintz. D.'s head, chest and eyebrows were completely shaved clean. I remember D. sitting mutely with a look of complete defeat on his face. This was not a solemn occasion for the therapists, as I remember the laughing and joking.

The same person wrote: 'An entry in my journal: November 11, 1975 finds N. still in a playpen in a straight jacket and diapers even though it was her birthday.'

The only result of all this exposure (many newspapers in Philadelphia carried the stories and clearly believed them) was that the Department of Public Welfare intervened and demanded that the Foundation be 'monitored' for six months.

I called Dr. Honig on November 2, 1986, and spoke with him. He told me that his foundation had recently been approved by the Joint Committee for the Accreditation of Hospitals. He said, pointedly, that *most* of the accusations made against him were false. He admitted having used a cattle prod, but had given it up because of the bad publicity. He said that it was a crazy method, but that it had seemed to work. I asked him if he continued to use other methods he had learned from John Rosen. He said that he did, using physical methods that included shaking patients, sitting on them, and wrestling with them. He said that times had changed, and that people were concerned about abuse and patients' rights and so on, and quite correctly so. Therefore, today he would use something like the cattle prod only experimentally. But he still continued to use the nurturing bottle containing warm milk, which a female therapist feeds, from her lap, to psychotic patients. Dr. Honig also told me of 'mother dolls,' life-sized dolls that patients can take to bed with them. He said that he didn't know what patients did with them, although they did at times destroy them. Dr. Honig also said that he had stopped using burials, a process wherein he had dug graves and buried 'parts of the insanity.' Dr. Honig now had about one hundred and twenty employees and about three dozen patients. The Foundation continues to provide training, consultation, and outpatient programming for hundreds of patients a month in the Bucks County area and beyond, as well as diagnostic and treatment services in forensic and correctional psychology. This means that the kind of abuse we have seen is not just tolerated by society, it is encouraged, and is spread to the wider community. One can only guess how many people's lives have been ruined or damaged by the spirit of John Rosen.

There seems to be no way to measure how widespread such abuse is. It is, of course, part of the thesis of this book that abuse of one form or another is built into the very fabric of psychotherapy –

that power corrupts, that psychiatric power corrupts just as political power does, and that the greater the power (and a psychiatrist's power is great indeed), the greater the propensity for corruption. Even more than politicians, therapists, by the very nature of their profession, are protected from usual forms of scrutiny. Psychotherapy is a self-policing profession. The psychotherapeutic relationship is a privileged one, protected by a tradition of secrecy (usually called 'confidentiality'). Psychotherapists almost always encourage their patients not to speak about what happens during a session. To do so is branded a form of acting out. Talking (and, by extension, talking about the faults of the therapist) outside the session about the session is considered to dilute the force of the therapy. It is a diversion of energy, so goes the rationalization, but one that, conveniently, insulates the patient from the community of family and friends. The very fact of investing in therapy, both financially and emotionally, means that one is bound to attempt to protect it from criticism. It is not unlike the reaction to well-meant attempts by outsiders to point to the flaws in one's mate: such criticism is rarely well received. The ways that a therapist can harm a patient are as varied as they are in any intimate relationship. A person can be harmed financially (paying more money than is comfortable, or, if rich, being exploited for financial information), emotionally, physically (e.g., becoming dependent on drugs), and sexually.

The profession has, by and large, ignored all of these possible areas of harm as fields of study, with the recent exception of the sexual exploitation of patients by therapists. For many years even this was almost never mentioned, except in private. I remember that one of the first seminars I attended when I was a candidate in psychoanalytic training was given by an elderly psychoanalyst from Montreal, who immediately informed us that a major part of his clinical practice consisted of analysts who had had sexual involvements with patients. He told us ten students that many of us, before our careers were finished, would become sexually involved with a patient. This was in the early 1970s, and there was virtually no literature on this topic. Nevertheless, we had no reason to believe that this distinguished analyst was in any sense exaggerating. Before the decade was over, an increasing body of literature addressed the subject. One reason, obviously, was that there were a number of landmark cases in which large awards were made to individuals who had sued therapists. There is no sense in pretending to the general public that something never happened when it is in the newspapers. But sexual involvement with patients, while privately tolerated, has never really been condoned. (I have never heard of a case where an analyst was dropped from the profession for sexual indiscretion, though several cases were much discussed in the analytic community. When a training analyst in London was openly sleeping with several of his patients, he was reprimanded to the extent of losing, temporarily, several of his official positions in the analytic society.) I believe the real reason that there has been recognition on the part of psychiatrists and psychotherapists generally of the danger of sleeping with patients is that it is a straw danger. It is easy to acknowledge and can then serve to cover up the many greater abuses that go on in daily practice which never reach public awareness. The value of the recent writing about this topic is that it dispels one of the myths that I am trying to combat in this book, namely, that such abuse is extremely rare. Just as the psychiatric profession admitted that incest and sexual assault in childhood existed, but dismissed their theoretical importance by claiming that such cases were one in a million (when in fact they are more like one in three[6]), so also psychiatrists were prepared to admit that sexual exploitation of patients happened, but so rarely that it need not be taken all that seriously. A review of the literature, therefore, will help us to see if this is really correct.

One of the most instructive cases is found early in the history of psychotherapy, but it only recently came to light. I am referring to Sabina Spielrein and her 'affair' with her analyst, Carl Jung.[7] Spielrein (1885–1941) came from a wealthy Russian Jewish family from Rostov-on-Don. She was raised speaking four languages (Russian, German, English, and French). At the age of fourteen she manifested what Jung was later to call symptoms of 'psychotic hysteria.' In 1904, when she was nineteen years old, her parents sent her to Zurich, to the Burghölzli Clinic, where her doctor was Carl Jung. From 1905 to 1909 she was an outpatient of Jung. Her analysis ended abruptly in 1909. In 1911 she completed her

[6] See, for example, Diana E. H. Russell, *The Secret Trauma: Incest in the Lives of Girls and Women* (New York: Basic Books, 1986).

[7] Although many analysts seem to believe she slept with Jung, there is no evidence in the historical documents that this actually happened.

medical studies in Zurich and became a doctor. In 1912 she married the Russian Jewish doctor Pawel Scheftel in Zurich, published her first psychoanalytic paper, and became a member of the Vienna Psychoanalytic Society. In 1913 she gave birth to a daughter, Renata. She spent some time in Geneva, where she was the analyst of Jean Piaget. In 1923 she and her husband and daughter returned to Russia. In 1925 she gave birth to a second daughter, Eva. In 1926 she returned, with her family, to Rostov, where she practiced psychoanalysis and became a training analyst. In 1938 her father and husband died. When the Germans invaded the Soviet Union in 1941, Spielrein was seen with her two daughters in Rostov-on-Don being herded into a synagogue, where she was shot by the Nazis.[8]

In 1980 a book by Aldo Carotenuto was published in Italy, and it appeared in English two years later as *A Secret Symmetry: Sabina Spielrein between Jung and Freud*.[9] This was a report on a series of documents found in the Palais Wilson in Geneva, which included a diary (1909–1912) by Sabina Spielrein, letters from Spielrein to Jung, letters from Spielrein to Freud, letters from Freud to Spielrein, and letters from Jung to Spielrein. (Permission was not given to publish the letters from Jung, but they have now been included in the German edition, published in 1986.)[10]

In 1908, while Spielrein was still being treated by Jung, they fell in love. Jung was married at the time, but had preached polygamy to Spielrein.[11] She refused that and apparently asked him to leave

---

[8]The information about her death comes from a Swedish journalist, Magnus Ljunggreen, in 'Sabina mellan Jung och Freud' (*Expressen* [1983]: 15).

[9]Translated by Arno Pomerans, John Shepley, and Krishna Wilson (New York: Random House, 1982); paperback edition, with commentary by Bruno Bettelheim (New York: Pantheon Books, 1984).

[10]*Tagebuch einer heimlichen Symmetrie: Sabina Spielrein zwischen Jung und Freud* (Freiburg: Kore Verlag, 1986). The German edition corrects the German text in many cases; the English version was based on an uncorrected German text. It also contains an excellent introduction by Johannes Cremerius, a Freudian analyst who is nonetheless willing to call it 'a terrible story' and one that reflects very badly on Freud, not to mention Jung.

[11]Jung's letters to Spielrein (1908–1919) are not particularly revealing. Nevertheless, there is no doubt that he gave her to believe he was searching for his beloved in her. In the second letter preserved, July 30, 1908, he told her:'You cannot believe how much it means to me to find a person I dare to love . . . How great would be my luck to find that person in you.' On December 4, 1908, he wrote to her: 'I am searching for the person who understands how

his wife, which he would not do, and the affair ended rather badly. It does not seem to have led to actual intercourse, only kissing. Spielrein refers to 'poetry' sessions but never makes clear what they consisted in; she did tell Freud, however, in a letter of June 10, 1909, that Jung was the first man to kiss her. Writing to Freud in 1907, Jung said that he was treating a patient who 'admits that actually her greatest wish is to have a child by me.'[12] He had already told Freud about Spielrein, but without indicating that he had any romantic interest in her. Then on March 7, 1909, he wrote Freud again, but this time he concealed the identity of the patient:

> The last and worst straw is that a complex is playing Old Harry with me: a woman patient, whom years ago I pulled out of a very sticky neurosis with unstinting effort, has violated my confidence and my friendship in the most mortifying way imaginable. She has kicked up a vile scandal solely because I denied myself the pleasure of giving her a child. I have always acted the gentleman towards her, but before the bar of my rather too sensitive conscience I nevertheless don't feel clean, and that is what hurts the most because my intentions were always honourable. But you know how it is – the devil can use even the best of things for the fabrication of filth [207].

Freud responded two days later:

> I too have had news of the woman patient through whom you became acquainted with the neurotic gratitude of the spurned. When Muthmann came to see me, he spoke of a lady who had introduced herself to him as your mistress, thinking he would be duly impressed by your having retained so much freedom.

---

[11] *Cont.* to love without punishing the other person, without imprisoning him or sucking him dry; I am searching for this person in the future who will make it possible for love to be independent of social prejudices or social disadvantages, so that love can always be its own goal, rather than only a means to a goal.' (*Ich suche den Menschen, der zu lieben versteht, ohne damit den Anderen zu strafen, einzusperren und auszusaugen; ich suche diesen zukünftigen Menschen, der es verwirklicht, dass Liebe unabhängig von sozialen Vor-oder Nachteilen sein kann, damit die Liebe immer Selbstzweck und nicht immer nur Mittel zum Zweck sei.*)

[12] July 6, 1907. *The Freud/Jung Letters*, ed. by William McGuire (Princeton: Princeton University Press, 1974), 72. All letters between Freud and Jung cited in this chapter are from this collection.

But we both presumed that the situation was quite different and that the *only possible explanation* was a neurosis in his informant. To be slandered and scorched by the love with which we operate – such are the perils of our trade, which we are certainly not going to abandon on their account [210]. [Italics added.]

Jung wrote back a hypocritical denial:

The story hawked round by Muthmann is Chinese to me. I've never really had a mistress and am the most innocent of spouses. Hence my terrific moral reaction! I simply cannot imagine who it might have been. I don't think it is the same lady. Such stories give me the horrors [212].

A few months later, on May 30, 1909, Sabina Spielrein wrote her first letter to Freud: 'I would be most grateful to you if you would grant me a brief audience! It has to do with something of greatest importance to me which you would probably be interested to hear about' (91).

Freud immediately wrote to Jung (June 3), enclosing the letter and telling Jung: 'Weird! What is she? A busybody, a chatterbox, or a paranoiac?' (226).

The next day Jung wrote a letter in which he attempted to hide from Freud what had really taken place:

Spielrein is the person I wrote you about. She was published in abbreviated form in my Amsterdam lecture of blessed memory. She was, so to speak, my test case, for which reason I remembered her with special gratitude and affection. Since I knew from experience that she would immediately relapse if I withdrew my support, I prolonged the relationship over the years and in the end found myself morally obliged, as it were, to devote a large measure of friendship to her, until I saw that an unintended wheel had started turning, whereupon I finally broke with her. She was, of course, systematically planning my seduction, which I considered inopportune. Now she is seeking revenge. Lately she has been spreading a rumour that I shall soon get a divorce from my wife and marry a certain girl student, which has thrown not a few of my colleagues into a flutter. What she is now planning is unknown to me. Nothing good, I suspect, unless perhaps you are imposed upon to act as a go-between. I need hardly say that I have made a clean break. . . . Gross and Spielrein are bitter experiences. To none of my patients have I extended so much friendship and from none have I reaped so much sorrow [228].

Freud responded on June 7:

Such experiences, though painful, are necessary and hard to avoid. Without them we cannot really know life and what we are dealing with. I myself have never been taken in quite so badly, but I have come very close to it a number of times and had *a narrow escape*. I believe that only grim necessities weighing on my work, and the fact that I was ten years older than yourself when I came to psychoanalysis, have saved me from similar experiences. But no lasting harm is done. They help us to develop the thick skin we need and to dominate 'countertransference,' which is after all a permanent problem for us. . . . The way these women manage to charm us with every conceivable psychic perfection until they have attained their purpose is one of nature's greatest spectacles [230].

The next day, June 8, Freud wrote to Spielrein:

Dr. Jung is my friend and colleague; I think I know him in other respects as well, and have reason to believe that he is incapable of frivolous or ignoble behavior . . . Did his readiness to help a person in mental distress perhaps kindle your sympathy? I am tempted to think so, for I know of many similar instances [113–114].

Two days later, Spielrein sent Freud the letter in which she indicated that Jung was the first man to kiss her and that he wrote that 'a kiss without consequences costs 10 francs.' The next day she sent him a full letter, in which she quoted from a most remarkable document, a letter that Jung sent to her mother (who had received an anonymous letter, possibly sent by Emma Jung, Jung's wife, that Jung was ruining her daughter):

A *doctor* and his *patient*, on the other hand, can talk of the most intimate matters for as long as they like, and the patient may expect her doctor to give her all the love and concern she requires. But the doctor knows his limits and will never cross them, for he is *paid* for his trouble. That imposes the necessary restraints on him. Therefore I would suggest that if you wish me to adhere strictly to my role as doctor, you should pay me a fee as suitable recompense for my trouble. In that way you may be *absolutely certain* that I will respect my duty as a doctor *under all circumstances.* . . . My fee is 10 francs per consultation [94].

The next letter is from Freud to Jung, dated June 18, 1909: 'Fräulein Spielrein has admitted in her second letter that her business has to do with you; apart from that, she has not disclosed her intentions' (234–35). It would appear from this statement that Spielrein did not send him the letter quoted above until a later date, if at all.[13] Freud goes on to say: 'In view of the kind of matter we work with, it will never be possible to avoid little laboratory explosions.'

Jung, however, took the problem more seriously than Freud did, and on June 21, he wrote him explaining that he had since learned that the rumor about him had not come from Spielrein, and that he had been less than candid with Freud:

[13] Carotenuto, in his introduction, wrote: 'Of the letters to Freud, only the first (30 May 1909) is complete. The other, written in several installments (between 10 June and 20 June 1909), lacks a few pages. . . . The letters to Freud are written on small folding cards and may actually be rough drafts, since there are a number of crossed-out words and corrections' (17). It seems likely, therefore, that this long letter was never sent to Freud, especially since there is no indication, anywhere, that he ever became aware of the contents of Jung's letter to Spielrein's mother. One can only wonder what his reaction would have been. Note that Cremerius, in the introduction to the German text (11–12), is under the impression that Freud received Spielrein's letter with an enclosed letter from Jung to her mother, and therefore judges Freud's response all the more harshly. But he seems to be mistaken here, though otherwise his introduction is excellent. Bruno Bettelheim, in his commentary in the paperback edition of Carotenuto's book, also assumes that Freud knew: 'Although Freud knew from this letter the impossible situation into which Spielrein had been projected by Jung's behavior, he still refused to meet her and continued to dissimulate to her' (30).

I discussed with her the problem of the child, imagining that I was talking theoretically, but naturally Eros was lurking in the background. Thus I imputed all the other wishes and hopes entirely to my patient without seeing the same thing in myself. When the situation had become so tense that the continued perseveration of the relationship could be rounded out only by sexual acts, I defended myself in a manner that cannot be justified morally. Caught in my delusion that I was the victim of the sexual wiles of my patient, I wrote to her mother that I was not the gratifier of her daughter's sexual desires but merely her doctor, and that she should free me from her. In view of the fact that the patient had shortly before been my friend and enjoyed my full confidence, my action was a piece of knavery which I very reluctantly confess to you as my father. I would now like to ask you a great favour: would you please write a note to Frl. Spielrein, telling her that I have fully informed you of the matter, and especially of the letters to her parents, which is what I regret most [236].

When Freud received the letter, he immediately (June 24, 1909) wrote a letter of apology to Spielrein:

Dear colleague:
I have today learned something from Dr. Jung himself about the subject of your proposed visit to me, and now see that I have divined some matters correctly but that I had construed others wrongly and to your disadvantage. I must ask your forgiveness on this latter count. However, the fact that I was wrong and that the lapse has to be blamed on the man and not the woman, as my young friend himself admits, satisfies my need to hold women in high regard. Please accept this expression of my entire sympathy for the dignified way in which you have resolved the conflict [114–15].

On January 20, 1913, Freud wrote to Spielrein: 'My personal relationship with your German hero has definitely been shattered. His behavior was too bad.[14] Since I received that first letter from

[14] The German reads: *Sein Benehmen war zu schlecht*. Freud means that Jung's behavior toward him was too bad to continue their relationship.

you, my opinion of him has greatly altered.' On May 8 of that same year, Freud told her bluntly: 'I imagine that you love Dr. J. so deeply still because you have not brought to light the hatred he merits.' When she tells Freud that she is going to have a child, Freud writes (August 28):

> I can hardly bear to listen when you continue to enthuse about your old love and past dreams, and count on an ally in the marvelous little stranger. I am, as you know, cured of the last shred of my predilection for the Aryan cause, and would like to take it that if the child turns out to be a boy he will develop into a stalwart Zionist [120].

Carotenuto continues to defend Jung when he writes: 'In the situation in which Jung found himself, Sabina must have expressed a typical image of the anima, attracting and repelling, wondrous and diabolical, exciting and depressing' [161]. In light of what happened, it is astonishing that he can write also:

> It is like appropriating the strength and courage of the analyst in order to face up to and accept the truth about oneself. One grows through the analyst's patience, his understanding, his sense of justice, and what is experienced as his unbounded wisdom [165].

Bruno Bettelheim, too, in an outrageous passage in his commentary ends by excusing Jung for his behavior on the grounds that it 'cured' the patient:

> Whatever may be one's judgment of Jung's behavior toward Spielrein, probably his first psychoanalytic patient, one must not disregard its most important consequence: he cured her from the disturbance for which she had been entrusted to his care. In retrospect we ought to ask ourselves: what convincing evidence do we have that the same result would have been achieved if Jung had behaved toward her in the way we must expect a conscientious therapist to behave toward his patient? However questionable Jung's behavior was from a moral point of view – however unorthodox, even disreputable, it may have been – somehow it met the prime obligation of the

therapist toward his patient: to cure her. True, Spielrein paid a very high price in unhappiness, confusion, and disillusion for the particular way in which she got cured, but then this is often true for mental patients who are as sick as she was [38].

This is a typical passage from a typical therapist. Even when forced to admit that behavior, by any standards, is wrong, the therapist can fall back on the excuse that the patient was 'very sick' even if this has merely to be assumed. How, after all, does Bettelheim know how 'sick' Sabina Spielrein was, except from the word of Jung, who, as even Bettelheim would acknowledge, had every reason to play up the degree of her illness to make his own achievement seem more important? Rosen, Honig, Jung, Bettelheim, all operate on similar assumptions, the very assumptions that underly all psychotherapy.

There have been a number of books on the topic of sexual abuse of patients, notably *Betrayal*, by Lucy Freeman,[15] *Therapist*, by Ellen Plaisl,[16] and *A Killing Cure*, by Evelyn Walker and Perry Deane Young.[17] Moreover, psychiatrists and psychoanalysts have addressed this topic for some time. A celebrated comment comes from Freud's admonishment to Ferenczi. Ferenczi reported to Freud that he was not opposed to kissing his patients from time to time. Freud wrote him an often-quoted letter in which he humorously disagreed with his student. There can be no doubt that Freud himself was opposed to any form of physical contact between the analyst and the patient. In an article called 'The Erotic Transference,' the analyst Leon J. Saul repeated the story about Freud and Ferenczi and warned against becoming sexually involved with patients.[18] Characteristically, Saul was still more concerned with fantasies and acting out by the patient rather than with reality and actions on the part of the analyst: 'The transference is in its essence infantile and incestuous . . . sexual elements are threatening in the

[15] Based on the personal account of Julie Roy (New York: Stein & Day, 1976).
[16] New York: St. Martin's Press, 1985.
[17] New York: Henry Holt and Co., 1986.
[18] *The Psychoanalytic Quarterly* 31 (1962): 54–61.

transference as they were in childhood toward parents.'[19] But Saul gave no evidence that children feel this toward parents. In fact, in a gesture rare for a psychoanalyst, he even admitted that 'analysts know too well the emotional warping caused in children by sexually seductive and abusive parents.'

When a distinguished psychoanalyst, Charles Clay Dahlberg, wrote an article called 'Sexual Contact Between Patient and Therapist,' he admitted that for years 'I had trouble getting this paper accepted by larger organizations where I had ... influence.'[20] The reason for the difficulty was that Dahlberg had the honesty to talk about what the analyst did. We should remember that only twenty-five years ago a petition was circulated demanding the resignation of Harold Greenwald from the New York State Psychological Association because he suggested at an annual meeting that the subject of therapist-client sex should be studied.[21] A certain amount of bad press was caused by the antics of two psychiatrists who publicly argued for the value of sleeping with patients (and admitted that they did so). Thus Dr. J. L. McCartney published an article in which he said that in forty years of practice, thirty percent of his adult women 'patients' 'expressed some form of Overt Transference, such as sitting on the analyst's lap, holding his hand, hugging or kissing him. About 10% find it necessary to act-out extremely, such as mutual undressing, genital manipulation or coitus.'[22] (Notice that McCartney implies that the patient is the sexual aggressor.) In 1972 the distinguished psychiatrist Judd Marmor, in an article called 'Sexual acting-out in psychotherapy,' began by admitting that psychiatrists and psychoanalysts had already written a great deal about the seductive patient, but almost nothing about the seductive therapist.[23] In 1973 the American Psychiatric Association adopted the American

[19] The term 'acting out' is just a smokescreen for actions the analyst doesn't like, so naturally the term refers to what the patient does; when the analyst does something that his colleagues don't like, if they find out about it, they call it 'acting in.'

[20] Contemporary Psychoanalysis 6 (1970): 107–24.

[21] However, this information comes from Martin Shepard's book The Love Treatment: Sexual Intimacy Between Patients and Psychotherapists (New York: Peter H. Wyden, 1971), which advocates sexual contact with some patients, so it must be taken with a grain of salt.

[22] 'Overt transference,' in Journal of Sex Research 2 (1966): 227–37.

[23] Psychiatry in Transition: Selected Papers of Judd Marmor, M.D. (New York: Brunner/Mazel, 1974).

Medical Association's blunt statement that 'sexual activity with a patient is unethical.'[24] (The American Psychological Association followed the next year.)

What was not known until 1973 was the number of psychiatrists who engaged in sexual practices with patients. In 1973 Sheldon H. Kardener, Marielle Fuller, and Ivan N. Mensh published 'A survey of physicians' attitudes and practices regarding erotic and non-erotic contact with patients,' in which they questioned four hundred and sixty physicians (including psychiatrists) and found that five to thirteen percent engaged in some kind of erotic behavior with their patients.[25] In an article the next year, Dr. Kardener is unequivocally against such contact, and ends by quoting Eric Berne: 'If you want the patient to be your therapist, be sure first that you can afford to pay him your usual fee.'[26] The American Psychological Association conducted an identical survey in 1977 and found that of seven hundred and three respondents 10.9 percent engaged in erotic contact.[27] Alan Stone, a psychiatrist and lawyer, wrote an article in 1976 in which he quotes the analyst Willard Gaylin as saying: 'There are absolutely no circumstances which permit a psychiatrist to engage in sex with his patients.' Nevertheless, Stone concludes, gloomily and unconvincingly: 'In the end, in this as in most other things, patients must depend on the decent moral character of those entrusted to treat them.'[28] This was a slender reed on which to depend, given that surveys were revealing that one out of ten psychotherapists had sexual contact with patients.

Psychiatrists are genuinely concerned with sexual abuse of

[24] 'The principles of medical ethics with annotations especially applicable to psychiatry,' *American Journal of Psychiatry* 130 (1973): 1058–64.

[25] *American Journal of Psychiatry* 130 (1973): 1077–81.

[26] 'Sex and the physician-patient relationship,' *American Journal of Psychiatry* 131 (1974): 1134–36. See, too, J. A. Perry, 'Physicians' erotic and nonerotic physical involvement with patients,' *American Journal of Psychiatry* 133 (1976): 838–40.

[27] Jean Corey Holroyd and Annette M. Brodsky, 'Psychologists' attitudes and practices regarding erotic and nonerotic physical contact with patients,' *American Psychologist* 32 (1977): 843–49.

[28] 'The legal implications of sexual activity between psychiatrist and patient,' *American Journal of Psychiatry* 133 (1976): 1138–41. There is a useful survey of the literature on this topic by Barbie J. Taylor and Nathaniel N. Wagner, 'Sex between therapists and clients: a review and analysis,' *Professional Psychology* 7 (1976): 593–601.

patients by members of their own profession. They have taken a clear stance against it, and one would be hard pressed to find a reputable psychiatrist to say that it could be harmless. Even the more-than-two-thousand-year-old Hippocratic Oath explicitly states that a physician must not seduce a patient:

> In every house where I come I will enter only for the good of my patients, keeping myself far from all intentional ill-doing and all seduction and especially from the pleasures of love with women or with men, be they free or slaves.[29]

State legislatures have made the same prohibition a matter of law. Nevertheless, there is some reason to believe that the professional societies have not been eager to take action to uphold their rules. This is demonstrated quite clearly in an article by Joseph R. Sanders and Patricia Keith-Spiegel of the Committee on Scholarly and Professional Ethics and Conduct of the American Psychological Association, in which they summarize the case of a psychologist who was accused by eight women of having made improper advances. He lost his license from the state. However, he did not wish to lose his membership in the American Psychological Society as well. It was brought to the society's attention, and a letter was sent to him asking for his explanation:

> The psychologist responded promptly and thoroughly. He admitted that he had a major problem but . . . he had been in individual therapy for almost one year and had joined a local self-help group for Ph.D. and MD level professionals with personal problems that had a negative effect on their ability to deliver quality services . . . His sincere desire and efforts to become rehabilitated led CSPEC to vote against expulsion.[30]

Feminists have been more sensitive to these issues than have psychiatrists, no doubt because women are the ones who suffer most from unethical behavior. As early as 1972, Phyllis Chesler, in her best-selling book *Women and Madness*, discussed the fact that

[29] Cited in William A. N. Dorland's *Illustrated Medical Dictionary*, 24th edition (Philadelphia: W. B. Saunders Company, 1965), 680.
[30] 'Formal and informal adjudication of ethics complaints against psychologists,' *American Psychologist* 35 (1980): 1096–1105.

women are so often sexually abused by their therapists as part of her penetrating analysis of the power imbalance in psychotherapy. (She did not wish to see psychotherapy dismantled, however, only reformed, a position I cannot share.)[31] Once women began to look into the matter in more statistical depth, the figures, not surprisingly, became higher. The latest survey (made in 1983) shows that something like fifteen percent of therapists have had sexual contact with a patient. And we must remember that these are only the number willing to talk about it.[32]

The problem with all these surveys is that they are taken of offenders. Imagine attempting to find out how many men had raped by asking nonconvicted rapists whether they were guilty of rape. Or imagine attempting to find the number of incest victims in a given community by asking all the fathers in that community how many of them had committed incest. No survey, as far as I know, has approached a representative sample of patients. I am sure that if this were done, the figures would be much higher. The profession itself is obviously not keen on doing sophisticated research in the field, or any research that would make the public more aware of the dangers. Recently insurance companies have refused to insure psychotherapists against sexual-abuse allegations. But when they were willing to do so, it was immeasurably more difficult to get a conviction. Remember that first the woman (it is almost always a woman) must get up the courage to accuse her therapist. Then she must be able to convince some official board to take action. The board itself must often convince a judicial branch to move, and so on.[33] In other words, the chances of the original abuse being discovered is minimal. Of even greater importance is the prejudice at every level against the woman who makes such an accusation. The most common response is not to

[31] New York: Doubleday & Co., 1972.

[32] See Jacqueline Bouhoutsos, 'Sexual intimacy between psychotherapists and clients: policy implications for the future,' in *Women and Mental Health Policy*, ed. by Lenore E. Walker (Beverly Hills: Sage Publications, 1984), 207–28.

[33] 'A very small number of victims ever complain to any authority. Roughly three quarters to one half of all victims are unaware that sex between therapists and patients is unethical or actionable. However, among those who are aware, only between one and four percent of victims ever take action.' *Report of the Senate Task Force on Psychotherapists' and Patients' Sexual Relations*. Prepared for the California Senate Rules Committee, March 1987. (Available from: Joint Publications, State Capitol, Box 90, Sacramento, CA 95814.)

believe her. A remarkable example of this comes from an article published in 1971:

> It seems fair to state that the greatest number of actions are brought by women who lead lives of very quiet desperation, who form close attachments to their therapists, who feel rejected or spurned when they discover that relations are maintained on a formal and professional level, and who then react with allegations of sexual improprieties.[34]

How does this man know that a woman who makes such an accusation is leading a life of quiet desperation? How does he know that such women feel rejected by being sexually refused, rather than feeling exploited by being sexually used? This article implies that almost all allegations of sexual abuse are false. The odds are otherwise: in every other area of sexual crime – rape, incest, child molestation – the reported instances have turned out to represent only a small fraction of the number of actual abuses that occur.

Just as no survey has examined the prevalence of sexual abuse by asking patients, so no systematic attempt has been made to discover the extent to which patients feel they have been abused in other ways – by being bullied, exploited, demeaned, degraded, ignored, ridiculed, taken advantage of, and so on. It may well be that people feel it is still worth the risk. But let us at least become aware of the actual dangers. Informed consent must include, I believe, a realization of the many ways in which psychotherapy may not do what it claims to do.

This brings up a topic that I had hoped to avoid, namely, the results of psychotherapy. I had wished to avoid it because it seemed to me such a subjective field. True, I had heard from many people who had been in analysis for many years that, in the end, they felt it had been a mistake, or a waste of time, or a waste of money, or harmful. But I had also heard, just as frequently, the opposite from other people, that psychoanalysis (or psychotherapy) had saved their lives, gotten them through a divorce or a death, been of immense benefit, saved them from some disaster or another (choosing the wrong partner, the wrong profession). Also, I had heard lukewarm accounts, from people who said that it was

[34] John J. Brownfain, 'The American Psychological Association Professional Liability Insurance Program,' *American Psychologist* 26 (1971): 648–52.

neither wonderful nor miserable, but simply okay, or it had helped them find out something about themselves. What could 'research' in this subjective area possibly teach us? But when I did finally read the literature I was impressed by how poorly psychotherapy seemed to fare. At least, I felt, one should be aware of this literature.

Awareness of the poor results of psychotherapy began in 1952, with a brief article by H. J. Eysenck, 'The effects of psychotherapy: an evaluation,' whose pessimistic, almost cynical conclusion unleashed great consternation among therapists:

> There appears to be an inverse correlation between recovery and psychotherapy; the more psychotherapy, the smaller the recovery rate ... roughly two-thirds of a group of neurotic patients will recover or improve to a marked extent within two years of the onset of their illness, whether they are treated by means of psychotherapy or not.[35]

The publication of this article resulted in a barrage of criticism by psychotherapists, who attempted to show how untrue Eysenck's results were.[36] Eysenck himself returned to the topic in 1960[37] and concluded:

> Psychologists and psychiatrists will have to acknowledge the fact that current psychotherapeutic procedures have not lived up to the hope which greeted their emergence 50 years ago. All methods of psychotherapy fail to improve on the recovery rate obtained through ordinary life experiences.

We must remember that Eysenck was pushing another brand of therapy, behavior modification, which was certainly not superior

---

[35] *Journal of Consulting Psychology* 16 (1952): 319–24.

[36] See A. E. Bergin, 'The evaluation of therapeutic outcomes,' in *Handbook of Psychotherapy and Behavior Change: An Empirical Analysis*, ed. by A. E. Bergin and S. L. Garfield (New York: John Wiley & Sons, 1971), 217–70; P. Meehl, 'Discussion of Eysenck, "The Effects of Psychotherapy,"' *International Journal of Psychiatry* 1 (1965): 156–57. The entire topic is discussed with elaborate bibliographical references in S. J. Rachman and G. T. Wilson, *The Effects of Psychological Therapy*, 2nd enlarged ed. (Oxford: Pergamon Press, 1980).

[37] *The Effects of Psychotherapy* (New York: International Science Press, 1960), last page.

to any of the therapies he criticized, no matter what kind of 'success' rates he achieved.

Nevertheless, Eysenck's discouraging conclusions have been replicated many times. Indeed, one of the most interesting studies came from somebody on the other side from Eysenck, which is why its results can be taken with some degree of confidence. The distinguished psychotherapy researcher Hans Strupp wrote an article in 1979 in which he concluded that 'patients undergoing psychotherapy with college professors [from unrelated disciplines] showed, on the average, quantitatively as much improvement as patients treated by experienced professional psychotherapists.'[38] If this is really the case, why then bother to have elaborate, expensive, and pretentious training institutes? As early as 1973 Strupp had concluded that

> contrary to my earlier views, I have become increasingly skeptical that psychotherapy has anything 'special' to offer, in the sense that its techniques exceed or transcend the gains that may accrue to a patient (or should we say learner?) from a highly constructive human relationship.[39]

Some psychologists have been willing to concede the real difficulties in psychotherapy,[40] and many thoughtful psychotherapists have also admitted that psychotherapy has the potential to cause great harm to patients.[41] If we think about it, we can see,

[38] 'Specific vs. non-specific factors in psychotherapy: a controlled study of outcome,' *Archives of General Psychiatry* 36 (1979): 1125–36.

[39] *Psychotherapy: Clinical Research and Theoretical Issues* (New York: Jason Aronson, 1973), 481.

[40] For example, Sol L. Garfield, in his 1980 speech to the American Psychological Association (from which he won the Distinguished Professional Contribution to Knowledge Award), called 'Psychotherapy: A Forty-Year Appraisal' (*American Psychologist* 36 [1981]: 174–83), seemed to concede the fact that no progress at all appeared to have been made in the field, or at least no progress that would be universally acknowledged.

[41] S. W. Hadley and Hans Strupp, in their article 'Contemporary views of negative effects in psychotherapy' (*Archives of General Psychiatry* 33 [1976]: 1291–1302), demonstrated that most psychotherapists agreed that the problem of harm was real (often leading, for example, to suicide). This is also the conclusion of M. J. Lambert, A. E. Bergin, and J. L. Collins in 'Therapist-induced deterioration in psychotherapy,' in *Effective Psychotherapy: A Handbook of Research*, ed. by Alan S. Gurman and Andrew M. Razin (New York: Pergamon Press, 1977), 452–81.

theoretically, the many ways in which psychotherapy can be harmful. But when we pass from theory to actual fact – that is, when we look at the evidence that can be accumulated without any great trouble, just as I have done in this chapter – we see case after case where psychotherapy, in actuality, was abused and people were harmed in concrete ways. It is true that we always have the option of saying that *these* cases represent exceptions. *These* cases represent the inversion of psychotherapy. But at what point do we begin to see that there must be something about psychotherapy itself that creates the conditions that make such abuse possible? For there is so much of it that it cannot be exceptional or our notion of a norm begins to lose its shape. Nevertheless, many readers may feel that I have concentrated only on the malevolent examples of therapy. Where are the benevolent therapists? Where are the therapists who, by universal recognition, are kind, compassionate, helpful human beings? In searching for a therapist with national recognition who could qualify for this position, I frequently came across the name of Carl Rogers. A number of my critics said to me that I should examine his work, that I would find none of the excesses of a Rosen or a Honig. In the next chapter, that is precisely what I do.

7

THE PROBLEM
WITH BENEVOLENCE:
Carl Rogers and Humanistic Psychology

After Rosen and Honig and therapists who sexually abuse their patients, Carl Rogers will seem like fresh air and goodness itself. The reader looking for fireworks such as those in the previous two chapters will not find them here. But the critique of Rogers is nonetheless important. To draw an inexact but perhaps illuminating analogy from political life, a benevolent depotism may make a better polity than a malign, Hitlerian one, but it remains a despotism, and is built, necessarily, on the same bedrock.

Perhaps the best-known critic of psychiatry is Thomas Szasz. But he has not widened his criticism to psychotherapy. In fact, quite the contrary. He believes that psychiatrists practice too little psychotherapy; that if they were more interested in psychotherapy, they would be better off. He has a preface to a recently published book in which he states this view, and he ends by saying: 'Real psychotherapy – that is to say, the humane and egalitarian "cure of souls," rather than the condescending paternalism of psychiatry, or the pretentious pseudo-science of psychoanalysis – is not about to disappear from the American scene.'[1] This view of the 'humane' value of psychotherapy, as opposed to its medical misuse, owes more to Carl Rogers (who died at the age of eighty-five in February 1987) than to any other person.

Carl Rogers's preeminence in the field of psychotherapy is almost universally acknowledged. For example, in a much-cited book, *Psychoanalysis and Psychotherapy: 36 Systems*,[2] Robert A. Harper says:

---

[1] *The Theoretic Dialogue: A Theoretical and Practical Guide to Psychotherapy*, by Soan Lal Sharma (Albuquerque: University of New Mexico Press, 1986).
[2] Englewood Cliffs, NJ: Prentice-Hall, 1959, 82.

The first system of psychotherapy of widespread prominence that has its roots almost exclusively in American psychology (as distinguished from psychiatry, on the one hand, and European sources, on the others) is what was originally called nondirective counseling and more recently client-centered therapy. The originator and outstanding exponent of the system is Carl Rogers.

Rogers's work reaches out to many other fields. As Richard Farson has written:

Professionals from education, religion, nursing, medicine, psychiatry, law, business, government, public health, law enforcement, race relations, social work – the list goes on and on – all came to feel that here, finally, was an approach which enabled them to succeed on the previously neglected human dimensions of their jobs, to reach the people for whom they felt responsible but were often unable to help.[3]

Carl Rogers was Professor of Psychology at the University of Chicago, President of the American Psychological Association (which gave him several awards, including the Distinguished Scientific Contribution Award and the Distinguished Professional Contributor Award), Fellow of the American Academy of Arts and Sciences. After resigning his position as Professor of Psychology and Psychiatry at the University of Wisconsin in 1963, he founded the Center for the Study of the Person in La Jolla, California. He was the author of books that have had a major impact on the general culture and on psychotherapy in particular.[4]

[3] Introduction to *Carl Rogers: The Man and His Ideas* by Richard I. Evans (New York: E. P. Dutton, 1975), xxx. Rogers himself said, in the same book: 'It means something to me to know that business executives read my stuff, educators at all levels, psychiatrists, psychologists, social workers, priests and ministers. The range of impact that my work has had is fantastic. I stand in awe of that myself' (112).

[4] These include: *Counseling and Psychotherapy: New Concepts in Practice* (1942), *Client-Centered Therapy: Its Current Practices, Implications, and Theory* (1951), *Psychotherapy and Personality Change* (1954), *On Becoming a Person* (1961), *The Therapeutic Relationship and Its Impact: A Study of Psychotherapy with Schizophrenics* (1967), *Person to Person: The Problem of Being Human* (1967), *Becoming Partners: Marriage and Its Alternatives* (1972), *Carl Rogers on Personal Power* (1977), *A Way of Being* (1980), and *Politics and Innocence: A Humanistic Debate (Rollo May, Carl Rogers, Abraham Maslow)* (1986). In addition, several books have been written about him, including Howard Kirschenbaum's *On Becoming Carl Rogers* (New York: Dell Publishing Co., 1979).

Rogers, with Rollo May and Abraham Maslow, is credited with being the founder, in the 1960s, of humanistic psychology (the 'third force,' to distinguish it from psychoanalysis and behaviorism), and he was one of the main figures in what is called 'the human potential movement.'

In the eyes of almost every therapist I have spoken to, Carl Rogers represents the opposite of John Rosen or Albert Honig. His method, many people have said to me, is what psychotherapy should be like. There are no horror stories from former clients (a word he popularized) of Carl Rogers. An examination of some of his ideas about psychotherapy, therefore, will certainly clarify for the reader my position on the dangers inherent in psychotherapy, no matter how benign it appears to be and how far removed from abuse.

It is unarguable that Rogers did away with some of the 'trappings' of the imbalance in the power relationship. He insisted on changing the designation 'patient' to 'client,' which, being more mercenary, is closer to the truth. He called his method 'client-centered' (or 'person-centered' or 'nondirective'), eschewing the label of expert or specialist. He demanded that training in psychotherapy be opened to all who showed talent, and not be restricted to those with professional or university degrees. He showed hostility to labeling and the use of diagnosis. He rejected the 'medical model of mental illness.' He was against all forms of manipulation within therapy. But it remains to be seen whether these modifications really touched the essential imbalance in the power relationship and the essential defects in the theory of therapy.

Rogers, in many publications, insisted that there were three conditions absolutely essential to successful therapy:

> First, and most important, is therapist congruence or genuineness – his ability to be a real person with the client. Second is the therapist's ability to accept the client as a separate person without judging him or evaluating him. It is rather an unconditional acceptance – that I'm able to accept you as you are. The third condition is a real empathic understanding . . . to find that here is a real person who really accepts and understands sensitively and accurately perceives just the way the world seems to me – that just seems to pull people forward.[5]

[5] *Carl Rogers: The Man and His Ideas*, 30.

But if we examine these conditions, we realize that they appear to be genuine only because the circumstances of therapy are artificial. Precisely because the client is seen for only a limited time (less than an hour, once a week), the therapist is (in theory; whether it actually happens is something else again) able to suspend his judgment. In fact, the therapist is *not* a real person with the client, for if he were, he would have the same reactions he would have with people in his real life, which certainly do not include 'unconditional acceptance,' lack of judging, or real empathic understanding. We do not 'really accept' everybody we meet. We are constantly judging them, rejecting some, avoiding some (and they us) with good reason. No real person really does any of the things Rogers prescribes in real life. So if the therapist manages to do so in a session, if he appears to be all-accepting and all-understanding, this is merely artifice; it is not reality. I am not saying that such an attitude might not be perceived as helpful by the client, but let us realize that the attitude is no more than playacting. It is the very opposite of what Rogers claims to be the central element in his therapy: genuineness.

Rogers believed that the ties he formed with his clients were central motivating forces in their lives. But this claim is totally at variance with the theories of Carl Rogers (and, from what I read, his life as well, for he refused to be a guru figure, though often given the opportunity). Thus, when asked about his views on Thomas Szasz's thesis concerning 'the myth of mental illness,' Rogers responded with an anecdote about a client hospitalized with a diagnosis of 'schizophrenic reaction – simple type.' Rogers saw him in the hospital twice a week for about a year and a half. Little was said. Some years later the client phoned to tell Rogers that he was doing well out of the hospital. Rogers commented:

> Now, was he schizophrenic? Oh, I don't know. He was a troubled person who was not able to cope with society, that was certain. The one thing that brought him out of it, I feel, was that we were able to form a close person-to-person relationship [95].

Rogers had not seen the person for eight years. He did not know what the client had been doing, whom he had been seeing. Nevertheless, he took credit for whatever 'cure' the client had achieved. He did not, evidently, do anything to help him get out of the institution. Yet he could confidently say that the relationship with him was the *one thing* that helped this man. Not only was this relationship completely one-sided, but also it was recounted exclusively from the viewpoint of the therapist. And we are led to believe that other factors in this man's life could not possibly have played the role that this supposedly 'real' relationship did. Here we can see that the therapist takes his therapy very seriously indeed.

Let us see how Rogers put these ideas more formally, in one of his best-known and much-anthologized pieces, 'The necessary and sufficient conditions of therapeutic personality change'[6]:

> For constructive personality change to occur, it is necessary that these conditions exist and continue over a period of time:
>
> 1 Two persons are in psychological contact.
> 2 The first, whom we shall term the client, is in a state of incongruence, being vulnerable or anxious.
> 3 The second person, whom we shall term the therapist, is congruent or integrated in the relationship.
> 4 The therapist experiences unconditional positive regard for the client.
> 5 The therapist experiences an empathic understanding of the client's internal frame of reference and endeavors to communicate this experience to the client.
> 6 The communication to the client of the therapists's empathic understanding and unconditional positive regard is to a minimal degree achieved.
>
> No other conditions are necessary. If these six conditions exist, and continue over a period of time, this is sufficient. The process of constructive personality change will follow.

There is no reason to believe that a therapist, any therapist, necessarily feels 'congruent' or 'integrated' in relationship to his client, any more than he would feel 'integrated' in any other relationship. Rogers explained what he meant by these terms:

[6] *Journal of Consulting Psychology* 21 (1957): 95–103.

The third condition is that the therapist should be, within the confines of this relationship, a congruent, genuine, integrated person. It means that within the relationship he is freely and deeply himself, with his actual experience accurately represented by his awareness of himself. *It is the opposite of presenting a façade*, either knowingly or unknowingly. [Italics added.]

What guarantee is there, what guarantee could there possibly be, that any given therapist is this genuine person Rogers posits him to be? The unconditional positive regard that Rogers wants the therapist to feel is something that cannot be legislated into existence any more than can love. We cannot feel these emotions upon command; either they are present or they are not. And the mere fact that somebody has come to you in need does not in and of itself mean that you will love that person. 'Unconditional regard' is not something that seems either likely or desirable. Faced with a brutal rapist who murders children, why should any therapist have unconditional regard for him? Or a wife batterer? What Rogers calls for is a very old idea in psychotherapy: empathy.

The fifth condition is that the therapist is experiencing an accurate empathic understanding of the client's awareness of his own experience. To sense the client's private world as if it were your own, but without ever losing the 'as if' quality – this is empathy, and this seems essential to therapy.

One of the signs, for Rogers, of a client's making progress was that 'he becomes increasingly able to *experience*, without a feeling of *threat*, the therapist's *unconditional positive regard*.'[7] Note the dilemma: if the client does *not* feel this, if the client feels the opposite, that the therapist is filled not with liking, but with loathing, then this is a sign that the patient is not yet well, still 'defensive,' still 'resisting,' that is, resisting the truth of the therapist's unconditional positive regard. But what if, in fact, the therapist does not feel such positive regard? How is that to be registered by the client? In Roger's scheme, it cannot, because the scheme does not encompass such negative possibilities.

[7] *Psychology: A Study of a Science*, vol. 3, *Formulations of the Person and the Social Context*, ed. by Sigmund Koch (New York: McGraw-Hill, 1959), 216.

This problem of negative vision, of not seeing what is there, permeates Rogers's theories. The history of psychology tells us that the ability to understand another person's inner world has been more honored in the breach than in practice. The history of psychology (and psychiatry) is replete with examples of therapists who have been completely unable to understand what their clients were telling them. Freud's misunderstanding of Dora's problems is a good example. So are the countless women who have attempted to convince a therapist that abuse (whether childhood sexual abuse or battering by a violent husband) really took place, when the therapist thinks it is only a fantasy; and, until the 1960s, the children who were physically abused but were not believed or even noticed by physicians, including pediatricians and psychiatrists (and no small number of therapists); and the large number of former psychiatric inmates who have reported terrible abuses in mental institutions. If such empathy is essential to therapy, it has been singularly lacking in the history of psychotherapy. Without taking a position on these essential points, and this means taking a political stance, the therapist cannot even acknowledge their reality, let alone understand and sympathize with the patient's experience of such abuse. *Nowhere in his writings does Rogers acknowledge the existence of such abuse, let alone ascribe to it any importance.* And how does one decide that a therapist does, in fact, possess empathy? Surely there is something absurd in Rogers's notion of measuring empathy by having 'trained judges rate the depth and accuracy of the therapist's empathy.'[8] Who would train the judges? And who would judge the judges' empathy? And would they not have to observe session after session to form a judgment? And what would the judges do if they decided that a particular therapist rates, say, only a B— in empathy?

It is clear that one of the things Rogers wanted a good therapist to be is a good friend. We all know that good friends are hard to come by, and cannot simply be purchased by the hour. But Rogers seemed to feel that a therapist, merely by announcing himself to be one, is automatically a better friend than even a real friend:

> It will be evident that for brief moments, at least, many good friendships fulfill the six conditions. Usually this is only

[8] *Journal of Consulting Psychology* 21 (1957), 99.

momentarily, however, and then empathy falters, the positive regard becomes conditional, or the congruence of the 'therapist' friend becomes overlaid by some degree of façade or defensiveness [*Journal* 21, 101].

Here Rogers assumed that friends will behave in a normal fashion, sometimes they like you and sometimes they don't, but that the therapist *always* likes you and is always genuine and nondefensive. What is impossible to achieve in real life is assumed to be automatically part of the good therapist's equipment. This is, I maintain, an unusually sanguine view of the world. Rogers showed this when he wrote:

Finally, in those programs – educational, correctional, military or industrial – which aim toward constructive changes in the personality structure and behavior of the individual, this formulation may serve as a very tentative criterion against which to measure the program [*Journal* 21, 103].

Did Rogers believe that the military and prisons really 'aim toward constructive changes'? It is a measure of just how profoundly optimistic his formulation is to read that he expected these, the most repressive of all possible institutions, to be capable of genuine empathy with dissent. And what he called 'constructive changes' is a catchall that can describe the most horrendous abuses of personal rights and liberty.

No doubt these beliefs were integral to Carl Rogers's thinking. In a book published in 1986 he wrote:

In 1969 I gave a talk on 'The Person of Tomorrow,' spelling out some of the characteristics of the new, powerful person emerging in our culture . . . I have had no reason since to materially change that picture. Take such a small example as the astonishing changes in the armed forces personnel regulations . . . we have the know-how, the skills to build this new America.[9]

[9] *Politics and Innocence*, ed. by Rollo May, Carl Rogers, and Abraham Maslow (Dallas: Saybrook, 1980), 31.

Rogers believed that the army had undergone a deep transformation. Many of us would find this hard to believe. But Rogers was committed to believing that such changes take place frequently and easily. He spent his life attempting to draw people in groups closer together and he must have believed that he had been successful. (For example, Rogers in the 1980s brought together racist whites and angry blacks in South Africa in American-style encounter groups; one cannot but question the lasting effect.)

In his autobiography[10] he spoke of his 'continuing attempt to resolve the tensions between psychiatry and psychology.' Later he spoke of his 'struggles with psychiatry' and said:

> These are the only two times I engaged in open combat with psychiatrists . . . I have endeavored to reconcile the two professions in their pursuit of a common goal . . . In 1957 I went to the University of Wisconsin, where, I am happy to say, my joint appointment in psychology *and* psychiatry was a pleasant resolution of these struggles.[11]

But what does this comment say of the depth of his concern with injustice in psychiatry? Could this injustice be set right merely by giving Carl Rogers a double appointment? In 'My Personal Growth' he had also written:

> These were years of great change and expansion in psychology following the war, and I was deeply involved in formulations regarding clinical training, the formation of the American Board of Examiners in Professional Psychology, and the continuing attempt to resolve the tensions between psychiatry and psychology [56].

An even more damaging sign that Rogers was willing to allow the superstructure of psychiatry to remain intact is the book he

---

[10] 'My Personal Growth,' originally written in 1965–1966 and published in *A History of Psychology in Autobiography*, vol. 5, ed. by E. G. Boring and G. Lindzey, (New York: Appleton-Century-Crofts, 1967); updated in 1971 for *Twelve Therapists*, ed. by Arthur Burton *et al.* (San Francisco: Jossey-Bass, 1972), 28–77.

[11] 'In Retrospect: Forty-Six Years,' *The American Psychologist* 29 (1974): 115–23.

edited and partly wrote, *The Therapeutic Relationship and Its Impact: A Study of Psychotherapy with Schizophrenics*.[12] It is the record of a study in which more than two hundred professionals worked, over a period of five years, with thirty-two 'chronic and acute schizophrenic' patients at the Mendota State Hospital, near Madison, Wisconsin. Almost all the patients there had electroshock or insulin treatments; Rogers selected those who had fewer than fifty treatments (24). He described them on the first page of his introduction as the 'disturbed, refractory, and apathetic individuals who were selected by the hand of fate (spelled "science") to be the human material for the study.' The plain fact is that these people did not volunteer for the study; they were coerced. This coercion is what Rogers first called 'the hand of fate,' then, recognizing that this was not true, changed it facetiously to 'science,' which was also false. To give some idea of what was involved, Rogers provided the following sample case from the research:

> Miss FAS was originally selected for the research in the fall of 1958. Another subject was paired with her and the flip of the coin indicated that Miss FAS was to be offered therapy. She was entered in the research design in December 1958. Test data and research instruments were collected from her, her therapist, and the staff at three-month and six-month intervals. Sample interviews were held every three months, although two such interviews were missed. At the time the table was constructed in 1961, she had completed four each of the Q-sort, WAIS, Rorschach, F Scale, Truax Anxiety Scale, and Stroop. She had taken five MMPI's, five TAT's, and six Relationship Inventories, and had participated in nine sampling interviews. The therapist had filled out seven Relationship Inventories and the ward personnel had returned seven Wittenborn Scales dealing with her ward behavior. This represents a total of 57 tests over a period of more than thirty months. During this time there were 238 tape-recorded therapy contacts with her. During this period Miss FAS was at times cooperative, more often indifferent, and

[12] Edited by Carl Rogers with the collaboration of Eugene T. Gendlin, Donald J. Kiesler, and Charles B. Traux (Madison: University of Wisconsin Press, 1967).

rather frequently, aggressively hostile. In behavior she was at times under complete restraint, at other times in an open ward. There were periods of marked progress and periods of marked regression. She was tested and recorded at every stage of her changing behavior [49–51].

He described the project this way:

It is the experience of a dozen therapists – sincere, dedicated workers who, each in his own way, were trying to establish helpful contact with their clients. Their ways *were* different. One, Buddha-like, sits through thirty hours of silence with a woman patient before she begins to reveal herself. Another, in a second interview, says, 'I won't listen to any more of that crap' [xv].

Again, we are warned, right from the beginning, that Rogers had already (like any therapist) prejudged the issue. Since these people were 'sincere, dedicated workers,' anything they did, no matter how intrusive, outrageous, or foolish, was automatically interpreted as 'helpful.' He even provided the example, refusing to judge the therapist who said 'I won't listen to any more of that crap.' Rogers, in other words, was accepting all positions, from Buddhalike silence to Rosenesque directness. Although some people have insisted that Rogers was as far from Rosen as therapy can go, in fact we learn from his article entitled 'Some Learnings from a Study of Psychotherapy with Schizophrenics' that Rogers specifically mentioned reading Rosen.[13] He also wrote:

Some of our therapists go further in their behavior. One in particular is moving more and more toward allying himself with the hidden and unrevealed person in the schizophrenic, and openly 'clobbering' the defensive shell. In his work there is a real similarity to Rosen or Withaker. He is sensitively and obviously committed to the person who is in hiding, but he is quite violently and sometimes sarcastically critical of the

[13] *Pennsylvania Psychiatric Quarterly*, Summer 1962. I have taken it from *Person to Person: The Problem of Being Human* by Carl Rogers and Barry Stevens (New York: Pocket Books, 1971), 183–96.

psychotic symptoms, the fear of revealing, the defences and avoidances. Perhaps partly because this approach is congenial to him as a person, he is finding it effective. As we listen to the recorded interviews of the various therapists in our group, we are gradually broadening the repertoire of behaviors which are real for each of us in dealing with our psychotic clients, and are slowly hammering out ways of facilitating movement in the unmotivated person [190].

John Rosen could not have said it any better.

In that article Rogers also had a passage describing the completely different approaches the therapists involved in the project took, and insisted that it really did not matter what they did, since he regarded them as good people:

Thus our sharply different therapists achieve good results in quite different ways. For one, an impatient, no-nonsense, let's put-the-cards-on-the-table approach is most effective, because in such an approach he is most openly being himself. For another it may be a much more gentle, and more obviously warm approach, because this is the way this therapist is. Our experience has deeply reinforced and extended my own view that the person who is able *openly* to be himself at that moment, as he is at the deepest levels he is able to be, is the effective therapist. Perhaps nothing else is of any importance [186].

But what about a sadistic therapist who is being himself? Or one who is not very helpful, or not very kind, or not very sensitive? Of course Rogers claimed that such qualities could not exist in the therapists trained according to his method. But why not? Surely one of the attractions of the Rogerian method is how simple it is to proclaim oneself a Rogerian therapist. The ideas in Rogers's work are simple, straightforward, and very few. One can learn them in a few hours. In fact, Robert Harper, in *Psychoanalysis and Psychotherapy*, notes how appealing Roger's therapy is to therapists who wish little training:

The client-centered way appeals to the young, insecure, inexperienced, prospective therapist as, at least superficially, the 'easy way.' It is unnecessary for the therapist to have any great knowledge of personality diagnosis or dynamics, and he takes no real responsibility for guidance of the disturbed client. He simply encourages the client to be more fully himself, he provides warmth and acceptance as the means whereby the client can achieve self-realization. Any permissive, warmly loving person can readily become a therapist via the client-centered system [83].[14]

The main fact to be remembered is that these patients were nonvoluntary, institutionalized patients whom the therapists described as 'chronic schizophrenics.' Most had been at the institution for years. They were seen twice a week, at the institution, but most of the time this was in flagrant violation of the patient's wishes: 'the therapist might force his presence on the patient, go to see him in the seclusion room (if the patient was confined there), or have him brought to the therapy office, more or less against his wishes, by ward aides' (57). Here Rogers acknowledged the use of force and manipulation, the very things that he repeatedly claimed never to have used. In a fascinating chapter entitled 'The Human Side of the Research,' he admitted something very important, namely, that most of the patients did not want to see the therapists for a simple, logical, and human reason: they were being used as guinea pigs, forced to undergo an enormous battery of psychological tests.

> One woman came to hate the testing violently. She felt guinea-pigged, evaluated, psychologically undressed. Each test experience seemed like an operation – one she was not sure she would survive. It took the very best efforts not only of the psychometrist, but in this case of the therapist as well, to persuade her to endure this 'torture' [64].

Clearly Rogers was aware of how invasive his 'treatment' appeared to his 'client.' Nevertheless, he persisted, and one begins

---

[14]This does not mean that Rogers was unconcerned with issues of training. In his book *Client-Centered Therapy*, he devotes one long chapter to 'The Training of Counselors and Therapists.' It is clear from this chapter that Rogers had no particularly revolutionary ideas on how to train or even to screen candidates.

to suspect that this had little to do with the good he thought he was doing. At one point, later in the book, he told a patient: 'I guess you know, *I* want you out of here. I am looking forward to meeting you in town, in my office. I really can't stand for you to be in here' (388). These are strong words, and I have no reason to doubt that Rogers believe them when he was saying them. But no matter how true the sentiments were, *in fact*, as Rogers admits, he could *not* get any patient out of the hospital, and the recognition of this fact on the part of the patients enraged them, quite justifiably: 'When it was gradually realized that the therapist did not have an authoritative administrative relationship to his client, this often had, at least temporarily, a negative effect on the relationship.' One patient told Rogers: 'What's the use of talking if you can't get me out of here?' (64—65) This is an excellent point, but it was totally lost on the therapists themselves. And so Rogers quoted one therapist who was

expressing some of the feelings experienced at one time or another by all our therapists. He says: 'The thing I have learned is that simply a supply of cooperative therapists such as ourselves will not suffice to clean out the back wards of the state hospitals. I have been quietly horrified by the monolithic acceptance of the status quo I have seen among the patients here. I must have thought that *any* new thing appearing on the ward would be welcome, let alone this most precious and specific hope for a new life that we can offer them. To find the patient so indifferent to a chance to talk with someone really stuns me' [68].

But this statement is even more stunning, since the therapist knows that the one thing the patient wants, to get out, he cannot provide. The acceptance of the status quo is precisely the fault the patients accuse the therapists of, namely, their inability to agree that the patients should not be incarcerated. It is incredibly self-serving on the quoted therapist's part to call therapy 'a precious . . . hope for a new life' when it could not offer them a new life at all, only the same life, with the addition of somebody else's interpretations. Do we think that slaves would have beenfited from the opportunity to talk to a sociologist about the inhumanity of their slavery?

It is to Rogers's credit that he recognized the problem, but to his shame that he took no meaningful action to resolve it. By offering therapy rather than freedom, he came down on the side of the hospital, one, he says, with 'a long and honorable history' (69). Rogers claimed that he was unable to free the patients from the institution by prior agreement, but it becomes clear that the reason he made this agreement in the first place was to protect his own interests (including his research interests), not those of the patients:

> It was consistent with our view of psychotherapy and a part of our agreement with the hospital that the therapists had no administrative authority or function in the hospital. Yet the carrying out of this policy created grave conflicts at times for the therapists. What does the therapist do when he feels that his patient has been kept in restraints for too long a period? How shall he behave when grounds privileges are consistently withheld from a patient who is struggling desperately toward independence? How can the therapist react when his patient behaves on the ward in a new, freer, and more independent fashion, and this behavior is perceived by the ward attendant simply as being troublesome? *Any course of action seems unsatisfactory. To stand up for the patient or to fight for what are perceived as his rights is to intrude on the hospital administration in a way that will surely and naturally be resented* [69]. [Italics added.]

It is not true that any course of action would have been unsatisfactory. What Rogers meant is that anything short of remaining silent would have created grave problems for the research project. No doubt had he stood up for the rights of the patients, the hospital staff would have resented it. But is this any argument for not doing it? All Rogers could say was that he had agreed, in advance, not to interfere. Clearly that is why the hospital allowed him in. But this means that he had to blind himself to injustice or live with the guilt of recognizing it and not doing anything about it. Since his lengthy book gives not a single detailed case of injustice (though Rogers in the passage quoted realized that it was ever-present), in fact, gives absolutely no sense of what it was like for the patients to be living in this oppressive environment, one can be certain that Rogers failed to see the very dilemma he claimed to have recognized. He willfully failed to see it, precisely because he knew, like the poor animals caught in one of the atrocious experiments to demonstrate 'learned helplessness,' that there was nothing he could do about it. But unlike the animals, and unlike the patients, who were coerced, nobody coerced Rogers, and there was something he could have done about it. He could have quit. But to do that he would have had to have been willing to question the very foundations of psychotherapy. And that, clearly, he was not prepared to do.[15]

One reason Rogers wanted to practice therapy in a hospital was that it had so often been said of his therapy that it was only suited to middle-class, mildly unhappy Americans. Rogers, like many crusaders, wanted to extend the reach of his teachings. In the general opinion of therapists, Rogers succeeded in showing that his work was applicable to 'schizophrenics.' Thus the psychiatrist Joel Kovel, in his popular *A Complete Guide to Therapy: From Psychoanalysis to Behaviour Modification*, says that 'Rogerian therapy is designed for a wide spectrum of emotional states. People from the relatively normal end have worked with it, as have hospitalized schizophrenics.' And then, in speaking of its limits, he says: 'Thus Rogerian treatment works best where the person doesn't have to go very far or deep – as with the student needing to steady

[15] This cannot fail to raise the much larger issue of psychotherapy under the Nazis. A book that received a great deal of favorable attention when it appeared in 1985 was Geoffrey Cocks, *Psychotherapy in the Third Reich: The Göring Institute*. In the book's last lines, the author writes that the 'nature of Nazi governance produced, on the institutional level, more opportunity than oppression for the evolving profession of psychotherapy.' This is no doubt true, but unlike Cocks, who stands in awe of this fact, I am appalled by it. For we cannot help, then, asking ourselves, whether there is something about the very nature of psychotherapy that allows it to be used by whatever oppressive regime happens to be in power. No doubt the anti-Nazi therapists (there were some, even in Germany) thought that they could best help their patients by remaining. But unless they were also activists (such as was the late Muriel Gardiner, an American psychoanalyst friend of the Freud family), they were bound, sooner or later, to play into the hands of the regime they secretly opposed. 'Internal emigration' and 'internal resistance' when unaccompanied by actions in the real world ultimately not only were of no use to others, but also appear to have destroyed the person's own self-worth. Karl Jaspers emigrated to Switzerland, and remained silent during the war. Hannah Arendt thought this admirable, but Jaspers himself was ashamed, and said so (after the war).

down – or where, practically speaking, he can't – as with chronic schizophrenics in a hospital.'[16]

Patients at the Mendota State Hospital lived in a state of oppression. In spite of his reputation for empathy and kindness, Carl Rogers could not perceive this. How could he have come to terms so easily with the coercion and violence that dominated their everyday existence? How could he remain so untouched by what he saw? Nothing in *The Therapeutic Relationship and Its Impact* or in his subsequent writings indicates any genuinely human response to the suffering he encountered in this large state hospital. Reading Rogers is such a bland experience that I found myself recalling the old adage that psychotherapy is the process whereby the bland teach the unbland to be bland. This reaction points to something lacking in Rogers and his writings, and that is sensitivity to people's real suffering. In reading through the many case histories that Rogers provided in his books, I was startled to see an almost total lack of the reporting of genuine traumas. Rogers, though he rejected most of psychoanalytic theory, clearly believed that 'troubles,' as he called them, came from within, not from the real world.[17] And just as clearly he conveyed this message to his clients, as surely as any psychoanalyst conveyed it to his patients. This is why such reports are lacking in almost all accounts of both kinds of therapy, in spite of the frequency of traumas in the actual lives of the people undergoing the therapy. The lack of sensitivity to abuse is conspicuous in a case history that Rogers reported in *The Therapeutic Relationship and Its Impact*. A patient is telling about hunting and the pleasure he gets from killing rabbits:

[16] New York: Pantheon Books, 1976, 116.
[17] In one of the last papers Rogers delivered, 'Rogers, Kohut and Erickson: A Personal Perspective on Some Similarities and Differences,' he contrasted Heinz Kohut's attempt to learn about the early childhood of his patients with his own approach: 'We can *never* know the past. All that exists is someone's current *perception* of the past. Even the most elaborate case history, or the most complete free association about the past, reveals only memories present *now*, "facts" as perceived *now*. We can never *know* the individual's past. I pointed out earlier that "the effective reality which influences behavior is at all times the perceived reality." We can operate theoretically from this base without having to resolve the difficult question of what *really* constitutes reality.' The paper appeared in *The Evolution of Psychotherapy*, ed. by Jeffrey K. Zeig (New York: Brunner/Mazel, 1987), 185.

Once in a while I'll kick up one, it's all right if you just go out there and just walk slow and look under the little piles, they just leap a little bit around holes – [Therapist laughs.] – A little dark in there and you bend down and look and you can see 'em – a lot of times you just take the gun butt and bust 'em in the head [481].

How is the patient to understand the therapists's laugh? Clearly it is a laugh of agreement, of pleasure in this cruel and sadistic account. The therapist doesn't raise the issue of cruelty because this behavior is something he approves of. This same patient then speaks about abusing children:

Well, I was talking about the time that I was sixteen that, I've always liked these, I've had quite a few relationships with queers [pause] I guess my biggest problem is from sex. Well, when I was six – sixteen [pause] [sighs] – I started to – molest young girls. I didn't want to hurt 'em – I never hurt 'em neither [486].

We are not told of any response by the therapist to this extraordinary confession. But when the psychiatrist Paul Bergman, of the National Institute of Mental Health, was asked by Rogers to comment on the excerpt, he said: 'I am very favorably impressed with the sturdy, firm, "masculine" tone of the therapist' (489). Could this be a reference to the macho laugh of the therapist? The psychiatrist O. Spurgeon English 'feels that Smith [this patient] indirectly admitted his anxiety about sex activity with girls his own age "and that he isn't up to feeling it yet," but that the therapist will get him there.' There is not a word by anybody about the admission that this man was sexually abusing young girls. Not only do the therapists refuse to take this in when it is reported by women patients as happening to them, but they cannot even admit it when it is confessed by a molester!

By contrast, the one area in which Rogers has been consistently criticized by other therapists is for his habit of repeating the client's words back in different words but with an identical meaning. It is indeed striking to read a case by Rogers, because of this habit of repeating. What Rogers most often did was avoid making any interpretation to the patient about the 'deeper significance' of his or her remarks to him. Rogers, somewhat to his credit, did not want to intrude on the thought processes of his patients; he only wished to mirror back what was said to him. But here there are insurmountable difficulties. For if he were a perfect mirror, he would merely echo words verbatim, and the client would undoubtedly say, 'That's what I just said' and eventually tire of the echo. And if he were not a perfect mirror, then he would, whether deliberately or not, alter his client's words, tone, context, and therefore appropriate them to his own use. That is a form of interpretation, something that Rogers claimed to avoid. Rogers reworded, changed the context, and added his own bias to what he was actually told. This is something we all do. But the therapist insists he or she does not. There is no way out of this dilemma. It is in the nature of therapy to distort another person's reality.

An examination of the work of Carl Rogers reveals nothing of the kind of excess we found in some of the other therapists examined in this book. He is not guilty of the kinds of abuse we saw in John Rosen or Albert Honig. Although he lacked the profundity of Freud and the sensitivity of Ferenczi, he was nonetheless representative of 'humane' psychotherapy as it is practiced today in the United States. He was respected by laymen and professionals alike. University departments of clinical psychology teach his ideas, and members of the therapeutic community make generous use of them. The faults of Carl Rogers examined in this chapter are not unlike the faults likely to be found in the average therapist working anywhere in this country in the 1980s. They are not the faults of individual therapists; they are the faults of therapy per se. No amount of reform could abolish these faults, because they are endemic to the very nature of psychotherapy. No school of therapy is exempt from them. That is why I have reserved for the last chapter a brief examination of the major forms of therapy popular in the United States today.

8

AND FURTHERMORE:
Family Therapy, Gestalt Therapy, Feminist Therapy, Incest-Survivor Therapy, Ericksonian Hypnotherapy, and Eclecticism

The criticisms I have made of the therapies examined in the previous chapters apply to many different kinds of psychotherapy not so far mentioned. I want to examine, in this chapter, a number of influential therapies to find the underlying assumptions about psychotherapy that are common to all of them.

FAMILY THERAPY

A family therapist who sees the entire family in therapy, like the more traditional one-to-one therapist, sets himself up as an arbiter of human values. By definition, a family therapist sees 'sick' families. It is then up to the therapist to define that 'sickness.' Frequently the therapist designates one member of the family as 'sick.' In a number of family case histories I have read, it is the adolescent daughter who is considered 'disturbed.' But suppose that the 'disturbed' adolescent girl is the victim of incestuous advances on the part of her father? Will the therapist discover this? Considering the fact that until the last few years not a single family therapist ever revealed such a situation in print, it is unlikely that this real and common problem was ever taken into account by a family therapist. The index of the *Journal of Marriage and the Family* from its inception through 1969 contains not a single reference to 'violence.'[1] To the extent that family therapists have recently become aware of violence within the family, they tend to take stances that conform to positions they held long before there was

---

[1] See J. E. O'Brien, 'Violence in divorce-prone families,' *Journal of Marriage and the Family* 33 (1971): 692–98.

any awareness of the reality of family violence. This means they have a tendency to blame the victims (usually women), or else they call these women 'unwitting collaborators.'[2] Often the only 'collaboration' was 'standing within arm's reach of their husbands.'[3]

Salvador Minuchin, one of the founders of family therapy, and still considered by many to be its most illustrious practitioner, wrote, quite recently, about a notorious case of child abuse in England:

> 'Maria Colewell was born on the 25th March, 1965, so that when she died, at the hands of her stepfather, William Kepple, on the night of the 6th/7th January, 1973, she was 11 weeks short of her eighth birthday.' This is the beginning of the Narrative of the Report of the Commission of Inquiry into the Care and Supervision Provided in Relation to the Child Maria Colewell, printed by her Majesty's Stationery Office in London in 1974.[4]

This little girl was starved and beaten to death by her stepfather for no apparent reason. When she died, she weighed only thirty-six pounds, and the physician who conducted the autopsy said that the bruising was the worst he had ever seen. Minuchin, faced with this grotesque example of child abuse, sees it from a 'family systems' perspective, and is therefore concerned with explaining (excusing?) the behavior of the family: 'The Kepples may have felt themselves in a Kafkaesque world full of accusers' (151). He goes on to maintain that the minority report by one member of the committee suggested that the stepfather was 'confused by the

---

[2] Evidence for this statement is to be found in several articles written by psychiatrists in the volume *The Abusive Partner: An Analysis of Domestic Battering*, ed. by M. Roy (New York: Van Nostrand Reinhold, 1982). See, in particular, N. Shainess's article 'Psychological Aspects of Wife-Battering.'

[3] See the excellent critique of family therapy by Michele Bograd, 'Family Systems Approaches to Wife Battering: A Feminist Critique,' *American Journal of Orthopsychiatry* 54 (no. 4) (October 1984): 558–68.

[4] *Family Kaleidoscope* (Cambridge, MA: Harvard University Press, 1984), 143. According to the book jacket, the *Journal of Child Psychiatry* said of this book: 'As one is swept along in Minuchin's powerful prose and conviction, it almost seems as if he has found the universal solvent in which all family griefs and violence can be dissolved.'

state's involvement in what he regarded as a purely private matter – the rearing of children.' Minuchin then comments: 'Was his forcing the children to defecate outside one way of commenting on the situation?' If one is not sufficiently alarmed by his interpretations by now, he offers a final one: 'Is it possible that beating Maria was a kind of declaration of independence?' (154) Supposing it somehow was, how would that help Maria? Suppose Maria had miraculously survived, would a family therapist's explanation of her stepfather's action help her? There is something morally offensive about attempting to explain, in psychological terms, an action that is so repellent.

In family therapy a large number of culturally sanctioned assumptions are brought into play as if they were brand-new insights. These assumptions are rarely more than prejudices of the time. For example, the psychiatrist and family therapist Ross Speck explained that when he visits a family at home (a common practice for family therapists), he observes signs of the 'sickness' immediately:

> In a middle-class living room there's always one overstuffed chair which *should* belong to Daddy. Sometimes a small child has usurped it because in a disturbed situation, the father is not acting his role of parent.[5]

This is related to what Speck calls 'a weak and passive father who abdicates his role in the family.' But these statements by Speck are nothing more than value judgments. Who, after all, has decided that 'weak' and 'passive' are necessarily vices? Even if they are, does a child in an armchair prove that? How does Speck divine so quickly the difference between 'weak' and 'mild' or between 'passive' and 'patient'? And how can Speck presume to know what anybody's role should be in a given family? Anyway, why does the overstuffed chair have to be Daddy's? Speck is merely giving voice to his own prejudices and opinions, and imposing them, as if they were scientific facts, on people who may not share these values.

In most family therapy, the therapist takes an active role. Virginia Satir, one of the founders of family therapy, made a habit of making her patients assume certain physical positions:

[5] Adelaide Bry, ed., *Inside Psychotherapy: Nine Clinicians Tell How They Work and What They Are Trying to Accomplish* (New York: Basic Books, 1972), 91.

I learned that if I put people in physical stances, they were likely to experience the feelings that went with that stance. For example, if I put someone in a placating stance he or she would begin to feel helplessness and also, often, rage.[6]

Playing the sage and behaving like a guru is endemic to family therapy. Indeed, it is prescribed in the standard textbooks in the field.[7] What is silently apparent in psychotherapy in general is made loudly clear here: the therapist knows best and in family therapy can abandon any pretense at modesty and boldly give orders. (Sometimes therapists are even expected to determine whether a child should remain with the parents or be removed to foster care.) This accounts for the growing popularity of engaging in paradoxical Zen-master-like behavior. Thus: 'A boy who compulsively soiled himself, despite all of the family's outrage and prohibition, stopped soon enough when the therapist ordered him to make in his pants and bring the product in.'[8]

Family therapists think of themselves as great pragmatists, and as having a firm grounding in social realities. Many family therapists believe that their treatment approach should extend beyond the family into society as a whole. But the vision of society as a whole that family therapists have is not a very profound one. The 'realities' they consider themselves experts in are the surface realities they have ingested from their own general culture without subjecting them to any deeper reflection. In the writings of family therapists, there is no class analysis, and no awareness of poverty, inequality, hunger, or traumas such as war, rape, and child abuse.

Family therapy owes its existence to the fact that it noted one serious defect in Freudian thinking about the individual: that it confines reality to the inside of one person, ignoring all the impingements of a larger, hostile or indifferent, external world. Shifting attention to the world of the family is still taking too narrow a view. And once we go beyond the family to society, the

[6] Jeffrey K. Zeig, *The Evolution of Psychotherapy* (New York: Brunner/Mazel, 1987), 68.

[7] For example, R. J. Green and J. L. Framo, eds., *Family Therapy: Major Contributions* (New York: International Universities Press, 1981).

[8] Joel Kovel, *A Complete Guide to Therapy: From Psychoanalysis to Behavior Modification* (New York: Pantheon Books, 1976), 188.

key concepts of psychotherapy prove of very little value. What it needed is a different kind of analysis, a political analysis.

GESTALT THERAPY

Gestalt (from the German for 'form,' meaning, here, the configuration of the whole) therapy refers to a system of beliefs and practices in which a patient is led to be more aware of total reality, especially through nonverbal manipulation. Sessions are usually in a group or a workshop, in which one person is placed in a chair called the 'hot seat' and speaks and responds physically and dramatically to various members of the group. Especially characteristic is the practice of dividing a person into topdog/underdog (Freud's superego/ego; Jung's anima/persona) and having 'them' engage in dialogue. The therapy can frequently take as little as fifteen minutes. Much is claimed for it by Gestalt practitioners:

> Gestalt Therapy is much more than a specific treatment or therapy. The gestalt philosophy underlying it claims to be a valid description of human functioning and problems that any person or group can use as a guide to fuller living and experiencing. Gestalt principles are as valid in everyday living as in the therapy situation, as valid with a gifted child as a disturbed one, as valid in the hospital as in the home. Besides the wide range of psychotherapeutic settings and populations, gestalt principles have also been applied to education, to the treatment of eyesight problems, and other physical illnesses.[9]

Miriam Polster, who is a professor in the Department of Psychiatry at the University of California, San Diego, writes:

> [Gestalt therapy] was born of the union between a fertile mind and a fertile milieu. What maintains the vitality of the theory is its growth in subtlety and application – through the enduring contributions of Perls and his colleagues, and through their

[9] John O. Stevens, *Legacy from Fritz* (Palo Alto: Science & Behavior Books, 1975), 1.

students. It is a rich and elegant theory, providing orientation and range for therapeutic choice.[10]

Frederick (Fritz) Perls, the founder and main figure of Gestalt therapy, was born in Berlin in 1893 and died in Chicago in 1970. His influence was at its peak during his tenure as Psychologist-in-Residence at the Esalen Institute in Big Sur, California, during the 1960s. Many of the terms common in psychotherapy today owe their origin to Perls: 'the here and now,' 'awareness,' 'the wisdom of the body,' 'excitement and growth' as key processes in the human organism, 'non-verbal cues,' and others.[11] Because Perls's therapy and techniques are so tied in to the man and his life, and because he was so open about his life, it is fairly easy to evaluate Gestalt. Perls was originally trained as a psychoanalyst (he had been most influenced by Freud, Reich, Rank, and Jung), and throughout his writings (which are not voluminous, some four volumes in all) he is preoccupied with comparing his achievement and his therapy with those of Freud. He leaves the reader in no doubt as to his importance. In his autobiography he wrote: 'Gestalt is not just another man-made concept . . . gestalt is – and not only for psychology – something that is inherent in nature.'[12] He believed that Gestalt was the only way mankind could be saved: 'Either American psychiatry would one day accept Gestalt therapy as the only realistic and effective form of understanding, or else it would perish in the debris of civil war and atomic bombs.' He takes no back seat to Freud: 'I accomplished the next step after Freud in the history of psychiatry.' And again: 'The crazy Fritz Perls is becoming one of the heroes in the history of science.' In this judgment he included not just the theory that he invented, but the

[10] In *The Evolution of Psychotherapy*, 322. For a useful source of articles about Gestalt therapy, see Chris Hatcher and Philip Himelstein, eds., *The Handbook of Gestalt Therapy* (New York: Jason Aronson, 1976).

[11] 'A good therapist doesn't listen to the content of the bullshit the patient produces, but to the sound, to the music, to the hesitations. Verbal communication is usually a lie. The real communication is beyond words.' Frederick Perls, *Gestalt Therapy Verbatim* (New York: Bantam Books, 1969), 57. Needless to say, only the seer, i.e., Perls himself, is in a position to determine when speech is genuine and when it is not.

[12] A year before he died, Perls wrote his autobiography, *In and Out of the Garbage Pail* (Lafayette, CA.: Real People Press, 1969). The book has no page numbers, and therefore the quotations that follow cannot be identified by page. The Bantam Books paperback edition had many printings.

practice as well: 'I believe that I am the best therapist for any type of neurosis in the States, maybe in the world.' All of the preceding quotations come from his autobiography, and it may well be that Perls intended the book to be humorous. But similar ideas are found in his other, more serious, works. Thus, in *Gestalt Therapy*, written with New York philosopher Paul Goodman, he states in a preface dated 1969: 'But how do we open the ears and eyes of the world? I consider my work to be a small contribution to that problem which might contain the possibility of the survival of mankind' (xi.)[13]

Clearly Perls thought of himself as a guru. He dressed the part and looked the part, with long white beard and hair, beads, sandals, and flowing robes. He behaved that way as well, in the tradition of the Zen master (having undergone some brief training in Zen in Japan), making paradoxical statements, shocking his listeners with his actions, which were sometimes violent, sometimes sexual. He used LSD frequently. But, like all gurus, he was unaware of how his language and his behavior were dictated by the times in which he lived. It is hard to hear the famous Gestalt prayer with which Perls began his group sessions (he thought individual therapy was something of a waste of his valuable time, because the audience was not large enough and could not be counted on to be appreciative enough) without a twinge of embarrassment. It would be trite at any time, but seems particularly wedded to the 1960s:

> I do my thing, and you do your thing.
> I am not in this world to live up to
>   your expectations.
> And you are not in this world to live
>   up to mine.
> You are you and I am I,
> And if by chance we find each other,
>   it's beautiful.
> If not, it can't be helped.[14]

[13] Frederick Perls, Ralph F. Hefferline, and Paul Goodman, *Gestalt Therapy* (New York: Bantam Books. 1980). First published in 1951.

[14] From *Gestalt Therapy Verbatim*, page 4. The Gestalt prayer is found in most of Perls's work. His explanation of it is found in the chapter entitled 'Gestalt Prayer,' pages 140–49 in *The Gestalt Approach and Eyewitness to Therapy*, by Fritz Perls (Palo Alto: Science & Behavior Books, 1973).

There are many puzzles about the adulation that Perls received. He is best known for his insistence on the primacy of feelings and his eagerness to denounce those for whom feelings did not matter or whose feelings he felt were not genuine. Yet he could demonstrate an almost unfathomable lack of feeling for those who had been part of his own family. In his autobiography he mentions his eldest sister, Else, only once, and coldly: 'She was a clinger . . . she also had severe eye trouble . . . when I heard of her death in a concentration camp I did not mourn much.' Perhaps even more astonishing, he has only one sentence about his only daughter: 'Renate is a phony.' His daughter told one of his admirers, the psychiatrist Martin Shepard: 'In the last six years that Fritz was alive we didn't even talk. I hadn't read *In and Out of the Garbage Pail* before he died. And after I read it, I thought that if he weren't dead, I'd kill him.'[15] She also tells how her father did not even know his own granddaughter: 'The last time Allison, my eldest daughter, saw Fritz, she was there with a girl friend. He went over to the friend and said, 'Hello Allison.' He couldn't even recognize his grandchild' (135).

Perls had a sign posted over the door to his house: 'No children allowed.' He was not at all reluctant to admit his distaste for children:

> The astonishing overestimation of children in our culture, that would have baffled the Greeks or the gentry of the Renaissance, is nothing but the reaction to the repression of the spontaneity of the adults (including the spontaneous urge to slaughter their children).[16]

One of the concepts that Perls found so upsetting in Freud was the 'repetition compulsion,' the need, according to Freud, many people have to repeat old wounds and traumas in order to master them. Perhaps Perls found this idea repellent because it seemed to fit his own life so perfectly. His remarks about his own father in his autobiography and as quoted in the book by Martin Shepard (page 19) paint a portrait of a father who hated his son and wanted

[15] *Fritz: An Intimate Portrait of Fritz Perls and Gestalt Therapy* (New York: E. P. Dutton, 1975), 136.
[16] *Gestalt Therapy*, 395.

nothing whatever to do with him, ever. His father called Fritz *ein Stück Scheisse*, 'a piece of shit,' a term he also employed for his wife, whom he regularly assaulted physically. Much as I dislike the psychoanalytic term 'insight,' I cannot help remarking that Perls seemed to have an inordinately small amount of it.

Perls's attitude toward women was remarkable for its callousness. Stories from his acquaintances are not needed to verify this, since Perls was only too happy to supply the information himself in his autobiography. He tells the story of how he physically fought with a woman in one of his groups, knocking her to the ground three times:

> I got her down again and said, gasping: 'I've beaten up more than one bitch in my life.' Then she got up, threw her arms around me: 'Fritz, I love you.' Apparently she finally got what, all her life, she was asking for, and there are thousands of women like her in the States. Provoking and tantalizing, bitching, irritating their husbands and never getting their spanking. You don't have to be a Parisian prostitute to need that so as to respect your man.

He mentions, too, in his autobiography, that his father was never faithful to his mother, and it was well known that Perls had sex with patients. Indeed, once again, he admitted it candidly and with seeming pride in his autobiography:

> I have affection and love – too much of it. And if I comfort a girl in grief or distress and the sobbing subsides and she presses closer and the stroking gets out of rhythm and slides over the hips and over the breasts – where does the grief end and a perfume begin to turn your nostrils from dripping to smelling?

One of the 'ideas' of modern therapy attributed to Perls is the notion that people have 'holes' in their personality. In the Author's Note to *Gestalt Therapy*, his best-known book, Perls writes: 'The worst hole I can think of is a person who has no ears. This is usually found in people who talk and talk and expect the world to listen' (x).

I can think of no more appropriate metaphor for the works of Fritz Perls.

The reason I have concentrated my criticism on the person of Fritz Perls in this section is that the Gestalt group-therapy technique depends on a single individual who acts as the leader and superego for the rest of the group. Perls made no bones about arrogating to himself all the privileges and power of a traditional guru. Implicit in this power is the ability to cause great pain and destruction to others, either directly or by causing the group to turn on, attack, and brutalize one of its members. Perls seemed positively to revel in the power he held over the people in his groups. This is the power that all cult leaders seek to obtain for themselves. It is not surprising, then, that many cults have incorporated aspects of psychotherapy into their rituals. All gurus – as the case of Bhagwan Shree Rajneesh makes clear – are only a few steps away from Jonestown.

FEMINIST THERAPY

My knowledge of feminist therapy is confined to the major writings that can easily be found in a university library. Much of what I say may not apply to the more grass-roots kind of feminist therapy. My knowledge is therefore only partial, and other criticisms of feminist therapy are possible. In the space available, I cannot offer any analysis of feminism. I agree with many of the feminist criticisms of traditional psychiatry and psychotherapy.[17] However, the problems in psychiatry and psychotherapy go deeper than just

[17]These criticisms go back some time now. I think of the influential book by Phyllis Chesler, *Women and Madness*, and another good book, by Dorothy Tennov, *Psychotherapy: The Hazardous Cure* (New York: Doubleday & Co., 1976). See also the article by Naomi Weisstein, 'Kinder, Küche, Kirche as Scientific Law: Psychology Constructs the Female,' in *Sisterhood Is Powerful*, ed. by Robin Morgan (New York: Vintage Books, 1970), and these collections and books: P. Susan Penfold and Gillian A. Walker, *Women and the Psychiatric Paradox* (Montreal: Eden Press, 1983); *Women Look at Psychiatry*, ed. by Dorothy E. Smith and Sara J. David (Vancouver: Press Gang Publishers, 1975); Patricia Perri Rieker and Elaine Hilberman Carmen, eds., *The Gender Gap in Psychiatry: Social Realities and Psychological Processes* (New York: Plenum Press, 1984). One of the earliest influential articles showed how therapists reflect stereotypic sexist attitudes as to what constitutes healthy, mature behavior: Inge K. Broverman, Donald M. Broverman, and Frank E. Clarkson, 'Sex-role stereotypes and clinical judgments of mental health,' *Journal of Counseling and Clinical Psychology* 34 (1970), 1–7.

patriarchal attitudes. Simply changing the gender might well solve one problem (sex bias, though even that is questionable), but it will not even begin to address other problems. Feminist therapists are part of a larger world of therapy in general. Like other therapists, they depend on colleagues for referrals. This means they must be part of a wider community to survive economically. Criticism of that wider community, then, must be softened. And indeed, in the literature I have seen, the criticism of the basic underlying principles of psychotherapy has been toned down in feminist therapy – so much so that there is now enormous renewed interest among feminist therapists (a label that is not conferred and can be taken by anyone) in Freudian psychoanalysis. Influential theorists and practitioners have endorsed major aspects of Freudian psychoanalysis.[18] After all, from where does feminist therapy derive its postulates, and its technique for psychotherapy? From more traditional forms of psychotherapy. Lucia Albino Gilbert has written:

> According to recent writers, no one theory underlies the practice of feminist therapy. Holroyd, for example, feels that feminist therapists can take any number of different orientations, including the psychoanalytic. She views feminist therapy as a combination of a radical therapy philosophy with humanistic therapy techniques ... feminist therapy is also thought to be heavily influenced by Rogers' self-theory.[19]

Once the accommodation process is set in motion, feminist therapists are bound to accept other aspects of traditional psychiatry. In the recent *Handbook of Feminist Therapy*, Lynne Rosewater wrote a chapter entitled 'Schizophrenia, Borderline, or Battered,'

[18] See Jean Baker Miller, *Toward a New Psychology of Women* (Boston: Beacon Press, 1976); Nancy Chodorow, *The Reproduction of Mothering* (Berkeley: University of California Press, 1978); Juliet Mitchell, *Psychoanalysis and Feminism* (New York: Random House, 1974). Sometimes the endorsement or acceptance of psychoanalytic ideas is more subtle, as in the influential book by Carol Gilligan, *In a Different Voice: Psychological Theory and Women's Development* (Cambridge, MA: Harvard University Press, 1982).

[19] 'Feminist Therapy,' in *Woman and Psychotherapy: An Assessment of Research and Practice*, ed. by Annette M. Brodsky and Rachel T. Hare-Mustin (New York: The Guilford Press, 1980), 250. The reference in the quotation is to J. Holroyd, 'Psychotherapy and Women's Liberation,' *Counseling Psychologist* (1976), 6, 22–28.

in which one might assume she would criticize and reject, from a feminist point of view, the labeling of women as 'schizophrenic' or 'borderline.'[20] Instead, she is concerned with a 'differential diagnosis,' how to differentiate a battered woman from a 'true' schizophrenic. In other words, she accepts all the traditional 'mental disease' categories without questioning them. She writes:

> In order to distinguish a battered woman from a schizophrenic (or borderline) woman, the therapist needs to have familiarity with the behavioral dynamics of battered women . . . sometimes a standardized test can be helpful in this process [216].

Not only does Rosewater, then, accept the specious medical diseases psychiatrists call schizophrenia and borderline, she also believes that equally specious psychological tests can help to distinguish a 'normal' person from a 'sick' one. She writes in her conclusion:

> There are some women who are *both* battered and borderline or schizophrenic. I have found that a test like the MMPI with the use of the Harris-Lingoes and Seerkownek subscale, can measure and help clarify the differences between these diagnostic categories [224].

Feminist therapists are very much like their more traditional male colleagues when it comes to seeking prestige, university backing, and funding, and do not appear to consider the many opportunities this offers for co-optation. They also suffer from some of the same elitism they rightly criticize in more traditional therapies.[21] An influential article by Annette M. Brodsky and Rachel T. Hare-Mustin, of Harvard University, lists this among its concluding

[20] Lynne Bravo Rosewater and Lenore E. A. Walker, *Handbook of Feminist Therapy: Women's Issues in Psychotherapy* (New York: Springer Publishing Co., 1985), 215–25.

[21] See *Big Mama Rag: A Feminist News Journal* 4 (no. 3), March 1976, 'Feminist Therapists Convene and Conflict,' by K. Terra *et al.*, a report on the January 1976 conference of feminist therapists in Boulder, Colorado, which points out the problems of professional elitism and lack of solidarity in the conference organization. See, too, Constance Perenyi, 'Enough Is Enough: Feminist Therapy and Other Bad Habits,' *Big Mama Rag* 7 (no. 11), November 1980.

priorities: 'The National Institute of Mental Health should take the lead in developing data banks and communications networks on clinical interventions with women and make known their availability.'[22] Even the language, here, is borrowed, and the dangers inherent in such an accommodation with NIMH are not even explored. Many categories that feminist therapists reject in principle they accept under a new name. Thus, while the notion of an expert is rejected, the same concept slips in unnoticed under the thin disguise of 'role model': 'The feminist model of therapy also stresses the function of the therapist in serving as a role model for female clients.'[23]

How does a role model differ from the guru/seer model, the wise person who is part and parcel of all traditional psychotherapies? Of course it doesn't:

> Role-modeling is an important part of the process. In feminist therapy, overt use is made of the person, experience, behaviors, and attitudes of the therapist. The goal is not to have the client become just like the therapist, but rather to set an example of a competent woman dealing effectively with her life.[24]

I have heard the same statement from many traditional male psychoanalysts. Why, after all, should one assume that the feminist therapist *is* 'a competent woman dealing effectively with her life' merely because she has become a therapist? If social position is enough to guarantee authenticity or competence, then surely the male therapist has as much right to lay claim to it as the feminist therapist. My point is that neither person can do so honestly.

Most of the ideas of feminist therapy about therapy per se derive from traditional psychotherapy. (I concede that the political ideas of empowerment and so on come from feminist theory, and with these I have no quarrel. Indeed, the earlier forms of peer consciousness-raising, where no money was exchanged and no

[22] 'Psychotherapy and Women: Priorities for Research,' in *Women and Psychotherapy*, 409.

[23] Susan Sturdivant, *Therapy with Women: A Feminist Philosophy of Treatment* (New York: Springer Publishing Co., 1980), 82.

[24] Mary Ballou and Nancy W. Gabalac, *A Feminist Position on Mental Health* (Springfield, IL: Charles C. Thomas, 1985), 32.

hierarchy existed, seemed to me far better than what they evolved into.) This is explicitly recognized by most feminist therapists. Thus Miriam Greenspan, in her widely used and highly readable book *A New Approach to Women and Therapy*,[25] provides an excellent criticism of humanistic psychology, but ends by adopting many traditional methods:

> In my own therapy practice, I am indebted to the growth therapies for certain active techniques to facilitate the expression of feelings, especially in cases where longstanding feelings have been blocked from consciousness and are interfering with the client's capacity to get on with her life. I might, for instance, suggest that a client use her fists or a tennis racket on a pillow as a means of coming face to face with her anger as a woman [131].

Greenspan accepts many of the values implicit in therapy, and in psychiatry generally; for example, that distrust of therapy is a problem of resistance, to be dealt with by the client. Thus she asks the question: 'How much of your distrust is something you would have to work out with *any* therapist, and how much of it is related to a profound conviction that this is not the therapy or therapist for you?' (340) This question implies that there are some people who would distrust any therapist, and that this is not 'healthy.'

Much of the 'soft' language of therapy is taken over by feminist therapists. Anica Vesel Mander, in her article 'Feminism as Therapy,' concludes:

> Feminism integrates the subjective and the objective, the rational and the intuitive, the mystical and the scientific, the abstract and the concrete aspects of the universe and considers
> . them harmonious parts of a whole, rather than opposites of one another.[26]

Dorothy Tennov, whose book *Psychotherapy: The Hazardous Cure* has been mentioned earlier, offers an excellent, feminist-oriented

[25] New York: McGraw-Hill, 1983.
[26] From the influential collection edited by Edna I. Rawlings and Dianne K. Carter, *Psychotherapy for Women: Treatment Toward Equality* (Springfield, IL: Charles C. Thomas, 1977), 298.

criticism of the sexism inherent in psychodynamic psychotherapy. But the alternative she proposes, behaviorism (which evidently she practices), is worse than the problem it is meant to solve. Feminist therapy, it seems, can mean a feminist orientation (which itself can mean many different things) combined with just about any other orientation the therapist is drawn to. Juliet Mitchell, Nancy Chodorow, and Jean Baker Miller are all Freudian psychoanalysts. Elizabeth Friar Williams identifies herself as a Gestalt feminist therapist.[27] Helen Block Lewis was a psychodynamically oriented clinical psychologist.[28] Her daughter, Judith Lewis Herman, who wrote an outstanding book on incest, is a psychiatrist.[29] This means that all the defects inherent in the various approaches examined in this book will seep, subtly or not so subtly, into 'feminist' therapy. I agree with Mary Daly's trenchant criticism of feminist therapy:

> Behind the more obviously misogynistic presuppositions of patriarchal psychotherapy (e.g., 'penis envy' and blaming the mother) there is a more subtle agenda, which is difficult to uproot and which seems to be endemic to the therapeutic situation in its various forms.[30]

INCEST-SURVIVOR THERAPY

Closely allied to feminist therapy is therapy for survivors of incest. Feminists like Judith Herman, Florence Rush, Louise Armstrong, Diana Russell, and the researcher David Finkelhor first provided the published data about incest upon which psychotherapeutic

[27] *Notes of a Feminist Therapist* (New York: Dell Publishing Co., 1976).
[28] *Psychic War in Men and Women* (New York: New York University Press, 1976).
[29] *Father-Daughter Incest* (Cambridge, MA: Harvard University Press, 1981).
[30] *Gyn/Ecology: The Metaethics of Radical Feminism* (Boston: Beacon Press, 1978), 281. I agree with Daly, too, that 'the concept of "feminist" therapy is inherently a contradiction' (282). However, once again I find myself out of sympathy with the alternative Daly proposes, a spiritually oriented celebration, though this is no way detracts from my agreement with her description of the problems with feminist therapy.

treatment depends.[31] But, except for Judith Herman, these authors do not promote therapy.[32] Therapists who do provide therapy for incest survivors are not necessarily feminist in orientation. They are often traditional therapists. The more traditional they are, the more likely they are to come from a tradition that has for many years denied the reality of sexual abuse (a theme of both my *Assault on Truth* and *A Dark Science*). It is alarming to see how, in the last year or two, many traditional male psychiatrists are now offering therapy for victims of sexual abuse, the very psychiatrists who a few years before denied that such a thing even existed. They have given it a name, identified the survivors as suffering from a syndrome, and claimed expertise in treating it. I have talked to psychiatrists who claim that nonprofessional women can only harm incest survivors by their lack of expertise and that treatment should be done in a hospital-based department of psychiatry. The chances that the woman who does wind up in such a place will be hurt in one form or another are very high. Many people seem to agree that the child who is sexually abused needs therapy. Dr. Suzanne M. Sgroi writes: 'We believe that all child victims of sexual abuse need some level of therapeutic intervention, regardless of the identity of the perpetrator.'[33] Standard textbooks in this field offer little guidance as to what kind of therapy should be used.[34] They don't even seem to be aware that there is a problem to consider. Some recent books offer no criticism at all of traditional therapies and naïvely assume that every therapist who has had

[31] Florence Rush, *The Best Kept Secret: Sexual Abuse of Children* (New York: McGraw-Hill, 1980); Louise Armstrong, *Kiss Daddy Goodnight* (New York: Hawthorn Books, 1978) and *The Home Front: Notes from the Family War Zone* (New York: McGraw-Hill, 1983); Diana E. H. Russell, *Sexual Exploitation: Rape, Child Sexual Abuse, and Workplace Harassment* (Beverly Hills: Sage Publications, 1984); David Finkelhor, *Sexually Victimized Children* (New York: The Free Press, 1979) and *Child Sexual Abuse: New Theory and Research* (New York: The Free Press, 1984).

[32] Louise Armstrong believes, as I do, that 'treatment' for incest is tied in to traditional psychiatry and therefore questionable when not downright harmful. See the Afterword to her *Kiss Daddy Goodnight: Ten Years Later* (New York: Pocket Books, 1987).

[33] *Handbook of Clinical Intervention in Child Sexual Abuse* (Lexington, MA: Lexington Books, 1982), 111.

[34] An example is *Sexual Assault of Children and Adolescents*, by Ann Wolbert Burgess, A. Nicholas Groth, Lynda Lytle Holmstrom, and Suzanne M. Sgroi (Lexington, MA: Lexington Books, 1978).

'specialized training' is competent to offer help. For example, *Incest and Sexuality: A Guide to Understanding and Healing* says:

> The degree is less important than the specialized training a counselor has had. Good backgrounds would include training and experience in incest treatment, sex therapy, couples counseling, family therapy, and depression treatment. A therapist with a background in incest and sex therapy is able to talk comfortably about sexual concerns while sensitively responding to underlying incest concerns.[35]

More sophisticated books – for example, *Sexual Abuse of Young Children* – do not address any of the problems inherent in psychiatry's attitudes toward incest.[36] Roland Summit, a psychiatrist and an advocate for abused children, writes in the Foreword to *Sexual Abuse of Young Children*: 'This book contains the most responsible, the most reliable, the most immediate, and the most useful experience ever compiled for the benefit of very young victims of child sexual abuse' (xv). Yet the book seems to endorse the treatment models of Parents United. Parents United, started in the 1970s, has had enormous influence on all treatment programs for incest survivors and incest perpetrators (note the confusion of perpetrator and victim, almost as if there could be a counseling service for Nazi guards and concentration-camp survivors). The philosophy can be found in Henry Giarretto's book *Integrated Treatment of Child Sexual Abuse: A Treatment and Training Manual*.[37] Giarretto explicitly recognizes that his treatment philosophy is based on humanistic psychology, and he mentions, among others, the names of Carl Jung, Carl Rogers, Karen Horney, and Erich Fromm (pages 10 and 11). This translates into 'people are what they are' and, therefore, 'act as they best know how to act.' The father who sexually assaults his daughter, then,

> did not behave out of conscious choice at that point in his life; self-abusive and abusive behavior was the only response he could make to discharge the chronic state of low self-worth

[35] By Wendy Maltz and Beverly Holman (Lexington, MA: D. C. Heath & Co., 1987), 112.

[36] Kee MacFarlane and Jill Waterman with Shawn Conerly, Linda Damon, Michael Durfee, and Suzanne Long, *Sexual Abuse of Young Children: Evaluation and Treatment* (New York: The Guilford Press, 1986).

[37] Palo Alto: Science & Behavior Books, 1982.

caused by unmet needs. The father-offender (or any offender) will stop being an offender when he is taught to become aware of all his needs for self-realization and to become personally responsible for meeting them [18].

Giarretto claims to have almost no recidivism among offenders who follow his program, but one can see that it would not be difficult for a manipulative person to learn this kind of psychobabble in a few minutes' time. The truth is that we have no idea why men abuse. Nor can I see how the victims of offenders will benefit from this therapy. The chapter in Giarretto's book by Ellie Breslin, 'Counseling Methods and Techniques,' is explicitly based on Gestalt therapy, which seems singularly ill-equipped to deal with people who have been victims of sexual abuse and which has, as we have seen, a potential for harm[38]

A very different and far more sophisticated approach is found in Judith Herman's *Father-Daughter Incest*. Herman, a psychiatrist, recognizes, in no uncertain terms, one problem within her profession:

> Most therapists lack the ability to help incest victims because they have never been trained to deal with the issue. In fact, they have been trained to avoid it. Psychoanalytic tradition has created an atmosphere of denial and disbelief within the mental health professions. Within training institutions, the result has been a perpetuation of ignorance from one generation of professionals to the next [180].

But Herman believes (as I do not) that this problem can be remedied. For her, the problem is rooted in the failure of therapists to recognize the reality of incest. She seems to believe that there is nothing in psychiatry per se that encourages this willful resistance to seeing the obvious: 'Many fully trained therapists, who handle other problems skillfully, still maintain a blind spot when it comes to incest' (181). It follows, therefore, that if a therapist does recognize incest, then he or she is in a position to help somebody deal with it by virtue of training in psychotherapy, which Herman accepts in its totality:

[38] Another such book is Adele Mayer, *Incest: A Treatment Manual for Therapy with Victims, Spouses and Offenders* (Holmes Beach, FL: Learning Publications, 1983).

First the supervisor offers an intellectual framework in which to understand the problem. References to the professional literature are often suggested. Second, the supervisors offer practical, problem-solving help with the strategies of therapy. Third and most important, the supervisors help the less experienced therapists to deal with the feelings of their own that have been evoked by the patients. With the support of competent supervisors, the therapists are usually able to master their own troubled feelings and put them in perspective. This done, the therapists are better able to attend to patients with empathy, and with a confidence in their ability to offer help [180].

Herman optimistically believes that 'the patient lucky enough to find such a therapist has the opportunity to undergo a corrective emotional experience.' She concludes: 'If the therapist is a woman, she herself becomes a model' (191). We are back in the world of traditional therapy, where all that is required to become a 'role model' for another person is to have 'expert training.' These are all assumptions that this book has rejected. But Herman has not questioned any of the fundamental values of psychiatry, which, considering the depth of her understanding of the devastation of incest, is surprising. It cannot be entirely accidental that psychiatry has for so long remained ignorant about violence toward women.

The contributions of feminist psychologists and psychiatrists to women's issues – such as Herman has brought to incest, Paula J. Caplan to masochism,[39] and Robert Seidenberg to agoraphobia[40] –

[39] *The Myth of Women's Masochism* (New York: E. P. Dutton, 1985). Caplan is certainly aware of her own ambiguity. Thus she writes: 'A psychoanalyst I know does superb work with a variety of patients and in his practice takes great care to support women's strengths and to help them stop attributing "sick" motives such as masochism to themselves. I have never hesitated to refer patients to him. Imagine my surprise when I heard him speak at a convention of mental health professionals, where he presented the case history of a former patient in a way that seemed to place the blame for a sexual harassment incident on her' (206). Needless to say, I do not find this surprising at all. I wonder if it made Caplan, whose book, except for her endorsement of therapy, is excellent, question her assumptions about the malleability of psychoanalysis.

[40] Robert Seidenberg and Karen DeCrow, *Women Who Marry Houses: Panic and Protest in Agoraphobia* (New York: McGraw-Hill, 1983). Although Seidenberg is a practicing psychoanalyst, he is also president of a local chapter of the National Organization of Women. His analyses of anorexia nervosa and of agoraphobia happily owe less to psychology than they do to feminist politics.

are valuable to the extent that they bring into focus problems that their more traditional colleagues would rather avoid. But the root of these problems will never be explored as long as the assumptions and presuppositions within psychology and psychiatry are not considered in depth.

Criticism similar to that which I have directed at feminist therapy and incest-survivor therapy can also be applied to so-called radical therapy, which has attempted to divorce itself from traditional therapy while retaining intact many of its most questionable assumptions.[41]

[41] Much radical psychiatry, which is now more or less defunct, has been influenced by Eric Berne and transactional analysis. See, for example, 'On Radical Therapy,' by Jeanette Hermes, in *Going Crazy: The Radical Therapy of R. D. Laing and Others*, ed. by Hendrik M. Ruitenbeek (New York: Bantam Books, 1972), 23–39: 'Another important thing that I encourage in group is what Berne called stroking. This is supporting a person's worth by affirming love for her by physically touching her and by telling her all the fine things we see in her.' Claude Steiner, who wrote the 'Radical Psychiatry Manifesto,' was a student of Eric Berne as well. He writes, in the 'Manifesto,' about seeing people in groups (which Berne encouraged): 'One-to-one contacts, of great value in crises, should become the exception rather than the rule . . . psychiatrists not proficient in group work are deficient in their training and should upgrade it,' in *The Radical Therapist*, ed. by Jerome Agel (New York: Ballantine Books, 1971), 281. Hogie Wyckoff, a disciple of Steiner, has explicitly acknowledged how 'radical psychiatry' is just another form of psychiatry: 'The radical psychiatry problem-solving group model has been developed through a synthesis of psychiatric theories borrowed from R. D. Laing, Fritz Perls, and Claude Steiner. Radical Psychiatry theory incorporates some basic transactional analysis (TA) assumptions about psychiatry and people. We assume, as Eric Berne did, that people are born OK and that they are made unhappy because of what they do to each other. We agree with Berne that the language of psychiatry should be simple and that people who practice psychiatry should communicate their opinions to group members rather than keep secrets and thus maintain a one-up stance.' From 'Radical Psychiatry for Women,' in *Psychotherapy for Women: Treatment Toward Equality*, ed. by Ena I. Rawlings and Dianne K. Carter (Springfield, IL: Charles C. Thomas, 1977), 370. For more on radical psychiatry, see *Rough Times*, ed. by Jerome Agel (New York: Ballantine Books, 1973); *Radical Psychology*, ed. by Phil Brown (New York: Harper & Row, 1973); *Readings in Radical Psychiatry*, ed. by Claude Steiner (New York: Grove Press, 1974). My rejection of radical psychiatry does not extend to the publications that are truly radical (and which reject psychiatry and psychotherapy), some of which are included in *Madness Network News* and *Phoenix Rising* (published in Toronto). See Sherry Hirsch *et al.*, eds., *Madness Network News Reader* (San Francisco: Glide Publications, 1974).

ERICKSONIAN HYPNOTHERAPY

The influence of Milton H. Erickson (1901–1980, and not to be confused with the Freudian psychoanalyst Erik H. Erikson) on psychotherapy has been steadily growing.[42] Although the general public has not been as responsive to the many books written by and about him, professionals, especially eclectic psychotherapists, have. He was important to Margaret Mead, Gregory Bateson, Paul Watzlawick, Don Jackson, Jay Haley, John Weakland, and many other well-known therapists. With the republication of the much-reprinted book by Jay Haley, *Uncommon Therapy*,[43] and the popular books by Bandler and Grinder,[44] Erickson became generally known as the father of brief strategic approaches to psychotherapy. Much of his fame within the profession is due to the

[42] According to Jay Haley in *Uncommon Therapy* (see n. 43), Erickson 'has long been known as the world's leading medical hypnotist' (18). (For the reader interested in learning more about hypnotism from an authoritative source, I would recommend Merton M. Gill and Margaret Brenman, *Hypnosis and Related States: Psychoanalytic Studies in Regression* (New York: International Universities Press, 1959). An erudite discussion of hypnosis can also be found in Theodore X. Barber, *LSD, Marihuana, Yoga, and Hypnosis* (Chicago: Aldine Publishing Co., 1970). See also Margaret Brenman and Merton Gill, *Hypnotherapy: With Appended Case Reports* (New York: International Universities Press, 1947). For more information on Erickson's life, see Jay Haley, ed., *Advanced Techniques of Hypnosis and Therapy: The Selected Papers of Milton H. Erickson, M.D.* (New York: Grune & Stratton, 1967). Erickson received his medical degree at the Colorado General Hospital and did his psychiatric training at the Colorado Psychopathic Hospital. He was at the Wayne County General Hospital and Infirmary as Director of psychiatric research and training, taught at the College of Medicine at Wayne State University, and was also Professor of Psychology at Michigan State University in East Lansing. In 1948 he settled in Phoenix, Arizona. He was a Fellow of the American Psychiatric Association, the American Psychological Association, and the American Psychopathological Association. He was the founding president of the American Society for Clinical Hypnosis, as well as editor of that society's professional journal. An excellent bibliography of books by and about Erickson can be found in William Hudson O'Hanlon, *Taproots: Underlying Principles of Milton Erickson's Therapy and Hypnosis* (New York: W. W. Norton & Co., 1987).

[43] *Uncommon Therapy: The Psychiatric Techniques of Milton H. Erickson, M.D.* (New York: W. W. Norton & Co., 1973). See also Haley's *Ordeal Therapy* (San Francisco: Jossey-Bass, 1984).

[44] R. Bandler and J. Grinder, *The Structure of Magic* (Palo Alto: Science & Behavior Books, vol. 1, 1975; vol. 2, 1976). See, too, the two volumes by J. Grinder, J. Delozier, and R. Bandler, *Patterns of the Hypnotic Techniques of Milton H. Erickson, M.D.* (Cupertino, CA: Meta Publications, 1975 and 1977).

praise he received from Gregory Bateson[45] and Jay Haley. Haley, in a recent introduction to a multi-volume collection of Erickson's conversations, writes:

> Milton H. Erickson, M.D., was the first strategic therapist. He might even be called the first *therapist*, since he was the first major clinician to concentrate on how to change people. Previously, clinicians devoted themselves to understanding the human mind; they were explorers of the nature of man. Changing people was of secondary interest. In contrast, Erickson had one major concern in his professional life — finding ways to influence people. Whether influencing people with hypnosis, persuasion, or directives, Erickson focused upon developing a variety of techniques to relieve psychological and physical distress. He seems to have been the first major therapist to expect clinicians to innovate ways to solve a wide range of problems and to say that the responsibility for therapeutic change lies with the therapist, rather than with the patient.[46]

Jay Haley is himself a prominent therapist who has considerable influence with other therapists. He is Director of the Family Therapy Institute of Washington, D.C., and has been Director of the Family Experiment Project at the Mental Research Institute, and Director of Family Therapy Research at the Philadelphia Child Guidance Clinic. An author of some seven books and a former editor of *Family Process*, Haley has been in the mainstream of psychotherapy research and practice since the 1950s. Therefore, his opinions about the direction that psychotherapy is taking today

---

[45] One can see the similarity between the early book of Jurgen Ruesch and Gregory Bateson, *Communication: The Social Matrix of Psychiatry* (New York: W. W. Norton & Co., 1951), in which the idea of the 'double-bind' originates, and the work by Erickson. The concept of the double-bind actually originated in an article by Gregory Bateson, D. D. Jackson, Jay Haley, and J. Weakland, 'Toward a Theory of Schizophrenia,' *Behavioral Sciences*, 1 (1956): 251–64, which acknowledges the influence of Erickson. The same authors wrote about it in 'A Note on the Double-Bind,' *Family Process* 2 (1963): 154–61. See also Gregory Bateson's essays in *Steps to an Ecology of Mind* (New York: Ballantine Books, 1975).

[46] Jay Haley, ed. *Conversations with Milton H. Erickson, M.D.*, vol. 1, *Changing Individuals* (New York: Triangle Press, 1985), vii.

are important. A conference on the Evolution of Psychotherapy was held in December 1986 in Phoenix, Arizona, under the auspices of the Milton H. Erickson Foundation. More than seven thousand therapists from all over the United States participated, including many of the most prominent names in psychotherapy: Albert Ellis, Virginia Satir, Carl Rogers, Rollo May, Judd Marmor, Aaron Beck, Thomas Szasz, Paul Watzlawick, Jay Haley, Joseph Wolpe, Bruno Bettelheim, R. D. Laing, Salvador Minuchin, and Lewis Wolberg.[47] The event received much coverage. Haley began his talk by saying: 'Among the mysteries of human life, there are three special ones. What is the nature of schizophrenia? What is hypnosis? What is the nature of therapy?' (17) These questions have been in the forefront of the history of psychotherapy. Freud asked these very questions, as had many of his colleagues (including Eugen Bleuler) before him, and almost all psychiatrists and therapists after him. Haley went on to make a historical statement that seems to me important, because it came from somebody who had taken the pulse of the nation's psychotherapists:

> If someone asked an analyst [in the past], 'Is it your job to change people?' the analyst would say it was not. The task was to help people understand themselves – whether they changed or not was up to them. The opposite posture seems more reasonable today in terms of accountability. The therapist is no longer a consultant but a people changer who fails if the case fails. As Erickson would put it, a therapist must learn many different ways to change many different kinds of people, or he should take up some other profession. In summary, the kind of therapy we have today as the mainstream is the opposite of what was done in the beginning. Some people have changed because of the influence of teachers, others out of trial and error, and others after examining therapy research. Today there is a generation of people who have seriously taken up the career of changing people. They are not advisors, consultants, objective observers, or diagnosticians. They are people whose task is to be expert at influencing another person. They are skilled at getting people to follow their

[47] Papers from this conference were published as *The Evolution of Psychotherapy*, ed. by Jeffrey K. Zeig (New York: Brunner/Mazel, 1987).

suggestions, including suggestions the person is not aware of receiving [27].

Such a change made Haley proud. It makes me very afraid. For how will Haley, or Erickson, or anyone else, for that matter, change people, if not in the direction of his or her own values?

Thus, a few pages after introducing Erickson as the greatest therapist of all time, in *Conversations with Milton H. Erickson, M.D.*, Haley asks his advice about a twenty-eight-year-old 'girl' who came to therapy because of severe menstrual cramps. Erickson asks Haley if she is pretty, and whether she thinks so herself. Then he explains that the body image is very important and that pretty girls often deprecate themselves:

> The girl with the painful menstruation – exactly what does she think about her body? Are her hips too large? Or her ankles too large? Is her pubic hair too scarce, too straight, too curly? Or what about it? It may be too painful a thing for her ever to recognize consciously. Are her breasts too large? Too small? The nipples not the right color? [3]

What are these if not cultural stereotypes, and, in fact, male ones to boot? Who are Erickson and Haley to tell a twenty-eight-year-old woman (whom they are still calling a 'girl') that she is pretty or to 'set her straight' about her body? There is nothing unusual about this case; Erickson's works are full of this statements to women that imply he is an authority on appearance and taste.

Thus he told a thirty-five-year-old professional woman who was 'plump' that he would see her only if she would allow him to 'assault' her verbally, which he proceeded to do, telling her that she was a mess: 'Her neck and ears were dirty, her teeth were in need of brushing, her hair sloppily combed, her steel-rimmed glasses, her lack of makeup.' He demanded that she clean herself up, and then he gave her instructions to take dance classes, see a beauty counselor at the local department store, sew her own formal gown, and go to the company dance. Then he told her:

> Grace, you have a very, very pretty patch of fur between your legs, now go home and think it over. Undress, get in the nude, stand in front of a mirror, and you will see the three beautiful

badges of womanhood . . . Grace you have a pretty patch of fur
between your legs.

He explains to Haley that telling this to her allowed her to meet a
man, marry, have children, and lead a happily married life: 'It was
all the raping that was necessary.' Erickson says: 'Grace later told
me that she had come to me with the realization in her mind that if
I thought it necessary to seduce her she would have yielded . . . I
had raped her, hadn't I?' (159–67) We should remember that
Erickson was describing a young woman he was treating in
Phoenix, in the late 1940s or early 1950s. Did he really help this
woman achieve something *she* wanted, or did he simply compel
her to adjust to the standards of the community in which she
lived? Such attitudes about women and how they should look and
behave were very common then and are still common among large
segments of the population. But this account was published in
1985, and not a single comment is made by Haley about the sexist
assumptions upon which Erickson's methods were based.

In reading this account by Haley, supposedly based upon tran-
scripts of interviews, one cannot help but wonder how accurate
Erickson's memory was. At the time Erickson wrote up the case, he
did not think he could publish the paper. However, it was published after his death.[48] The paper itself is more interesting, different from, and more alarming than Erickson's memory of it (it
concerns the same woman). First of all, we learn that Erickson
heard from 'an unmarried man of her own age' that he could get
seriously interested in her 'if that damned girl would comb her
hair, wash her ears and neck, put on a dress that didn't look like an
ill-fitting gunnysack, straighten her stockings, and polish her
shoes.' Erickson sided with him completely and added his own
sexist philosophy: 'In summary, her appearance epitomized her
problem.' Erickson agreed to see her on his terms only:

> These terms are absolute, full, and complete obedience in
> relation to every instruction I give you regardless of what I
> order or demand. . . . You will be told what to do, and you will

[48] In *Innovative Hypnotherapy: The Collected Papers of Milton H. Erickson on Hypnosis*, vol. 4, ed. by Ernest L. Rossi (New York: Irvington Publishers, 1980), 482–90.

do it. That's it. If I tell you to resign your position, you will resign. If I tell you to eat fresh garlic cloves for breakfast, you will eat them. . . . I want action and response – not words, ideas, theories, concepts. . . . Once you come, you are committed to therapy, and your bank account belongs to me as does the registration certificate for your car. . . . I will tell you what to do and how to do it, and you are to be a most obedient patient.

Erickson then put her into a trance and told her:

'Ann [Grace], you are five feet three inches tall, and you weigh about 130 pounds; you have trim ankles, an excellent figure, a beautiful mouth and beautiful eyes. . . .' Then in a tone of voice of utter intensity, in manner of conveying a vitally important message, she was asked the following question: 'Ann, did you know that you have a pretty patch of fur between your legs?' For some minutes Ann stood staring at the author, blushing deeply and continuously, apparently too cataleptic to close her eyes or to move in any way. 'You really have, Ann, and it is definitely darker than the hair on your head. Now at least an hour before bedtime, let us say at nine o'clock tonight, after you take your shower, stand in the nude before the full length mirror in your bedroom. Carefully, systematically, thoroughly examine your body from the waist down. . . . Try to realize how much you would like to have the right man caress your pretty pubic hair and your softly rounded belly. Think of how you would like to have him caress your thighs and hips.'

He then told her to 'look well at the two emblems of womanhood you wear on your chest. Examine them carefully, both visually and tactually.' He then proceeded to berate her in great detail for her bad taste in clothes, the dirt in her fingernails, her hair, teeth, how she needed deodorants, and so on. He then ordered her to leave with total amnesia for all that had been said: 'Let me see no more of you until you keep your next appointment as a "vision of delight."' He then gives us the sequel, his word for it, of course, that the woman married a physician, had four children, 'appeared to be not over 40' though she was forty-five, 'and the entire family was obviously happy and well-adjusted.' 'Obviously happy and well-adjusted'? By whose standards? By Erickson's, of course. And obviously he knew almost nothing about the woman and her family. Why then was he so certain they had achieved this pinnacle of happiness? Because *if* they did, then that justified what he had done to the woman. He had to believe that his 'therapy' worked, that it was successful, magically so, and that he had, like the wizard and magician so many other therapists took him to be, transformed the ugly duckling into a happy, beautiful princess all in the space of a single interview. His cases read like fairy tales, but ones designed to glorify Milton H. Erickson.[49] One therapy session, a few words of wisdom, and the person (usually a woman) is transformed for life into Erickson's ideal.

One of the hidden prerogatives in inducing change is the right to infallible opinions. If, as Haley says, the business of the therapist is to change a patient fast, then the therapist must know what is real, what is true, what is good, and must force the patient into accepting the therapist's definition so that change can occur immediately. This Erickson achieved through trance induction and suggestion, often made in an offhand manner so that the person receiving the suggestion (usually posthypnotic, i.e., made during hypnosis for later action) would not even know that a suggestion has been made. It is, by Erickson's own admission, the imposition of the will of the therapist upon that of the patient to change in the direction chosen by the therapist. But the change is only as good as the therapist's wisdom. Whether the values of the therapist coincide with the values of the patient was, for Erickson, largely irrelevant, since clearly he believed he has discovered, in his own life, the correct way to be in the world.

[49] It is only fair to add that Erickson surmounted extraordinary physical disabilities both as a child and as an adult. At seventeen, he came down with a severe case of polio; he was completely paralyzed, able only to speak and move his eyes, and was not expected to survive. By sheer dint of effort he achieved amazing mobility and a very strong upper body. In later life he lost his powerful shoulder muscles to such an extent that he frequently had to use both hands to raise an eating utensil. Eventually he was restricted to a wheelchair. His wife wrote a very inspiring account in a letter, which is reproduced in Jeffrey K. Zeig's *Experiencing Erickson: An Introduction to the Man and His Work* (New York: Brunner/Mazel, 1985), 7–12. Perhaps it was this disability that made Erickson sensitive to other people's bodies in ways that appear more offensive to a reader than they were to the people directly faced with him.

In one case a woman in her thirties consulted Erickson because of an obsession with other people's sexual lives.[50] She was married and had three children; her husband had had a vasectomy after the third child. Erickson put her into a trance and gave her the posthypnotic suggestion that she talk freely:

> 'A torrent of words poured forth in the language of the street. . . . She had not realized that a vasectomy would constitute so serious a deprivation for her. . . . In her obsessional interest in love affairs, rumored or published in the news, the only ones that had interested her were those of men, married or divorced, who had fathered children. She went on to declare, in direct Anglo-Saxon terms, that the essence of her problem was a compelling desire, once more, to have sex relations with a biologically complete man, even at the risk of an illegitimate pregnancy.'

Erickson decided that she really wished to have an affair, that he did not think it a good idea, and instead induced another trance, and gave her the posthypnotic suggestion that she would have many erotic, satisfying dreams, and upon awakening 'she would recall them and engage in a fantasy about them . . . culminating spontaneously in an intense orgasm.' This happened, much to Erickson's satisfaction.

> 'Then in the morning, when wide awake and reviewing her dream behavior, she had deliberately chosen to fantasize about one of the men she had previously named, and had been delighted to experience an orgasm as a result. That afternoon she picked up her husband at his office. While waiting for him, she had greeted his business associate, a married man with a large family, and had quietly and immediately had an orgasm. That evening she had insisted that she and her husband call on a married couple she admired greatly. While playing cards with the host as her partner, she had an orgasm.'

One cannot help wondering, in reading this account, just how accurate it is. Is Erickson's pleasure in the account the woman

[50] 'Vasectomy: A Detailed Illustration of a Therapeutic Reorientation,' in *Innovative Hypnotherapy*, 386–91.

presumably gave him purely objective? The whole thing is tinged with fantasy and has a feeling of unreality about it. So many of Erickson's accounts seem designed to provide him with direct sexual pleasure. Of course, he never discusses whether he got sexual pleasure from what he did, but an account such as the following suggests that he may have. He tells the story of a young woman who kept putting off her marriage to the man she loved. Furthermore, to Erickson's displeasure, 'every time the subject of sex was raised she developed deafness. She just turned blank. Apparently couldn't see you or hear you.' So Erickson instructed her to buy 'the shortest pair of short shorts imaginable.' Then he told her:

> 'Now you're going to listen to me when I discuss sex, or I'll have you take those off and put them on in my presence.' She listened to me on the subject of sex. Then I told her, 'Now this is the first of July; you've got until the seventeenth of this month to marry that guy. You're coming in tomorrow. I'm going to get you all ready to marry the guy' [127].

The next day the woman came in, and Erickson said:

> 'Now you need to know how to undress and go to bed in the presence of a man. So start undressing.' Slowly, in an almost automatic fashion, she undressed. I had her show me her right breast, her left breast, her right nipple, her left nipple. Her belly button. Her genital area. Her knees. Her gluteal [buttocks] regions. I asked her to point where she would like to have her husband kiss her. I had her turn around. I had her dress slowly. She dressed. I dismissed her [128].[51]

In spite of wishing to play the wise and kindly sage of Eastern legends, Erickson was, in reality, a psychiatrist, armed with all the powers of medicine and psychiatry. Once, a young woman came to see him because she desperately wanted an abortion. When Erickson refused to send her to somebody who could help, she threatened to commit suicide. One is prepared to hear another

[51] *Conversations with Milton H. Erickson*, vol. 2, *Changing Couples*, in the section entitled 'Sex, Fun and Impotency.'

miracle cure, but, instead, Erickson immediately called three policemen to get her out of his office. Haley asked him why: 'How come you didn't try and manipulate her out of it in that situation instead of bringing in the police?' His reply is, at least, honest:

> Because she was a university student over at Temple, and her roommate knew that she had called me. If that gal committed suicide or went to an abortionist where would my professional standing be? The only thing to do is protect myself. Get the police in.[52]

Erickson made liberal use of restraints when he worked at the Arizona State Hospital. He writes that he gave a well-attended presentation 'on the desirability of physical restraint. . . . I had my patients put in straitjackets.'[53] With so-called psychotic patients, Erickson's methods are reminiscent of John Rosen's. When a male patient told Erickson that he did not believe he had a colon, Erickson put him in restraints, 'slipped a cathartic in his tube feeding,' and when the man yelled to be taken to the bathroom, Erickson said, 'But you've got no colon.'[54] The man then told him that he could not drink from a glass. 'In tube-feeding him I put plenty of salt in him to dehydrate him in a most gosh awful fashion. He was literally dehydrated. He was dying of thirst.' The man drank a glass of milk, as Erickson predicted he would. These are cruel, crude jokes. Sometimes the crudity of the wording and the thinking coincide, as when Erickson tells about a woman

> who told me that she was sick and tired of being so frightfully inhibited. Her mother's life had been one of complete inhibition by a hostile husband. She and her sisters had patterned after their mother. They led inhibited lives. She wished she would get over being inhibited. I told her she ought to get off the ice or skate. That's what her other psychotherapist had said many times. 'All right, I will say it to you once. Get off the pot, or shit.'[55]

[52] Conversations, vol. 1, 200.
[53] Experiencing Erickson, 108.
[54] Conversations, vol. 1, 227.
[55] Experiencing Erickson, 141.

Erickson believes that this single comment freed her from a life of inhibition. Much of what Erickson does and says makes me think of a kind of prison-camp therapy. He boasts that he makes no interpretations. But his directives are basically no different from interpretations. It is frightening to think that this is the direction in which therapy is moving, yet that seems to be the case. Haley writes:

At the time these conversations began Erickson and his therapy was so unique that it was difficult for us to understand. The standard psychodynamic therapy of the time assumed the therapist was a non-directive, passive listener. In that framework Erickson's therapy seemed different and strange and we struggled to understand what would seem more obvious, at least to us, a decade or two later. Although he was in isolation at the time of these conversations, in the sense of doing a therapy different from his colleagues, since that time the field had gone in his direction and seeing couples and families, as well as doing a directive strategic therapy, is assumed to be the correct way to change people.[56]

Jeffrey Zeig has written that 'Ericksonian methods are probably the fastest-growing field of psychotherapy in the Western world.'[57] Even if this is an exaggeration, there can be little doubt of the enormous influence exercised by Erickson and his school on psychotherapy in the 1980s.

The Ericksonian technique epitomizes, in a seemingly nonviolent way, what Rosen epitomizes in a violent way – the therapist-as-boss. Hypnotherapists are frank about what they seek to achieve: to put somebody into a vulnerable, defenseless condition, in which the person can be told what to do. It is not surprising

[56] *Conversations*, vol. 2, viii.

[57] Some idea of the range of application of Erickson's principles can be seen in Jeffrey K. Zeig, ed., *Ericksonian Psychotherapy*, vol. 1, *Structures*, vol. 2, *Clinical Applications* (New York: Brunner/Mazel, 1985), xiii. See also: 'Erickson was called the world's greatest communicator. Alternately, it has been said that he was the premier psychotherapist of the century . . . history will demonstrate that what Freud contributed to the theory of psychotherapy, Erickson will be known as contributing to the practice of psychotherapy.' From *A Teaching Seminar with Milton H. Erickson*, ed. Jeffrey K. Zeig (New York: Brunner/Mazel, 1980), xix.

that Erickson succumbed to the opportunity to abuse his patients, as the examples quoted make clear.

ECLECTIC THERAPY

Most therapists in private practice today would describe themselves as eclectic, which means, according to *Webster's Collegiate Dictionary*, 'the method or practice of selecting what seems best from various systems.' It is important to keep in mind that the systems from which they have selected the 'best' features are none other than the ones I have examined in this book.

About half of the psychologists who practice therapy describe themselves as eclectic.[58] Most psychologists believe that 'eclecticism offers the best hope for a truly comprehensive approach to treatment.'[59] Eclectics say that most recent studies demonstrate that whether therapy is successful or not has almost nothing to do with the specific therapy chosen. They are *all* good, so they say, or pretty much effective, or at least no one theory seems preferable to any other.[60] Sol L. Garfield, the former editor of the *Journal of Consulting and Clinical Psychology* (and President of the American Psychological Association's Division of Clinical Psychology), has written:

[58] See S. L. Garfield and R. Kurtz, 'a Study of Eclectic Views,' *Journal of Consulting and Clinical Psychology* 45 (1977): 78–83; also J. C. Norcross and J. O. Prochaska, 'A National Survey of Clinical Psychologists: Affiliations and Orientations,' *The Clinical Psychologist* 35 (1982): 4–6. In 1983, Prochaska and Norcross asked respondents to select one of four theoretical perspectives underlying their eclecticism. Among this group, 45 percent chose psychodynamic (i.e., psychoanalytic), 25 percent humanistic-existential, 17 percent behavioral, and 13 percent other. See J. O. Prochaska and J. C. Norcross, 'Contemporary Psychotherapists: A National Survey of Characteristics, Practices, Orientations, and Attitudes,' *Psychotherapy: Theory, Research and Practice* 20 (1983): 161–73.

[59] See D. S. Smith, 'Trends in Counseling and Psychotherapy,' *American Psychologist* 37 (1982): 802–9. For an excellent overview of eclecticism, see *Handbook of Eclectic Psychotherapy*, ed. by John C. Norcross (New York: Brunner/Mazel, 1986).

[60] See M. L. Smith, G. V. Glass, and T. I. Miller, *The Benefits of Psychotherapy* (Baltimore: Johns Hopkins University Press, 1980), a work that is generally considered to be the most sophisticated survey of psychotherapy-outcome studies.

It thus appears that some type of explanation offered by the therapist during psychotherapy has a positive impact on the patient. It seems that whether or not the explanation or interpretation given is 'true' in the theoretical or scientific sense is really of little significance in the therapeutic situation. This is a rather strong pronouncement on my part, and when I have presented this view to groups of therapists, I have been aware that it tends to be rather coolly received – and understandably so. It challenges the therapists's own professional-scientific belief system and appears also to denigrate his or her professional work. Nevertheless, the implications of comparable outcomes among the major forms of psychotherapy, particularly recently, should make us face this issue in a forthright manner.[61]

Eclecticism is not new. In a sense, one could claim that every therapist is an eclectic, even when he would call himself a strict Freudian psychoanalyst, for example. This was a point made by the acerbic British psychoanalyst Edward Glover when he became Chairman of the Training Committee of the British Psycho-Analytical Society. In 1937 he conducted a survey of practices by British psychoanalysts and noted an astonishing lack of uniformity in the technique of psychoanalysis, even though most of the analysts had similar training. He concluded:

To put the matter quite simply: when psychoanalysts differ on important points of doctrine, one or other of the contesting parties must, however unwillingly, be practicing suggestion on his patients instead of analyzing them.[62]

---

[61] 'An Eclectic Psychotherapy,' in *Handbook of Eclectic Psychotherapy*, 151.

[62] *The Technique of Psycho-Analysis* (New York: International Universities Press, 1955), vii. The survey was first published in 1940 under the title *An Investigation of the Technique of Psycho-Analysis*. The survey is still astonishingly up to date, perhaps because, as Glover noted, 'therapeutic slogans, those harbingers of technical rigidity, do change of course from time to time; but these are rather indications of anxiety and uncertainty than concentrates of new analytical wisdom . . . I have reason to know that even if the present-day student couches his difficulties in a more complex, sometimes more pretentious, argot, the underlying uncertainties are identical with those experienced by his predecessors' (vii).

'Suggestion' in the history of psychoanalysis represents abuse of the purity of analysis. It means telling patients what to do, rather than allowing them to discover what they should do. Glover's point is that differences in point of view from analyst to analyst have important implications, and are not consistent with the theoretical pretensions of classical psychoanalysis. While one might readily agree, it is not all that easy, as Glover was to discover in his acrimonious battle with Melanie Klein and members of her school, to agree on who is doing the analysis and who the suggesting.

Eclectic or not, no one can practice psychotherapy without having made some sorts of theoretical decisions. How would one decide, for example, whether to see the patient alone, or with a spouse, or with family, or in a group, and for how long, and how often, and so on, without some theoretical framework? Should one interpret, confront, comfort, question, agree, or simply say nothing? In spite of recent efforts to consider eclecticism a separate theoretical orientation, in fact eclecticism is simply an amalgam of all the different schools or at least the different theoretical orientations.[63] When one asks eclectic therapists to name the people and schools to whom they are most indebted, a surprisingly small number are named. Most will mention Freud and the later Freudians (Anna Freud, Otto Fenichel, Heinz Hartmann, Phyllis

[63] Probably the term most commonly used by an eclectic therapist to describe the theory is 'psychodynamically oriented pyschotherapy.' This is another term for psychoanalytically oriented psychotherapy; it derives from attempts in the 1950s to base therapy upon psychoanalytic principles. The issue was much discussed in early numbers of the *Journal of the American Psychoanalytic Association*, especially in volume 2, published in 1954. The influence of these papers upon the practice of psychotherapy in America has been enormous. Most important were: Leo Rangell, 'Similarities and Differences Between psychoanalysis and Dynamic Psychotherapy' (734–44); Merton M. Gill, 'Psychoanalysis and Exploratory Psychotherapy' (771–97); and Frieda Fromm-Reichmann, 'Psychoanalysis and General Dynamic Conceptions of Theory and of Therapy: Differences and Similarities' (711–21). See, too, her selected papers, *Psychoanalysis and Psychotherapy*, ed. by Dexter M. Bullard (Chicago: University of Chicago Press, 1959). Many of the more influential 'primers' on how to do therapy belong to this orientation; for example, the perennially popular book by Sidney Tarachow, *Introduction to Psychotherapy* (New York: International Universities Press, 1970), and Kenneth Marc Colby's *Primer for Psychotherapists* (New York: John Wiley & Sons, 1951).

Greenacre, Bertram Lewin, Erik Erikson[64]), especially Ferenczi and possibly Wilhelm Reich, and from current schools Melanie Klein, Heinz Kohut[65]; the neo-Freudians, Karen Horney, Erich Fromm[66]; something from Harry Stack Sullivan and Frieda Fromm-Reichmann; something from Jung, from Rogers and non-directive therapy; from Perls and Gestalt; from existentialism, Rollo May, Abraham Maslow, Ludwig Binswanger, and even the psychoanalytic existentialist R. D. Laing,[67] and the controversial psychiatrist Thomas Szasz. Many therapies are no longer influential in mainstream pyschotherapy, for example, Eric Berne's transactional analysis[68] and Arthur Janov's primal scream,[69] and therefore have not been discussed here.[70] After all, therapies proliferate at an extraordinary rate.

In 1959 Robert A. Harper identified thirty-six distinct therapies.[71] By 1980 there were well over two hundred fifty mentioned in two separate books.[72] I could not possibly address each school individually. Nevertheless, this book has addressed

[64] For a criticism of Erikson, see my 'India and the Unconscious: Erik Erikson on Gandhi,' *International Journal of Psychoanalysis* 55 (1974): 519–26.

[65] For a critique of Kohut, see Charles Hanly and J. M. Masson, 'A Critical Examination of the New Narcissism,' *International Journal of Psychoanalysis* 57 (1979): 49–66.

[66] For a good criticism of the neo-Freudians, R. D. Laing, and others, see Russell Jacoby, *Social Amnesia: A Critique of Contemporary Psychology from Adler to Laing* (New York: Beacon Press, 1976).

[67] For a good criticism of Laing, see Thomas Szasz, *Schizophrenia: The Sacred Symbol of Psychiatry* (New York: Basic Books, 1976), 50–83.

[68] A criticism of TA can be found in Joel Kovel's *A Complete Guide to Therapy*.

[69] For an incisive criticism of primal scream and some other faddish therapies (e.g., co-counseling, rebirthing, est), see R. D. Rosen, *Psychobabble: Fast Talk and Quick Cure in the Era of Feeling* (New York: Atheneum, 1978).

[70] I have excluded from this book the physical therapies and therapies based on the many forms of behavior modification, including cognitive therapy, learning theory, sex therapy, not because I have no criticism of them, but for reasons of space and also because they have already been much and well criticized (usually, however, from the point of view of a rival therapy, rather than on principle). As for other forms of physical therapy, such as electro-shock, I would urge the reader to consult the excellent anthology edited by Leonard Roy Frank, *Shock Treatment: A Crime Against Humanity* (Boston: South End Press, 1987).

[71] *Psychoanalysis and Psychotherapy: Thirty-Six Systems* (Englewood Cliffs, NJ: Prentice-Hall, 1959).

[72] R. J. Corsini, ed., *Handbook of Innovative Psychotherapies* (New York: John Wiley & Sons, 1981), and R. Henrik, ed., *The Psychotherapy Handbook* (New York: Meridian Books, 1980).

most of the major figures directly. Many of the authors just mentioned who have not been dealt with directly were themselves influenced by people I did discuss. Thus Karen Horney was indebted to Ferenczi, for example. With the exception of Honig, all the therapists I have concentrated on in this book have been a force to contend with in therapy. Even John Rosen, one of the more egregious examples of a therapist who abuses his patients, has been frequently invoked in the eclectic psychotherapy literature. Jay Haley, in *Strategies of Psychotherapy* (100), and Frieda Fromm-Reichmann[73] both refer to his theories uncritically.

Most important is the fact that the basic underlying principles are the same for all therapies, whatever their theoretical orientation or the techniques of their practice. I am referring to a state of mind that takes precedence over any particular orientation, the very decision to offer therapy in the first place. While some individual therapists are warm, accepting, loving human beings, no therapist, regardless of background or school, escapes the criticisms I have made in these pages. By virtue of the simple fact that they are offering *therapy*, they are subject to the criticism I have been making. As individuals they may be of high character and intelligence, but once they don the invisible robe of authority that psychotherapy invests them with they have entered an entirely different realm. None of the literally thousands of books and articles about psychotherapy I have consulted in writing this book has questioned the very *idea* of therapy. Not even the many psychotherapists who have given up the profession have questioned this idea. Usually, they quit because they are 'burned out' or they think they are lacking something because working as a therapist no longer gives them the great satisfaction it once did. So taboo is the notion of criticizing the endeavor of therapy that most of them have not even considered the possibility that the fault does not lie with them but with an idea that has outlived its usefulness, if indeed it ever had any.

Government statistics estimate that thirty-four million Americans are affected by some 'mental disorder.'[74] In 1980 there

---

[73] 'Note on the Development of Treatment of Schizophrenics by Psychoanalytic Psychotherapy,' in *Specialized Techniques in Psychotherapy*, ed. by Gustav Bychowski and J. Louise Despert (New York: Grove Press, 1958), 168.

[74] Quoted by John M. Darley *et al.*, in *Psychology* (Englewood Cliffs, NJ: Prentice-Hall, 1984), 503.

were 25,523,915 office visits to psychiatrists in the United States, and 26,887,870 office visits to psychologists. Nearly ten million people had one or more visits for ambulatory mental-health care.[75] Psychotherapy is a multibillion-dollar business. It is time to conduct a searching examination of the foundations of this profit from other people's misery. That has been my aim in this book.

[75] Carl A. Taube *et al.*, 'Patients of Psychiatrists and Psychologists in Office-Based Practice: 1980,' *American Psychologist* 39 (1984): 1435–47. These statistics are based on a National Medical Care Utilization and Expenditure Survey. Morton Hunt, in an article entitled 'Navigating the Therapy Maze,' in the *New York Times Magazine* (August 30, 1987), writes: 'Today, one American in three has been in psychotherapy, and in 1987 15 million of us will make roughly 120 million visits to mental health professionals – nearly twice as many visits as to internists.'

CONCLUSION

Every therapy I have examined in this book (with the exception of radical and feminist therapies, which are beset with other problems) displays a lack of interest in social injustice. Each shows a lack of interest in physical and sexual abuse. Each shows an implicit acceptance of the political status quo. In brief, almost every therapy shows a certain lack of interest in the world.

A therapist, like anybody else, sees people's problems in terms of what the therapist already knows. If what the therapist is told doesn't fit his theories, it will have to be bent so that it will fit. Self-interest impels therapists to pretend to knowledge they do not possess. Therapists attempt to impose their own structures on their patients. It is easier to make the assumptions necessary to remain a member of the profession of psychotherapy, for example, that everybody is responsible for his or her own situation in life. Once one of these tenets is abandoned, the whose structure threatens to collapse.

I believe that therapy is never honest. This is not to say that all therapists are dishonest. Most are not. Most want to be helpful; but what they actually can offer, under the best of circumstances, falls far short of what they would like to offer. It cannot be otherwise. Because therapy depends for its existence on the postulate that the truth of a person's life can be uncovered in therapy, the therapist is rarely willing or able to acknowledge that the profession itself is fraudulent.

One of the ways therapists avoid questions that might lead to a fundamental reassessment of the very nature of psychotherapy is to accept certain clichés as profound truths. Therapists, in time, begin to respond automatically to oft-repeated myths. It is important to identify these myths.

One of the myths is a version of 'he came to me after he had tried everything else,' or 'she tried this particular kind of therapy as a last resort.' What is assumed, first of all, is that the statement is true. But since it is so self-serving, it is likely to be false much of the time.[1] Freud began using this myth in his early *Studies on Hysteria*, written in 1895, and hardly a therapist since then has not said this of at least some patients. We have seen that John Rosen and Albert Honig said it of their patients, and, of course, the psychiatrists who administer electroshock say it of theirs. Always the assumption of the 'last-resort theory' is that the patient was about to die, to be locked away permanently, or to have something terrible and irremediable happen were it not for his or her finding this particular therapist and this particular therapy. It *sounds* good, because nobody wants to question something that has saved somebody's life.

There is a related myth that stems from the patient: the testimonial 'I would be dead without his or her help,' or 'this therapy benefited me enormously.' We hear from many patients and former patients how much benefit they have derived from a certain person or treatment. We hear it from people who are given electroshock, from people on dangerous psychiatric drugs, and from people who have been lobotomized. I am not questioning their belief that they have been helped. But a little reflection suggests that it would be difficult for some people to believe otherwise given the indoctrination process they are subjected to both inside and outside institutions (society at large accepts,

[1] A related question involves the belief most therapists have that the particular method they have been trained in is the best one available. Werner Wolff distributed a questionnaire to psychotherapists of different orientations to which 70 percent answered that they believed their particular form of therapy was best, 'Fact and Value in Psychotherapy,' *American Journal of Psychotherapy* 8 (1954); 466–86. Jerome Frank, acknowledging this research, says that it 'raises uncomfortable questions about the goals of training programs in psychotherapy. Until we have a rational basis for choice of specific therapies, one may well ask whether there is any point in mastering any particular one, especially since all have so much in common.' But his conclusion – that it does not matter which therapy one studies, so long as one studies some therapy – is opposite to the one I would draw, namely, that there is no point in studying any therapy. *Psychotherapy and the Human Predicament: A Psychosocial Approach*, ed. by Park Elliott Dietz (New York: Schocken Books, 1978), 18.

unthinkingly, psychiatric values). Even when therapy is voluntary, there is an emotional and mental coercion that is rarely examined by members of the professions. When therapy is not voluntary, the opportunities for oppression become even greater.

Another myth is found in the comment 'Granted there are abuses in psychotherapy, they are the exception. The average therapist is not likely to harm a patient.' When I was practicing as a psychoanalyst, I frequently heard other psychoanalysts talk about the frauds in the field. I remember asking a prominent psychoanalyst from a famous institute in New York how many colleagues he would be willing to refer a relative to. He responded that he did not trust the vast majority of his colleagues. I have heard this over and over, though no analyst I know has ever stated it publicly.

I do not believe that abuse in the field of psychotherapy is unusual. It is just not talked about much. The reason for the enormous increase in the number of lawsuits brought against psychotherapists for malpractice is not because abuse is increasing; it is only because more people are willing to seek redress.[2] From an examination of a large cross-section of cases of psychotherapy reported in the nineteenth-century literature, few therapists would deny that by today's standards almost all would fall under the category of gross negligence, gross ignorance, or malpractice. Is there any reason to believe that in the next century people will not say the same thing of the cases reported today?

Another myth is that *all* therapy helps, regardless of the theoretical orientation of the therapist. This point of view has been most cogently expressed by Jerome D. Frank in his influential book *Persuasion and Healing: A Comparative Study of Psychotherapy*: 'The hypothesis of this book is that features common to all types of

[2] The literature on malpractice is by now enormous. Here are only a few of the better-known books and articles: D. J. Dawidoff, *The Malpractice of Psychiatrists: Malpractice in Psychoanalysis, Psychotherapy and Psychiatry* (Springfield, IL: Charles C. Thomas, 1973); R. Slovenko, *Psychiatry and Law* (Boston: Little, Brown, 1973); Daniel B. Hogan, *The Regulation of Psychotherapists*, vol. 13, *A Review of Malpractice Suits in the United States* (Cambridge; MA: Ballinger Publishing Co., 1979); A. A. Stone, 'The *Tarasoff* Decisions: Suing Psychotherapists to Safeguard Society,' *Harvard Law Review*, 90 (1976): 358–78; P. F. Slawson, 'Psychiatric Malpractice: A Regional Incidence Study,' *American Journal of Psychiatry* 48 (1970): 50–64; Ronald Jay Cohen, *Malpractice: A Guide for Mental Health Professionals* (New York: The Free Press, 1979).

psychotherapy combat a major source of the distress and disability of persons who seek psychotherapeutic help.'[3] What counts, people like Frank claim, is the relationship that develops between any therapist and any patient. The more 'liberal' critics of psychotherapy from within the field, such as Hans H. Strupp, stress that 'the therapist does not treat a disease or a disorder but rather a human being who experiences more or less specific difficulties in his adjustment to life.' Strupp believes that 'future research efforts must be aimed at matching a particular patient with a particular therapist for the purpose of achieving a human relationship in which the patient as a human being can feel respected, accepted, and understood,'[4] But all therapists claim to respect, accept, and understand the people they treat. All therapists tend to believe that a relationship with them is good for a patient. No therapist says: 'A relationship with me is a dangerous and terrible experience.' If anyone ever developed the ability to make the 'match' Strupp has written about, there would be no divorce. Such expectations are unreasonable and impossible. This does not reflect the *difficulties* of doing psychotherapy; it reflects the *impossibility* of doing psychotherapy, a conclusion with which Strupp would strongly disagree. The claim that any relationship with any therapist is 'curative' obviously cannot be true. For example, a woman had an adverse reaction to marijuana and entered 'rage reduction therapy' with a Californian psychotherapist. Was her 'relationship' with him helpful? She was diagnosed as an 'incipient schizophrenic' and 'treated with more than ten hours of the newly developed therapy . . . she was poked, beaten and tortured during this time . . . and suffered severe bruising of the upper half of the

[3] Baltimore: Johns Hopkins University Press, 1961; rev. ed., New York: Schocken Books, 1974, xvi.

[4] 'Critical Assessment of Psychodynamic Psychotherapy,' in Maurice Dongier and Eric Wittkower, eds., *Divergent Views in Psychiatry* (New York: Harper & Row, 1981). These later views are considerably less optimistic than the earlier ones, which are unfortunately far better known and more popular; Hans H. Strupp, Ronald F. Fox, and Ken Lessler, *Patients View Their Psychotherapy* (Baltimore: Johns Hopkins University Press, 1969). In the book, Strupp concludes: 'The psychotherapeutic situation is a unique vehicle for personal growth and maturation. It has much in common with other interpersonal experiences – openness, acceptance, and understanding . . . at its best, individual psychotherapy creates a learning situation unequaled by anything else that human ingenuity has been able to devise' (142).

body, and complete kidney failure.'[5] And clearly, as we have seen, therapy did not help the patients of John Rosen or Albert Honig. But for the sake of argument let us exclude these cases, and imagine for a moment that they are not representative of psychotherapy in general. 'It is generally agreed,' writes Jerome Frank in *Persuasion and Healing*, 'that the success of a psychotherapist depends in part on his genuine concern for the patient's welfare' (183). Strupp and his colleagues, in a study of one hundred thirty-one patients who had received at least twenty-five interviews of intensive psychotherapy in a university hospital outpatient clinic, found that the 'good therapist' is a 'keenly attentive, interested, benign and concerned listener – a friend who is warm and natural, is not averse to giving direct advice, who speaks one's language, makes sense and rarely arouses intense anger.'[6] What does it mean to have a 'relationship' with such a person when a true relationship is possible only with an equal? In fact, those qualities can only be ascribed to somebody we really know. Many therapists can appear to be warm and interested and benign and concerned. But this does not guarantee that they actually possess those qualities, or that such qualities exist *outside* the therapeutic relationship. After all, the therapist, every therapist, is paid for the attention he or she supplies to the patient. It is not difficult to appear to be attentive when one is rewarded

---

[5] See *APA Monitor*, March 1973, 5: 'Rage Reduction Therapy Pioneer Battles to Keep California License.' Z-therapy, as it is also called, has been endorsed as having limited application 'for some autistic children and some depressed patients' by the American Psychiatric Association Commission on Psychiatric Therapies. The commission gives the following account of this cruel therapy: 'Therapy consists of holding the autistic child down (i.e., using physical restraint) and, in addition, tickling the child so as to produce violent rage reactions. Once the rage is produced, the therapist will release the child and be loving and affectionate to him.' With the adult, 'The patient is physically restrained while the therapist asks sharp questions designed to evoke traumatic experiences from the past. At the same time the questions are asked, or afterward, the therapist tickles or painfully prods the patient's rib cage to stimulate a rage reaction. No matter how vigorously the patient struggles or cries, the restraints are firmly maintained until the patient is literally wild with rage and expressing it in the most direct and violent fashion. Sessions may go on for several hours at a time (the typical session lasts four to eight hours) until the patient is totally exhausted and has stopped struggling.' *The Psychiatric Therapies*, chaired by Toksoz B. Karasu (Washington, DC: American Psychiatric Association, 1984), 562–63.

[6] *Patients View Their Psychotherapy*, 117.

handsomely. If we place our trust in somebody, it matters very much whether that person only appears to be worthy of our trust, or actually *is* worthy. And these are things we find out only over time, and in a relationship without power and hierarchy. The therapeutic relationship *always* involves an imbalance of power. One person pays, the other receives. Vacations, time, duration of the sessions are all in the hands of one party. Only one person is thought to be an 'expert' in human relations and in feelings. Only one person is thought to be in trouble. This cannot but affect the judgment and perception of the party less powerful.

One of the most highly praised psychiatrists of his time was D. Ewen Cameron (1901–1967). He was Chairman of the Department of Psychiatry at McGill University, in Canada, Director of the famed Allan Memorial Institute, and Professor of Psychiatry at the Albany Medical College. He was also President of both the American Psychiatric Association and the World Psychiatric Association. During the Second World War he was part of an international committee of psychiatrists and social scientists who studied the origins and nature of Nazi culture. After the war, during the Nuremberg trials, he was selected to evaluate some of the Nazi defendants, including Rudolf Hess. Hardly any psychiatrist has received more honors than Dr. Cameron. After his death, the *American Journal of Psychiatry* quoted this comment:

> His world-wide success in his profession was, of course, due principally to his great knowledge and brilliance. But surely a great factor was also the softness – one is tempted to say loveliness – of his personality. Those who were privileged to know him, even briefly, will not soon forget the warmth and the kindliness of this understanding man.[7]

But there are at least fifty-three people, most of them women, who came to the Allan Memorial Institute between 1957 and 1961 seeking help for various problems who have not forgotten something else about Cameron. With funds from the Central Intelligence Agency, which was interested in the new brain-washing techniques developed by Cameron, these fifty-three people were subjected to megadoses of LSD, 'sleep therapy' (via drugs) for up to

[7] 124 (1967): 261.

sixty-five consecutive days, and a particularly intense form of electroshock. In addition, they were forced to hear repeated recorded messages during sixteen-hour intervals, which Cameron called 'psychic driving.' None of these patients consented to the experiment, nor were they told they were being used for research. A group of nine former patients filed suit (still pending) in U.S. District Court in Washington in December 1980 against the United States government. In an excellent article in the *Washington Post* (July 28, 1985) entitled 'Twenty-Five Years of Nightmares,' David Rennic writes:

> Dr. Mary Morrow approached Cameron for a fellowship in psychiatry, but Cameron thought, after a physical exam, that Morrow appeared 'nervous' and admitted her as a patient instead. For 11 days Morrow says she underwent depatterning experiments that included electroshock treatment, and barbiturates. The treatment resulted in brain anoxia – not enough oxygen reaching the brain – and she was hospitalized. Today Morrow suffers from prosopagnosia – she cannot recognize people's faces.

The depatterning treatment undergone by Morrow has been described by Cameron in an article published in a leading psychiatric journal.[8] So many electroshocks were given to a patient in a single day that 'the patient developed an organic brain syndrome with acute confusion, disorientation and interference with his learned habits of eating and bladder and bowel control.' The idea was to bring the person to the level of a four-year-old child, then restructure the patient's memory. Cameron hoped to become as famous as Freud for this new treatment of 'schizophrenics.'[9] When

[8] 'The Depatterning Treatment of Schizophrenia,' *Comprehensive Psychiatry* 3 (1962): 65–76.
[9] Ironically, it was a well-known Freudian analyst, Gregory Zilboorg, writing an appreciation of Cameron in *The American Journal of Psychiatry* (July, 1963, 12), who said: 'He has confirmed psychoanalysts on his staff, and he sees Freud as a part of the total evolution of psychiatric thought,' which shows that analysts could accept Cameron. On the other hand, when the psychiatrist who succeeded Cameron at the Allan Memorial Institute, R. A. Cleghorn, ordered a follow-up study of Cameron's patients, the results were anything but optimistic: 'A questionnaire designed to examine memory function in detail was completed by 27 former patients who had received the intensive ECT . . . The

he first wrote about his method in 1958, in an article entitled 'Treatment of the Chronic Paranoid Schizophrenic Patient,' he said: 'We are presenting a method of treatment which we have found to be more successful than any hitherto reported.'[10] (When patients were not cooperative, Cameron, in this article, called their reactions 'paranoid.') The CIA hoped it could obliterate memories of CIA operations by former agents.[11] It was particularly interested in an article that Cameron published in 1960 in which he spoke of a patient who, after treatment, had 'complete amnesia for all events of his life.'[12] According to Cameron, differential amnesia, i.e., forgetting specific events, can be 'for ten years prior to treatment' and total amnesia for five years.

One of Cameron's patients has been called 'a human guinea pig, a poor pathetic man.'[13] His son, Dr. Harvey Weinstein, a psychiatrist, is the Director of Student Health Services at Stanford University. On May 4, 1987, in a telephone conversation, I asked him if what Cameron had done to his father had changed his view of psychiatry in general or electroshock in particular. He said it had not. He personally would not give electroshock, because of the connotations it had in his own mind. But 'under the right circumstances, with the proper controls, and for the right patient,' he had no objection to its use. I argued that Cameron's having been President of the American, Canadian, and World Psychiatric Associations clearly meant that his practices fell well within the con-

[9]*Cont.* dependence on others for recall of past events is reported by 63 percent of the sample. A persisting amnesia retrograde to the depatterning and ranging in time from six months to ten years is reported by 60 percent of the respondents.' The study concludes: 'The incidence of physical complications and the anxiety generated in the patient because of real or imagined [!] memory difficulty argue against the administration of intensive electroconvulsive shock as a standard therapeutic procedure.' A. E. Schwartmann and P. E. Termansen, 'Intensive Electroconvulsive Therapy: A Followup Study.' *Journal of the Canadian Psychiatric Association* 12, suppl. (April 1967): 92–95.

[10] *Journal of the Canadian Medical Association* 78 (1958): 92–95.

[11] For twenty years, between 1953 and 1973 (and possibly beyond), the CIA spent at least twenty-five million dollars in attempts to learn how to control the human mind. See John Marks, *The Search for the 'Manchurian Candidate': The CIA and Mind Control,* (New York: Quadrangle/The New York Times Book Co., 1979).

[12] 'The problem of differential amnesia as a factor in the treatment of schizophrenia,' *Comprehensive Psychiatry* 1 (1980): 26–34.

[13] A phrase used in the article, 'Twenty-Five Years of Nightmares.'

fines of psychiatry; he was hardly a pariah. On the contrary, he was one of the most honored members of his profession. Surely this says something about the state of psychiatry? Dr. Weinstein felt that it says something only about the state of psychiatry *then*, not now, and adduced as evidence the fact that many of his psychiatric colleagues in this country are appalled when they learn what Cameron did. If this is true, how is it that there has not been a single article condemning Cameron's practices in any psychiatric journal since 1977, when the CIA's partial funding of them was made public? Some psychiatrists might claim that what Cameron did is only an *abuse* of psychiatry. It is virtually impossible to find a practicing psychiatrist who can see that what Cameron did is the very purpose of psychiatry, that this is its *use*, not its abuse.

The myth of training also deserves mention. Therapists usually boast of their 'expertise,' the 'elaborate training' they have undergone. When discussing competence, one often hears phrases like 'he has been well trained,' or 'he has had specialized training.' People are rather vague about the nature of psychotherapy training, and therapists rarely encourage their patients to ask in any detail. They don't for a good reason: often their training is very modest. To receive a degree in marriage, family, and child counseling (the MFCC), for example, one need study only one year after receiving a bachelor's degree. The most elaborate and lengthy training programs are the classic psychoanalytic ones, but this is not because of the amount of material that has to be covered. (I spent eight years in my psychoanalytic training. In retrospect, I feel I could have learned the basic ideas in about eight hours of concentrated reading.) Instead, it is because the training is an elaborate indoctrination program, a way of becoming a 'professional.' This process is recognized, indeed encouraged:

> Professional training, if it truly succeeds, leads to a psychologic amalgamation of the person with the function that he is to perform. We speak then not of having a job, but of being a member of a profession. Professional people are strongly identified with what they do, they derive pleasure and pride from the status which their function affords them in their community, and they find it difficult to think in terms of change even if greater economic security is offered, because their deepest satisfactions stem from carrying on their pro-

fession which has become part of their life. This sense of professional identity is an essential attribute in a profession such as psychotherapy, and its acquisition must be considered one of the important training goals.[14]

In short, one is learning to become a loyal member of a select group. A natural response to criticism is to attack the critic, because loyalty to one's profession is considered essential. How is it possible to carry on serious, critical examination of the basic postulates of a field in which your personal identity is tied up? The reason we so casually accept a statement like the one made by Ekstein and Wallerstein above is that it corresponds to the general structure of our society. Indeed, how could psychotherapy, part of the very structure of our society, place itself outside society and criticize it? Psychotherapists, like the rest of us, are taught to be good and obedient citizens. I would agree with the conclusion of Eliot Freidson to his excellent book *Profession of Medicine:*

> It is my own opinion that the profession's role in a free society should be limited to contributing the technical information men need to make their own decisions on the basis of their own values. When he preempts the authority to direct, even constrain men's decisions on the basis of his own values, the professional is no longer an expert but rather a member of a new privileged class disguised as expert.[15]

I think by now there is general agreement that no psychotherapy can be value free, and that no psychotherapist can avoid instilling or attempting to instill his or her values in patients. David Rosenthal, who did research in this area as early as the 1950s, concluded that patients accept the values of their therapists, which is what we would expect.[16] Nathan Hurvitz put the matter well

[14] Rudolf Ekstein and Robert S. Wallerstein, *The Teaching and Learning of Psychotherapy* (New York: Basic Books, 1958), 66.
[15] *Profession of Medicine: A Study of the Sociology of Applied Knowledge* (New York: Dodd, Mead & Co., 1972), 382. See, too, Elliott A. Krause, *Power and Illness: The Political Sociology of Health and Medical Care* (New York/Amsterdam: Elsevier, 1972).
[16] 'Changes in Some Moral Values Following Psychotherapy,' *Journal of Consulting Psychology* 19 (1955): 431–36.

when he concluded: 'In this way psychotherapy creates powerful support for the established order – it challenges, labels, manipulates, rejects or co-opts those who attempt to change the society.'[17] Erving Goffman, in his much-celebrated book *Asylums*, writes: 'It is understandable that a large part of psychotherapy consists of holding the sins of the patient up to him and getting him to see the error of his ways. And in a sense, I do not see how it can or should be otherwise.'[18]

Whether one agrees with Goffman's perception of what happens in psychotherapy or not, his last comment, that he does not see how it could or should be otherwise, strikes me as wrong. Of course, in a sense, it *cannot* be otherwise because psychotherapy is merely an extension of the views of the dominant society. Psychotherapy could and *should* be otherwise by ceasing to exist. It can and should be replaced by open and searching criticisms of the very foundation of our society, a reexamination of its basic postulates, including, of course, a rigorous examination of the basic underlying postulates of psychotherapy, along with some explanation for how society has made psychotherapy so popular and so destructive. Kate Millett was recently asked what she would 'do' with somebody who was arguing all the time, and breaking things, and acting weird. Her response is enlightening:

A great many people might argue and argue and argue because they're so exasperated, being hounded by somebody, or in one of those emotional love/hate family/sibling/divorce situations, that they behave madly because they're so mad in the old American sense of angry at the people around them. There's no reason to believe that when they go outside where they're not met with hostility and antagonism that they wouldn't be just fine. What if you and I had an enormous argument about, say, even this topic, and circumstances were

[17] 'Psychotherapy as a Means of Social Control,' *Journal of Consulting and Clinical Psychology* 40 (1974): 237. See, too, Phil Brown, ed., *Mental Health Care and Social Policy* (Boston: Routledge & Kegan Paul, 1985). Lillian Ross's stories in *The New Yorker*, later published as the book *Vertical and Horizontal* (New York: Simon & Schuster, 1963), give a lively sense of the distorted values of a psychoanalyst opposed to the more natural values of his patient, who escaped just in time.

[18] *Asylums: Essays on the Social Situation of Mental Patients and Other Inmates* (Garden City, NY: Doubleday & Co., 1961), 366.

okay for you to lift up the phone and call the white squad and win the argument by having me dragged off in an ambulance? Well, that's what families do. While if you *didn't* call the white squad, I could just get back on the airplane and live my own life. I'm saying that people have a right to their own lives, and if you can't help somebody, you ought to get out of their way.[19]

It is difficult to find a therapist who does not feel loyalty to the profession. Professional loyalty means subordinating human impulses to what is considered most advantageous to the profession as a whole. Therapists depend on a social network for referrals. So even if an individual therapist is completely opposed to somatic intervention – drugs or electroshock, for example – working in a setting where these are used is often difficult to avoid, and the opposition then becomes internalized, i.e., silenced. This is another step along the road of corruption. And even those therapists who are not part of a hospital setting are nevertheless part of a larger therapeutic community that will not take lightly any departure from professional solidarity. A therapist who takes a strong stance against electroshock, for example, risks social isolation by his peers, or even worse. That is one reason so few therapists have spoken out publicly against electroshock. Even, then, if therapists do not use electroshock themselves, they are part of a professional world that sanctions, even encourages, its use. Witness how Carl Rogers was sucked into the life of the institution he had only come to study. It is impossible to remain silent in the face of tyranny without, by this very act of silence, becoming an agent of that tyranny.

It is the world of therapy, it is *therapy* itself that is at the core of the corruption I have described in this book. Every therapist, no matter how kindly and benign in appearance and behavior, is sooner or later drawn into that corruption, because the profession itself is corrupt. A profession that depends for its existence on other people's misery is at special risk. The very mainspring of psychotherapy is profit from another person's suffering. Historically

---

[19]This is from an interview with Kate Millett about the difficulty she has had for the last three years, and is still having, getting her book *The Loony Bin Trip* published. See Andrea Freud Loewenstein, 'Kate Millett's *Loony Bin Trip* . . .,' *Sojourner* (June 1987), 12–15.

therapists have never been in the forefront of the struggle for social change. It is not in the interest of the profession to create conditions that would lead to the dissolution of psychotherapy.

As was seen in the last chapter, radical therapists and feminist therapists (both contradictions in terms) are no exception to these remarks. Both profit from a system that exploits people's unhappiness and both place their loyalty to the profession above that of the people they see, no matter how much rhetoric they use to camouflage this fact. It is the lack of a courageous stance against the many forms of tyranny within psychiatry that I find so upsetting. I know of no group of feminist therapists, for example, that publicly opposes electroshock. I have heard ex-inmates of psychiatric institutions say they were sent there by radical therapists or by feminist therapists.

Kurt R. Eissler, the distinguished Freudian psychoanalyst and former Director of the Freud Archives, wrote an article, published in 1963 in Germany (*Psyche* 17, 241–301), with the arresting title 'Die Ermordung von wievielen seiner Kinder muss ein Mensch symptomfrei ertragen können, um eine normale Konstitution zu haben?,' which translates as: 'The death of how many of his children must a man be able to bear, without developing symptoms, in order to be said to have a normal constitution?' The article is an impassioned argument against German psychiatrists who reject Jewish claims for restitution, based upon psychological damage from having been in a concentration camp, on the grounds that these people are either simulating, or inventing (fantasy!), or their constitution predisposed them to have a traumatic reaction. I found Eissler's article, written with genuine outrage, persuasive. Nevertheless, I could not help thinking how deeply imbued our culture has become with psychiatric thinking. For Eissler's point is that when the trauma is great enough, we cannot distinguish a normal constitution from an abnormal one, we cannot tell a *real* shizophrenic from a false one. But Eissler has not subjected the very concepts of normal and abnormal constitutions or schizophrenia to any searching examination. He simply believes that there *is* such a thing as a normal constitution and an abnormal one, that there is such a thing as genuine schizophrenia, and furthermore that an experienced psychiatrist (a term he uses often) will be able to distinguish one from the other. But the German psychiatrists who wrote their reports denying the relevance of trauma were also experienced psychiatrists. Quite possibly these German psychiatrists were anti-Semitic, but there seems a more fundamental problem at work here, one that Eissler and other psychiatrists completely ignore: Once we give *anybody* the right to decide who or what is normal and abnormal we have abdicated a fundamental intellectual responsibility (to repudiate the very idea of making such distinctions) and we should not be surprised when it is 'misused' by people who come from a different psychiatric orientation. It cannot but be misused.

Everybody should know, then, that to step into the office of a psychotherapist, regardless of the latter's persuasion, is to enter a world where great harm is possible. In California any therapist can send a person to a psychiatric institution involuntarily or can persuade (often by coercion) that person to enter one 'voluntarily.' Psychiatric drugs or electroshock are almost certain to be used inside (nor are they absent from 'office' psychiatry either), not to mention the everyday dehumanizing process that is built into *every* psychiatric institution, from the state mental hospital to the most expensive private sanatorium.

How many therapists can honestly say that they have never been responsible for sending anyone to an institution? Even those people who appear not to be at risk of being sent to such a place have entered a world where they are automatically at some risk. Therapists wield enormous power, whether or not they seek it. Imbalance in power rarely leads to compassionate behavior. Yet it is precisely such compassion (and knowledge) that we have been conditioned to expect from a therapist, any therapist. My criticism in this book is not directed at the 'patient,' the person who expects compassion from a therapist, because that is what we have been taught to expect. No matter how many times a person is disappointed by a therapist, there is always the hope that the next therapist will prove to be the wise, virtuous, and kindly guru, completely dedicated to listening and to easing another person's pain, whom most of us hope to find when we seek out a therapist. My criticism is directed both at the profession at large and at individual therapists. For they have fostered this myth when they know it is false. They know, often in exquisite detail, the failings of their colleagues and often regale each other with horror tales from the battlefield of psychotherapeutic practice. They also know enough of their own faults and inadequacies to realize that their 'clients' are bound to get less than they hoped or had been led to expect. Many times I sat behind a patient in analysis and became acutely and painfully aware of my inability to help. Many times, indeed, I did feel compassion. But at times I also felt bored, uninterested, irritated, helpless, confused, ignorant, and lost. At times I could offer no genuine assistance, yet rarely did I acknowledge this to the patient. My life was in no better shape than that of my patients. Any advice I might have had to offer would be no better than that of a well-informed friend (and considerably more expensive). I must assume that none of this was unique to me. Everything I experienced in the situation must have been felt by other therapists as well. The only reason, I think, that I can acknowledge these deficiencies in my capacity as a therapist is that I made the decision (not an easy one from economic and social points of view) to stop getting paid for an activity that was so artificial and so basically flawed as psychotherapy.

The corruption I have discerned in psychotherapy and discussed in this book is not unique to this one discipline. Psychotherapy is not, as the profession and individual therapists claim, the instrument that will allow us to detect corruption elsewhere. Psychotherapy cannot be reformed in its parts, because the activity, by its nature, is harmful. Recognizing the lies, the flaws, the harm, the potential for harm, the imbalance in power, the arrogance, the condescension, the pretensions may be the first step in the eventual abolition of psychotherapy that I believe is, one day in the future, inevitable and desirable.

AFTERWORD
TO THE SECOND EDITION
The Tyranny of Psychotherapy

After the publication of *Against Therapy: Emotional Tyranny and the Myth of Psychological Healing* the most common criticism I heard as I lectured around the United States was that my book was merely a list of all the worst therapists who have ever lived, and that it was as if I had set out to uncover the worst abuses these worst therapists had ever perpetrated, and that no matter how many individual examples of corruption among psychotherapists I can provide, this does not necessarily reflect on the discipline of psychotherapy as a whole.[1] I am not sure this is true. After all,

[1] Glenn Collins, for example, in his review of *Against Therapy* in the *New York Times* (November 13, 1988), accuses me of taking the reader on 'the grand tour' of horror stories in therapy, as if this were some fundamental failing in my character, or evidence of sadism directed at the reader. He seems to feel it was wrong of me to 'revive assertions that Carl Jung collaborated with the Nazis during World War II' as if this were some how a lapse in good taste, or to point out that the 'founding deities of therapy were paternatistic, sexist, authoritarian and all too fallible'. But he never says I am mistaken, or why, precisely, it is wrong to raise these questions. Most importantly, Mr. Collins writes that I 'suggest that psychotherapy has not come to terms with sexual assault, child abuse, rape, battering, torture, concentration camp victimization and other atrocities.' I do more than suggest it, I state it flat out, many times. I believe it, and I believe it on the basis of much historical evidence. I can go even further, and suggest that any new-found concern for oppression on the part of the profession of psychiatry should be viewed with a generous degree of skepticism, especially when the primary oppressors have been the psychiatrists themselves: lobotomy, electroshock, medications that cause tardive dyskinesia (a grotesque and irreversible Parkinsonian neurolgical impairment), forced incarceration in psychiatric institutjons, sexual abuse of patients, the list goes on and on. True, recently, psychotherapists are eager to exploit the

there are a finite number of psychotherapists, and after a while, when you continue to find evidence of abuse, you begin to ask yourself whether there is not something inherently corrupting about the very process of becoming a psychotherapist. It seems that the less we know about an individual therapist, the more likely we are to worship him or her. 'Knowledge' inevitably leads to disillusion. And it usually takes some years for incriminating information to become available. Especially during the lifetime of powerful psychotherapists, people are reluctant to come forward to bear witness to their own negative experience.

An important example of this process of demystification is the reassessment that has come about due to the New information has recently come to light about Bruno Bettelheim that necessitates a complete reassessment of his place in the history of psychotherapy. When Bettelheim committed suicide in a Maryland nursing home in March 1990 at the age of 86, obituaries in the *New York Times* and elsewhere, could not praise him highly enough. Without exception, he was called one of America's great psychoanalysts, and the man who had pioneered child psychotherapy, a brilliant theoretician, a man of enormous compassion and love, and so on.[2] Of course psychoanalysts knew that he was never a psychoanalyst, merely somebody interested in psychoanalysis.[3] (It would be like my calling myself a medical doctor on the grounds that I was interested in and had

---

[1]*Cont.* new public interest in sexual abuse. They say, for example, that they are 'experts' in its treatment, and that women need to seek a psychiatrist to be 'healed.' But permit me to be skeptical of a profession which claims expertise in child abuse when a few years back they claimed it hardly existed.

[2]One example among many: 'For Bettelheim, the privilege of being a psychoanalyst and of practicing, teaching, transmitting, and modifying psychoanalytic theory and practice, consisted in a deeply ingrained respect for the human being, for his or her own privacy, individual uniqueness, struggles, quest for truth, aspirations towards personal forms of liberation, creativity, and playfulness.' David James Fisher, 'Homage to Bettelheim,' *Partisan Review* 4, vol. 57, no. 4 (1990).

[3]I have often heard people say that Bettelheim did not refer to himself as a psychoanalyst, only others did so. But this is not entirely true. For example, in *The Informed Heart*, he wrote: 'It took several years of intensive analysis, and many more years of its practice, to teach me how far psychological experiences can change the personality of a man . . . ' [10]

contributed to medicine, even though my degree is in Sanskrit.)
As for his compassion to children, we heard this mainly from
Bettelheim himself, in his many books, such as *Love is Not
Enough: The Treatment of Emotionally Disturbed Children*, and *The
Uses of Enchantment*. We had not yet heard from the children.
Well, many of the children who were in the Sonia Shankman
Orthogenic (a prejudiced word, that refers to so-called 'mental
defects' that need correction) School at the University of Chicago,
originally diagnosed as 'autistic' or 'chronic schizophrenic' (now
miraculously cured; would Bettelheim claim that their current
anger is proof that he 'cured' them?) have now started to come
forth and speak, and the story they tell is a chilling one, in
complete contrast to the ones that Bettelheim told about himself.
Articles in the *Chicago Reader*, *Commentary*, and the *Washington Post*,
reveal a different Bruno Bettelheim.[4] Alida Jatich, for example,
who was in the school from 1966 to 1972, and is now a computer

[3]*Cont.* which certainly implies that he practiced psychoanalysis.
Moreover, in the last interview he gave before his death, 'Love and
Death' to Celeste Fremon (*Los Angeles Times Magazine*, January 27, 1991,
21) Bettelheim said, 'Now, I will not say that psychoanalysis doesn't
help in many ways. After all, if I didn't believe that, I wouldn't be a
psychoanalyst.' In fact, he was not a psychoanalyst.

[4]The letter that started the discussion was printed anonymously in
the *Chicago Reader*, under the title 'Brutal Bettelheim' on April 6, 1990,
and stated, among other things, 'it's agonizingly difficult to write about
this. I've been trying to put these memories behind me for a long time.
These memories have robbed the joy from my life. But when I saw
those obituaries that painted Bettelheim as a hero, I could keep silent
no longer . . . Bruno Bettelheim did not help children at his school;
instead, he damaged everyone he came in contact with. Bettelheim
and his life's work is a fraud.' The writer was Alida M. Jatich (personal
communication). Charles Pekow, another inmate, wrote the next article,
in the *Washington Post*, entitled 'The Other Dr. Bettelheim: The Revered
Psychologist Had a Dark, Violent Side' (August 26, 1990). Pekow's article
reveals the same world: 'In the four books he wrote about the school,
Bettelheim never mentioned hitting. But he created a climate of fear – we
could never tell when he would attack us for any arbitrary reason. Once,
after a boy returned from a visit home, Bettelheim spent five minutes
slapping him in the face, hitting him in the sides with fists and pulling his
hair. Midway through, he revealed why: the lad had told his brother to
"do well in school." He had no right to "push" his brother around. To be
sure, the blows he struck, though often painful and humiliating, did

programmer in Chicago, wrote in the *Chicago Reader* that 'In person, he was an evil man who set up his school as a private empire and himself as a demigod or cult leader. He bullied, awed, and terrorized the children at his school, their parents, school staff members, his graduate students and anyone else who came into contact with him.' He made no secret of the fact that, a clumsy man himself, he abhorred clumsiness in others. Bettelheim theorized that awkwardness was a sign of hidden aggression, and all aggression, even unconscious aggression, must be punished. Here is her story in her own words:

> I was at his school from 1966 to 1972 and I lived in terror of him. He beat me for bumping into people, on the theory that there is no such thing as an accident. Another time he dragged me out of the shower without any clothes on and beat me in front of a roomful of people. No, I don't understand what prompted him to do that, and I don't suppose I ever will. I didn't dare try to defend myself. Children who didn't 'behave' would be threatened with being sent to a state asylum where they would be given shock treatments and drugs.[5]

Ronald Angres, in his fine article 'Who, Really, Was Bruno

[4]*Cont.* not physically damage people. But I often saw Bettelheim drag children across the floor by their hair and kick them. He even hit autistic children who couldn't speak clearly . . . I heard him proclaim that even sporting collisions were always the result of deliberate aggression (even from children with motor problems lacking normal nerve controls). And I saw him hit children who had such accidents.' Pekow also pointed out that Bettelheim's methods were similar to those used in concentration camps. All of these articles are excellent; the one by Ronald Angres, discussed below, is especially beautifully written and tightly argued. Much to be recommended, too, is an article by Ron Grossman, published in the *Chicago Tribune* (November 11, 1990), which points to the puzzles in Bettelheim's degree (it is not at all certain he had any degree at all in psychology) and reveals that 'the senior counselors also regularly laid down on Bettelheim's couch to be analyzed, with Bettelheim sharing the results with the rest of the staff.' See too the article in the *New York Times* by Richard Bernstein: 'Accusations of Abuse Haunt the Legacy of Dr. Bruno Bettelheim' (November 4, 1990, Section E, 6).

[5]Letters column, *University of Chicago Magazine*, October 1990.

Bettelheim'[6] writes that Bettelheim was 'widely mourned as a paragon both of insight and of compassion; but to me, in the twelve years I spent as his student/patient, he was a bully, a tormentor, and a liar.' Angres, whose account reveals considerable consistency and astuteness, wrote that

> ... though Bettelheim routinely proclaimed in print and speech that no one should *ever* use corporal punishment on children, he himself just as routinely administered it. And so I lived for years in terror of his beatings, in terror of his footsteps in the dorms – in abject, animal terror. I never knew when he would hit me, or for what, or how savagely. For Bettelheim prized his unpredictability, no less than his unconventionality: as someone who saw into the secret depths of men's souls, he gloried in defying ordinary notions of which offenses were important, or even what constituted an offense. 'What a hostile character!' he would say of me, and countless other boys, as he beat us publicly. These beatings, which made the greatest impression on me of anything that I have known in life, stick in my memory as grand performances of exultant rage.

Astonishingly, this outstanding article in *Commentary* called down the wrath of Ernst Federn (the psychoanalyst Paul Federn's son) who wrote an almost incoherently angry letter to the editor in which he says: 'Bettelheim was a pioneer in what in the field is called "milieu therapy" the only effective form of therapy for severely disturbed patients. Anyone who has some knowledge or experience with this type of treatment knows that it cannot exclude violent acting out, not only from the side of the patients but from the therapists and the caretakers as well. This violence is not corporal punishment in the sense of chastisement but the consequences of the disturbed behavior and is integrated into the therapy itself.' An astonishing letter.[7] Bettelheim first attracted the

---

[6] *Commentary* 90, no. 4, October 1990, 26–30.
[7] The letter, sent to the editors of *Commentary*, was not published. I have seen it through the courtesy of Ron Angres. The editors did publish (February 1991) a large number of letters on this article, along

attention of American academics, when he wrote a bizarre paper entitled 'Individual and Mass Behavior in Extreme Situations'[8] about his experiences in Dachau and Buchenwald (he was there in the late 1930s for several months), one of the first, perhaps the very first, article to blame the victims, by stating that to some degree the Jews provoked some of the actions of the Nazis. (This was a theme later taken up with a vengeance by Raul Hillberg in his book *The Destruction of the European Jews* and by Hannah Arendt in her equally outrageous *Eichmann in Jerusalem* a book that Bettelheim defended in print when other more careful scholars distanced themselves from her views.)

In Bettelheim's obituary in the *New York Times* (March 13, 1990) a close friend of Bettelheim, the psychoanalyst Rudolph Eckstein is quoted as saying, 'He told me that once you were in a camp, you could never escape the cruelty. He turned it upside down when he started his school for disturbed children. It was a protected, caring environment, the mirror opposite of the camps. The door was locked to the outside, but always open from the inside.' In fact, Bettelheim seems to have turned the school into yet another version of a concentration camp, as Angres and other survivors of his school point out. (Of course Bettelheim has been defended by the staff and the present director of the school, Jacquelyn Sanders.)[9] This was recognized in an excellent letter to the *New York Times* by Roberta Redford who was an inmate in the school from 1967 to 1974, titled 'Bettelheim Became the Very Evil He Loathed' (Tuesday, November 20, 1990) who

---

[7]*Cont.* with a fine response by Angres. Most of the letters, many from former patients, were supportive but there were a few like that by Federn.

[8]*Journal of Abnormal and Social Psychology,* vol. 38 (1943) reprinted in Bruno Bettelheim, *The Informed Heart: Autonomy in a Mass Age* (Illinois: The Free Press, 1960).

[9]She wrote a memorial tribute in the *University of Chicago Chronicle* (October 25, 1990, page 2) which ends with these words: 'Not only did Dr. B. know what I had to say about him, he also knew of the plan to establish a Bettelheim Center for Research and Training at the Orthogenic School, so that there can long continue to be, in his name and in his memory, a very personal place that, as part of a great University, can bring heart and mind together so that the light necessary for us and others on similar quests to explore the dark shadows of children's

wrote: 'Perhaps it was the power he held over so many lives for so many years that corrupted him. I would like to believe that at the beginning his motives were pure. By the time I knew him, he was a megalomaniac, twisted and out of control. We were terrified of him, and lived for those days when he was out of town ... We had nobody on our side. We were falsely imprisoned, falsely labeled as insane and then publicly beaten and humiliated. This was a loving milieu that was supposed to turn the Nazi methods upside down? No. This was a replica of the Nazi milieu Bettelheim supposedly loathed.' Is the fact that Bettelheim beat the children news? Not really. As Ron Angres points out: 'Everyone who worked at the Orthogenic School knew. His beatings, after all, were usually performed in front of staff members and, almost as often, in front of classmates or dorm mates. Yet those who observed these scenes for the most part kept silent.' *Newsweek* (September 10, 1990) in an article titled 'Beno Brutalheim'? pointed out that 'there are indications that at least the local psychiatric community knew exactly what was going on, and did nothing. Chicago analysts scathingly referred to the doctor as "Beno Brutalheim".' But not, note, in print!

Even Anna Freud has not proven immune from criticism from her own analysands. Esther Menaker, in her book *Appointment in Vienna: An American Psychoanalyst Recalls her Student Days in Pre-War Austria*,[10] is the first intrepid analysand of Anna Freud to point to serious flaws in that great daughter of Sigmund's method of analysis:

> Anna Freud must have sensed my attachment to Elizabeth and experienced it as competitive with her relationship to me, for she reacted strongly, even unprofessionally, to a trivial incident. Elizabeth had given me a rather chic silk dress that had become too small for her. I remember it well: a black silk print with a small yellow flower, close-fitting and rather elegant on a slim young figure. One day, for reasons I no longer remember, I wore it

[9]*Cont.* suffering can continue to grow.' She is not, needless to say, referring to the suffering caused by Dr. Bettelheim.
[10]New York: St. Martin's Press, 1989, 113–14

to my analytic session. Feeling that it was not particularly appropriate for the occasion, I made some comment about this, referring to the fact that it was a gift from Elizabeth. With considerable emotion and a palpable sense of relief, Anna Freud said, 'I thought the dress was not yours. It's not your style or taste.' The remark left me somewhat conflicted, although I said nothing. (I must have been learning that I could not be outspoken with impunity.) Actually, I liked the dress, although it did differ from my usual style. But it was precisely this change that I enjoyed. Anna Freud's lack of joyousness, of abandon, of even a bit of flamboyance, put a damper on some of my natural inclinations in these directions.

The problem of Anna Freud's understanding of her own sexuality has come to play some role in probing the limits of her understanding of other people's sexuality. David Viscott, a prominent psychiatrist in Los Angeles with his own radio and television show, recently suggested the possibility that Anna Freud was sexually assaulted by her father, Sigmund Freud. He does not have any direct evidence, only circumstantial. This is not the place for me to address this intriguing question, but I merely wish to note that in 1981, the year before she died, Anna Freud contributed two pages to the book *Sexually Abused Children and Their Families* edited by Patricia Beezley Mrazek, Instructor of Pediatrics at the University of Colorado Health Sciences Center, and the late C. Henry Kempe, Professor of Pediatrics at the Medical School of the University of Colorado (Oxford: Pergamon Press, 1981). The last paragraph of her contribution (on page 34) is worth quoting in full:

Far from existing only as a phantasy, incest is thus also a fact, more widespread among the population in certain periods than in others. Where the chances of harming a child's normal developmental growth are concerned, it ranks higher than abandonment, neglect, physical maltreatment

or any other form of abuse. It would be a fatal mistake
to underrate either the importance or the frequency of its
actual occurrence.

The last sentence is particularly important: if it is really a
'fatal mistake' to underrate the importance or the frequency
of its actual occurrence, what explanation would Anna Freud
provide for the fact that over her entire illustrious career, she
did precisely this? In her voluminous writings about children
(more than eight volumes), during a long and successful career,
apart from this one outstanding statement, Anna Freud consistently failed to address the question of the sexual abuse of
children.[11] Are these words intended to be self-incriminatory?
Or is she looking beyond herself, possibly to her father? Could
this, in fact, be a kind of veiled accusation? After an initial courageous stance, her father wound up underrating both
the importance and the frequency of the actual occurrence
of the sexual abuse of children. In fact, so successful was
Sigmund Freud's 'reasoning' on this point, that he convinced
generations of psychiatrists that the sexual abuse of children
was neither important nor frequent. I need not remind my
readers that the standard *Comprehensive Textbook of Psychiatry* as
late as 1975 was still speaking about the actual incidence of

[11]It is widely recognized that Anna Freud had little interest in
the actual circumstances of her patients. '. . . She also places all of
adolescent pathology in the young people's inner space, with very
little interest in their social environment. During a Hampstead Clinic
discussion of a clinical presentation, she was troubled when some
clinicians suggested that the source of pathology might be located in
the adolescent's family, and she pointed out that the parents were
clearly well-meaning, middle-class, and benevolent, overlooking that
none of these qualities negated a possible pathological family system.'
(Sophie Freud, *My Three Mothers and Other Passions* (New York: New York
University Press, 1988), 304). However, Sophie Freud, the daughter of
Esti Freud, Freud's daughter-in-law, does not agree with my criticisms:
'Yet the recent criticism that Sigmund Freud or Anna Freud relegated
all accusation against parents to the realm of fantasy is unjustified' (314),
evidently a reference to my position, now shared by many others, and
she cites a passage from Anna Freud to prove her point: 'In actual life
it is as a rule far more important to protect the child from the father's
violence than the father from the child's hostility.'

incest as one per million in the general population.[12] The latest edition (1988) of the *New Harvard Guide to Psychiatry* lists, in its index, under incest, only one entry: 'Delusional disorder.'[13] By contrast, Diana Russell's sophisticated research shows that the actual prevalence of sexual abuse before the age of 18 is something like 38 per cent of the female population.[14]

Again, people have come to me with the objection that even if Freud were wrong about sexual abuse, this need not compromise his other contributions. It is worth considering for a moment whether this is so. It cannot be denied, I think, that Freud's views on women were compromised from the beginning by his characterizing women's genuine memories of sexual abuse as mere fantasies. His theories on female sexual development were tainted by his belief that these 'imaginings' must be grounded in psychological need (the 'Oedipus Complex'), which also vitiated his view of childhood sexuality. Since he could not acknowledge that men were violating women and children in fact and not just in fantasy, he was unable to give a convincing portrait of male sexual development either. Nonetheless, these very real and

[12]D. James Henderson, 'Incest,' in ed. by A. M. Freedman, H. I. Kaplan and B. J. Sadock, *Comprehensive Textbook of Psychiatry*, 2nd ed. (Baltimore: Williams and Wilkins, 1975) 1532. See Judith Lewis Herman, *Father–Daughter Incest* (Cambridge: Harvard University Press, 1981).

[13]*The New Harvard Guide to Psychiatry*, ed. by Armand M. Nicholi (Cambridge: Harvard University Press, 1988).

[14]Diana E. H. Russell, 'The Incidence and Prevalence of Intrafamilial and Extrafamilial Sexual Abuse of Female Children', *Child Abuse* 7 (1983) 133–46. This generally considered the most serious and reliable of the studies in this area, and it has now been replicated several times. Her conclusion (see page 145) reads: 'Over one-quarter of the population of female children have experienced sexual abuse before the age of 14, and well over one-third have had such an experience by the age of 18 years.' Her definition of extrafamilial child sexual abuse is: 'one or more unwanted sexual experiences with persons unrelated by blood or marriage, ranging from petting (touching of breasts or genitals or attempting at such touching) to rape, before the victim turned 14 years, and completed or attempted forcible rape experiences from the ages of 14 to 17 years (inclusive)'. Her definition of infrafamilial child sexual abuse was defined as 'any kind of exploitive sexual contact that occurred between relatives, no matter how distant the relationship, before the victim turned 18 years old'.

important systemic defects did not prevent Freud from certain recognitions that have proved real and enduring: the reality of the unconscious; the reality of certain psychological devices to protect us against unbearable emotional pain, the importance of trauma as a factor in human misery, the importance of early childhood experiences in general, the fact that dreams are significant, and can reveal important biographical information, and so on. These are theoretical advances. They do not, however, translate directly into therapeutic devices. Thus while recognizing the reality of the unconscious, it does not follow that the ability to interpret another person's unconscious is easily achieved, learned, or passed on. This general statement is also true of interpretive efforts in general. Too often interpretations are used as disguised insults, or ways of forcing another person to accept the analyst's opinions. 'Insight' comes no easier to the so-called analyst than it does to the so-called patient. Freud's own 'insights' were often shockingly manipulative. One has to think only of the great case histories to realize how often Freud was wrong: he handed over his first analytic patient (Emma Eckstein) to a quack (Wilhelm Fliess) who performed a disastrous operation that disfigured her, yet Freud could never acknowledge what happened and insisted the injuries were psychosomatic in origin; he dismissed Dora's real problems as hysterical in nature and only grudgingly recognized her insights into the politics of her own family; he assured the Wolf Man that he would recover memories to vindicate Freud's interpretations (such memories never came); he analyzed Schreber's so-called delusions on the basis of unconscious homosexual longings for his father, instead of on that father's sadistic physical manipulations of the young boy, and so on. It would be a good idea if all therapists could acknowledge that if the founder of their 'science' was so prone to errors in psychological judgment, apparent to most of us fifty years later, their own efforts might be viewed in a similar light some years hence. Humility and skepticism should be the order of the day in all psychology.

I have also had to come to terms with the fact that people with whom I am in almost complete agreement, for example Thomas Szasz, part company with me when it comes to the value of therapy. When I decided to publish my unpopular views about child sexual abuse, it was Alice Miller who first came to my aid, encouraging me to stand up against the combined might of the psychoanalytic establishment. In many conversations, however, it became obvious to me that while Alice Miller could break decisively with orthodox psychoanalytic theory, it was not possible for her to include psychotherapy in general in her criticisms. This has become increasingly clear in her last three books, the most important of which, *Banished Knowledge: Facing Childhood Injuries*, is recently published. In that book she tells how she was finally able to be 'healed' and face her own childhood abuse (though what, precisely, it consisted of we are never told) by seeking out a Swiss psychotherapist who practices a form of primal therapy which he calls Primäre Therapie. This man, J. Konrad Stettbacher, is only known in the United States through Alice Miller's references to him. Indeed, he was more or less unknown in Switzerland as well until Alice Miller wrote about him in her last books. (I understand that his schedule is full for life now.) He has just published a book, still only available in German, entitled *Wenn Leiden einen Sinn haben soll: Die heilende Begegnung mit der eigenen Geschichte* [If Suffering Is To Have Meaning: The Healing Encounter With One's Own History] with a foreword by Alice Miller. In her four-page Introduction, Alice Miller cannot praise the book enough. She says, for example, that it is 'a breakthrough to an entirely new concept of help and self-help, without any trace of pedagogy, and at the same time a breakthrough to a new view of man, to an anthropology with as yet unimagined perspectives.' Such extravagant praise is completely out of place. The small book is filled with prescriptions about what to do and not to do when undergoing his form of psychotherapy (which he warns is very expensive). The therapist, of course, is to be obeyed, as long as the therapist is 'well-trained' and, lo and behold, how does one know if a therapist has been 'well trained'? If he has been trained in the Stettbacher method! It is a modified version of primal therapy crossed with Miller's own views about childhood (which, in and of themselves – that is, divested of their therapeutic cloak – I find unobjectionable). The dust-jacket of the book in German tells us little about him: 'J. Konrad Stettbacher was born in 1930 in Bern, Switzerland and since 1972 has had a private practice in "primary" psychotherapy, something he himself developed.'[15] It would seem that neither Alice nor Stettbacher have engaged in any fundamental re-evaluation of therapy, the underlying structure remains the same.

One has to ask the broader questions. How can clients or patients really know to whom they are talking? What can be asked? 'Are you faithful to your wife? Are you a good father? Do you frequently lie, cheat, steal? What are your politics? How do you feel about animals, race, the war?' And can honest answers be expected in the unlikely event that the therapist would answer such questions? What is involved in full disclosure? Can we expect honesty and introspection about all those signs which point to bias, prejudice and a lack of objectivity? Can these qualities be reasonably expected in therapy? Can therapy proceed without them? And what guarantee can there be beyond blind faith that such qualities will be available, merely because the practitioner was 'well-trained'? (As if anybody will admit to poor training.) What is training, anyway? Can there be an institute for the instillation of human kindness? Can such matters ever be taught? Yet without them, is therapy not dangerous? At most colleges and universities today, the students put out a guide book, grading their teachers openly and frankly, in a way that cannot be found in the more formal publications put out by the universities themselves. There is no equivalent consumers' guide to therapists, warning them away from the dullards, the frauds, and the narcissists. A guild protects its members from such possible narcissistic wounds. And a guild needs to feed on itself to survive, hence the cult-like atmosphere evidenced in all training institutes. There is reverence for a founder around whom legends accrue. These legends are then passed on. They are not just about Freud. Many of the lesser names, as time passes, take on some of the reflected glory of the first master, and so we think, with some reverence, of Adler, Rank, Stekel, and so on, though if we read their actual words (as spoken during the famous Wednesday night meetings, in the published Protocols, for example) we are reminded of how human, humanly

[15]Alice Miller, *Banished Knowledge: Facing Childhood Injuries* (New York: Doubleday, 1990). J. Konrad Stettbacher, *Wenn Leiden einen Sinn haben soll: Die heilende Begegnung mit der eigenen Geschichte* (Hamburg: Hoffmann und Campe, 1990).

flawed that is, they were. Most of their comments were banal, some were downright silly, others were dogmatic, irrelevant or plain wrong. But this council of elders, the further it is removed from us in time, takes on an aura of sanctity and wisdom. Freud began passing on rings to his favorite disciples. These ring-bearers then bequeathed their rings to favorite disciples, and otherwise reasonable people see them as possessing some fetishistic essence. Old values are then conserved and the penalty for questioning them or revolting is disbarment. We are no longer in the realm of science. It is the mythical world of fairy-tales we have entered. In this sense psychoanalytic institutions are not at all like a university. In a university tolerance and diversity are greater. There is an avenue to seek redress and air grievances. There is no such thing as an ombudsman in psychoanalytic institutes. How, then, can an individual be protected from the power imbalance that exists in his own analysis? The temptation to abuse, misuse, profit from, and bully is constant. All access to power offers the opportunity for corruption. Within the therapeutic setting, emotional power, at the very least, is almost absolute.

This 'impossible' profession makes demands that simply cannot be met. No therapist can consistently and permanently avoid the temptation to abuse the inevitable and inherent power imbalance. Even the kindest therapist may well experience envy of somebody else's capacity for love, or anger that they are leading a more interesting life, or that they are richer, smarter, better looking, deeper, happier, more amusing, or whatever quality they have and the therapist lacks. We may be tested and tempted by our friends in this same regard in real life, but we have no strangle-hold on them, nothing that is built into the relationships we do or do not form. But in therapy that strangle-hold is preordained.

Freud is supposed to have told Richard Sterba, 'During my whole life I have endeavored to uncover truths. I had no other intention and everything else was completely a matter of indifference to me. My single motive was the love of truth.'[16] A noble sentiment, no doubt, but is it true? One can't help but wonder how somebody could be so clear as to his motivation,

[16]R. E. Sterba, *Reminiscences of a Viennese Psychoanalyst* (Detroit: Wayne State University Press, 1982), 115.

and yet so rigid when it came to contemplating another point of view. Freud had few minor foibles. But he had large ones. He had a superb intellect, but a small heart. And this means there were things he simply could not understand. Such as another person's suffering.

The message I wish to reinforce is that the consent we presumably give to psychotherapy must be genuinely informed. In order to be informed, we must hear more from the critics of psychiatry and psychotherapy than we have been accustomed to.[17] It is alarming to see how far from this ideal practicing psychiatrists can be. The most flagrant example I have seen is from a Chicago psychiatrist, J. Dennis Freund who is quoted by the *Chicago Tribune* as saying in a new book *A Psychiatrist Speaks Out*: 'I am strongly for civil rights, but a patient who is deprived of reality, whose mind is suffused with delusions, has lost her civil rights. Only a hospital, and a physician, can give her her civil rights back.' I am alarmed at psychiatry's fear of taking an unsentimental and unflinching look at its own past. The role of psychiatry in Nazi Germany, where over 300,000 mental patients were killed by psychiatrists, a prelude to the killing of Jews and gypsies, has been glossed over or ignored by world psychiatry until very recently, and even now, the best research is coming, not from the psychiatrists, but from people outside the field.[18] Anna

[17]On the plus side are the few new books that raise fundamental questions concerning psychiatry. I would in particular recommend Kate Millett's *The Loony Bin Trip* (New York: Simon & Schuster, 1990), a powerful indictment of forced commitment. Peter Breggin's new book *Toxic Psychiatry* (London: Fontana, 1992) is one of the most scathing critiques of psychiatry ever to appear. Also being reprinted (by Harpers) is what I consider the single best book against psychiatry ever written, Janet and Paul Gotkin's *Too Much Anger Too Many Tears*. I too have recently published *Final Analysis: The Making and Unmaking of a Psychoanalyst* (London: Fontana, 1992) which tells the story of my analytic training and the reasons why I left the field.

[18]See the outstanding book by the geneticist Benno Mueller-Hill *Murderous Science: Elimination by Scientific Selection of Jews, Gypsies, and Others in Germany 1933–1945*, trans. by George R. Fraser (Oxford: Oxford University Press, 1988). I consider Robert J. Lifton's 1987 book, *The Nazi Doctors* to be something of a whitewash of psychiatry. Lifton, an American psychiatrist, does not make it clear who, precisely, the perpetrators were, and certainly never indicts anybody outside of

Freud, in an article entitled Child Observation and Prediction (*Psychoanalytic Study of the Child* 13 (1958): 112–16) wrote:

> I was impressed by the story of a boy who, at 4$^{1}/_{2}$ years, had escaped with his family from enemy-occupied territory. A subsequent analysis showed which elements of the experience had been singled out for traumatic value: he had suffered a severe shock from the fact that the invaders had deprived his father of his car. This, to him, meant that the father had been robbed of his potency. Besides this all-important oedipal experience, everything else (loss of home, security, friends) paled into insignificance.

This is a good demonstration of the incapacity of analysts to see beyond their theoretical constructs. It is typical that psychoanalytic interpretations avoid external reality and focus on predetermined events that *must* loom large in the child's psyche. Psychoanalysts were well prepared, because for so many years they too had ignored the real world that National Socialism created around them.

Klaus Hoppe, a psychoanalyst in Los Angeles who specializes in treating Jewish concentration camp survivors (in spite of the fact that he admits to having been a member of the Hitler Youth, though of course he would distance himself from it today – see

[18]*Cont.* Germany, though the silence of the international psychiatric community deserves condemnation. (I know of no study yet of the reaction, though preliminary research I have done shows that there were almost no voices of protest raised outside of Germany either.) In fact, psychiatric professionals (including holders of prestigious chairs of psychiatry in German universities) enthusiastically pursued the elimination of about 80 per cent of the population of psychiatric institutions. In 1942 Foster Kennedy, chief of Neurology at Bellevue Hospital and president of the American Neurological Association, wrote about 'unfit and feeble-minded children of at least five years' whom he described as 'useless and foolish and entirely undesirable' and thought they should be euthanized. The *Journal of the American Psychiatric Association* in July 1942 endorsed this view. Recently, some new information has come to light about the French killing of mental patients too. See Max Lafont, *L'extermination douce: La mort de 40,000 malades mentaux dans les hôpitaux psychiatriques en France, sous le Régime de Vichy* (Paris: Éditions de l'Arefppi, 1987).

Psychoanalytic Reflections on the Holocaust: Selected Essays, ed. by Steven A. Luel and Paul Marcus (New York: Ktav, 1984) 94) – writes:

> Sometimes the expert may use a combination of projection upon and identification with the survivor, i.e. 'altruistic surrender.' He thus gratifies his own libidinal needs and simultaneously liberates inhibited aggressive drives. In addition, he puts himself into the role of an alter ego of the survivor: he attacks the German officials, giving in to the manipulative wishes of the survivor, who is still afraid of the authorities. (Op. cit., p. 105)

In other words, if a concentration-camp survivor wishes to receive compensation from the German government (*Wiedergutmachung*) for his suffering, Hoppe might well 'interpret' this as a 'manipulative wish' and warns the psychiatrist that his desire to help such a patient maybe no more that an expression of an aggressive drive against Germans! I can see nothing wrong with releasing such aggression. Why would this be a bad thing? Here psychoanalytic theory is enlisted as an aid to salve the conscience of a German psychoanalyst at the expense of the real needs of those who suffered the most, namely his Jewish patients.

Psychiatry has not distinguished itself by fighting in the front lines for social justice and against human oppression. It is time this fact was recognized and the implications drawn.

A final historical example: There is a letter Freud wrote to his daughter Anna, on September 3, 1932, that is now in the Library of Congress. It is, curiously enough, the one passage in the entire correspondence between father and daughter where Freud clearly speaks with some passion about an event in psychoanalysis that seems to have exercised him more than any other. It is found very late in the letters. It concerns Sandor Ferenczi, Freud's favorite disciple and the most beloved of all the analysts, and his turning from orthodox Freudian doctrine. I have given all the details of this strange case in my book *The Assault on Truth* (reissued by Fontana Paperbacks in 1992), but at that time, of course, I had not seen this letter to Anna Freud. It does not change the story, but it does add some interesting details, and it is fascinating in the context of the letters. This is because Freud is writing on a rather delicate subject, the sexual abuse of children, to his own daughter, Anna, and the person about whom he is writing is somebody he once called 'my beloved son' and somebody who he had once hoped would marry Anna. Moreover, Anna Freud made no secret of the special affection she held for Ferenczi. She told me about it quite openly, and was visibly shaken when I told her that the letters I found in her father's desk revealed clearly that Freud had not been fair to Ferenczi. The letter is worth quoting in full:

> The two of them came in before 4. She was as charming as always, but from him there emanated an icy coldness. Without further question or any greeting, he began: I want to read you my paper. He did so, and I listened in shock. He has suffered a total regression to the etiological views that I believed in 35 years ago and renounced, [namely] that the general cause of the neuroses are severe sexual traumas in childhood, and he said it almost with precisely the same words I used at the time. No word about the technique by means of which he retrieves this material. It also contains remarks about the hostility of patients and the necessity of accepting their criticism and admitting one's errors in front of them. The results are confused, unclear, artificial. The whole thing is really stupid, or seems so because it is so dishonest and incomplete. Well, by now you have already heard the paper and can judge for yourself. In the middle of his reading Brill came in (he later caught up on what he had missed). The paper seemed to me harmless, it can hurt only him, and will certainly spoil the mood of the first day [of the Congress]. I asked only two questions. The first, I said, would be asked as well by his audience. How did he come by these trance phenomena which the rest of us never see? His answers were evasive and reticent; when he was asked about his contradictions [sic] against the Oedipus Complex etc., he explained that Brill's comments were incomprehensible, and admitted certain deviations from his views that I however could not understand. Brill whispered to me: 'He is not sincere.' [In English in the original.] It is the same as with Rank, only much sadder. My second question was what he

had in mind in reading me the paper? Here also he revealed his coldness. It came out that he does want to be president [of the International Psycho-Analytical Association] after all. I told him that I would not attempt to influence the vote. My only motive against him is that in this case you could unburden yourself of your position; I think, though, that his paper will create hostility toward him.

It is impossible for a modern reader to read these words without thinking how profoundly right Ferenczi was and how completely mistaken Freud was. Ferenczi's paper is a gem, one of the great documents in the history of psychology. Never before (or since) had any man penetrated so deeply into the mysteries of the sexual abuse of children. The very trance phenomena that Freud claimed never to see is commonly referred to by victims of sexual assault: they go into an altered state as a means of warding off the full reality and thus the full impact of the attack. When this state is deliberately or accidentally achieved in analysis, buried memories of the event become available.

What was it about this paper that Freud feared would spoil the mood of the Congress in Wiesbaden in 1932? It was simply this: Ferenczi was asking deep and important questions about psychoanalysis that no analyst, including Freud, wanted to hear. He was really calling into question his own practice and the very fabric of psychoanalysis. If psychoanalysts from Freud on could miss something so common and so essential to childhood, then how could it possibly be what it claimed to be, a method of discovering truth? The greatest truth it had seen (and Freud had seen it clearly in 1896) it had repudiated. Ferenczi in his paper talked openly about the hypocrisy of the analysts, and how important it was to recognize that patients knew more about the truth than did the analyst. Freud was incensed. It clearly offended his sense of dignity to be asked to recognize errors in front of a patient. Freud, certainly by then, was no seeker of truth, and Ferenczi, to his everlasting credit, was.

What happened to psychoanalysis, why did it become so dry and so inhuman? It did not begin that way. The early letters of Freud, those to his fiancée, and those to his best friend, Fliess, are filled with life, passion, emotions. Not so, though, the later letters. Once

Freud had 'made it,' once psychoanalysis was a recognized science, something happened both to him and to his discovery. They both aged. They lost something essential. Freud and psychoanalysis slowly became respectable and that may have squeezed the life out of both. Reading the early Freud, from the *Studies on Hysteria*, the great essay 'The Aetiology of Hysteria,' 'Screen Memories,' *The Interpretation of Dreams*, is to enter an exciting, passionate world. The later Freud is always elegant, eloquent, but something has gone out of it, something is missing, some essential passion has disappeared.

Finally, I must address the concern, widely expressed, that I have not offered any alternative to psychotherapy. I have repeatedly expressed my resistance to being placed in the position of pretending to have a solution. I did not, and still do not feel that in order to criticize the current state of affairs in psychotherapy I must offer a better alternative. Still, I have been forced, by the large number of people who have challenged me in this matter, to think about it more than I had when I wrote *Against Therapy*. Exposing oppression, injustice and all the many evils our times are subject to is itself a healthy activity. In fact, I cannot think of a better therapy than exposing the inadequacies of psychotherapy itself. Politicizing oneself by joining with other survivors in political actions is an excellent antidote to the powerlessness that psychiatry induces in its subjects. Becoming active in the struggle against psychiatry (and other forms of injustice) even in one's own mind, is a good alternative to the helplessness that psychiatry encourages in patients. Writing up one's own story, even if only for the instruction of other friends, especially if nothing is omitted, is to offer people the other side of the official story – and more of these personal stories are being published every year. Finally, becoming informed, the hard way, by active investigation is still the best way of exposing the truth.

BIBLIOGRAPHY

This bibliography contains books consulted and used in the writing of this book. However, it does not contain books that were specifically cited in the text itself. An asterisk indicates a book of particular value.

Adams, Joe Kennedy. *Secrets of the Trade: Madness, Creativity, and Ideology.* New York: The Viking Press, 1971.

Aftel, Mandy, and Robin Lakoff. *When Talk Is Not Cheap.* New York: Warner Books, 1985.

Alexander, Franz G., and Sheldon T. Selesnick. *The History of Psychiatry.* New York: Harper & Row, 1966.

Amada, Gerald. *A Guide to Psychotherapy.* New York: Madison Books, 1985.

*Bart, Pauline, B., and Patricia H. O'Brien. *Stopping Rape: Successful Survival Strategies.* New York: Pergamon Press, 1985.

Basaglia, Franco, and Franca Basaglia Ongaro, eds. *Crimini di Pace: Ricerche sugli intellettuali e sui tecnici come custodi di istituzione violente.* 3rd ed. Torino: Einaudi, 1975.

—— *Scritti, I, 1953–1968: Dalla psichiatria fenomenologica all'esperienza di Gorizia.* Torino: Einaudi, 1981.

—— *Scritti, II, 1968–1980: Dall'apertura del manicomio alla nuova legge sull'assistenza psichiatrica.* Torino: Einaudi, 1982.

Beck, Aaron T. *Cognitive Therapy and the Emotional Disorders.* New York: International Universities Press, 1976.

—— *The Diagnosis and Management of Depression.* Philadelphia: University of Pennsylvania Press, 1967.

Beck, Aaron T., *et al.*, *Cognitive Therapy of Depression.* New York: The Guilford Press, 1979.

Benziger, Barbara Field. *Speaking Out: Doctors and Patients, How They Cure and Cope with Mental Illness Today.* New York: Walker & Co., 1976.

Berenson, Bernard G., and Robert R. Carkhuff, eds. *Sources of Gain in Counseling and Psychotherapy: Readings and Commentary*. New York: Holt, Rinehart & Winston, 1967.

Bergin, Allen E., and Hans H. Strupp. *Changing Frontiers in the Science of Psychotherapy*. Chicago: Aldine, Atherton, 1972.

Bettelheim, Bruno. *The Informed Heart: Autonomy in a Mass Age*. Glencoe, IL: The Free Press, 1962.

*Blackbridge, Persimoon, and Shiela Gilhooly. *Still Sane*. Vancouver: Press Gang Publishers, 1985.

Bourgignon, Odile. *Mort des enfants et structures familiales*. Paris: Presses Universitaires de France, 1984.

Boyers, Robert, ed. *Psychological Man*. New York: Harper & Row, 1975.

Boyers, Robert, and Robert Orrill, eds. *R. D. Laing and Anti-Psychiatry*. New York: Harper & Row, 1971.

Braginsky, Dorothea D., and Benjamin M. Braginsky. *Hansels and Gretels: Studies of Children in Institutions for the Mentally Retarded*. New York: Holt, Rinehart & Winston, 1971.

—— *Mainstream Psychology: A Critique*. New York: Holt, Rinehart & Winston, 1974.

Brandt, Anthony. *Reality Police: The Experience of Insanity in America*. New York: William Morrow & Co., 1975.

*Breggin, Peter Roger. *Electroshock: Its Brain-Disabling Effects*. New York: Springer Publishing Co., 1979.

*—— *Psychiatric Drugs: Hazards to the Brain*. New York: Springer Publishing Co., 1983.

—— *The Psychology of Freedom*. Buffalo: Prometheus Books, 1980.

Brody, Eugene B., and Frederick C. Relich, eds. *Psychotherapy with Schizophrenics*. New York: International Universities Press, 1952.

Bruch, Hilde. *Learning Psychotherapy*. Cambridge, MA: Harvard University Press, 1974.

Bychowski, Gustav, and J. Louise Despert, eds. *Specialized Techniques in Psychotherapy*. New York: Basic Books, 1952.

Castel, Robert. *L'age d'or de l'aliénisme*. Paris: Les Éditions de Minuit, 1976.

—— *La gestion des risques: De l'anti-psychiatrie à l'après-psychanalyse*. Paris: Les Éditions de Minuit, 1981.

—— *Le psychanalysme*. Paris: Maspero, 1973; Flammarion, 1981.

Castel, Robert, Françoise Castel, and Anne Lovell. *The Psychiatric Society*. New York: Columbia University Press, 1982.

*Chamberlin, Judi. *On Our Own: Patient-Controlled Alternatives to the Mental Health System*. New York: McGraw-Hill, 1979.

Chessick, Richard D. *Why Psychotherapists Fail*. New York: Science House, 1971.

*Chorover, Stephan L. *From Genesis to Genocide: The Meaning of Human Nature and the Power of Behavior Control*. Cambridge, MA: MIT Press, 1980.

Clare, Anthony. *Psychiatry in Dissent: Controversial Issues in Thought and Practice*. Philadelphia: Institute for the Study of Human Issues, 1976.

Coleman, Lee. *The Reign of Error*. Boston: Beacon Press, 1984.

Condidaris, Matthew G., Dale F. Ely, and Jack T. Erikson. *1986 Edition: California Laws for Psychotherapists*. San Diego: Harcourt Brace Jovanovich, 1986.

Doctor Caligari's Psychiatric Drugs. Berkeley: Network Against Psychiatric Assault, 1984.

Donaldson, Kenneth. *Insanity Inside Out*. New York: Crown Publishers, 1976.

Dongier, Maurice, and Eric D. Wittkower, eds. *Divergent Views in Psychiatry*. New York: Harper & Row, 1981.

*Drigalski, Dörte von. *Flowers on Granite: One Woman's Odyssey Through Psychoanalysis*. Berkeley: Creative Arts Book Co., 1986.

Edwards, Rem B., ed. *Psychiatry and Ethics: Insanity, Rational Autonomy, and Mental Health Care*. Buffalo: Prometheus Books, 1982.

Ennis, Bernice. *Guide to the Literature in Psychiatry*. Los Angeles: Partridge Press, 1971.

Ennis, Bruce J. *Prisoners of Psychiatry: Mental Patients, Psychiatrists, and the Law*. New York: Harcourt Brace Jovanovich, 1972.

Eschenröder, Christof T. *Hier irrte Freud: Zur Kritik der psychoanalytischen Theorie und Praxis*. 2nd, enlarged ed. Munich: Urban & Schwarzenberg, 1986.

Estroff, Sue E. *Making It Crazy: An Ethnography of Psychiatric Clients in an American Community*. Berkeley: University of California Press, 1981.

Farber, Leslie H. *The Ways of the Will*. New York: Harper & Row, 1966.

Fenichel, Otto. *The Collected Papers of Otto Fenichel*. Edited by Hannah Fenichel and David Rapaport. 2 vols. New York: W. W. Norton & Co., 1953–1954.

—— *Problems of Psychoanalytic Technique*. Translated by David Brunswick. New York: Psychoanalytic Quarterly, 1941.

Finkelhor, David, and Kersti Yllo. *License to Rape: Sexual Abuse of Wives*. New York: Holt, Rinehart & Winston, 1985.

Fisher, Seymour, and Roger P. Greenberg, eds. *The Scientific Evaluation of Freud's Therapy*. New York: Basic Books, 1978.

Fliess, Robert, ed. *The Psychoanalytic Reader*. New York: International Universities Press, 1948.

Fontana, Vincent J. *Somewhere a Child Is Crying: Maltreatment – Causes and Prevention*. Rev. ed. New York: New American Library, 1983.

Foucault, Michel. *Histoire de la folie à l'age classique*. Paris: Éditions Gallimard, 1972.

Frank, K. Portland. *The Anti-Psychiatry Bibliography and Resource Guide*. 2nd ed., rev. Vancouver: Press Gang Publishers, 1979.

*Frank, Leonard Roy, ed. *The History of Shock Treatment*. San Francisco: privately printed by author, 1978.

Franks, Violet, and Vasanti Burtle, eds. *Women in Therapy: New Psychotherapies for a Changing Society*. New York: Brunner/Mazel, 1974.

Friedberg, John. *Shock Treatment Is Not Good for Your Brain*. San Francisco: Glide Publications, 1976.

Friedenberg, Edgar, *Z. R. D. Laing*. New York: The Viking Press, 1974.

Fromm-Reichmann, Frieda. *Principles of Intensive Psychotherapy*. Chicago: University of Chicago Press, 1950.

—— *Psychoanalysis and Psychotherapy: Selected Papers*. Edited by Dexter M. Bullard. Chicago: University of Chicago Press, 1959.

Furst, Sidney, ed. *Psychic Trauma*. New York: Basic Books, 1967.

Geuter, Ulfried. *Die Professionalisierung der deutschen Psychologie im Nationalsozialismus*. Frankfurt am Main: Suhrkamp Verlag, 1984.

Giovannoni, Jeanne M., and Rosina M. Becerra. *Defining Child Abuse*. New York: The Free Press, 1979.

Glenn, Michael, ed. *Voices from the Asylum*. New York: Harper & Row, 1974.

Glover, Edward. *On the Early Development of Mind*. New York: International Universities Press, 1956.

—— *The Technique of Psycho-Analysis*. New York: International Universities Press, 1955.

Gordon, David, and Maribeth Meyers. *Phoenix: Therapeutic Patterns of Milton H. Erickson*. Cupertino, CA: Meta Publications, 1981.

*Gotkin, Janet, and Paul Gotkin. *Too Much Anger, Too Many Tears: A Personal Triumph over Psychiatry*. New York: Basic Books, 1975.

Green, Hannah. *I Never Promised You a Rose Garden*. New York: Holt, Rinehart & Winston, 1964.

Greenacre, Phyllis. *Trauma, Growth and Personality*. London: The Hogarth Press, 1953.

Greenson, Ralph. *The Technique and Practice of Psychoanalysis*. New York: International Universities Press, 1967.

Gross, Martin L. *The Psychological Society*. New York: Simon & Schuster, 1978.

Haley, Jay. *Strategies of Psychotherapy*. New York: Grune & Stratton, 1963.

Halleck, Seymour L. *The Politics of Therapy*. New York: Science House, 1971.

Havens, Leston L. *Approaches to the Mind: Movement of the Psychiatric Schools from Sects Toward Science*. Boston: Little, Brown & Co., 1973.

Hemminger, Hansjörg, and Vera Becker. *Wenn Therapien schaden: Kritische Analyse einer psychotherapeutischen Fallgeschichte*. Reinbek: Rowohlt, 1985.

Henry, William E., John H. Sims, and S. Lee Spary. *Public and Private Lives of Psychotherapists*. San Francisco: Jossey-Bass, 1973.

Hernik, Richie, ed. *The Psychotherapy Handbook*. New York: New American Library, 1980.

Hill, Lewis B. *Psychotherapeutic Intervention in Schizophrenia*. Chicago: University of Chicago Press, 1955.

Hinsie, Leland E., and Robert J. Campbell. *Psychiatric Dictionary*. 4th ed. New York: Oxford University Press, 1970.

Hogan, Daniel B. *The Regulation of Psychotherapists*. Vol. 1: *A Study in the Philosophy and Practice of Professional Regulation*. Vol. 2: *A Handbook of State Licensure Laws*. Vol. 3: *A Review of Malpractice Suits in the United States*. Vol. 4: *A Resource Bibliography*. Cambridge, MA: Ballinger Publishing Co., 1979.

Hollingshead, August B., and Frederick C. Redlich. *Social Class and Mental Illness*. New York: John Wiley & Sons, 1958.

Holt, Robert R., and Lester Luborsky. *Personality Patterns of Psychiatrists*. New York: Basic Books, 1958.

Horowitz, Mardi, and others. *Personality Styles and Brief Psychotherapy*. New York: Basic Books, 1984.

Ingleby, David, ed. *Critical Psychiatry: The Politics of Mental Health*. New York: Pantheon Books, 1981.

Katz, Jay, Joseph Golstein, and Alan M. Dershowitz. *Psychoanalysis, Psychiatry and Law*. New York: The Free Press, 1967.

Kelly, Delos H., ed. *Deviant Behavior: A Text-Reader in the Sociology of Deviance*. New York: St. Martin's Press, 1984.

Kopp, Sheldon B. *Guru: Metaphors from a Psychotherapist*. Palo Alto: Science and Behavior Books, 1971.

Kubie, Lawrence S. *Practical and Theoretical Aspects of Psychoanalysis*. 2nd ed., rev. New York: International Universities Press, 1975.

—— *Symbol and Neurosis: Selected Papers of Lawrence S. Kubie.* Edited by Herbert J. Schlesinger. New York: International Universities Press, 1978.

Laing, R. D. *Wisdom, Madness and Folly: The Making of a Psychiatrist.* New York: McGraw-Hill, 1985.

Lasch, Christopher. *The Minimal Self: Psychic Survival in Troubled Times.* New York: W. W. Norton & Co., 1984.

Lerner, Barbara. *Therapy into Ghetto: Political Impotence and Personal Disintegration.* Baltimore: Johns Hopkins University Press, 1971.

Lewin, Bertram. *The Psychoanalysis of Elation.* New York: Psychoanalytic Quarterly, 1961.

—— *Selected Writings of Bertram D. Lewin.* Edited by Jacob A. Arlow. New York: Psychoanalytic Quarterly, 1973.

Light, Donald. *Becoming Psychiatrists: The Professional Transformation of Self.* New York: W. W. Norton & Co., 1980.

London, Perry. *The Modes and Morals of Psychotherapy.* New York: Holt, Rinehart & Winston, 1964.

Mcdougall, Joyce. *Théâtres du Je.* Paris: Éditions Gallimard, 1982.

Madness Network News Reader. Edited by Leonard Roy Frank and others. San Francisco: Glide Publications, 1974.

Mannoni, O. *Prospero and Caliban: The Psychology of Colonization.* 2nd ed. Translated by Pamela Powesland. New York: Frederick A. Praeger, 1956.

Menninger, Karl. *A Psychiatrist's World: The Selected Papers of Karl Menninger.* New York: The Viking Press, 1959.

—— *Theory of Psychoanalytic Technique.* New York: Science Editions, 1961.

Miller, Alice. *The Drama of the Gifted Child.* New York: Basic Books, 1981.

—— *For Your Own Good: Hidden Cruelty in Child-Rearing and the Roots of Violence.* New York: Farrar, Straus & Giroux, 1983.

—— *Thou Shalt Not Be Aware: Society's Betrayal of the Child.* New York: Farrar, Straus & Giroux, 1984.

Miller, Jonathan. *States of Mind.* New York: Pantheon Books, 1983.

Miller, Peter, and Nikolas Rose, eds. *The Power of Psychiatry.* Cambridge, MA: Polity Press, 1986.

Mullahy, Patrick. *The Beginnings of Modern American Psychiatry: The Ideas of Harry Stack Sullivan.* Boston: Houghton Mifflin Co., 1973.

Nahem, Joseph. *Psychology and Psychiatry Today: A Marxist View.* New York: International Publishers, 1983.

Nicholi, Armand M., Jr., ed. *The Harvard Guide to Modern Psychiatry.* Cambridge, MA: Harvard University Press, 1978.

Offer, Daniel, and Melvin Sabshin. *Normality: Theoretical and Clinical Concepts of Mental Health*. New York: Basic Books, 1966.

Offit, Avodah K. *Night Thoughts: Reflections of a Sex Therapist*. New York: Congdon & Weed, 1981.

Pagelow, Mildred Daley. *Woman-Battering: Victims and Their Experiences*. Beverly Hills: Sage Publications, 1981.

Patterson, C. H. *Theories of Counseling and Psychotherapy*. New York: Harper & Row, 1973.

Perry, Helen Swick. *Psychiatrist of America: The Life of Harry Stack Sullivan*. Cambridge, MA: Harvard University Press, 1982.

Peterson, Dale. *A Mad People's History of Madness*. Pittsburgh: University of Pittsburgh Press, 1982.

Quetel, Claude, and Pierre Morel. *Les fous et leurs médecins de la Renaissance au XXᵉ siècle*. Paris: Hachette, 1979.

Richter, Horst-Eberhard. *Die Chance des Gewissens: Erinnerungen und Assoziationen*. Hamburg: Hoffmann & Campe, 1986.

Robitscher, Jonas. *The Powers of Psychiatry*. Boston: Houghton Mifflin Co., 1980.

Rogow, Arnold A. *The Psychiatrists*. New York: G. P. Putnam's Sons, 1970.

Roman, Paul M., and Harrison M. Trice, eds. *The Sociology of Psychotherapy*. New York: Jason Aronson, 1974.

Rosen, George. *Madness in Society: Chapters in the Historical Sociology of Mental Illness*. Chicago: University of Chicago Press, 1968.

Rosenbaum, Max, and Melvin Muroff, eds. *Anna O.: Fourteen Contemporary Reinterpretations*. New York: The Free Press, 1984.

Rothman, David J. *The Discovery of the Asylum: Social Order and Disorder in the New Republic*. Boston: Little, Brown & Co., 1971.

Rothman, David J., and Sheila M. Rothman. *The Willowbrook Wars: A Decade of Struggle for Social Justice*. New York: Harper & Row, 1984.

Ruesch, Jurgen. *Disturbed Communication: The Clinical Assessment of Normal and Pathological Communicative Behavior*. New York: W. W. Norton & Co., 1957; rpt. 1972.

—— *Therapeutic Communication: A Descriptive Guide to the Communication Process as the Central Agent in Mental Healing*. New York: W. W. Norton & Co., 1961.

Ruitenbeck, Hendrik M. *The New Group Therapies*. New York: Avon Books, 1970.

Rycroft, Charles. *Psychoanalysis and Beyond*. Chicago: University of Chicago Press, 1985.

Sarbin, Theodore, R., and James C. Mancuso. *Schizophrenia: Medical Diagnosis or Moral Verdict?* New York: Pergamon Press, 1982.

Scheff, Thomas J. *Being Mentally Ill: A Sociological Theory*. Chicago: Aldine Publishing Co., 1966.

Scheff, Thomas J., ed. *Labeling Madness*. Englewood Cliffs, NJ: Prentice-Hall, 1975.

—— *Mental Illness and Social Processes*. New York: Harper & Row, 1967.

Schrag, Peter. *Mind Control*. New York: Pantheon Books, 1978.

Schrag, Peter, and Diane Divoky. *The Myth of the Hyperactive Child and Other Means of Child Control*. New York: Pantheon Books, 1975.

Schur, Edwin M. *The Awareness Trap: Self-Absorption Instead of Social Change*. New York: McGraw-Hill, 1976.

—— *Labeling Deviant Behavior: Its Sociological Implications*. New York: Harper & Row, 1971.

Schwender, Rolf, ed. *Psychiatrie und Antipsychiatrie im Ausland*. Munich: A. G. Spak, 1983.

*Scull, Andrew, ed. *Madhouses, Mad-Doctors, and Madmen: The Social History of Psychiatry in the Victorian Era*. Philadelphia: University of Pennsylvania Press, 1981.

Sedgwick, Peter. *Psycho-Politics: Laing, Foucault, Goffman, Szasz and the Future of Mass Psychiatry*. New York: Harper & Row, 1982.

Shakow, David, and David Rapaport. *The Influence of Freud on American Psychology*. Cleveland: Meridian Books, 1964.

Sharpe, Ella Freeman. *Collected Papers on Psycho-Analysis*. Edited by Marjorie Brierly. London: The Hogarth Press, 1968.

—— *Dream Analysis*. London: The Hogarth Press, 1961.

Shutts, David. *Lobotomy: Resort to the Knife*. New York: Van Nostrand Reinhold Co., 1978.

Singer, Erwin. *Key Concepts in Psychotherapy*. 2nd ed. New York: Basic Books, 1970.

Small, Leonard. *The Briefer Psychotherapies*. New York: Brunner/Mazel, 1971.

Strupp, Hans H., and Jeffrey L. Binder. *Psychotherapy in a New Key: A Guide to Time-Limited Dynamic Psychotherapy*. New York: Basic Books, 1984.

Sullivan, Harry Stack. *The Collected Works*. 2 vols. Edited by Helen Swick Perry and Mary Ladd Gawel. New York: W. W. Norton & Co., 1953.

Szasz, Thomas. *The Ethics of Psychoanalysis: The Theory and Method of Autonomous Psychotherapy*. Rev. ed. New York: Basic Books, 1974.

—— *Law, Liberty, and Psychiatry: An Inquiry into the Social Uses of Mental Health Practices*. London: Routledge & Kegan Paul, 1974.

*—— *The Manufacture of Madness: A Comparative Study of the Inquisition and the Mental Health Movement*. New York: Harper & Row, 1970.

—— The Myth of Mental Illness: Foundations of a Theory of Personal Conduct. Rev. ed. New York: Harper & Row, 1974.

—— The Myth of Psychotherapy: Mental Healing as Religion, Rhetoric, and Repression. Garden City, NY: Doubleday & Co., 1978.

—— Sex by Prescription. Garden City, NY: Doubleday & Co., 1980.

—— The Therapeutic State: Psychiatry in the Mirror of Current Events. Buffalo: Prometheus Books, 1984.

Szasz, Thomas, ed. The Age of Madness: The History of Involuntary Mental Hospitalization. New York: Jason Aronson, 1974.

Tarachow, Sidney. An Introduction to Psychotherapy. New York: International Universities Press, 1963.

*Timpanaro, Sebastiano. The Freudian Slip: Psychoanalysis and Textual Criticism. New York: Schocken Books, 1976.

Torrey, E. Fuller. The Death of Psychiatry. New York: Penguin Books, 1975.

—— Witchdoctors and Psychiatrists: The Common Roots of Psychotherapy and Its Future. Rev. ed. New York: Harper & Row, 1986.

Valenstein, Elliot S. Great and Desperate Cures: The Rise and Decline of Psychosurgery and Other Radical Treatments for Mental Illness. New York: Basic Books, 1986.

—— ed. The Psychosurgery Debate: Scientific, Legal and Ethical Perspectives. San Francisco: W. H. Freeman & Co., 1980.

Walkenstein, Eileen. Don't Shrink to Fit: A Confrontation with Dehumanization in Psychiatry and Psychology. New York: Grove Press, 1975.

Wallerstein, Robert S. Forty-Two Lives in Treatment: A Study of Psychoanalysis and Psychotherapy. New York: The Guilford Press, 1986.

Weddin, Dan, and Raymond J. Corsini, eds. Great Cases in Psychotherapy. Itasca, IL: F. E. Peacock Publishers, 1979.

Weinberg, George. The Heart of Psychotherapy. New York: St. Martin's Press, 1984.

Wertham, Fredric. A Sign for Cain: An Exploration of Human Violence. New York: Paperback Library, 1969.

Wheelis, Allen. The Quest for Identity. New York: W. W. Norton & Co., 1958.

Wolman, Benjamin B., ed. Psychoanalytic Techniques: A Handbook for the Practicing Psychoanalyst. New York: Basic Books, 1967.

Wood, Garth. The Myth of Neurosis: Overcoming the Illness Excuse. New York: Harper & Row, 1986.

Zilbergeld, Bernie. The Shrinking of America: Myths of Psychological Change. Boston: Little, Brown & Co., 1983.

INDEX

My Mother/My Self

Nancy Friday

Why are women the way they are? Why, despite, everything, do we find so much of ourselves mysterious? Where do the dependence, the longing for intimacy, the passivity come from?

Drawing on her own and other women's lives, Nancy Friday shows compellingly that the key lies in a woman's relationship with her mother – that first binding relationship which becomes the model for so much of our adult relationships with men, and whose fetters constrain our sexuality, our independence, our very selfhood.

'Brilliant. Courageous. Moving. One of the most important books I have ever read about my mother, myself and my life.'

Washington Post

'A book most women will want to read and every man ought to.'
Michael Korda

Breaking the Bonds

Understanding Depression, Finding Freedom

Dorothy Rowe

'The light at the end of the tunnel'   Jill Tweedie

Depression: the imprisoning experience of isolation and fear which comes when we realize that there is a serious discrepancy between what we thought our life to be and what it actually is.

From birth onwards we create our own secure worlds of meaning. Challenged seriously enough, these worlds can crumble, leaving us despairing, frightened, isolated, helpless. But we are not helpless. We can resolve to save ourselves by embarking on a journey of understanding and self-acceptance, and finally and for ever break free of the bonds of depression.

Dorothy Rowe, the internationally renowned psychologist and expert on depression, brings together in this book what her twenty-five years of research have shown her about depression, and shows us how every one of us can take charge of our life and find the way to happiness, hope and freedom.

'Wise and witty, factual and poetic, and a luminous path to self-understanding for all of us'   Jill Tweedie

'Wisdom, says Rowe, is knowing your worst fear and why you have it. *Breaking the Bonds* takes us to it and, if we're smart, into the nirvana of beginning to know what we want . . . this is a smashing book'   *New Statesman*

'This splendid book is a vastly readable, greatly enjoyable lifeline. Use it if you're depressed, to help yourself. Read it if you're not, so that you can help others. Either way, *read* it'   Claire Rayner

ISBN 0 00 637565 0

Dorothy Rowe's Guide to Life

'Dorothy Rowe is full of robust good sense, rare intuitive wisdom and unhurried sensitivity ... she is a giver of courage'

NIGELLA LAWSON, *The Times*

The central theme of all Dorothy Rowe's work is that, while the world and ourselves might *seem* to be solid and real, the way in which we are constituted means that we can never know reality directly, only the meanings we have created about reality.

It is when we don't understand this, when we mistakenly think that we, our life and the world are fixed, unalterable parts of reality which we have to put up with and cope with as best we can, that we find we can't handle life's problems – we make mistakes, feel trapped, and often despair.

When we do understand it, we realize that we are free to change.

Dorothy Rowe has helped tens of thousands of people reach this understanding through her books on fear, depression and unhappiness. She has shown how, by understanding our nature, we can end our suffering. Her *Guide to Life* is a summation of this wisdom but with more besides, for there is no end to self-understanding. Like all her books, it is clear and compassionate, witty and wise.

ISBN 0 00 638422 6

Wanting Everything
The Art of Happiness

Dorothy Rowe

'I would like to see it on every bookshelf in the country. We would be the happier for it'   FAY WELDON

To be human is to suffer. We enter this world expecting that we can have everything, but we learn very quickly that we can't always get what we want. The accompanying and constant feelings of loss, frustration, anger, aggression, resentment and sadness can dominate us for the rest of our lives.

The strategies we evolve to cope with these feelings – greed for possessions or power, a propensity for assuming responsibility for everything, saddling ourself with guilt for the world, martyrdom, envy or utter selfishness – do not lead to happiness. But Dorothy Rowe shows us how, once we understand the nature of our longing and the conditions that prevent its fulfilment, we can arrive at a state of wanting which does hold the possibility of fulfilment, and which does lead to happiness.

'Dorothy Rowe is essentially a chronicler of emotional pain, a suggester of solutions. Her perspective on existence acknowledges sadness, pain, anger, but it instantly makes things seem meaningful'   *Guardian*

ISBN 0 00 637430 1

The Courage to Live

Discovering Meaning in a World of Uncertainty

Dorothy Rowe

The way in which we perceive death shapes the fundamental pattern of our lives, the very core of our existence.

Fear death, and we live pessimistically in its shadow; learn to accept it, and life's possibilities open up as splendidly varied, infinitely exciting, precious beyond price.

Drawing on personal interviews and her deep insight into the practices of psychotherapy today, eminent psychologist Dorothy Rowe reveals how we structure our lives – how, out of the formless chaos of reality, we give meaning and purpose to our existence through the influences of different cultures, languages and beliefs.

With true warmth and humour, Dorothy Rowe challenges us to find our own ways of living with the uncertainty of death, encouraging us to embrace the freedom of a life without fear.

ISBN 0 00 637736 X

Beyond Fear

Dorothy Rowe

Fear is the great unmentionable. We fear loss, bereavement, old age, death, rejection, failure – most of all, we fear annihilation of the self. Yet all of this we keep to ourselves, afraid of being thought weak.

Denying our fear of self-destruction, around which our entire sense of self is built, can have profound effects upon ourselves and those around us in later life. It can lead to physical illness, like anorexia, or to mental problems, such as panic attacks, depression and schizophrenia.

It lies within our power to break this pattern, discovering greater happiness in our lives. In *Beyond Fear* eminent psychologist Dorothy Rowe explains how to recognize the need for change and how to bring it about.

'This is a most extraordinary and valuable book and Dorothy Rowe is a most extraordinary and valuable person. Not only is she phenomenally wise, but she imparts her wisdom in a kind of prose poetry that moves, enlightens, reforms, beguiles and educates all at once' Fay Weldon

ISBN 0 00 637101 9